Lecture Notes in Computer Science 4340

Commenced Publication in 1973
Founding and Former Series Editors:
Gerhard Goos, Juris Hartmanis, and Jan van Leeuwen

Radu Prodan   Thomas Fahringer

Grid Computing

Experiment Management, Tool Integration,
and Scientific Workflows

 Springer

Authors

Radu Prodan
Thomas Fahringer
University of Innsbruck, Institute for Computer Science
Technikerstr. 21a, 6020 Innsbruck, Austria
E-mail: {radu,thomas.fahringer}@dps.uibk.ac.at

Library of Congress Control Number: 2006939015

CR Subject Classification (1998): C.2, D.4, F.3, H.4, H.3, C.4, I.2.8

LNCS Sublibrary: SL 2 – Programming and Software Engineering

ISSN   0302-9743
ISBN-10   3-540-69261-4 Springer Berlin Heidelberg New York
ISBN-13   978-3-540-69261-4 Springer Berlin Heidelberg New York

Springer is a part of Springer Science+Business Media

springer.com

© Springer-Verlag Berlin Heidelberg 2007
Printed in Germany

Typesetting: Camera-ready by author, data conversion by Markus Richter, Heidelberg
Printed on acid-free paper   SPIN: 11965800   06/3142   5 4 3 2 1 0

To our families

Preface

In the last decade, the interest in computational Grids has increasingly grown in the scientific community as a means of enabling the application developers to aggregate resources scattered around the globe for solving large-scale scientific problems. As applications get larger, more complex and dynamic, the use of software tools becomes vital for tuning application parameters, identifying performance leaks, or detecting program defects. Extensive efforts within academia and industry over the last decade resulted in a large collection of tools for practical application engineering. Available tools of broad interest include program source and structure browsers, editors, static program analysers, performance predictors, optimising compilers, schedulers, execution control and monitoring environments, sequential and parallel debuggers (providing deadlock detection and deterministic replay mechanisms), checkpointers, data and execution visualisers, performance analysers, or various program tracers.

Despite all these extensive efforts, building applications that can effectively utilise the Grid still remains an art due to the lack of appropriate high-level tools to support the developers. In this monograph, we address four critical software development aspects for the engineering and execution of applications on parallel and Grid architectures.

First of all, existing available performance analysis tools target single application execution which is not sufficient for effective performance tuning of parallel applications. The most popular performance metrics such as speedup or efficiency require repeated execution of the application for various machine sizes for which no automatic tool support exists so far. Additionally, parallelising and tuning of applications for a certain compute platform requires repeated experimentation for various data distributions, loop iteration scheduling strategies, or compiler optimisation options, which is known to be an NP-complete problem.

Second, tool portability is critical since tools are often based on a monolithic design that does not isolate the inherent platform dependencies required to support advanced and in-depth analysis. For example, when using a new parallel system the users must in most cases learn about and familiarise themselves with new tools with different functionality and interfaces, which is in many cases very time consuming and can be a major barrier in using novel modern computer architectures.

Third, existing tools cannot be used in cooperation on the same application instance to enhance the performance and correctness debugging engineering process since they are not designed for interoperability and often are based on incompatible instrumentation or monitoring systems.

Fourth, the workflow model that recently emerged as a new attractive paradigm for programming loosely coupled Grid infrastructures requires novel tools that offer appropriate high-level support, including abstract specification mechanisms, optimised scheduling, and scalable fault-tolerant execution, which are of paramount importance to effectively running distributed large-scale applications. These topics attract a lot of interest within the Grid community that aims to evolve the Grid to a commodity platform that transparently aggregates high-performance resources scattered around the globe in a single virtual supercomputer for performing scientific simulations.

In this monograph, we first propose a new directive-based language called ZEN for compact specification of wide value ranges of interest for arbitrary application parameters, including problem or machine sizes, array or loop distributions, software libraries, interconnection networks, or target execution machines. We design the ZEN directives as problem-independent with global or fine-grain scopes that do not change the semantics of the application, nor require any application modification or special preparation. Irrelevant or meaningless experiments can be filtered through well-defined constraints. Additionally, the ZEN directives can be used to request a wide range of performance metrics to be collected from the application for arbitrary code regions.

Based on the ZEN language, we develop a novel experiment management tool called ZENTURIO for automatic experiment management of large-scale performance and parameter studies on parallel and Grid architectures. ZENTURIO offers automatic analysis and visualisation support across multiple experiments based on the performance and output data collected and organised in a common shared data repository. In contrast to existing parameter study tools, ZENTURIO requires no special preparation of the application, nor does it restrict the parametrisation to input files or to global input arguments. We validated the functionality and usefulness of ZENTURIO on several real-world parallel applications from various domains, including theoretical chemistry, photonics, finances, and numerical mathematics.

We designed ZENTURIO as a comprehensive distributed service-oriented architecture for interoperable tool development based on the latest state-of-the-art Web and Grid services technologies. We illustrate how a service-oriented architecture facilitates the integration of a broad set of tools and enables a range of useful tool interoperability scenarios that facilitate the engineering effort of applications. We illustrate a variety of novel adaptations of state-of-the-art Web technologies for Grid computing which anticipated several existing standardisation efforts.

Based on the ZENTURIO experiment management architecture, we propose a generic optimisation framework that integrates general-purpose meta-heuristics for solving NP-complete performance and parameter optimisation problems in an exponential search space specified using the ZEN experiment specification language. We illustrate a generic problem-independent realisation of the search engine using a genetic algorithm that allows new optimisation problems to be formulated through appropriate objective functions, for example, a performance metric using the ZEN language. We illustrate three case studies that instantiate the framework for Grid workflow scheduling, throughput scheduling of parameter studies, and performance tuning of parallel applications on the Grid using irregular array distributions.

Finally, we propose a timely approach for modelling and executing scientific workflows in dynamic and heterogeneous Grid environments. We introduce an abstract formal model for hierarchical representation of complex directed graph-based workflows using composite activities (such as parallel and sequential loops or conditional activities) interconnected through control and data flow dependencies comprising advanced collective communication patterns such as broadcast, scatter, and gather. We propose and comparatively analyse three heuristic-based algorithms for scheduling two real-world scientific workflows from material science and meteorology domains. The scheduled applications achieve good performance on the Austrian Grid environment using advanced runtime techniques such as partitioning, workflow optimisation, and load balancing. We design a steering algorithm that performs runtime monitoring and workflow schedule adaptations which ensure that certain quality of service performance contracts are preserved during execution of the workflow. We conclude with a classification of the most important performance overheads that may slow down the performance of scientific workflows and validate them through several experiments.

Innsbruck, October 2006   Radu Prodan
                                                      Thomas Fahringer

Contents

List of Figures

List of Tables

List of Algorithms

1

Introduction

Before 1990, the world wide *Internet* network was almost entirely unknown outside the universities and the corporate research departments. The common way of accessing the Internet was via command line interfaces such as `telnet`, `ftp`, or popular Unix mail user agents like `elm`, `mush`, `pine`, or `rmail`. The usual access to information was based on peer-to-peer email message exchange which made the every day information flow slow, unreliable, and tedious. The advent of the *World Wide Web* has revolutionised the information flow though the Internet from obsolete message passing to world wide Web page publication. Since then, the Internet has exploded to become an ubiquitous global infrastructure for publishing and exchange of (free) digital information.

Despite its global success and acceptance as a standard mean for publishing and exchange of digital information, the World Wide Web technology does not enable ubiquitous access to the billions of (potentially idle) computers simultaneously connected to the Internet providing peta-flops of estimated aggregate computational power. Remote access to computational power is highly demanded by applications that simulate complex scientific and engineering problems, like medical simulations, industrial equipment control, stock portfolio management, weather forecasting, earthquake simulations, flood management, and so on.

Nowadays, the common policy of accessing high-end computational resources is through manual remote `ssh` logins on behalf of individual user accounts. Similar to the World Wide Web that revolutionised the information access, *computational Grids* are aiming to define an infrastructure that provides dependable, consistent, pervasive, and inexpensive access to the world wide computational capabilities of the Internet [77]. In this context, computational Grids raise a new class of important scientific research opportunities and challenges regarding, e.g.:

- secure resource sharing among dynamic collections of individuals and institutions forming so called *Virtual Organisations* [77];
- solving large scale problems for which appropriate local resources are not available;

- improving the performance of applications by increasing the parallelism through concurrent use of distributed computational resources;
- course-grain composition of large-scale applications from off-the-shelf existing software services or application components;
- exploiting (or stealing) unused processor cycles from idle workstations (e.g. desktop, network) to increase the overall computational power;
- appropriate distribution and replication of large data files near to places where subsequent computations will likely take place;
- incorporation of semantic Web technologies [51].

1.1 Motivation

In the past years, the interest in *computational Grids* has increasingly grown in the scientific community as a mean of enabling application developers to aggregate resources scattered around the globe for solving large scale scientific problems. Developing applications that can effectively utilise the Grid, however, still remains very difficult due to the lack of high level tools to support developers.

In this monograph, we aim to contribute to various research aspects regarding integrated tool development for efficient engineering and high performance execution of scientific applications in Grid environments.

1.1.1 Performance Tuning

Computational Grids have the potential to harness remote high performance platforms for efficient execution of scientific applications. Existing parallel applications that leverage the currently successful parallel programming standards [49, 164], however, require to be tuned to the characteristics of each particular parallel architecture in order to achieve high performance. The compiler technology has proven to be inefficient in transparently parallelising the applications and still relies on the manual user support. In addition, existing performance tools (e.g. [128]) offer help for advanced analysis of single experiments only, which is not sufficient for efficient application performance tuning.

In a traditional approach, the performance tuning of parallel applications is a cyclic multi-experimental process. The most popular performance metrics, such as efficiency or speedup, require the investigation of numerous problem and machine sizes for, e.g. various compiler options and data or control flow distributions. This process involves many cycles of code editing, compilation, execution, data collection, performance analysis, and data visualisation, which is tedious and error prone to be managed manually. To this date there is no automatised support for performance analysis of parallel applications across multiple experiments.

1.1.2 Parameter Studies

In the last decade, large scale parameter studies have become feasible through the appearance of parallel compute engines with multi-gigabyte memories and terabyte disk farms. Such parameter studies require repeated invocation of the same application on a variety of input data sets combined with appropriate organisation of the output data files for subsequent analysis and visualisation. Existing parameter study tools like Nimrod [5] or ILAB [197] require special preparation of the application, which is usually the main obstacle for a tool in achieving user acceptance. The application developers are in general very reluctant in changing their applications to the peculiarities of each tool and prefer to write special purpose scripts hard coded for their specific parameter studies, rather than using general purpose tools that can give them enhanced graphical interfaces and fault tolerance support.

1.1.3 Optimisation

Exhaustive performance and parameter studies describe the complete evolution of the performance metric or the output parameter under investigation as a function of the indicated input parameters. While such studies provide invaluable information on the application behaviour, they often produce an overflow of data which is irrelevant for further studies. In many cases parameter spaces become so large that they are impossible to be exhaustively traversed. On the other hand, users are often only interested in finding parameter combinations that optimise a certain performance metric or an output parameter, rather than conducting the complete set of experiments for all parameter combinations. This is typically an NP-complete optimisation problem [183], such as performance tuning and scheduling, that requires heuristic-based algorithms to find approximate or satisfactory solutions. There are currently no tools to support the users in defining and solving general NP-complete optimisation problems for scientific applications in Grid environments.

1.1.4 Scheduling

Fine-grained performance analysis and tuning, as is usually performed on traditional parallel computers, is often unrealistic to be applied to world wide course-grain computational Grid infrastructures. The problem of high performance execution of scientific applications gets shifted from fine-grained performance analysis and tuning to appropriate scheduling onto the available computational Grid resources.

Application scheduling in a classical approach is an NP-complete optimisation problem. The scheduling search space, which exponentially depends on the (potentially unbounded) number of resources and tasks, can achieve particularly huge dimensions on the Grid which have not been previously addressed. In addition, static scheduling as an optimisation problem has to be enhanced with steering capabilities that consider the dynamic availability of the Grid resources over space and time in order to be effective.

While scheduling is a topic extensively addressed in the past in the distributed systems, parallel processing, and compiler communities, there is currently little effort to transfer the existing practice and technology to the Grid computing field. Most of the current Grid projects approach the scheduling problem in an ad-hoc manner using simple opportunistic matchmaking techniques [152].

1.1.5 Parametrisation Language

One reason why there is no tool support for automatic experiment management regardless the ultimate goal (i.e. performance studies, parameter studies, optimisations) is the lack of appropriate languages to define experiments. Currently each user takes own ad-hoc approaches in defining value ranges for relevant application parameters by writing hard coded scripts that serve a very specific experimental purpose. Moreover, existing performance and parameter study tools that offer some support for automatic experiment management, approach the parameter specification problem in a similar ad-hoc manner through special purpose external scripts that force the developers to export application parameters to external global variables [4]. Other tools that aim for a more user friendly parameter specification through graphical annotations are restricted to input files [197].

We identified the following limitations in existing parameter specification approaches as being critical for an end-user:

1. the parameter specification is restricted to input files or program arguments;
2. only global variables or program arguments can be expressed;
3. local variables cannot be parameterised;
4. parallelization strategies (e.g. array and loop distributions), or other application characteristics that were not considered during tool design, cannot be expressed;
5. the parametrisation forces the user to perform undesired modifications and adaptations of the application;
6. there is no formal approach to define a general purpose experiment specification language.

1.1.6 Instrumentation

Program instrumentation is a common task that all performance analysis tools need to perform for measuring and collecting the runtime application data needed to perform the analysis. The various instrumentation technologies that we encountered so far have the following drawbacks:

1. *source code instrumentation* [18, 153] forces the user to manually insert probes in the application which, apart from being tedious to perform, often introduces undesired source code modifications that are bound to the profiling library used;

2. *compiler instrumentation* through external flags as performed by most commercial compilers has serious limitations in specifying fine-grained local source code regions for which to the collect performance data;

3. *dynamic instrumentation* [31] and

4. *binary rewriting* [95] do not interfere with the original source code, but are limited to binary executables, impossible to be reversibly mapped to the original source code. In addition, the portability of these technologies is very critical;

5. *object code wrapping* [30] is limited to pre-compiled software libraries statically augmented with instrumentation probes.

1.1.7 Portability

The set of tools available on each individual platform is usually heterogeneous in functionality and the user interface provided. Before using a new parallel system, the users must in most cases learn and familiarise themselves with new tools with different functionality and interfaces. This requires (often unnecessary) extra time and effort and can be a major deterrent against using more appropriate computer systems. The main reason for tools not being available on a large set of platforms is their limited portability.

1.1.8 Tool Interoperability

The cooperative use of software tools can significantly improve the application engineering process. For instance, an experiment management tool can make use of a performance monitor for cross-experiment performance analysis and tuning. On the other hand, the use of online performance tools in conjunction with correctness debuggers can significantly improve the performance steering process by applying on-the-fly program modifications based on online performance data analysis.

Unfortunately, most of the tools supporting different phases of the application engineering process cannot be used in cooperation to further improve the user efficiency because they are insufficiently integrated into a single coherent environment. The main reason for the lack of interoperability between existing tools are their incompatible monitoring systems and the critical (not isolated) platform dependencies. Each tool requires special preparation of the application which is in most cases the main incompatibility cause.

1.1.9 Grid Services

The Grid community acknowledged Web services [193] as the fundamental technology for building service-oriented infrastructures for the Grid. The Web services standards, purposely designed by industry for modeling persistent and stateless business processes, have fundamental limitations in modeling Grid resources that are by definition transient and stateful. While there are present approaches that aim to define new standards for modeling Grid resources with Web services [13, 46], there were little efforts to analyse and validate their appropriateness by the time we carried out the work presented in this monograph.

1.1.10 Scientific Workflows

Workflow modeling originating in business process modeling field [187] is gaining increased interest as the potential state-of-the-art paradigm for programming Grid applications. Despite this general consensus, there is little work to formally define the model and characteristics of scientific workflows suitable for being executed in Grid environments [198]. For example, while business workflows are in most cases Directed Acyclic Graphs (DAG) that consist of a limited number of nodes, scientific workflows that implement Grid applications are often based on a Directed Graph (DG) model and require large iterative loops that implement a dynamic convergence behaviour or a recursive problem definition. In addition, there is still little tool support that tries to automatise the runtime execution cycle of scientific workflows on dynamic and unreliable computational Grids, in particular with regard to scheduling, fault tolerance, and performance analysis. While these topics have been extensively studied in other fields like business modeling, heterogeneous, distributed, and parallel systems, or compiler construction, there is little effort that tries to apply existing technology and practice to scientific workflows in Grid environments.

1.2 Goals

We address the motivating problems outlined in the previous sections in the context of a novel experiment management tool and an open architecture for integrated tool development in Grid infrastructures.

1.2.1 Experiment Specification Language

We propose a new *directive-based language* called ZEN [139, 143] to facilitate the specification of arbitrary application parameters through annotations of arbitrary application files. We define so called ZEN directives as language independent comments with a well-defined syntax that do not change the semantics of the application source files, as they are ignored by compilers or interpreters that are unaware of their semantics. The scope of the ZEN directives can be global or restricted to arbitrary code regions, which allows local fine-grained parametrisation. We associate simple macro-processor-based string replacement semantics to ZEN directives to ensure that they are not specific to any particular language or problem and can express new parameters that were not thought during the language design. We introduce constraint directives to filter invalid experiments and performance directives to specify the metrics to be measured and computed for fine-grained code regions, without altering the application source code with instrumentation probes. The directive-based approach gives the users the privilege to perform easy and flexible parametrisation that does not require any inconvenient modification or adaptation of their application.

1.2.2 Experiment Management Tool

We propose a novel general purpose *experiment management tool* called ZEN-TURIO [140, 144] that we purposely design to perform large scale *performance and parameter studies* for parallel and Grid applications. ZENTURIO uses the ZEN directive-based language to define potentially large value ranges for arbitrary application parameters, including program variables, file names, compiler options, target machines, machine sizes, scheduling strategies, or data distributions, with no intrusion in the source code and without forcing the developer to perform any undesired modification or adaptation to the application. We designed ZENTURIO as a distributed service-oriented tool consisting of the following client and service components:

1. A graphical *User Portal* is the only entry point for interacting with the tool and enables the user to easily create, manipulate, and online monitor large sets of executing experiments;
2. An *Experiment Generator* service parses application files annotated with ZEN directives and generates synthetic experiments based on the semantics of the directives encountered;
3. An *Experiment Executor* service retrieves a set of experiments and automatically compiles, executes, and monitors them on the target machine;
4. Optionally upon the completion of each experiment, the Experiment Executor automatically stores the output files and performance data into an *Experiment Data Repository* for post-mortem multi-experiment performance and parameter studies;
5. An advanced *Application Data Visualiser* portlet of the User Portal assists the user in automatically querying the repository and provides a wide set of analysis diagrams [67] to visualise the variation of any performance metric or output parameter as a function of arbitrary defined parameters.

1.2.3 Optimisation

As a next natural step, we enhanced ZENTURIO with a *modular framework* for solving customisable *NP-complete optimisation problems* [145]. The user can flexibly instantiate the framework for large scale performance and parameter optimisation problems by providing two (optionally three) inputs:

1. the *parameter space* by means of ZEN directive-based parameterisations [139, 143];
2. an *objective function* that must implement a *problem independent interface* defined by the framework. As case studies, we provide three objective function instantiations for three optimisation problems:
   a) application specific analytical prediction function for single static workflow scheduling [145, 146];
   b) random function for simulated independent task-set scheduling [145];
   c) performance metric for performance tuning of parallel applications, provided using the ZEN language and computed through experiment execution [147];
3. optionally, an encoding of the heuristic-based *search engine* to find a point in the parameter space that maximises the objective function, or employ existing algorithms that we predefine as part of the framework implementation.

We implement generic *meta-heuristics* that can be applied to any optimisation problem to surf the search space defined through ZEN directives for an experiment that maximises the objective function. We illustrate a generic encoding of the search engine using a *genetic algorithm* and target various other algorithms, including subdivision, simplex, and simulated annealing, as future work.

1.2.4 Scientific Workflows

As the workflow model emerged as an attractive paradigm in the Grid community for efficiently executing scientific applications in loosely coupled Grid environments, we contribute to the state-of-the-art practice in the field in the following aspects [69]:

1. *formal specification of scientific workflow model* [70] with regards to:
   a) *scalable representation* of large workflows structures consisting of hundreds to thousands of so called activities interconnected through control flow and data flow dependencies;
   b) support for formal specification of *dynamic workflows* with runtime changing structures, comprising dynamic shape, variable number of activities, variable execution paths, or variable data dependencies;
   c) support for concise specification of *complex data transfer models* between large numbers of workflow activities, including collective communication patterns like broadcast, scatter, and gather;

   d) support for DG-based workflows with sequential recursive *loops*, often
      characterised by statically unknown number of iterations, for example
      due to application specific dynamic convergence criteria;
2. transfer of *scheduling technology* techniques [145, 189, 190] from distributed computing and compiler optimisation fields for optimised mapping of
   complex workflow structures onto the computational and network Grid
   resources. We bring enhancements to existing scheduling algorithms that
   are limited to DAG-based structures and do not consider sequential loops
   in the mapping and execution process [146];
3. *scalable execution* that tries to minimise the rather crude overheads introduced by the Grid middleware technologies through a distributed architecture, workflow partitioning, and optimisation techniques [58, 61];
4. incorporation of *fault tolerance* techniques, especially from the distributed systems field, including replication, migration, and various levels of
   checkpointing mechanisms [59];
5. *dynamic steering* techniques for runtime adaptation of workflow static
   schedules and runtime executions to dynamically changing Grid environments. We propose a novel hybrid approach for dynamic steering of DG-
   based workflow applications that adapts the optimised static schedules to
   the heterogeneous and dynamically changing Grid resources upon well-
   defined rescheduling events, including performance contracts established
   during the scheduling process (as a form of negotiation) [146];
6. *overhead analysis* that tries to systematically classify and understand the
   major sources of overheads encountered when executing large scientific
   workflows in distributed Grid environments [58, 133].

1.2.5 Service-Oriented Grid Architecture

The main reason why each computing platform has its own heterogeneous
set of tools is their limited portability. In addition, the tools are usually designed as stand-alone and cannot be used in cooperation to improve the user
efficiency in the application engineering process. We approach the portability and interoperability issues through a distributed *multi-layered service-
oriented architecture* with the following design principles [110, 111]:

1. the platform dependencies are isolated within stand-alone distributed
   services and sensors exporting a platform independent interface. The user
   tool is therefore decoupled from the intimate hardware and operating
   system dependencies which significantly increases the tool portability;
2. we identified and implemented a set of general purpose middleware services that provide enhanced functionality to support the tool development
   in Grid environments, including factory, registry, experiment generation
   and execution, aggregation, instrumentation, and scheduling;
3. the recommendation that every computer vendor provides a core set of
   tool services with a platform independent interface significantly eases the
   tool development and multi-platform availability;

4. the functionality of each tool is no longer implemented by a single monolithic tool acting as a big black-box. Enabling light weight portals easily to be installed and managed on local client machines significantly simplifies the use of Grid environments by non-expert users;

5. the services are designed such that they can be concurrently accessed by multiple clients. This enables multiple tools interoperate by sharing common services which possibly monitor the same target application processes;

6. an asynchronous event framework enables the services to notify the clients about interesting application and system events. Events are important for detecting important status information about the system and application and can be used to avoid expensive continuous polling.

Beyond the provisioning of an open framework for tool development, we identify and study various practical scenarios how *interoperable use of software tools* can significantly improve the productivity of the application engineering process [111, 150].

1.2.6 Grid Services

We contribute with several proposals regarding enhancements and adaptations of the Web services technology for implementing services that model *stateful Grid resources* [142, 144]:

1. we define and implement of the factory design pattern for on-the-fly service instantiation on remote Grid sites;

2. we design and implement a registry service for high throughput service discovery;

3. we define a service compatibility operation for functionality-based service discovery (i.e. green pages lookup operation);

4. we adapt existing Web services standards for publishing persistent service implementations (rather than persistent instances);

5. we model service state and lifecycle using non-standard extensions provided by existing Web services implementation toolkits;

6. we comparatively analyse and benchmark existing ongoing standards for modeling transient and stateful Grid services and their underlying implementations [141, 144].

1.3 Outline

Chapter 2 presents the Grid architectural model which represents the foundation on top of which we will elaborate the concepts presented in this monograph.

Chapter 3 presents a complete formal specification of the ZEN directive-based language used to specify application parameters and performance metrics.

Chapter 4 is devoted to a detailed description of the ZENTURIO experiment management tool with particular focus on the tool functionality applied to a broad range of real-world applications.

Chapter 5 describes the open service-oriented architecture for interoperable tool development, in the frame of which we designed the ZENTURIO experiment management tool. We present in detail the set of sensors, the Grid services, the event framework, and several prototype online tools, together with various tool interoperability types and scenarios.

Chapter 6 presents the ZENTURIO optimisation framework validated by three case studies: workflow scheduling, throughput scheduling, and performance tuning of parallel applications.

In Chapter 7 we present a timely approach to modeling, scheduling, fault tolerant scalable execution, and overhead analysis of scientific workflow applications in dynamic and heterogeneous Grid environments.

Chapter 8 outlines the most relevant related work in all the fields touched by the previous chapters: experiment management, performance studies, parameter studies, tool interoperability, scheduling, and scientific workflows.

Chapter 9 summarises the research work presented in this monograph.

2
Model

2.1 Introduction

The mostly used attempt to define Grid computing [77] is through an analogy with the electric power evolution around 1910. The truly revolutionary development was not the discovery of electricity itself, but the electric power grid that provides standard, reliable, and low cost access to the associated transmission and distribution technologies. Similarly, the Grid research challenge is to provide standard, reliable, and low cost access to the relatively cheap computing power available nowadays.

Definition 2.1. *A computational Grid was originally defined as a hardware and software infrastructure that provides dependable, consistent, pervasive, and inexpensive access to high-end computational capabilities [77]. With the time, the Grid concept has been refined and better formulated, e.g. as a persistent infrastructure that supports computation and data intensive collaborative activities that spawn across multiple* Virtual Organisations.

The natural starting point in building computational Grids is the existing world wide Internet infrastructure that aggregates a potentially unbounded number of resources. Analogous to the World Wide Web that provides ubiquitous access to the information over the Internet, the computational Grids explore new mechanisms for ubiquitous access to computational resources and quality of service beyond the best effort provided by the Internet protocol (IP).

There are currently two recognised architectural approaches for building scalable Grid infrastructures:

1. *Service-oriented architectures* [89] are based on the aggregation of portable and reusable programs called services that can be accessed by remote clients over the network in a platform and language independent manner.

   Definition 2.2. *A* service *is a self-contained entity program accessible through a well-defined protocol and using a well-defined platform and language independent interface that does not depend on the context or the state of other services.*

A service-oriented architecture is suitable for implementing Grid environments due to several significant advantages that it offers:

   a) it increases the *portability* and facilitates the *maintenance* of the system by isolating platform dependent services to appropriate sites accessible using a well-defined platform independent interface;

   b) it enables *interoperability* by providing well-defined standard network protocols for communicating with the remote services;

   c) it enables *light-weight clients* which are easy to be installed and managed by unexperienced users by isolating complex implementation functionality within external services;

   d) it *decouples* the clients from the rest of the system and allows the users to *move*, *share*, and *access* the services from different Grid locations;

2. *Peer-to-peer architectures* [17] are an aggregation of equivalent programs called *peers* situated at the edges of the Internet that provide functionality and share part of their own hardware resources with each other (e.g. processing power, storage capacity, network link bandwidth, printers) through network contention without passing through intermediate entities. The strength of peer-to-peer architectures is the high degree of *scalability* and *fault tolerance*.

We build the integrated tool environment presented in this book on the foundation of a generic service-oriented architectural model that is the scope of the remaining part of this chapter.

2.2 Distributed Technology History

The realisation of service-oriented architectures for building distributed Grid infrastructures is the outcome of a long track of research and industry experience on distributed services and component technologies.

Distributed applications require a protocol which defines the communication mechanism between two concurrent remote processes. Traditionally, there have been two communication protocol models for building distributed applications: message passing/queuing and request / response. While both models have their individual advantages, either one can be implemented in terms of the other. For example, messaging systems can be built using lower level request / response protocols, which was the case of the Microsoft's *Distributed Computing Environment (DCE)* [156]. For the (Sun) *Remote Procedure Call (RPC)* [163] applications, the synchronous request/response design style is usually a natural fit. In the 1980s, the communication protocol models focused on the network layer, such as the *Network File System* [174] developed originally by Sun Microsystems (which most networked Unix systems currently use as their distributed file system) and Microsoft DCE RPC applications on Windows NT.

In the 1990s, the object-oriented community pushed for an *Object RPC (ORPC)* protocol that links application objects to network protocols. The

primary difference between ORPC and the proceeding RPC protocols is that
ORPC codifies the mapping of a communication endpoint to a language level
object. This mapping allows the server-side middleware locate and instantiate
a target object in the server process. The *Common Object Resource Broker
Architecture (CORBA)* [120] designed by the Object Management Group and
the Microsoft's *Distributed Component Object Model (DCOM)* [158] have
dominated and competed for many years for an ORPC protocol industry
standard. Although CORBA and DCOM have been implemented on various
platforms, the reality is that any solution built on these protocols is largely
dependent on a single vendor implementation. Thus, if one were to develop
a DCOM application, all the participating nodes in the distributed application would have to be running a flavour of Windows. In the case of CORBA,
every node in the application environment would need to run the same *Object Request Broker (ORB)* product. While there are cases when CORBA
ORBs from different vendors do interoperate, that interoperability does not
extend to higher level services such as security and transaction management.
Furthermore, any vendor specific optimisations in this situation is lost.

Other efforts such as the *Java Remote Method Invocation (RMI)* [93] from
Sun Microsystems enhanced with the *Jini* [64] network awareness are bound
to the Java language and fail to fulfill the language independence requirement
of Grid computing. The *Enterprise Java Beans* [157] server-side component
technology for the Java 2 Enterprise Edition (J2EE) platform [105] failed
to become a standard due to incompatible data formats, limited network
transport layer security, the use of non-Web-based communication protocols,
and the lack of semantic information in the data representation.

2.3 Web Services

In the year 2000, a consortium of companies comprising Microsoft, IBM,
BEA Systems, and Intel defined a new set of XML (eXtensive Markup Language) [94] standards for programming Business-to-Business (B2B) applications called *Web services* [89], which are currently being standardised under
the umbrella of the World Wide Web Consortium (W3C) [193]. The motivation behind the Web services is to solve existing barriers between traditional Enterprise Java Beans businesses collaborating in electronic transactions
such as incompatible data formats, security issues, Web access, and semantic
information. Web services are a technology for *deployment* and *access* of business functions over the Web that compliments existing standards like J2EE,
CORBA, DCOM, RMI, or Jini, which are technologies for *implementing* Web
services.

Definition 2.3. *A* Web service *is an interface that describes a collection of
operations of a service (see Definition 2.2) that are network accessible through
standardised XML messaging.*

2.3.1 Web Services Stack

The key for interoperability between Web services the outcome of a three layer *Web services stack* [113] depicted in Figure 2.1.

1. *The Hyper Text Transfer Protocol (HTTP)* is a bottom simple and firewall friendly RPC-like protocol that is the current defacto standard for Web communication over the TCP/IP protocol. Additionally, HTTP can operate on top of the Transport Layer Security (TLS) (or its Secure Socket Layer (SSL) predecessor) to provide secure communication using authentication and encryption mechanisms provided by the Public Key Infrastructure (PKI) [19];

2. *The Simple Object Access Protocol (SOAP)* is the XML-based message passing standard for communication between remote Web services using both message passing and request/response communication models on top of HTTP. SOAP is open to additional underlying network protocol bindings beyond HTTP, such as File Transfer Protocol (FTP), Simple Mail Transfer Protocol (SMTP), Message Queuing (MQ) Protocol, Java Remote Method Protocol (JRMP), or CORBA Internet Inter-ORB Protocol (IIOP). However, in contrast to the popular belief, Web services do not mandate the use of SOAP for Web services communication;

3. The *Web Service Description Language (WSDL)* [38] is the XML standard for the specification of Web services interfaces, analogous to the CORBA Interface Definition Language. A WSDL document is commonly divided into two distinct parts [113]:

   a) *service interface* is the abstract and reusable part of a service definition, analogous to an abstract interface in a programming language, that can be instantiated and referenced by multiple service implementations. A service interface consists of the following XML elements:

      i. `wsdl:types` contains the definition of complex XML schema data types [195] which are used by the service interface;

      ii. `wsdl:message` defines the data transmitted as a collection of logical parts (`wsdl:parts` – e.g. input arguments, return argument,

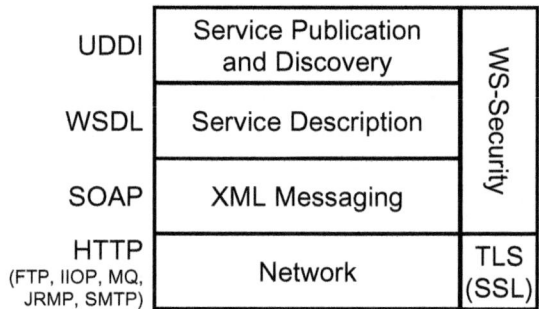

Fig. 2.1. The interoperable Web services stack.

and exception messages), each of which being associated with a different type;

iii. `wsdl:operation` is a named endpoint that consumes an input message and returns an output message and a fault message (corresponds to a Java class method);

iv. `wsdl:portType` defines a set of abstract operations (corresponds to a Java interface definition);

v. `wsdl:binding` describes the protocol and the data format for the operations of a `portType`;

b) *service instance* part of a WSDL document describes an instantiation of a Web service. A Web service instance is modeled as a `wsdl:service`, which contains a collection of `wsdl:port` elements (i.e. usually one). A `port` associates one network endpoint (e.g. URL) with a `wsdl:binding` element from a service interface definition.

A common practice is to define the service interface in a separate *abstract interface WSDL document* which is further included into the *instance WSDL document* through an `import` element;

4. *The Universal Description, Discovery and Integration (UDDI)* [137] is a specification for distributed Web-based information registries of business Web services. The WSDL interface and the URL address of persistent Web services are typically published in a centralised UDDI Service Repository for remote discovery and access. The UDDI best practices document [41] requires that the interface part of the WSDL document be published as a UDDI `tModel` and the instance part as a `businessService` element (i.e. as URLs), as shown in Figure 2.2. The `businessService` UDDI element is a descriptive container used to group related Web services. It contains one or more `bindingTemplate` elements which contain information for connecting and invoking a Web service. The `bindingTemplate` contains a pointer to a `tModel` element which describes the Web service meta-data. An `accessPoint` element is instantiated with the SOAP address of the service `port`;

5. *The Web Services Security (WS-Security)* [131] specification describes enhancements to the SOAP messaging that provide quality of protection through message integrity (through XML digital signature), message confidentiality (through XML encryption), and single message authentication. These mechanisms can be used to accommodate a wide variety of security models and encryption technologies, including PKI (see Section 2.4). We can observe in Figure 2.1 that security can be applied at two different layers in the Web services stack:

a) *network layer* over the TLS protocol;

b) *message layer* based on WS-Security for signing and encrypting XML-based SOAP messages.

Security at the message layer is more powerful than the security at the network layer, since the data encryption happens at a higher level of

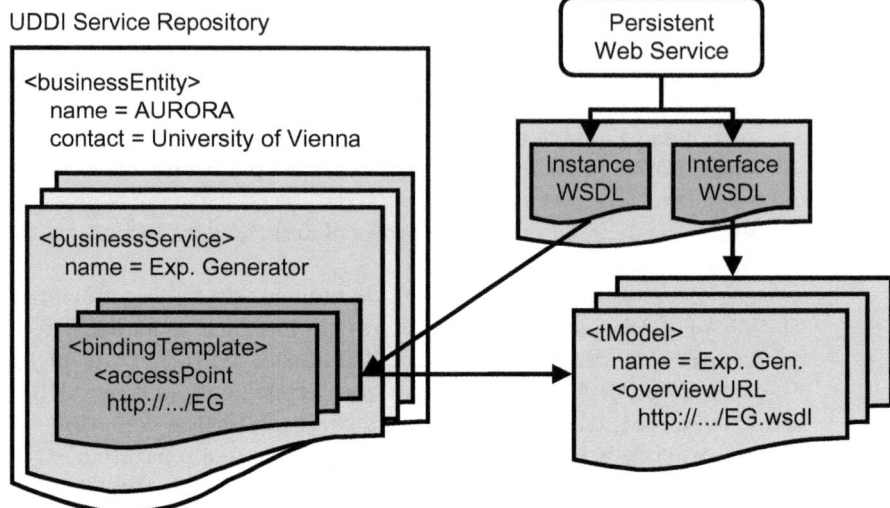

Fig. 2.2. The best practices of publishing a Web service into a UDDI Service Repository.

abstraction (i.e. it is easier to read a credit card number from an ASCII SOAP message than from a network packet). A higher degree of security can be achieved through authentication and data encryption at both network and message layers, however, at accumulated security overhead costs.

2.3.2 Web Services Runtime Environment

The Web services standards omit on purpose to specify any runtime environment that implements the service-oriented architecture based on XML document exchange. Java is currently the most popular programming language supported by high level Web services implementations due to its platform independent interpreted object code design. Figure 2.3 illustrates the most common runtime architectural design implemented by existing advanced industry or open source Web services toolkits for Java [11, 103, 129, 173, 186].

Following the CORBA RPC-based model, advanced implementation toolkits completely shield the client application from the underlying XML-based technologies. Existing tools transform / generate the WSDL description of a Web service into / from a (Java) interface definition which is understood by the (Java) clients. Automatically generated *stubs* that export the Web service interface in the client implementation language perform automatic parameter marshaling and (SOAP) message routing.

The Java implementation of the SOAP-based communication infrastructure can be based either on the synchronous JAX-RPC (Java API for XML

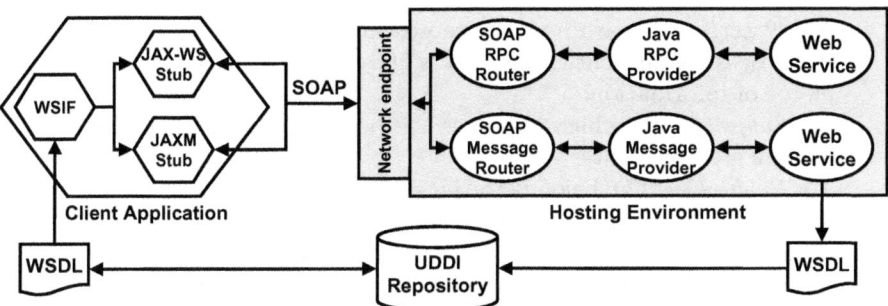

Fig. 2.3. The Web services runtime environment.

RPC), JAX-WS (Java API for XML Web Services), or the asynchronous JAXM (Java API for XML Messaging) libraries designed by Sun Microsystems. These interfaces are used for mapping each remote call from a Java client into a SOAP message. Additionally, the *Web Services Invocation Framework (WSIF)* [62] enables the invocation of WSDL-described services independently of the underlying (SOAP) protocol implementation.

Similar to the Enterprise Java Beans component model, Web services typically run within a *hosting environment*, such as J2EE [105], JBoss [73], Tomcat [119], Weblogic [134], or Websphere [97], which is an HTTP server and servlet engine responsible for deploying and managing the service lifecycle. The Web service functionality is typically encoded as a Java class that implements the service WSDL interface and deployed using the hosting environment specific tools. Upon receiving a message at the network endpoint of the hosting environment, a SOAP RPC / message router (servlet) unmarshals the message and forwards it to a Java RPC / message provider. The Java provider loads the Java class specified in the SOAP message (if not already loaded) that implements the Web service and invokes the appropriate method. The results of the method are returned to the SOAP router which marshals and transfers them to the requesting client.

2.4 Grid Security Infrastructure

The abstract Grid architectural model that we describe in this chapter implicitly assumes the use of the *Grid Security Infrastructure (GSI)* [78] as the defacto standard for authentication and secure communication across applications and services. GSI has the following distinguishing characteristics that makes it suitable for being applied in Grid environments:

1. *Public key cryptography* [19] based on private and public key pairs is the fundamental technology used for encrypting and decrypting messages;
2. *Digital signatures* are employed for insuring data integrity over the network;

3. *X.509 certificates* are used for representing the identity of each user in the process of authentication. An X.509 certificate includes four primary pieces of information:
    a) *Subject name* which identifies the person or the object that the certificate represents;
    b) *Public key* that belongs to the subject;
    c) *Certificate Authority* that signed the certificate and certifies that the public key and the subject name belong to the same trusted subject;
    d) *Digital signature* of the trusted certificate authority;
4. *Mutual authentication* is a protocol which ensures that the two parties involved in communication identify each other and trust their certificate authorities;
5. *Secure private keys* promote the encrypted store of the user private key exclusively on the local personal computer (i.e. laptop) or on cryptographic smartcards;
6. *Single sign-on* restricts the user authentication to one single password (keyboard) specification during a working session;
7. *Proxy cryptography* creates a new private and public key-pair digitally signed by the user that temporarily represents the user's Grid identity. This allows the true private key of the user be un-encrypted for a minimum amount of time until the signed proxy is generated which minimises the danger of loosing the identity;
8. *Proxy delegation* allows remote services behave on behalf of the client through the creation of remote proxies that impersonate the user (see Figure 2.4).

2.5 Globus Toolkit

Since 1995, the *Globus Toolkit (GT)* [76] is the driving force in Grid computing, developing middleware technology aimed to support and ease the

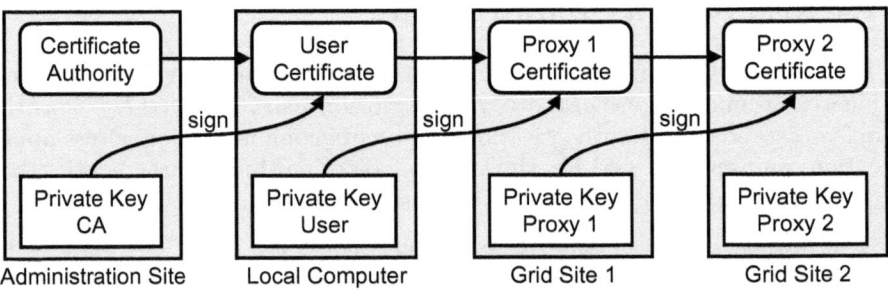

Fig. 2.4. The GSI single sign-on and proxy delegation chain of trust.

development of high level Grid infrastructures and applications with special focus on high performance scientific computing.

The version two of GT, in short GT2, was the most successful and stable Globus release at the time we carried out this research, which provides the following three categories of fundamental services for building higher level Grid infrastructures:

1. *Resource management services* for executing applications on remote Grid sites, which comprise:
   a) *Grid Resource Allocation Manager (GRAM)* [47] that provides a single GSI-enabled interface for allocating and using remote computational resources on top of existing local resource managers like Condor [123], Load Sharing Facility [201], Maui, Portable Batch System (PBS) [29], Sun Grid Engine [172], or simple Unix `fork` [168] system call;
   b) *Dynamically-Updated Request Online Coallocator (DUROC)* [48] that employs multiple GRAM services for co-allocation of several Grid sites for executing the same application instance. DUROC requires reservation functionality from the local resource manager in order to work effectively in real Grid environments;
   GRAM and DUROC use the *Resource Specification Language (RSL)* to formulate resource requirements;
2. *Information services* implemented by the *Monitoring and Discovery Service (MDS)* [72] that comprises:
   a) *Grid Resource Information Service (GRIS)* that provides information about a particular site using an underlying sensor like the Ganglia [126] for machine information;
   b) *Grid Index Information Service (GIIS)* that provides hierarchical means of aggregating multiple GRIS services for a coherent Grid system image and efficient high performance resource query support;
3. *Data Grid services* represented by the:
   a) *Global Access to Secondary Storage (GASS)* [25] libraries and utilities which simplify the process of porting and running of applications in a Grid environment by installing a transparent distributed file system that eliminates the need for manual login to remote Grid sites;
   b) *GridFTP* [6] which is a high performance, secure, and reliable data transfer protocol optimised for high bandwidth use of wide area networks based on the highly popular FTP protocol;
   c) *Globus Replica Catalogue* [169] which is a mechanism for maintaining a catalogue of data set replicas;
   d) *Globus Replica Management* [169] which is a mechanism that ties together the Replica Catalogue and the GridFTP technologies for remote management of large data set replicas.

The Globus Replica Catalogue and Replica Management services are very specific to data Grid and therefore we no longer consider them as part of our computational Grid architectural model presented in this chapter.

Despite its enormous success in the user Grid research community, GT2 on its own suffers from substantial integration and deployment problems, which is mostly due to its scripting or C language-based interface and implementation. The Java Commodity Grid Kit (CoG) [184] adds a layer on top of GT2 that exports a platform independent Java interface to the Globus services. GT2 and Java CoG, augmented with GSI and Web services support, represent an excellent starting point for implementing higher level Grid architectures, like the model that we describe in this chapter.

2.6 Grid Architectural Model

In conformance with the informal recommendations for building Grid environments formulated by the *Open Grid Services Architecture (OGSA)* [79] within the Global Grid Forum [37], we base our work on tool integration and development (see Chapter 7) on a service-oriented architecture depicted in Figure 2.5 which consists of three layers:

1. *The machine layer* is represented by a broad set of heterogeneous high performance computational resources that build in aggregation the hardware Grid infrastructure, while providing a set of monitoring sensors that export intimate machine information using a portable interface;
2. *The Grid services layer* is the middleware that builds a common bridge across heterogeneous resources by providing a broad set of high level functionality required for developing Grid applications such as registries, factories, schedulers, enactment engines, resource managers, or various instrumentation, aggregation, and filtering services. Beyond portability achieved through machine independent interfaces, communication using standard Web services-based SOAP protocol is the key for achieving interoperability between end-user applications;
3. *The application layer* is instantiated by user friendly portals or special purpose tools that interoperate through standardised SOAP message exchange on top of the Grid middleware services.

2.6.1 Machine Layer

The machine layer is represented by the set of computational resources, also called for brevity reasons *machines*, interconnected through conventional Internet protocols that build in aggregation the physical Grid hardware infrastructure. The machines can have a broad variety of architectures, ranging from single sequential computers to complex parallel architectures.

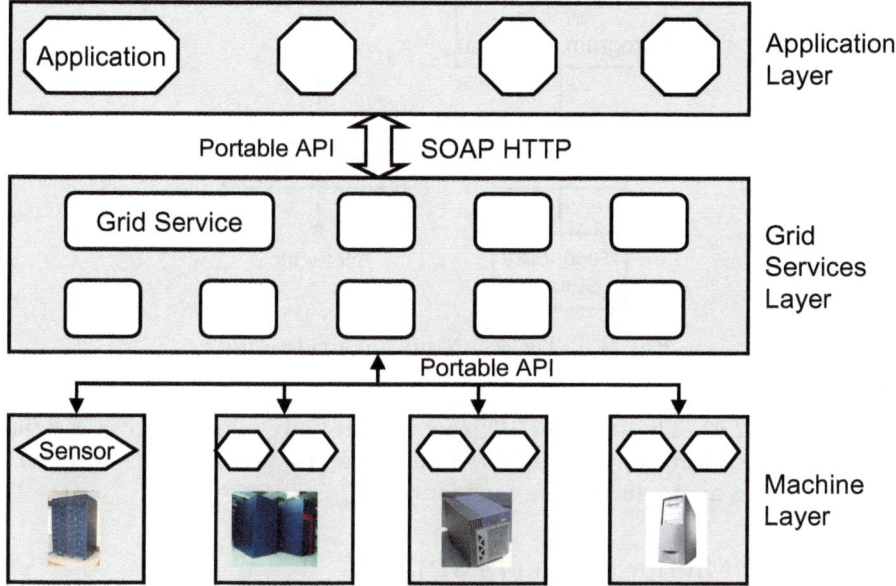

Fig. 2.5. The Grid architectural model.

In addition, all machines provide a set of low level platform dependent sensors that expose online monitoring information about the underlying capabilities and provide instrumentation and manipulation functionality using a machine independent interface. Isolating platform dependencies within sensor under a portable interface reduces the effort of porting n services onto m platforms from $n \times m$ to $n + m$.

Definition 2.4. *A* sensor *is a small light-weight background program, often also referred as* daemon, *that monitors and collects low level intimate information about running processes and the underlying computational resources. It additionally exports and provides remote access to this information by means of a well-defined platform independent interface.*

In the following, we summarise some of the most representative computer architectures that we commonly encounter in today's Grid environments.

Sequential Computers

Most of the past and present computers are based on the same machine model called the *von Neumann architecture*. A von Neumann computer comprises a single *Central Processing Unit (CPU)* connected to a single storage structure which holds both the set of instructions that dictates how to perform the computation, and the data produced or required by the computation

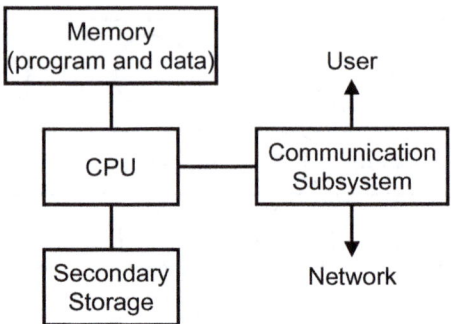

Fig. 2.6. The von Neumann architecture.

(see Figure 2.6). The unique CPU can execute only one stream of instructions and therefore supports only the Single Instruction Single Data (SISD) programming model in Flynn's taxonomy [74].

Symmetric Multiprocessors (SMP)

A Symmetric Multiprocessor (SMP) is a parallel computer consisting of two or more identical CPUs connected to a single shared main memory via a common bus (see Figure 2.7). The cost of accessing the shared memory is the same for all CPUs, for which reason SMPs are also called *Uniform Memory Access (UMA)* architectures. Each CPU, however, may have its local cache to exploit data locality and reduce the crude memory access latencies. The SMP architecture supports the Single Instruction Multiple Data (SIMD) and Multiple Instructions Multiple Data (MIMD) programming models in Flynn's taxonomy. One important aspect is that an SMP machine uses a single operating system and all CPUs share the same input and output resources. SMP computers allow any CPU work on any task, no matter where the data for that task is located in memory. With proper operating system support, SMPs can easily move processes between CPUs to balance the workload effectively.

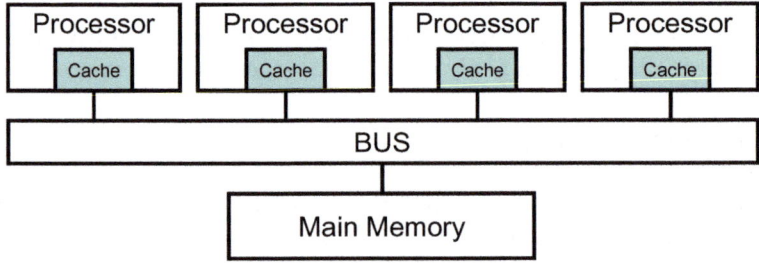

Fig. 2.7. The Symmetric Multiprocessor (SMP) architecture.

The disadvantage of SMPs is their limited scalability in accessing the shared memory through the common bus that becomes rapidly saturated.

Massively Parallel Processors (MPPs)

Massively Parallel Processors (MPPs) are huge and expensive supercomputers, consisting of possibly thousands of processors. The processor types used in an MPP machine are the ones commonly present in personal computers or workstations and are typically interconnected through a high performance proprietary network designed to achieve low latency and high bandwidth. The structure of the interconnecting network normally employs hypercube, tree, or two respectively three-dimensional mesh topologies.

Clusters of Workstations (COWs)

A Cluster of Workstations (COW), often also called Network of Workstations (NOW), is a collection of loosely coupled computers (compared to SMPs) that work together closely so that in many respects they can be viewed as a single parallel computer (see Figure 2.8). Clusters are commonly, but not always, connected through fast local area networks such as Fast Ethernet, Gigabit Ethernet, Myrinet, or Infiniband. Clusters are usually deployed to improve speed and reliability of single (sequential, SMP, MPP) computers, while typically being much more cost effective than single computers of comparable speed or reliability.

As any other distributed memory computer, COWs are typically accessible through manual remote login shells to one front-end (or master) computer shared by multiple end-users for source code editing, environment setup, compilation, and job management purposes. A local resource manager gives the users access (usually exclusive) to the compute nodes (or slaves), typically by submitting jobs to various cluster queues that run the computational intensive parallel applications.

SMP Clusters

SMP clusters combine the advantage of SMPs with the scalability of distributed memory computers (see Figure 2.9). An SMP cluster consists of a large set of SMP nodes interconnected through high performance commodity networks. This is presently the most successful parallel computer architecture employed by almost all supercomputers of today's top 500 ranking [57].

Cache Coherent Non-Uniform Memory Access (ccNUMA)

The rise in popularity of the single memory image offered by SMP computers, coupled with the desire to scale systems beyond the limits of bus or

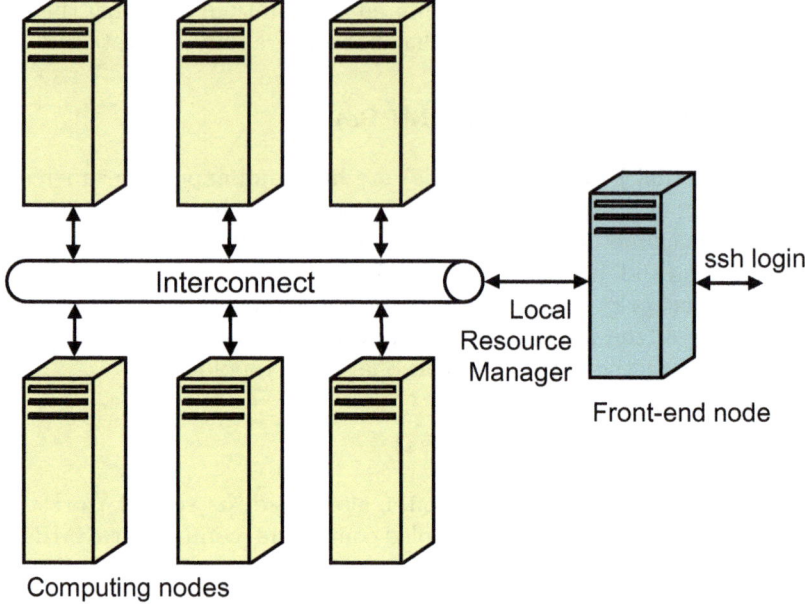

Fig. 2.8. The Cluster of Workstation (COW) architecture.

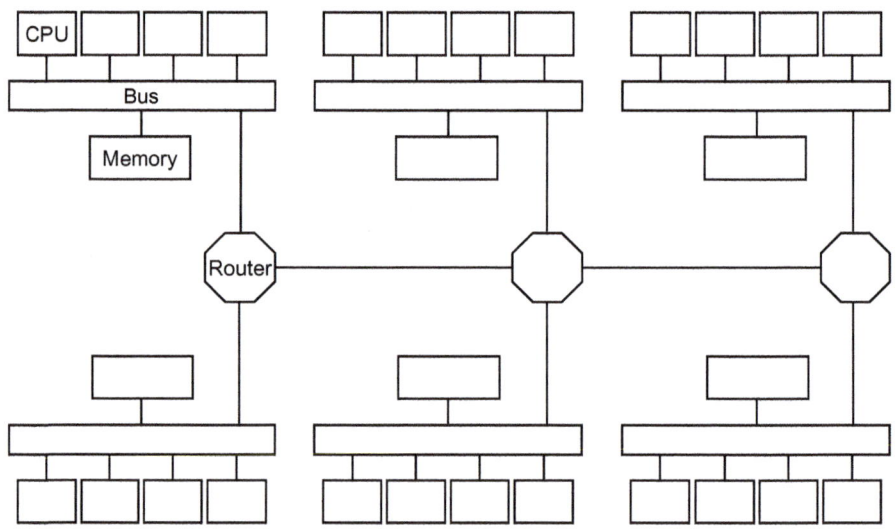

Fig. 2.9. The SMP cluster architecture.

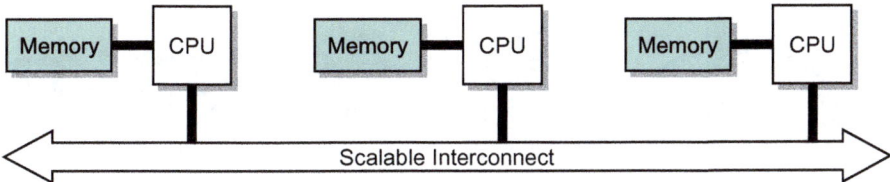

Fig. 2.10. The Cache Coherent Non-Uniform Memory Access (ccNUMA) architecture.

crossbar-based systems, led to the development of distributed shared memory architectures. In this model, memory is physically distributed at the hardware level but the system still presents a single logical memory image to the end-user (see Figure 2.10). Naturally, the processors will access their local memory much more quickly than that of a neighbour, thus giving rise to the term *Non-Uniform Memory Access (NUMA)*. This architecture presents problems in ensuring that the caches belonging to different processors are maintained in a coherent state, requiring additional hardware logic.

Although simpler to design and build, non-cache coherent NUMA parallel computers become prohibitively complex to program in the standard programming model of von Neumann architectures. As a result, all NUMA computers sold to the market use special purpose hardware to maintain cache coherence, and are therefore referred as cache coherent NUMA (ccNUMA) parallel computers. Typically, cache coherence takes place by using inter-processor communication between cache controllers (also called hubs) to keep a consistent memory image when more than one cache stores the same memory location. For this reason, ccNUMA performs poorly when multiple processors attempt to access the same memory area in rapid succession. Operating system support for NUMA attempts to reduce the frequency of this kind of access by allocating processors and memory in NUMA friendly ways and by avoiding expensive scheduling and locking algorithms.

A good example of leading edge ccNUMA parallel computers are SGI Origin and Altix range of servers.

Grid Infrastructures

Grid computing represents the next evolution step after cluster computing in aggregating cheap and widely available computing power required by high performance scientific applications. The scope of Grid computing is to aggregate and provide coordinated use of large sets of heterogeneous distributed resources, ranging from sequential and parallel computers, to storage systems, software, and data, all connected through the Internet-based wide area (high performance) network (see Figure 2.11). In contrast to dedicated clusters characterised by close (local area) proximity of their computing nodes and often homogeneous hardware and software infrastructures, Grids are characteri-

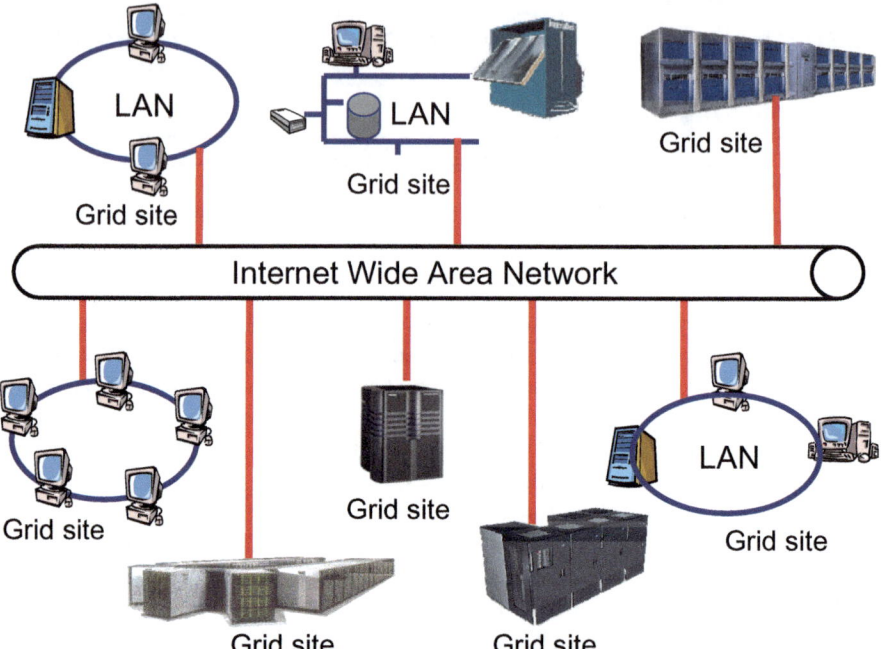

Fig. 2.11. The Grid hardware architecture.

sed by the distant proximity of large numbers of aggregated sites, inherently heterogeneous in terms of hardware, operating systems, and software.

Definition 2.5. *We define a* Grid site *(and often simply call* site *for brevity reasons) a sequential or parallel computer accessible through one hosting environment (see Section 2.3.2) and one single Grid Resource Allocation Manager (GRAM) service (introduced in Section 2.5) using polices establishes by local administration authorities usually through a local resource allocation manager.*

2.6.2 Grid Services Layer

The Grid services layer largely consists of a set of distributed services that provide generic high level functionality for advanced tool development, composition, integration, and interoperability.

The Grid community has generally acknowledged Web services as the defacto standard technology for the realisation of the service-oriented Grid architectures. However, the standard Web services technologies that we summarised in Section 2.3 are designed for integration of *persistent and stateless business processes*, in contrast to the Grid services that need to model *transient and stateful Grid resources*. Examples of target stateful resources include parallel applications, data repositories, local job management queues, or Grid sites with limited availability.

In this context, the *Open Grid Services Architecture (OGSA)* [79] is the generic broad architectural model currently being defined within the Global Grid Forum [37] that defines design mechanisms to uniformly expose Grid services semantics, to create, name, and discover transient Grid service instances, to provide location transparency and multiple protocol bindings for service instances, and to support integration with underlying native platform facilities. Extensive joint efforts in both Grid and Web communities are currently working towards defining a widely accepted standard for building OGSA compliant interoperable Grid services [13].

Definition 2.6. *A* Grid service *is a* Web service *enhanced with standard interface support for expressing* lifecycle, state, *and* asynchronous events *required for modeling and controlling* dynamic, stateful, *and* transient *Grid* resources.

A Grid site can host multiple Grid services within its hosting environment that can be remotely accessed using Web services XML-based document exchange. We define in our model two persistent Grid services that are required to exist in a Grid environment:

1. *Factory* for creating transient Grid service instances on arbitrary remote Grid sites;
2. *Registry* for light-weight publication, management and high throughput discovery of transient Grid services.

While there were several attempts in the Grid community that aimed to standardise the specification of state within Grid services [13, 46], there was no mature and widely accepted standard by the time we have carried out the work presented in this monograph. We can generally distinguish two orthogonal design patterns for modeling state within Grid services:

1. *Encapsulation* uses the Java Beans model of accessing and manipulating the service state through `get` and `set` interface methods. In this model illustrated in Figure 2.12(a), a *stateful Grid service* specialises the stateless Web service with methods concerning service state and lifecycle. The main advantage of the encapsulation model is the natural object-oriented design that facilitates specialised extensions through *inheritance*. The disadvantages are the non-standard extensions brought to the Web services technology and the poor fault tolerance due to the one-to-one association between the resource and the Grid service as a single point of failure. The encapsulation approach was taken by the currently obsolete Open Grid Services Infrastructure (OGSI) standard [46].
2. *Delegation* interposes a stateless Grid service (that remains a pure Web service) between the client and a *driver* that manages the stateful resources (see Figure 2.12(b)). While the implementation of the Grid service

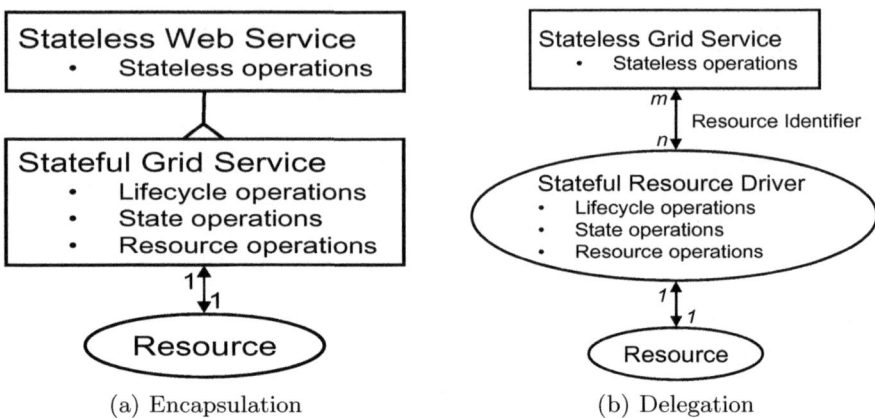

(a) Encapsulation   (b) Delegation

Fig. 2.12. The stateful Grid service design alternatives.

is stateless, the *interface* of the service is *stateful*. The state of the service within the service interface is represented by the *context* [32] that identifies and maps a request to an existing stateful resource (for instance by providing its reference handler). The advantages of the delegation model over encapsulation are its full compliance with the Web services principles and the high degree of fault tolerance due to the m to n association between the stateless Grid service and the modeled resource (i.e. multiple Grid services can be used for accessing a stateful resource). The task of providing fault tolerance is naturally deferred to the specialised resource driver. The delegation approach is currently being taken by the Web Services Resource Framework (WSRF) [13] specification.

2.6.3 Application Layer

The application layer is represented in our architecture by the portable and interoperable end-user applications, typically represented by graphical user portals or special purpose applications and tools, built on top of the Grid middleware services underneath.

In this section, we present three generic models that represent some of the most representative types of applications that are currently successful in harnessing the computational power provided by existing Grid environments: single site parallel applications, workflows, and parameter studies.

Single Site Applications

Single site Grid applications (see Definition 2.6) are typically represented by traditional *sequential* and tightly coupled *parallel applications* running on the computer architectures that we introduced in Section 2.6.1. In this section, we give an abstract execution model of parallel applications depicted in Figure 2.13, that represents the foundation for the multi-experimental performance analysis addressed in this monograph (see Chapters 3 and 4).

A parallel application consists of a set of distributed memory processes. Each process executes a program which is divided in sequential and parallel regions. A process may dynamically fork, synchronise, and terminate threads during its execution. All the threads of a process share the same address space. In a sequential region only one thread of the process is active. In a parallel region several threads may be active and execute simultaneously. Depending on the language implementation, the threads may be spawned at the beginning of the program or at the beginning of each parallel region.

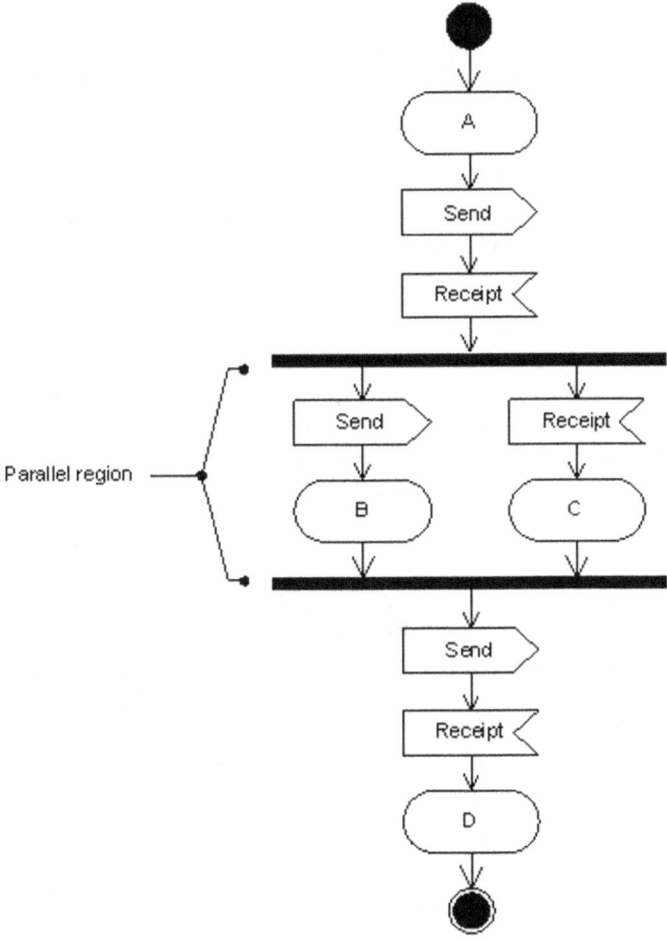

Fig. 2.13. The parallel application execution model.

At the end of the parallel region the active threads may be synchronised, for example through a barrier or a join operation. Following the parallel region, all the parallel threads except the one that continues to execute the sequential region are either terminated or stopped. A stopped thread can be resumed by a subsequent parallel region or terminated at the end of the program execution. The threads active within the same process exchange data through a common shared memory segment. The distributed memory processes exchange data through generic *send* and *receive* message passing operations, executed either by the sequential processes or by the parallel threads. All the parallel processes and all the threads are terminated at the end of the execution of the parallel application.

There are currently two widely accepted standards that implement in cooperation this hybrid distributed and shared memory parallel application model:

1. *Message Passing Interface (MPI)* [164] for explicit message passing between processes on distributed memory architectures (i.e. COW, NOW, MPP);
2. *Open Multiprocessing (OpenMP)* [49] for implicit compiler-based parallelization on shared memory architectures (i.e. SMP, ccNUMA).

Figure 2.14 displays a typical generic scenario for executing parallel single site applications in a Grid environment:

1. *query* the *Monitoring and Discovery Service (MDS)* information service for the remote parallel computers and the underlying hardware and software configurations (e.g. processor speed, memory and disk size, compiler and software libraries available, queue load and permissions) required to execute the application. Each parallel computer represents in our model a computational Grid site (see Definition 2.5);
2. *transfer* the parallel application to the remote Grid site using the GridFTP file transfer protocol. Remotely running a (C or Fortran) par-

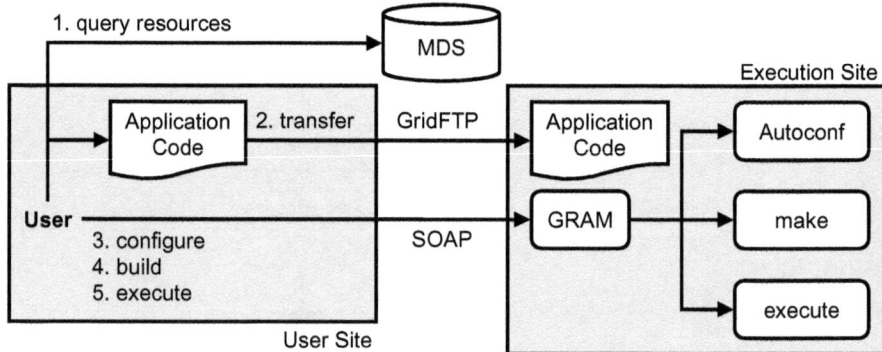

Fig. 2.14. The execution model of parallel applications on the Grid.

allel application is bound to difficult software dependencies, such as the availability of shared libraries, or non-standard options required for compiling and linking the application. A pragmatic solution for solving such complex remote dependencies is to build *static binary executable code* on a local computer compatible with the remote architecture and operating system, however, at a certain performance penalty. In cases when the transfer of the source code to the remote Grid site cannot be avoided, the next execution steps are required;

3. *configure* the application source code for the target architecture, typically by executing a remote auto-configuration program (like *Autoconf* [82] employed by the GNU software) using GRAM;
4. *build* (i.e. compile and link) the application, typically by executing a `make` command on the remote execution site front-end processor using GRAM;
5. *execute* and *monitor* the application using GRAM, typically configured to interact with an available back-end local resource manager [29, 102, 123, 172, 201] that gives access to the computing nodes (slaves). Automatic input and output file staging is automatically performed using GASS functionality.

Workflow Applications

Workflow modeling is a well established area in computer science that is strongly driven and influenced by the business process modeling field [187]. Recently, the Grid community has generally acknowledged that orchestrating Grid services in a workflow represents an important class of loosely coupled applications suited for programming large scale Grid environments. The Grid services are usually wrappers around off-the-shelf applications (often also called components) that solve a well-defined atomic problem.

In this section, we introduce a generic low level workflow model that represents our fundamental internal representation for scheduling and scalable execution in Grid environments, to which any higher level (user-oriented) workflow specification needs to be compiled (see Chapter 7).

Definition 2.7. *We model a workflow application as a Directed Acyclic Graph (DAG):* $\mathcal{A} = (Nodes, C\text{-}edges)$, *where Nodes is the set of workflow* activities *and C-edges is the set of directed* control *flow dependencies. We classify the workflow activities in two distinct categories:*

$$Nodes = Nodes^{CA} \cup Nodes^{DA} :$$

1. Computational activities, *denoted as* $CA(z) \in Nodes^{CA}$, *where z is the abstract site where the CA activity executes. We ignore in our representation the concrete type and location (beyond site) of the computational activity for simplicity and clarity reasons (required in Chapter 6);*

2. Data transfer activities, *denoted as* $DA(z_1, z_2) \in Nodes^{DA}$, *where* z_1 *and* z_2 *are the source, respectively the destination abstract sites of the transfer. We ignore in our representation the concrete name and location (exact path on one site) of the data transfer activity for the same simplicity and clarity reasons.*

Let $succ(N)$ *denote the set of* successors *of one activity* $N \in Nodes$:

$$N_s \in succ(N) \iff \exists \, (N, N_s) \in \textit{C-edges}.$$

Similarly, let $pred(N)$ *denote the set of* predecessors *of one activity* $N \in Nodes$:

$$N_p \in pred(N) \iff \exists \, (N_p, N) \in \textit{C-edges}.$$

If $pred(N) = \emptyset$, *where* $\emptyset$ *denotes the empty set, then* N *is a* start *activity. Similarly, if* $succ(N) = \emptyset$ *then* N *is an* end *activity. Additionally, we refer to the set of predecessors and successors of rank* p *of an activity* N *as:*

$$pred^p(N) = pred(\ldots pred(N)),$$

respectively:

$$succ^p(N) = succ(\ldots succ(N))$$

(p calls). Two activities N_1 *and* N_2 *are* independent *if and only if* $\nexists \, p$ *such that* $N_1 \in pred^p(N_2) \lor N_1 \in succ^p(N_2)$.

We model a *CA* activity as a single site Grid application, as described in Section 2.6.3, remotely allocated and manipulated using GRAM. An *DA* activity uses the GridFTP high performance network communication protocol to physically transfer a file between two (i.e. source and destination) Grid sites. We transparently employ GSI for control flow activity authentication as well as GridFTP control and data channel security.

A workflow can have an arbitrary number of start and end activities. Additionally, we express input and output *file staging* in this simple model through *DA* workflow activities having predefined fixed (instead of abstract) source, respectively destination sites.

Parameter Studies

Parameter studies, also called parameter sweeps, are large sets of independent experiments that represent the same application executed on different input parameter configurations. The scope of parameter studies is to analyse the evolution of important output results as a function of various input parameter values.

We can model parameter studies as a specialisation of the workflow model: $\mathcal{A} = (Nodes, \textit{C-edges})$ introduced in Definition 2.7, where:

1. the set of activities exclusively consists of CA activities: $Nodes = Nodes^{CA}$;
2. the set of DA (i.e. data transfer) activities is empty: $Nodes^{DA} = \emptyset$;
3. the set of control flow dependencies between the parameter study activities is empty: $C\text{-}edges = \emptyset$.

We assume that file staging to the Grid sites available to the parameter study is done either offline or through GASS functionality.

2.7 Summary

In this section we defined a general Grid architectural and computing model based on several abstract concepts supported by mature implementation platforms. We introduced the Web services technology stack that defines the key middleware standards for achieving interoperability in a service-oriented Grid environment. Afterwards, we presented the Grid Security Infrastructure that extends the standard Public Key Infrastructure with functionality required by the users to access large scale and distributed Grid infrastructures, including proxy cryptography supporting single sign-on and delegation capabilities. Finally, we presented a three-tier abstract Grid architectural model comprising:

1. *the machine layer* that aggregates high performance computers based on today's most modern parallel computer architectures;
2. *the Grid services layer* that enhances the stateless and persistent Web services technology with functionality for modeling state and lifecycle of resources, which is one of the main differences that distinguishes Grid computing from business Web applications;
3. *the application layer* instantiated by end-user scientific applications or software tools. In this context, we introduced abstract models for representing and executing parallel applications, parameter studies, and scientific workflows in Grid environments.

3

The ZEN Experiment Specification Language

Existing parameter study tools provide support to specify value ranges for application parameters of interest, e.g. by means of external scripting languages [5], or through graphical annotation of input files [197]. All these approaches, however, force the user to export the application parameters to global input files or program arguments, which often requires undesired source code adaptation for using the tool. Additionally, there are no tools that combine the experiment specification and management with cross-experiment performance analysis. All currently existing performance tools are restricted to single experiment analysis, which is not enough for efficient application performance tuning, that is inherently a multi-experimental process.

3.1 Functionality and Use Cases

Under this motivation, we designed the ZEN language that addresses the parameter specification problem for performance and parameter studies using a directive-based approach [139, 143]. We define so called *ZEN directives* as program comments that can be inserted in any source file to specify value ranges for arbitrary application parameters.

One main advantage of the directive-based approach over an external script [5] is the ability to specify experiments at a more detailed granularity, e.g. associate local scopes to directives, restrict parametrisation to specific local variables, evaluate different scheduling alternatives for individual loops, or various distribution options for parallel arrays. Moreover, the ZEN directives do not change the semantics of the code, as they are ignored by language processors that are unaware of their semantics. We designed the ZEN directives as language independent and, therefore, can apply them in the context of any programming language.

Example 3.1 shows six sample ZEN directives valid, in descending order, in the context of the following programming languages: FORTRAN 77, Fortran 90/95, C, C++/Java, Lisp, and shell scripting language.

Example 3.1 (Sample ZEN directives in various programming languages).

```
CZEN$  A = { 1, 2, 3 }
!ZEN$  A = { 1, 2, 3 }
/*ZEN$ A = { 1, 2, 3 }*/
//ZEN$ A = { 1, 2, 3 }
;ZEN$  A = { 1, 2, 3 }
#ZEN$  A = { 1, 2, 3 }
```

We defined in the ZEN language four categories of directives:

1. *Substitute directives*, formally specified in Section 3.2.3, assign a set of values to an application parameter. Each value from the set represents an experimental value for the parameter that shall be used by the application scientist in a separate experiment. The parameter instantiation is performed through plain string substitution that replaces all occurrences of the parameter name with its experimental value (in the scope of the directive);

2. *Assignment directives*, formally specified in Section 3.2.6, have analogous specification semantics as the substitute directive with the difference that the parameter instantiation is performed by inserting an assignment statement in place of the directive, which assigns the experimental value to the parameter name (as program variable);

3. *Constraint directives*, formally specified in Section 3.2.8, define a boolean condition over multiple parameters which restricts the set of possible experiments to a meaningful subset;

4. *Performance directives*, formally specified in Section 3.2.9, are used to request a wide variety of performance metrics for specific code regions of the program. The scope of the ZEN language is therefore not restricted to parameter studies.

3.1.1 Shared Memory Application Scalability

OpenMP [49] is a directive-based language which represents the defacto standard defined by industry for programming shared memory architectures (see Section 2.6.3). One typical optimisation problem that concerns the users running OpenMP applications is to determine the *"optimal" number of threads* to execute a parallel region, expressed by the NUM_THREADS clause of the PARALLEL directive. The typical procedure for a user to achieve this goal is to manually change the number of threads parameter to this clause (or through a special hard-coded script), recompile the application, and observe the change in the execution time.

In our generic approach, the user simply inserts a global ZEN substitute directive d1, as illustrated in Example 3.2, that substitutes all occurrences of the parameter NUM_THREADS(4) in the enclosing file with the elements from the set:

$$\mathcal{V}^{\text{NUM\_THREADS}(4)} = \bigcup_{i=1}^{4} \text{NUM\_THREADS}(i).$$

As a result, four experiments will be automatically generated, each one executing the loop using a different number of parallel threads.

Example 3.2 (OpenMP parallel region scalability).

```
d1:  !ZEN$ SUBSTITUTE NUM_THREADS\(4\)={ NUM_THREADS({1:4}) }
d2:  !ZEN$ CR CR_P, CR_OMPPA PMETRIC WTIME, OSYNC
     !$OMP PARALLEL NUM_THREADS(4)
     .  .  .
     !$OMP END PARALLEL
```

In addition, the user can employ ZEN performance directives to specify the metrics of concern that should be collecting upon the execution of all experiments. The advantage of the directive-based approach in this case is that the user does not alter the original source code with tool or library specific instrumentation probes that can often be rather large in number and intrusive for parallel applications. The directive **d2** requests the wall-clock time (mnemonic WTIME) and the synchronisation time (mnemonic OSYNC) from the entire enclosing program unit (mnemonic CR_P) and all OpenMP parallel regions (mnemonic CR_OMPPA).

It is important to notice that the code shown in this example is semantically valid for both ZEN-aware and ZEN-unaware compilers, i.e. that understand or ignore the ZEN directives.

3.1.2 ZEN Transformation System

A file parameterised with ZEN directives, which we call ZEN file in Figure 3.1 (and formally define in Section 3.2.2, Definition 3.12), is given as input to a *ZEN Transformation System* that parses the ZEN directives and generates the corresponding (so called) ZEN file instances that instantiate each parameter with one concrete value. The ZEN Transformation System can be seen as a source-to-source language processor. The scanner and parser modules examine the ZEN directives and construct an abstract syntax tree representation of the ZEN file. The code generator is different from a conventional compiler unparser, as it commonly generates a possibly large number of ZEN file instances (instead of one). The code generation rules are specified by the semantics of the ZEN directives that annotate the ZEN file.

The number of the ZEN file instances is given by the cardinality of the value set of the ZEN file which we will formally define in Section 3.2.7.

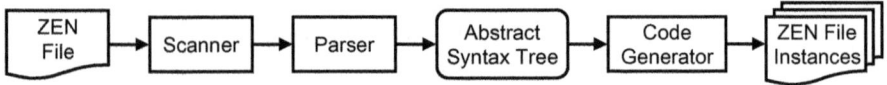

Fig. 3.1. The ZEN Transformation System.

3.1.3 Shared Memory Loop Scheduling

Appropriate *scheduling of parallel loops* is another critical optimisation decision for OpenMP parallel programs. Example 3.3 contains one parallel loop expressed through one OpenMP directive d2 with a default static scheduling strategy. We can easily express various other *scheduling strategies* combined with different so called *chunk sizes* [49] for all parallel loops of the enclosing file by means of a ZEN substitute directive d1, as follows:

STATIC scheduling means that the iterations are assigned to all parallel threads (i.e. four in this example) statically, before the parallel loop starts its execution;

DYNAMIC scheduling means that each thread dynamically receives a new set of iterations after it finishes the iterations assigned;

GUIDED scheduling means that the iteration space is divided into scheduling pieces, where the size of each successive piece is exponentially decreased.

The chunk size indicates the number of loop iterations to be scheduled atomically. The ZEN directive d1 replaces the original OpenMP scheduling clause STATIC with every element from the set[1]:

$$\mathcal{V}^{\text{STATIC}} = \{\underline{\text{STATIC},10}\ ,\ \underline{\text{STATIC},100}\ ,\ \underline{\text{DYNAMIC},10}\ ,\ \underline{\text{DYNAMIC},100}\ ,$$
$$\underline{\text{GUIDED},10}\ ,\ \underline{\text{GUIDED},100}\}$$

in different experiments.

Example 3.3 (OpenMP loop scheduling).

```
d1: !ZEN$ SUBSTITUTE STATIC = { STATIC\,{1,10:100:10},
                                DYNAMIC\,{1,10:100:10}, }
                                GUIDED\,{1,10:100:10} }
d2: !$OMP PARALLEL DO SCHEDULE(STATIC) NUM_THREADS(4)
     .  .  .
    !$OMP END PARALLEL
```

---

[1] We have <u>underlined</u> each individual set element to avoid potential confusion and allow the reader distinguish between commas as set element delimiters and commas as regular string characters.

3.1.4 Distributed Processor Arrays

High Performance Fortran (HPF) [98] is a directive-based language designed in the late 1990s to improve the productivity of writing data parallel programs. HPF has failed to achieve general acceptance in the parallel processing community due to its poor performance compared to explicit message passing based programs (i.e. MPI-based) and the rather limited support for expressing irregular problems. It is, however, widely recognised that the HPF ideas deserve further attention as a high productivity paradigm for programming next generation high performance computing architectures [167].

To examine the scalability of HPF programs, the user commonly varies the *number of parallel processors* organised in an array expressed through a PROCESSORS directive. The HPF code shown in Example 3.4 defines an 2×2 two-dimensional processor array (see directive d2) onto which the arrays defined by the programmer are distributed using a DISTRIBUTE directive (see directive d4). The ZEN substitute directive d1 causes the replacement of all occurrences of the string P(2,2) with one element from the associated value set:

$$\mathcal{V}^{P(2,2)} = \{P(2,2), P(4,2), P(6,2), P(8,2), P(2,4), P(4,4),$$
$$P(6,4), P(8,4)\}.$$

Therefore, eight experiments will be generated, each of which investigates the scalability of the application on a different processor matrix.

Example 3.4 (HPF array and independent loop distributions).

```
d1:  !ZEN$ SUBSTITUTE P\(2,2\) = { P({2:8:2},{2,4}}) } BEGIN
d2   !HPF$ PROCESSORS P(2,2)
d1:  !ZEN$ END SUBSTITUTE
       . . .
d3:  !ZEN$ SUBSTITUTE CYCLIC = { CYCLIC({2:10:2},20) } BEGIN
d4:  !HPF$ DISTRIBUTE A(BLOCK, CYCLIC) ONTO P
d3:  !ZEN$ END SUBSTITUTE
       . . .
d5:  !ZEN$ SUBSTITUTE A\(i,j\) = { A(i,j), B(I(i)) } BEGIN
d6:  !HPF$ INDEPENDENT, ON HOME(A(i,j))
d5:  !ZEN$ END SUBSTITUTE
       DO i = 1, N
         . . . A(i,j) . . .
         . . . B(I(i)) . . .
       ENDDO
```

3.1.5 Distributed Memory Arrays

Beyond the specification of appropriate machine sizes, the *distribution of array* elements across processors is another non-trivial optimisation that can

significantly influence the overall performance of data parallel HPF applications. The HPF standard defines two regular patterns for distributing an array
A(N) onto a processor array PROC(P):

BLOCK(M) distribution indicates that the elements of array A are distributed
in contiguous blocks of size M onto the elements of PROC. If the optional
block size M is omitted, it is as if it were present with $M = \left\lceil \frac{N}{P} \right\rceil$. The data
distribution function that maps the data array index dimension $[1..N]$ to
the processor array index dimension $[1..P]$ is defined as follows:

$$\texttt{DISTR}_M : [1..N] \rightarrow [1..P], \ \texttt{DISTR}_M(i) = \left\lceil \frac{i}{M} \right\rceil, \ where \ M \geq \left\lceil \frac{N}{P} \right\rceil ;$$

CYCLIC(M) distribution indicates that the elements of array A are distributed
in a round-robing fashion across the elements of PROC in blocks of size
M. If the optional block size M is omitted, it is as if it were present with
$M = 1$. The data distribution function that maps the data array index
dimension $[1..N]$ to the processor array index dimension $[1..P]$ is defined
as follows:

$$\texttt{DISTR}'_M : [1..N] \rightarrow [1..P], \ \texttt{DISTR}'_M(i) = \left\lfloor \frac{i-1}{M} \right\rfloor \ mod \ P.$$

The ZEN substitute directive d3 in Example 3.4 defines a parameter CYCLIC
with the value set:

$$\mathcal{V}^{\texttt{CYCLIC}} = \{\texttt{CYCLIC(2)}, \texttt{CYCLIC(4)}, \texttt{CYCLIC(6)}, \texttt{CYCLIC(8)},$$
$$\texttt{CYCLIC(10)}, \texttt{CYCLIC(20)}\} .$$

Every parameter value represents a different array distribution with a different pattern and block size that substitutes the original CYCLIC distribution.
Figure 3.2 illustrates a sample CYCLIC(2) column-wise distribution and a
BLOCK row-wise distribution of a two-dimensional array $A(8,4)$ onto a two-
dimensional processor array $P(2,2)$.

The ZEN substitute directive can be similarly employed to examine different options of the HPF REDISTRIBUTE directive.

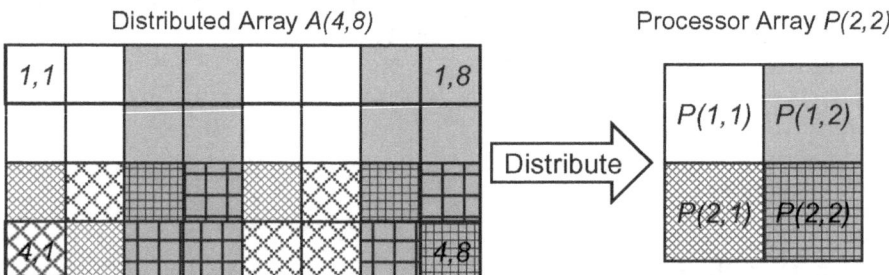

Fig. 3.2. The (CYCLIC(2), BLOCK) distribution of array $A(8,4)$ onto processor
array $P(2,2)$.

3.1.6 Work Distribution

Similar to the OpenMP loop scheduling (and complementary to the data distribution approach), the HPF ON and the ON HOME directives allow the programmer to control the *distribution of the computation* (i.e. the control flow) across the processors of a parallel machine. The ON HOME directive requests the work distribution of a parallel loop be derived according to an array section provided as argument. Such loops often contain references to array elements that are distributed using various patterns that are not related to each other and, therefore, it is NP-hard to determine the optimal distribution of iterations.

Example 3.4 defines an HPF INDEPENDENT loop (see directive d6) which accesses the elements of two distributed arrays A and B. The ZEN substitute directive d5 specifies two different scheduling strategies for the loop iteration i: the processor A(i,j) and the processor B(I(i)).

An important detail one can notice in Example 3.4 is that the ZEN substitute directives d1, d3, and d5 have a local scope within the file in which they are defined, specified through pairs of BEGIN / END directives. This allows the user to focus the parameter specification to certain relevant regions of the code that require particular analysis or tuning. For example, the local ZEN substitute directive d5 ensures that the string A(i,j) is replaced only within the INDEPENDENT directive and not further in the parallel loop.

3.1.7 Parameter Studies

Parameter studies [5, 197] are applications that are executed for different input parameters to examine their effect on the corresponding output results. In a typical application encoding, the output parameter values are written to a distinct output file for every experiment.

Example 3.5 (Parameter study).

```
d1:  !ZEN$ CONSTRAINT INDEX Input1 == Output1 BEGIN
d2:  !ZEN$ SUBSTITUTE Input1 = { Input{1:100} }
     OPEN(UNIT=2, IOSTAT=IOS, FILE='INPUT1', STATUS='OLD')
d2:  !ZEN$ END SUBSTITUTE
        . . .
d3:  !ZEN$ SUBSTITUTE Output1 = { Output{1:100} }
     OPEN(UNIT=2, IOSTAT=IOS, FILE='Output1', STATUS='NEW')
d3:  !ZEN$ END SUBSTITUTE
d1:  !ZEN$ END CONSTRAINT
```

Example 3.5 illustrates a scenario how ZEN directives can be employed to manage such parameter studies. The (local) ZEN substitute directives d2 and d3 are used to specify the different input and output data files to be

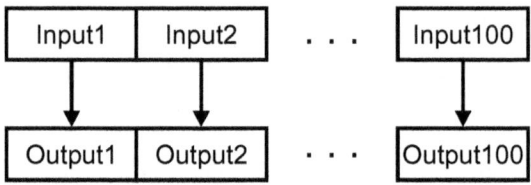

Fig. 3.3. The ZEN constraint defined by Example 3.5.

used in each experiment, respectively. The (local) ZEN constraint directive
d1 associates every input file with a correct output file which avoids invalid
input and output file combinations (see Figure 3.3):

$$\mathcal{V}^{\texttt{Input1}} = \bigcup_{i=1}^{100} \texttt{Input}i;$$
$$\mathcal{V}^{\texttt{Output1}} = \bigcup_{i=1}^{100} \texttt{Output}i;$$
$$\mathcal{V}(\texttt{Input1}, \texttt{Output1}) = \bigcup_{i=1}^{100} (\texttt{Input}i, \texttt{Output}i).$$

Thus, 100 parameter study experiments are generated (instead of $100 \times 100 = 10000$), each of them reading the data from and writing the data to different
input and output files.

3.2 Formal Language Specification

In previous section we gave an introduction to the basic functionality of the
ZEN language through several of the most relevant use cases that were at
the origins of our design motivations. In this section we formally define the
syntax of the ZEN directive-based language for performance and parameter
study experiment specification.

3.2.1 ZEN Set

One important goal we had in designing the ZEN language was to express
wide value ranges for application parameters using a compact and practical
syntax. For this purpose, we designed a special stand-alone language construct called ZEN set.

Definition 3.6. *A ZEN set is a totally ordered set of (integer or real) numbers or strings, with a well-defined syntax and a well-defined evaluation function ε, defined by the Equation 3.1. An element of a ZEN set is called ZEN
element.*

We define the ZEN sets with the following regular expression-based syntax:

zen-set	**is**	" {" *elem-list* " }"
elem-list	**is**	*elem* ["," *elem*]*
elem	**is**	*num*
	or	*comp-elem*
num	**is**	*low:up*[:*stride*]
	or	*number*
comp-elem	**is**	(*zen-num-set* | *zen-string*)+
low	**is**	*number*
up	**is**	*number*
stride	**is**	*number*
number	**is**	*integer*
	or	*real*
integer	**is**	[+|−]?[0–9]
real	**is**	[+|−]?[0–9]+"."[0–9]*
zen-num-set	**is**	" {" *num-list* }
num-list	**is**	*num* ["," *num*]*
zen-string	**is**	([^\n{},:] | "\{" | "\}" | "\," | "\:")*

Let · denote the string concatenation operator, also referred in the following using one blank character. Let $\mathcal{P}$ denote the power set and $\mathbb{R}$ the set of real numbers. The semantics (i.e. the concrete set of elements) of a ZEN set is given by the evaluation function:

$$\varepsilon : \textit{zen-set} \rightarrow \mathcal{P}(\mathbb{R} \cup \textit{string}), \ \varepsilon \left(\bigcup_{i=1}^{n} \textit{elem}_i \right) = \bigcup_{i=1}^{n} \bar{\varepsilon}(\textit{elem}_i), \qquad (3.1)$$

where *string* denotes an arbitrary string, $\mathcal{P}(\textit{string})$ denotes the set of strings, and the function $\bar{\varepsilon}$ is defined in Figure 3.4.

Informally, an *elem* construct of a ZEN set can be expressed as:

1. a regular real *number* (see Example 3.7, Equation 3.2);
2. a *low:up:stride* pattern evaluated to a set of numbers ranging from *low* to *up* with the increment *stride* (see Example 3.7, Equations 3.4 and 3.6). The stride is optional and has a default value of one, therefore:

$$\bar{\varepsilon}(\textit{low:up}) = \bar{\varepsilon}(\textit{low:up:1});$$

3. a composite element *comp-elem* that alternates multiple sets of numbers denoted as *zen-num-set*, with multiple ZEN strings denoted as *zen-string*. The composite element is evaluated to a set of elements by computing the cross product of the *zen-num-set*s and replacing each *zen-num-set* with the corresponding tuple element (see Example 3.7, Equations 3.7, 3.9, 3.11, and 3.13). The *zen-string* elements must obey the syntax defined by the evaluation function $\bar{\varepsilon}_s$ defined in Figure 3.4, with the following informal meaning:

$$\bar{\varepsilon} : elem \rightarrow \mathcal{P}(\mathbb{R} \cup string),$$

$$\bar{\varepsilon}(e) = \begin{cases} low + k * stride \mid k \in 0.. \frac{up - low}{stride} & , e \text{ is } low{:}up{:}stride; \\ \{e\}, & e \text{ is } number; \\ X, & e \text{ is } (zen\text{-}num\text{-}set \mid zen\text{-}string)+, \end{cases}$$

$$(zen\text{-}num\text{-}set \mid zen\text{-}string)+ = zen\text{-}string_1 \ \{num_{11}, \ldots, num_{1n_1}\} \ \ldots$$
$$zen\text{-}string_p \ \{num_{p1}, \ldots, num_{pn_p}\} \ zen\text{-}string_{p+1},$$

$$X = \{\bar{\varepsilon}_s(zen\text{-}string_1) \ n_1 \ldots \bar{\varepsilon}_s(zen\text{-}string_p) \ n_p \ \bar{\varepsilon}_s(zen\text{-}string_{p+1}) \mid$$
$$\forall \ (n_1, \ldots, n_p) \in \varepsilon(\{num_{11}, \ldots, num_{1n_1}\}) \times \ldots \times \varepsilon(\{num_{p1}, \ldots, num_{pn_p}\})\},$$

$$\bar{\varepsilon}_s : string \rightarrow string,$$

$$\bar{\varepsilon}_s(s) = \begin{array}{ll} s, & \forall \ e \in \{"\backslash","\backslash\{","\backslash\}","\backslash:"\}, \ e \notin s; \\ \bar{\varepsilon}_s(s_l) \ c \ \bar{\varepsilon}_s(s_r), & s = s_l \ \backslash c \ s_r, \ \forall \ c \in \{`,`,`\{`,`\}`,`:`,``\}. \end{array}$$

Fig. 3.4. The ZEN set element evaluation function.

a) *commas* inside a *zen-string* must be prefixed by one '\' character which distinguishes them from the value delimiters of a *zen-num-set*:

$$\bar{\varepsilon}(string_l \ \backslash, \ string_r) = string_l \ , \ string_r,$$

where ',' $\notin string_l \wedge$ ',' $\notin string_r$ (see Example 3.7, Equations 3.8, 3.10, 3.11, 3.12, and 3.13);

b) *braces* inside a *zen-string* must be prefixed by one '\' character which avoids *zen-num-sets* inside *zen-strings*:

$$\bar{\varepsilon}(\backslash\{num_1\backslash, \ldots \backslash, num_n\backslash\}) = \{num_1, \ldots, num_n\}$$

(see Example 3.7, Equations 3.8 and 3.10);

c) *colons* inside a *zen-string* must be prefixed by one '\' character which allows the pattern *low:up:stride* be a *zen-string*:

$$\bar{\varepsilon}(low\backslash : up\backslash : stride) = low : up : stride$$

(see Example 3.7, Equations 3.5, 3.10, and 3.12).

Example 3.7 (ZEN set evaluation examples).

- Numerical value set enumeration:

$$\varepsilon(\{1, 2, 3\}) = \{1, 2, 3\}; \tag{3.2}$$

- Alphanumerical (i.e. ZEN string) value set enumeration:

$$\varepsilon(\{a, b, c\}) = \{a, b, c\}; \tag{3.3}$$

- Numerical value ranges using the *low:up:stride* pattern:

$$\varepsilon(\{1 : 10 : 2\}) = \{1, 3, 5, 7, 9\}; \tag{3.4}$$

- The *low:up:stride* pattern as ZEN string through colon escape:

$$\varepsilon(\{1\backslash : 10\backslash : 2\}) = \{1 : 10 : 2\}; \tag{3.5}$$

- Mixed numerical enumeration and *low:up:stride* value range:

$$\varepsilon(\{0, 1 : 10 : 2, 11\}) = \{0, 1, 3, 5, 7, 9, 11\}; \tag{3.6}$$

- Function parameter variation:

$$\varepsilon(\{foo(\{10, 20, 30\})\}) = \{foo(10), foo(20), foo(30)\}; \tag{3.7}$$

- Inner *zen-num-set* avoidance through escaped braces and commas:

$$\varepsilon(\{foo(\backslash\{10\backslash, 20\backslash, 30\backslash\})\}) = \{foo(\{10, 20, 30\})\}; \tag{3.8}$$

- Variation of array distribution [98]:

$$\varepsilon(\{\texttt{BLOCK}(\{4 : 12 : 4\}), \texttt{CYCLIC}(\{8, 16\})\}) = \\ \{\texttt{BLOCK}(4), \texttt{BLOCK}(8), \texttt{BLOCK}(12), \texttt{CYCLIC}(8), \texttt{CYCLIC}(16)\}; \tag{3.9}$$

- Inner *zen-num-set* avoidance through escaped braces, colons, and commas:

$$\varepsilon(\{\texttt{BLOCK}(\backslash\{4\backslash : 12\backslash : 4\backslash\})\backslash, \texttt{CYCLIC}(\backslash\{8\backslash, 16\backslash\})\}) = \\ \{\texttt{BLOCK}(\{4 : 12 : 4\}), \texttt{CYCLIC}(\{8, 16\})\}; \tag{3.10}$$

- Two-dimensional matrix index annotation through escaped commas:

$$\varepsilon(\{A(\{0 : 10 : 5\}\backslash, \{4 : 12 : 4\})\}) = \{A(0, 4), A(0, 8), A(0, 12), \\ A(5, 4), A(5, 8), A(5, 12), A(10, 4), A(10, 8), A(10, 12)\}; \tag{3.11}$$

- One-dimensional matrix index annotation through escaped commas and colons:

$$\varepsilon(\{A(\{0 : 10 : 5\}\backslash, 4\backslash : 12\backslash : 4)\}) = \\ \{A(0, 4 : 12 : 4), A(5, 4 : 12 : 4), A(10, 4 : 12 : 4)\}; \tag{3.12}$$

- Loop scheduling variation [49][2]:

$$\varepsilon(\{\underline{\text{STATIC}\backslash}, \{4, 8\}, \underline{\text{DYNAMIC}\backslash}, \{1 : 4\}\}) = \{\underline{\text{STATIC}, 4}, \underline{\text{STATIC}, 8},$$
$$\underline{\text{DYNAMIC}, 1}, \underline{\text{DYNAMIC}, 2}, \underline{\text{DYNAMIC}, 3}, \underline{\text{DYNAMIC}, 4}\}. \quad (3.13)$$

The *total order* of the ZEN elements, denoted by the operator $\prec$, in a ZEN set:

$$zen\text{-}set = \bigcup_{i=1}^{n} elem_i$$

is given by the following ordering rules:

1. The order of the elements separated by commas is their enumeration order (see Example 3.7, Equations 3.2, 3.3, 3.7, 3.10, and 3.13):

$$\forall \, elem_i, elem_j \in \varepsilon \left(\bigcup_{i=2}^{n} elem_i \right), \, \forall \, i, j \in [1..n], \, elem_i \prec elem_j \iff i < j;$$

2. The element order specified by a *low:up:stride* value range pattern is the ascending element sequence from *low* to *up* with the increment *stride* (see Example 3.7, Equations 3.4, 3.6, 3.12, and 3.13):

$$\forall \, e_i, e_j \in \bar{\varepsilon}(low\text{:}up\text{:}stride), \, e_i \prec e_j \iff$$
$$e_i = low + k_i * stride \, \wedge \, e_j = low + k_j * stride \, \wedge \, k_i < k_j;$$

3. The cross product tuples are ordered lexicographically (see Example 3.7, Equations 3.9, 3.11, and 3.13):

$$\forall \, (n_1, \dots, n_p), (n_1', \dots, n_p') \in \varepsilon \left(\bigcup_{i=1}^{n_1} num_{1i} \right) \times \dots \times \varepsilon \left(\bigcup_{j=1}^{n_p} num_{pj} \right),$$

$$string_1 \, n_1 \dots string_p \, n_p \, string_{p+1} \prec string_1 \, n_1' \dots string_p \, n_p' \, string_{p+1}$$
$$\iff \exists \, i \in [1..n] \text{ such that } \left(\forall \, j \in [1..i-1] : n_j = n_j' \right) \wedge n_i \prec n_i'.$$

Definition 3.8. *Let $(A, \prec)$ and $(B, \prec)$ denote two totally ordered sets with the same ordering operation $\prec$. The* union *of the totally ordered sets A and B is the totally ordered set $(A \cup B, \prec)$ obtained by appending $B \backslash A$ to A:*

$$\forall \, a, b \in A \cup B, \, a \prec b \iff a \in A \, \wedge \, b \in B \subset A \, \vee$$
$$(a, b \in A \, \vee \, a, b \in B \subset A) \, \wedge \, a \prec b.$$

We will need the total order of ZEN sets when defining the ZEN index constraint directive in Section 3.2.8.

---

[2] To avoid any potential confusion and allow the reader distinguish between commas as set element delimiters and commas as regular characters of a string, the ZEN set elements have been underlined.

3.2.2 ZEN Directives

We designed ZEN as a directive-based language that does not change the semantics of the code, unless parsed by a ZEN-aware compiler (i.e. preprocessor).

Definition 3.9. *A* ZEN directive *is a comment line that starts with the prefix* ZEN$.

The characters that mark the beginning (and eventually the end) of a comment are the only programming language specific features of ZEN. Example 3.1 of Section 3.1 showed six sample ZEN directives valid, in descending order, in the context of the following programming languages: FORTRAN 77, Fortran 90/95, C++ (or Java), C, Lisp, and shell scripting language.

We associate to every ZEN directive d, except the assignment directive, a scope denoted as *scope*(d) which refers to the code region to which the directive applies.

Definition 3.10. *A* ZEN variable *is an arbitrary application parameter defined by a ZEN substitute or a ZEN assignment directive. A ZEN variable is a sequence of characters that must obey the following syntax constraints:*

1. *equality and blank characters must be escaped by a* \ *' character, which distinguishes them from the assignment character and eventual neighbouring blank characters in a ZEN directive (e.g.* count\=4 *in Example 4.3);*
2. *arithmetical* ($+$, $-$, $*$, $/$, $\%$, $\char`^$)*, relational* ($==$, $!=$, $<$, $>$, $<=$, $>=$)*, and logical(*!*,* &&*,*||*) operators, as well as left and right parentheses must be escaped by a* \ *' character, which distinguishes them from the parentheses and operators of a ZEN constraint (e.g.* BLOCK\(4\) *in Example 3.4);*

Definition 3.11. *The* value set *of a ZEN variable z, denoted by $\mathcal{V}^z$, is the totally ordered ZEN set $(\mathcal{S}, \prec)$ associated with z:*

$$\mathcal{V}^z = \varepsilon(\mathcal{S}),$$

where the value function ε and the operator $\prec$ were defined in Section 3.2.1.

We will illustrate the need for the total order of elements in the value set in Section 3.2.8.

Definition 3.12. *An arbitrary application file $\mathcal{Z}$ (e.g. source file, input data file, makefile), annotated with ZEN directives that define n ZEN variables $z_1, \ldots, z_n$, is called* ZEN file *denoted as $\mathcal{Z}(z_1, \ldots, z_n)$. A* ZEN file instance *denoted as $\mathcal{ZI}(e_1, \ldots, e_n)$ is an instantiation of the ZEN file $\mathcal{Z}$, obtained by instantiating each ZEN variable z_i with one ZEN element from its value set: $e_i \in \mathcal{V}^{z_i}$, $\forall\, i \in [1..n]$.*

ZEN File Instance (𝒵ℐ)	Generated Code
𝒵ℐ(NUM_THREADS(1))	!$OMP PARALLEL NUM_THREADS(1)
𝒵ℐ(NUM_THREADS(2))	!$OMP PARALLEL NUM_THREADS(2)
𝒵ℐ(NUM_THREADS(3))	!$OMP PARALLEL NUM_THREADS(3)
𝒵ℐ(NUM_THREADS(4))	!$OMP PARALLEL NUM_THREADS(4)

Fig. 3.5. The ZEN file instances generated by Example 3.2.

In cases when the ZEN variables are irrelevant, we will denote for brevity reasons the ZEN files and the ZEN file instances as $\mathcal{Z}$ and $\mathcal{ZI}$, respectively.

Informally, a ZEN file represents a parameterised application file. A ZEN file instance instantiates each application parameter of the ZEN file with one concrete parameter value. For example, Example 3.2 of Section 3.1 illustrated an excerpt of a ZEN file that we denote as $\mathcal{Z}(\texttt{NUM\_THREADS(4)})$, which defines four machine sizes for running the OpenMP parallel region within four ZEN file instances, depicted in Figure 3.5.

The ZEN variables can have three different types: *integer*, *real* and *string*. The motivation for including the integer and real types along side string (which would have been enough otherwise) are the value set constraints that we will introduce in Section 3.2.8.

Definition 3.13. *The type τ of a ZEN variable z is determined by the ZEN Transformation System, introduced in Section 3.1.2, in the parsing phase based on the values of the associated ZEN elements, as follows:*

$$\tau(z) = \begin{cases} "integer", & \forall\ e \in \mathcal{V}^z,\ e\ is\ integer; \\ "real", & \forall\ e \in \mathcal{V}^z,\ e\ is\ number\ \wedge\ \neg\ (\forall\ e \in \mathcal{V}^z,\ e\ is\ integer); \\ "string", & \forall\ e \in \mathcal{V}^z,\ e\ is\ zen\text{-}string\ \wedge\ \neg\ (\forall\ e \in \mathcal{V}^z,\ e\ is\ number). \end{cases}$$

3.2.3 ZEN Substitute Directive

The *ZEN substitute directive* employs a conventional macroprocessor-based string replacement mechanism to overwrite application parameters with value instances of interest within ZEN files. This is expressed in the ZEN language by assigning a ZEN set to a ZEN variable. This directive is commonly employed to examine various language specific parallelization patterns, as we illustrated earlier in Section 3.1, e.g. machine sizes (see Example 3.2), work scheduling strategies (see Example 3.3), data distributions (see Example 3.4), or problem sizes (see Example 3.5).

One flavour of the ZEN substitute directive is the *global substitute directive* whose scope comprises the entire ZEN file in which is defined with the following syntax:

global-substitute-dir **is** `SUBSTITUTE` *zen-var* $=$ *zen-set*
zen-var   **is** `([^-\+\*/%"^"=<>!&\|\(\): \t\r\n\f]|"\="|`
                         `"\+"|"\-"|"\*"|"\/"|"\%"|"\^"|"\=="|"\!="|`
                         `"\ <"|"\ >"|"\ <="|"\ >="|"\!"|"\&&"|"\||"|`
                         `"\("|"\)"|"\:"|"\")+`

The ZEN Transformation System introduced in Section 3.1.2 replaces all occurrences in the entire file of the name of a ZEN variable z with one element $e \in \mathcal{V}^z$. It is the responsibility of the user to ensure that the global substitution produces a correct outcome (i.e. ZEN file instance). Eventual erroneous substitutions usually produce subsequent faulty file compilations or faulty application executions.

3.2.4 Local Substitute Directive

It often occurs in practice that the user needs to apply a parameter substitution to a specific restricted code region, for instance to a certain OpenMP loop from a file that contains many other loops. The local ZEN substitute directive restricts the scope of the global version to a specific region of the ZEN file through the following syntax:

local-substitute-dir **is** `SUBSTITUTE` *zen-var* $=$ *zen-set* `BEGIN`
                        code-region
                        `END SUBSTITUTE`

Example 3.4 of Section 3.1 illustrated the use of several local ZEN substitute directives to express various array and work distribution options for different machine (processor array) sizes in the context of an HPF parallel program.
  The local substitute directives can be also nested.

3.2.5 Homonym ZEN Variables

Example 3.14 defines one global ZEN substitute directive d1 and one local substitute directive d2, with the peculiarity that the ZEN variables they define have the same name `STATIC`. Despite their identical name, the two ZEN variables are distinct, each one having its own scope and value set. Intentionally or not, such situations often happen in practice and need special care. In this particular example, keeping the default `STATIC` distribution for both parallel loops, as well as a semantically proper ZEN variable naming (i.e. `STATIC`), may be of importance for the user.

Example 3.14 (OpenMP loop scheduling).

```
d1:  !ZEN$ SUBSTITUTE STATIC = { STATIC\,{1,10:100:10},
                                 DYNAMIC\,{1,10:100:10} }
     !$OMP PARALLEL DO SCHEDULE(STATIC) NUM_THREADS(4)
       . . .
d2:  !ZEN$ SUBSTITUTE STATIC = { GUIDED } BEGIN
d3:  !$OMP PARALLEL DO SCHEDULE(STATIC) NUM_THREADS(4)
d2:  !ZEN$ END SUBSTITUTE
```

Definition 3.15. *If the textual name of two or more ZEN variables in a ZEN file is identical, these ZEN variables are called* homonyms.

We define the impact of the homonym ZEN variables to the semantics of the global and local ZEN substitute directives as follows:

1. No homonym global ZEN substitute variables are allowed within one ZEN file;
2. A local ZEN substitute directive d_i with a ZEN variable z_i, defined in the scope of any global or local ZEN substitute directive d_j with an associated ZEN variable z_j, where z_i and z_j are homonym augments the value set of z_j as follows:

$$\mathcal{V}^{z_j} = \mathcal{V}^{z_j} \cup \mathcal{V}^{z_i},$$

where the union of two totally ordered value sets was defined in Definition 3.8.

A ZEN variable z is therefore characterised by the:

1. *textual name* denoted in the following as $\nu(z)$;
2. *ZEN directive* d which assigns a value set $\mathcal{V}^z$ to z;
3. *ZEN file* $\mathcal{Z}$ which contains the directive d.

We use the following convention for naming ZEN variables for the remainder of this chapter:

1. if no homonym ZEN variables were defined, the plain textual name of the ZEN variable is used for brevity reasons;
2. if other homonym ZEN variables were defined, the ZEN variable is referred through its textual name subscripted with a unique ZEN directive identifier.

Therefore, the directive **d2** from Example 3.14 defines the following value set for the ZEN variable $STATIC_{d2}$:

$$\mathcal{V}^{STATIC_{d2}} = \mathcal{V}^{STATIC_{d1}} \cup \{GUIDED\}.$$

3.2.6 ZEN Assignment Directive

The substitute directive must be used with care as it might replace undesired occurrences of the ZEN variable in the corresponding scope. For instance, if the variable D in Example 3.16 must be substituted in a given scope, then every occurrence of this character will be replaced, even in keywords such as `DO` or `END`. This problem is particularly critical for shortly named variables (e.g. one character long) that are commonly used by programmers (even as global external variables), which are problematic or simply inconvenient to be renamed.

To overcome this limitation and give the user extra flexibility in defining application parameters, we introduce a new type of directive called *ZEN assignment directive* that inserts arbitrary assignment statements into ZEN files. The purpose of this directive is to indicate the values of interest for a specific program variable which must be defined in the context of the directive location in the ZEN file. Formally, a ZEN assignment directive assigns a ZEN set to a ZEN variable using the following syntax (where *zen-var* was defined in Section 3.2.3 and *zen-set* in Section 3.2.1):

assignment-dir **is ASSIGN**   *zen-var* = *zen-set*

The ZEN Transformation System introduced in Section 3.1.2 textually replaces a ZEN assignment directive with a statement which assigns one element $e \in \mathcal{V}^z$ to the ZEN variable z. The assignment statement must conform to the syntax of programming language in which the ZEN file is written. For example, if the ZEN file represents a C program, the assignment statement must adhere to the C language syntax. The ZEN Transformation System does not apply any type checking or examine whether the (ZEN) variable was declared in the scope of the directive (using the target language syntax and semantics). An eventual *"variable not found"* syntax error will be detected by a subsequent compilation of the ZEN file instance.

Example 3.16 (Shortly named ZEN variables).

```
        INTEGER D, i
  s:    D = 50
  d:    !ZEN$ ASSIGN D = { 2**{6:12} }
        DO i = 1, D
```

The ZEN assignment directive d in Example 3.16 assigns seven values to a ZEN variable D that represents the upper bounds of the immediately following `DO` loop, where $**$ denotes the Fortran power operator:

$$\mathcal{V}^D = \left\{ 2^6, 2^7, 2^8, 2^9, 2^{10}, 2^{11}, 2^{12} \right\}.$$

First of all, one can notice that the code is semantically valid for both ZEN-aware and ZEN-unaware compilers. The ZEN-aware compilers replace the

ZEN directive **d** with an assignment statement that assigns one element $e \in \mathcal{V}^D$ to the (ZEN) variable D. In this example, the default assignment statement **s** becomes redundant and will be eliminated as dead code by subsequent optimised compilation. It is worthwhile to further notice that using a substitution in place of the assignment directive would also replace the character **D** in the keyword **DO** which would produce an erroneous program.

3.2.7 Multi-dimensional Value Set

It is clear that one ZEN directive implies a number of ZEN file instances equal to the cardinality of the value set that it defines. This section describes how multiple ZEN directives defined within a single ZEN file impact the number of ZEN file instances generated.

Definition 3.17. *The* multi-dimensional value set *of n distinct ZEN variables $z_1, \ldots, z_n$, denoted as $\mathcal{V}(z_1, \ldots, z_n)$, is the cross product of their value sets:*

$$\mathcal{V}(z_1, \ldots, z_n) = \mathcal{V}^{z_1} \times \ldots \times \mathcal{V}^{z_n}.$$

The value set *of a ZEN file $\mathcal{Z}(z_1, \ldots, z_n)$, denoted as $\mathcal{V}(\mathcal{Z}(z_1, \ldots, z_n))$ or simply $\mathcal{V}^{\mathcal{Z}}$, is the entire set of ZEN file instances generated from the multi-dimensional value set of its ZEN variables:*

$$\mathcal{V}(\mathcal{Z}(z_1, \ldots, z_n)) = \bigcup_{\forall (e_1, \ldots, e_n) \in \mathcal{V}(z_1, \ldots, z_n)} \mathcal{Z}\mathcal{I}(e_1, \ldots, e_n).$$

For instance, Example 3.14 of Section 3.2.5 defined two ZEN directives **d1** and **d2**, whose multi-dimensional value set is given by the cross product of their value sets:

$$\mathcal{V}(\text{STATIC}_{d1}, \text{STATIC}_{d2}) = \mathcal{V}^{\text{STATIC}_{d1}} \times \mathcal{V}^{\text{STATIC}_{d2}},$$

with the cardinality:

$$|\mathcal{V}(\text{STATIC}_{d1}, \text{STATIC}_{d2})| = |\mathcal{V}^{\text{STATIC}_{d1}}| \cdot |\mathcal{V}^{\text{STATIC}_{d2}}| = 22 \cdot 23 = 506.$$

Definition 3.18. *A* ZEN application, *denoted as $\mathcal{A}(\mathcal{Z}_1, \ldots, \mathcal{Z}_n)$ or simply $\mathcal{A}$, consists of a set of ZEN files:*

$$\mathcal{A}(\mathcal{Z}_1, \ldots, \mathcal{Z}_n) = \bigcup_{i=1}^{n} \mathcal{Z}_i.$$

A ZEN application instance, *denoted as $\mathcal{A}\mathcal{I}(\mathcal{Z}\mathcal{I}_1, \ldots, \mathcal{Z}\mathcal{I}_n)$ or simply $\mathcal{A}\mathcal{I}$, is a set of ZEN file instances which instantiate each ZEN file of the ZEN application:*

$$\mathcal{A}\mathcal{I}(\mathcal{Z}\mathcal{I}_1, \ldots, \mathcal{Z}\mathcal{I}_n) = \bigcup_{i=1}^{n} \left\{ \mathcal{Z}\mathcal{I}_i \mid \mathcal{Z}\mathcal{I}_i \in \mathcal{V}^{\mathcal{Z}_i} \right\}.$$

From an informal perspective, a ZEN application represents a Grid application annotated with ZEN directives that confirms to one of the models that we introduced in Section 2.6.3.

Definition 3.19. *The* value set *of a ZEN application, denoted in the following as* $\mathcal{V}(\mathcal{A}(\mathcal{Z}_1, \ldots, \mathcal{Z}_n))$ *or simply* $\mathcal{V}^{\mathcal{A}}$, *is the set of application instances generated by the cross product of the value sets of its constituent ZEN files:*

$$\mathcal{V}(\mathcal{A}(\mathcal{Z}_1, \ldots, \mathcal{Z}_n)) = \bigcup_{\forall (\mathcal{Z}\mathcal{I}_1, \ldots, \mathcal{Z}\mathcal{I}_n) \in \mathcal{V}^{\mathcal{Z}_1} \times \ldots \times \mathcal{V}^{\mathcal{Z}_n}} \mathcal{A}\mathcal{I}(\mathcal{Z}\mathcal{I}_1, \ldots, \mathcal{Z}\mathcal{I}_n).$$

3.2.8 ZEN Constraint Directive

The plain cross product of the value sets often produces a large number of ZEN element combinations that have no correct or useful practical meaning. The consequence can be a dramatic increase in the number of experiments and the time needed to conduct them, for instance in the context of a parameter study. We therefore introduce the *ZEN constraint directive* to filter the meaningless or irrelevant the parameter combinations from the multi-dimensional value set.

Similar to the substitute directive, we define the ZEN constraint directives with global and local scopes, where local constraint directives can be also nested:

global-constraint-dir	**is**	CONSTRAINT *type b-expr*
b-expr	**is**	*bool-expr(zen-var-list)*
type	**is**	VALUE
	or	INDEX

local-constraint-dir	**is**	CONSTRAINT *type b-expr* BEGIN
		code-region
		END CONSTRAINT

The term *b-expr* refers to a boolean expression which contains constants and ZEN variables as operands. The set of arithmetical operators allowed in a *b-expr* is: $\{+, -, *, /, \%, \char94\}$, the set of relational operators: $\{==, ! =, <, > , <=, >=\}$, and the set of logical operators: $\{!, \&\&, ||\}$. The symbols % and ^ denote the modulo, respectively the power operators. The operators assume the standard mathematical associativity which can be overwritten using parentheses. The arithmetical operators have precedence over the relational operators which have precedence over the logical operators. An arithmetical operation over a set of integers produces an integer result. An operation over a set of mixed integer and real numbers produces a real result.

There are two types of ZEN variables that can appear in a ZEN constraint:

1. *local ZEN variables* that must be defined in the scope of the ZEN constraint;

2. *external ZEN variables* that must be globally defined in a different ZEN file, referred by prefixing the ZEN variable with the ZEN file name followed by a colon (see Example 4.4 in Chapter 4, Section 4.2.1).

A ZEN constraint directive denoted as d, which defines the boolean expression *bool-expr(zen-var$_1$, ..., zen-var$_n$)*, refers to all ZEN variables in the scope of the directive with the name in $\{zen\text{-}var_1, \ldots, zen\text{-}var_n\}$. If there exist homonym ZEN variables in the scope of the directive with the name in $\{zen\text{-}var_1, \ldots, zen\text{-}var_n\}$, the following set of constraints is generated:

$$\bigcup_{\substack{\forall\,\{z_1,\ldots,z_n\}\subset scope(d)\wedge \\ \nu(z_i)=zen\text{-}var_i,\,\forall\,i\in[1..n]}} bool\text{-}expr\,(z_1,\ldots,z_n)\,,$$

where $\nu(z_i)$ is the textual name of a ZEN variable as defined in Section 3.2.5.

The ZEN constraint directive defines two types of constraints, which depend on the type of the ZEN variables involved (see Definition 3.13):

1. *value set constraint* defines a boolean expression over a set of ZEN variables of type integer and real;
2. *index domain constraint* defines a boolean expression over a set of ZEN variables of any type, including string.

Value Set Constraint

The *value set constraint* is indicated by the VALUE clause of the ZEN constraint directive and defines a boolean expression over a set of ZEN variables of types integer and real. We defined the type of a ZEN variable in Definition 3.13.

Definition 3.20. *Let* $z_1, \ldots, z_n$ *denote a set of ZEN variables. The tuple* $(e_1, \ldots, e_n) \in \mathcal{V}^{z_1} \times \ldots \times \mathcal{V}^{z_n}$ *is called* value-valid *if and only if the following condition holds:*

$$valid(e_1, \ldots, e_n) \iff \alpha\,(\Pi_{j_1,\ldots,j_m}\,(e_1,\ldots,e_n)) = true,$$

$\forall\,\alpha : \mathcal{V}^{z_{j_1}} \times \ldots \times \mathcal{V}^{z_{j_m}} \rightarrow boolean$ *a value set constraint, where:*

$$\{z_{j_1}, \ldots, z_{j_m}\} \subset \{z_1, \ldots, z_n\},\ \forall\,j_k \in [1..n],\ \forall\,k \in [1..m]\ \wedge\ m < n.$$

The notation $\Pi_{j_1,\ldots,j_m}(e_1,\ldots,e_n)$ *denotes the* projection *of the tuple element* $(e_1,\ldots,e_n)$ *from the n-dimensional space* $\mathcal{V}^{z_1} \times \ldots \times \mathcal{V}^{z_n}$ *onto its m-dimensional subspace* $\mathcal{V}^{z_{j_1}} \times \ldots \times \mathcal{V}^{z_{j_m}}$.

Informally, a tuple $(e_1, \ldots, e_n) \in \mathcal{V}^{z_1} \times \ldots \times \mathcal{V}^{z_n}$ is value-valid if and only if it satisfies all the value set constraints defined across any subset of the ZEN variables involved. A value set constraint is evaluated by instantiating each ZEN variable z_i with the corresponding ZEN element e_i from the tuple $(e_1, \ldots, e_n)$, $\forall\,i \in [1..n]$. All the invalid tuples are eliminated from the multidimensional value set.

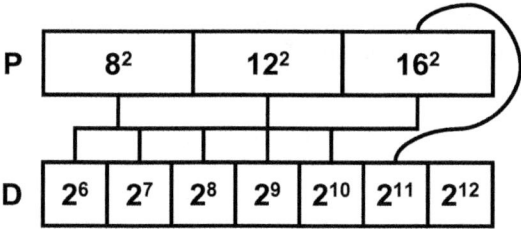

Fig. 3.6. The value set constraint defined in Example 3.21.

Example 3.21 (Value set constraint).

```
INTEGER D, P, i
!ZEN$ ASSIGN P = { {8:16:4}**2 }
D = 50
!ZEN$ ASSIGN D = { 2**{6:12} }
DO i = 1, D
!ZEN$ CONSTRAINT VALUE D^3 / P < 40000000
```

In Example 3.21, the ZEN variable P defines a set of three square numbers from 8^2 to 16^2 with the stride 4. Similarly, the ZEN variable D is assigned a set of seven power of 2 elements from 2^6 to 2^{12}.

$$\mathcal{V}^P = \{8^2, 12^2, 16^2\};$$
$$\mathcal{V}^D = \{2^6, 2^7, 2^8, 2^9, 2^{10}, 2^{11}, 2^{12}\}.$$

The value set constraint directive filters the ZEN elements from the cross product $\mathcal{V}^N \times \mathcal{V}^P$ such that the boolean expression defined yields true (see Figure 3.6):

$$\mathcal{V}(D, P) = \bigcup_{\forall (e_1, e_2) \in \mathcal{V}^D \times \mathcal{V}^P \wedge \frac{e_1^3}{e_2} < 4 \cdot 10^7} (e_1, e_2).$$

Assuming that D represents the size of a three-dimensional array and P the number of the available processors onto which the array is distributed, the constraint restricts the value set to those combinations which need less than 40 megabytes of memory on each processor.

Index Domain Constraints

While the boolean expression defined by a value set constraint is meaningful over ZEN variables of types integer and real, it is problematic to comprise ZEN variables of type string. This is the main reason for which we defined in Section 3.2.2 (see Definition 3.11) the value set of a ZEN variable as a totally ordered set that associates a unique index to each ZEN element, as specified by the following definition.

Definition 3.22. *The* index domain *of a ZEN variable* z, *denoted as* $\mathcal{I}^z$, *is the totally ordered set of elements* $\mathcal{I}^z = (\mathcal{S}, <)$, *where:*

$$\mathcal{S} = \bigcup_{i=1}^{|\mathcal{V}^z|} i$$

and $\mathcal{S} \subset \mathbb{N}^*$, *where* $\mathbb{N}^*$ *denotes the set of positive natural numbers (i.e. non-zero). The total order of elements in* $\mathcal{I}^z$ *is the natural element order. The* value function *of a ZEN variable* z *is the total bijective function:*

$$\vartheta : \mathcal{I}^z \to \mathcal{V}^z,$$

which associates to each element $\vartheta(i) \in \mathcal{V}^z$ *an index* $i \in \mathcal{I}^z$ *such that:*

$$\forall\, i, i_1, i_2 \in \mathcal{I}^z,\ i_1 < i < i_2 \iff \vartheta(i_1) \prec \vartheta(i) \prec \vartheta(i_2).$$

The index function*:*

$$\vartheta^{-1} : \mathcal{V}^z \to \mathcal{I}^z$$

is the inverse of the value function.

For example, the ZEN directives defined in Example 3.21 of the previous subsection define the following index sets and value functions:

$$\mathcal{I}^P = \{1, 2, 3\};$$
$$\vartheta_P : \mathcal{I}^P \to \mathcal{V}^P,\ \vartheta_P(i) = (8 + 4 \cdot (i-1))^2;$$
$$\mathcal{I}^D = \{1, 2, 3, 4, 5, 6, 7\};$$
$$\vartheta_D : \mathcal{I}^D \to \mathcal{V}^D,\ \vartheta_D(i) = 2^{i+5}.$$

The *index domain constraint*, indicated by the **INDEX** clause of the ZEN constraint directive, defines a boolean expression over the index domains of the ZEN variables involved.

Definition 3.23. *Let* $z_1, \ldots, z_n$ *denote a set of ZEN variables. The tuple* $(e_1, \ldots, e_n) \in \mathcal{V}^{z_1} \times \ldots \times \mathcal{V}^{z_n}$ *is called* index-valid *if and only if the following condition holds:*

$$valid\left(\vartheta^{-1}(e_1), \ldots, \vartheta^{-1}(e_n)\right) \iff$$
$$\iff \beta\left(\Pi_{j_1, \ldots, j_m}\left(\vartheta^{-1}(e_1), \ldots, \vartheta^{-1}(e_n)\right)\right) = true,$$

where $\Pi_{j_1, \ldots, j_m}\left(\vartheta^{-1}(e_1), \ldots, \vartheta^{-1}(e_n)\right)$ *was defined in Definition 3.20,* $\forall\, \beta :$ $\mathcal{V}^{z_{j_1}} \times \ldots \times \mathcal{V}^{z_{j_m}} \to boolean$ *an index domain constraint, where:*

$$\{z_{j_1}, \ldots, z_{j_m}\} \subset \{z_1, \ldots, z_n\},\ \forall\, j_k \in [1..n],\ \forall\, k \in [1..m]\ \wedge\ m < n.$$

Informally, a tuple $\left(\vartheta^{-1}(e_1), \ldots, \vartheta^{-1}(e_n)\right) \in \mathcal{I}^{z_1} \times \ldots \times \mathcal{I}^{z_n}$ is index-valid if and only if it satisfies all the index domain constraints defined across any subset of the ZEN variables involved. An index domain constraint is evaluated by instantiating each ZEN variable z_i with the index of the corresponding ZEN element e_i from the tuple $(e_1, \ldots, e_n)$, $\forall \; i \in [1..n]$. All the invalid tuples are eliminated from the multi-dimensional value set.

Example 3.5 of Section 3.1.7 showed a typical use of the index constraint directive for associating input and output data files in the context of a common parameter study experiment. Clearly, value set constraints cannot be used to express the association between the value set elements of type string of the Input1 and Output1 ZEN variables, which demonstrates the need for the index constraint directive.

Multi-dimensional Value Set

In the following definition we redefine the multi-dimensional value set, initially introduced in Definition 3.17, to take the ZEN constraints into consideration.

Definition 3.24. *We define the* multi-dimensional value set *of a set of ZEN variables* $z_1, \ldots, z_n$ *as the set of tuples that are both value-valid and index-valid:*

$$\mathcal{V}(z_1, \ldots, z_n) = \bigcup_{\substack{\forall \, (e_1, \ldots, e_n) \in \mathcal{V}^{z_1} \times \ldots \times \mathcal{V}^{z_n} \, \wedge \\ valid(e_1, \ldots, e_n) \, \wedge \, valid\left(\vartheta^{-1}(e_1), \ldots, \vartheta^{-1}(e_n)\right)}} (e_1, \ldots, e_n).$$

3.2.9 ZEN Performance Directive

For performance-oriented program development, the user commonly requires information about the execution of specific code regions such as the overall execution time, the number of cache misses, the communication time, the synchronisation time, or the floating-point operations per second. To address multi-experimental performance analysis, we include support in the ZEN language to specify performance metrics to be measured for specific code regions of the application through *ZEN performance directives*.

In contrast to the other ZEN directives that have general applicability, the ZEN performance directives is only meaningful in the context of parallel applications following the shared and distributed processing model introduced in Section 2.6.3. The parallel programming paradigms supported in our implementation are MPI, OpenMP, and HPF. The scope of the ZEN performance directive can be global to the entire enclosing ZEN file or can be limited to a local code region:

> *global-perf-dir* **is CR**   *cr_mnem-list*   **PMETRIC**   *pm_mnem-list*
> *local-perf-dir* **is CR**   *cr_mnem-list*   **PMETRIC**   *pm_mnem-list*   **BEGIN**
>   *code-region*
>   **END CR**

The ZEN performance directive defines two clauses associated with two sets of mnemonics:

1. *Code region mnemonics (cr_mnem)* are associated with the CR clause and define the code regions within the scope of the directive that are going to be instrumented;
2. *Performance metric mnemonics (pm_mnem)* are associated with the PMETRIC clause and define the performance metrics to be measured for the indicated code regions.

Definition 3.25. *A code region $\mathcal{CR}$ is a quadruple that associates a ZEN application $\mathcal{A}$, a ZEN file $\mathcal{Z}$, a start line number l_s, and an end line number l_e:*

$$\mathcal{CR} = (\mathcal{A}, \mathcal{Z}, l_s, l_e),$$

where $l_s, l_e \in \mathbb{N}^*$. A performance measurement, denoted as $\mathcal{M}$, is an association between a performance metric and a code region:

$$\mathcal{M} = (pm\_mnem, \mathcal{CR}).$$

Let $d \in \mathcal{Z}$ denote a ZEN performance directive that specifies a set of n code regions and p performance metric mnemonics. The set of performance measurements defined by d and denoted as $\mathcal{M}(d)$ is given by to the cross product of the two mnemonic lists:

$$\mathcal{M}(d) = \bigcup_{j=1}^{p} pm\_mnem_j \times \left(\bigcup_{i=1}^{n} \bigcup_{\substack{\forall \mathcal{CR} \in scope(d) \, \wedge \\ \mathcal{CR} \ is \ cr\_mnem_i}} \mathcal{CR} \right).$$

Informally, a global performance directive d collects performance metrics for all the code regions of the ZEN file that contains d. The code region types are specified in the CR clause and the performance metrics in the PERF clause of d. The local performance directive restricts the performance metrics and the code regions to the corresponding local scope. The local performance directives can be also nested.

Example 3.26 presents an excerpt of a hybrid parallel application designed for SMP clusters that uses OpenMP for intra-node parallelization and MPI for inter-node communication. This example defines one global ZEN performance directive d1, one local ZEN performance directive d2, the entire program code region CR_P, one OpenMP parallel region CR_OMPPA, and one OpenMP parallel loop CR_OMPDO. The metrics specified by the two ZEN performance directives are the wall-clock execution time WTIME, the data movement ODATA (i.e. the MPI communication time), the level two data cache misses L2_DCM, and the control of parallelism (i.e. OpenMP fork, join, loop scheduling, and barrier). This example generates therefore the following set of performance measurements given the directive nests displayed:

$$\mathcal{M}(d1) = \{(\text{WTIME}, \text{CR\_P}), (\text{WTIME}, \text{CR\_OMPPA}), (\text{WTIME}, \text{CR\_OMPDO}),$$
$$(\text{ODATA}, \text{CR\_P}), (\text{ODATA}, \text{CR\_OMPPA}), (\text{ODATA}, \text{CR\_OMPDO})\};$$
$$\mathcal{M}(d2) = \{(\text{L2\_DCM}, \text{CR\_OMPDO}), (\text{OCTRP}, \text{CR\_OMPDO})\}.$$

Example 3.26 (ZEN performance directive).

```
d1:         !ZEN$ CR CR_P, CR_OMPPA PMETRIC WTIME, ODATA
            . . .
CR_OMPPA:   !$OMP PARALLEL NUM_THREADS(4)
            . . .
CR_OMPPA:   !$OMP END PARALLEL
d2:         !ZEN$ CR CR_OMPPA PMETRIC L2_DCM, OCRTP BEGIN
            . . .
CR_OMPDO:   !$OMP PARALLEL DO NUM_THREADS(4)
            . . .
CR_OMPDO:   !$OMP END PARALLEL
d2:         !ZEN$ END CR
```

We implement the ZEN performance directives based on the SCALEA [181] instrumentation engine and overhead analysis tool built on top of the Vienna Fortran Compiler [21] that translates HPF programs into mixed OpenMP and MPI source code equivalents. We currently support approximately 50 code regions (e.g. CR_P = entire program, CR_L = all loops, CR_OMPPA = all OpenMP parallel loops) and 140 performance metric mnemonics (e.g. ODATA = data movement, OSYNC = synchronisation, ODATA_L2 = number of level 2 cache misses) for the OpenMP, MPI, and HPF programming paradigms. We give a complete list of the code regions and the performance metric mnemonics supported by our implementation in Appendix 10.2 and 10.4, respectively.

Definition 3.27. *Let $\mathcal{M}(\mathcal{A})$ denote the set of a performance measurements of a ZEN application defined through ZEN performance directives:*

$$\mathcal{M}(\mathcal{A}) = \bigcup_{\forall d \in \mathcal{Z} \land \forall \mathcal{Z} \in \mathcal{V}^{\mathcal{A}}} \mathcal{M}(d).$$

We define an experiment as a tuple $(\mathcal{AI}, M)$ that associates a ZEN application instance $\mathcal{AI} \in \mathcal{V}^{\mathcal{A}}$ with a target execution site M. A performance data is a function which quantifies each performance measurement for one experiment:

$$\delta_M : \mathcal{M}(\mathcal{A}) \times \mathcal{V}^{\mathcal{A}} \to \mathbb{R}.$$

A performance study experiment *is a triplet* $(\mathcal{AI}, M, \delta_M (\mathcal{M}(\mathcal{A}) \times \mathcal{AI}))$ *where* $\mathcal{AI} \in \mathcal{V}^{\mathcal{A}}$ *and* $\delta_M (\mathcal{M}(\mathcal{A}) \times \mathcal{AI})$ *is the image of the performance data function projected over the sub-domain* $\mathcal{M}(\mathcal{A}) \times \mathcal{AI}$.

Informally, a performance study experiment associates an experiment with the complete set of performance data collected after executing the experiment on a certain site, as specified by the complete set of ZEN performance directives.

3.2.10 Parameter Study Experiment

In this section we use the opportunity to define a parameter study experiment as natural side-effect of the formalism presented in this chapter.

Definition 3.28. *Let* $\mathcal{Z}_o$ *denote an output file of a ZEN application* $\mathcal{A}$. *We represent an* output parameter *as a tuple* $(\mathcal{Z}_o, string\text{-}pattern)$, *where string-pattern is a unique pattern that prefixes the output parameter within the output file* $\mathcal{Z}_o$. *Let* $\mathcal{OP}(\mathcal{A})$ *denote the complete set of output parameters of the ZEN application* $\mathcal{A}$. *We define an* output data *as a function:*

$$\epsilon : \mathcal{OP}(\mathcal{A}) \to \mathbb{R},$$

and a parameter study experiment *as a tuple:* $(\mathcal{AI}, \epsilon(\mathcal{OP}(\mathcal{A})))$, *where* $\mathcal{AI} \in \mathcal{V}^{\mathcal{A}}$, *and* $\epsilon(\mathcal{OP}(\mathcal{A}))$ *is the image of the output data function.*

Definition 3.28 illustrates that the target execution site of a parameter study experiment is irrelevant.

3.2.11 Experiment Generation Algorithm

The ZEN constraints act as a filter over the cross product of all the ZEN variable value sets of a ZEN application. In this section we present an efficient algorithm for generating the valid tuples of ZEN elements, as defined by the multi-dimensional value set in Definition 3.24.

A straight-forward algorithm which evaluates according to Definition 3.24 all the p constraints for all the tuples of the cross product $\mathcal{V}_1 \times \ldots \times \mathcal{V}_n$, has a mathematical complexity of $\mathcal{O}(p \cdot n^o)$, where o denotes the average cardinality of the value sets. This complexity can be reduced by shifting the focus from the value sets to the ZEN constraints, which are likely to be defined over a significantly smaller subset of ZEN variables. The idea of our algorithm is to filter the invalid tuples from the beginning without generating the full cross product which avoids further unnecessary and redundant constraint tests. With this approach, the complexity of the algorithm is reduced to $\mathcal{O}(p\overline{n}^o)$, where $\overline{n}$ is represents the average number of ZEN variables in a ZEN constraint logical expression. The improvement comes obviously from the fact that $\overline{n} \ll n$.

Definition 3.29. *Let* $S_{i_1}, \ldots, S_{i_r}, S_{j_1}, \ldots, S_{j_s}$ *denote* $r + s$ *arbitrary sets,* $(v_{i_1}, \ldots, v_{i_r}) \in S_{i_1} \times \ldots \times S_{i_r}$ *and* $(v_{j_1}, \ldots, v_{j_s}) \in S_{j_1} \times \ldots \times S_{j_s}$. *We define the* composition operator $\otimes$ *between two tuples as follows:*

$$
\begin{array}{c}
(v_{i_1}, \ldots, v_{i_r}) \\
\otimes \\
(v_{j_1}, \ldots, v_{j_s})
\end{array}
=
\begin{cases}
(v_{k_1}, \ldots, v_{k_t}), & \forall\, S_{i_u} = S_{j_w} \in \{S_{i_1}, \ldots, S_{i_r}\} \cap \{S_{j_1}, \ldots, S_{j_s}\}, \\
& 1 \le u \le r \,\wedge\, 1 \le w \le s,\; v_{i_u} = v_{j_w}; \\
(\ ), & \exists\, S_{i_u} = S_{j_w} \in \{S_{i_1}, \ldots, S_{i_r}\} \cap \{S_{j_1}, \ldots, S_{j_s}\}, \\
& 1 \le u \le r \,\wedge\, 1 \le w \le s \,\wedge\, v_{i_u} \ne v_{j_w},
\end{cases}
$$

where:

$$
\begin{aligned}
(v_{k_1}, \ldots, v_{k_t}) &\in S_{k_1} \times \ldots \times S_{k_t}; \\
\{S_{k_1}, \ldots, S_{k_t}\} &= \{S_{i_1}, \ldots, S_{i_r}\} \cup \{S_{j_1}, \ldots, S_{j_s}\}; \\
(v_{i_1}, \ldots, v_{i_r}) &= \Pi_{i_1, \ldots, i_r}(v_{k_1}, \ldots, v_{k_t}); \\
(v_{j_1}, \ldots, v_{j_s}) &= \Pi_{j_1, \ldots, j_s}(v_{k_1}, \ldots, v_{k_t}).
\end{aligned}
$$

The composition operator $\otimes$ has the following properties:

1. *commutativity:* $A \otimes B = B \otimes A$;
2. *associativity:* $A \otimes (B \otimes C) = (A \otimes B) \otimes C$;
3. *idempotency:* $A \otimes A = A$;
4. *neutral element:* $A \otimes (\ ) = A$;
5. $(\mathcal{G}, \otimes)$ is an *Abelian group*, where $\mathcal{G} = S_{k_1} \times \ldots \times S_{k_t}$.

Lemma 3.30. *Let* $z_1, \ldots, z_n$ *denote* n *ZEN variables and let* $\gamma_1, \ldots, \gamma_p$ *denote* p *(value set or index domain) constraints over the* n *ZEN variables, where log-expr denotes a logical expression:*

$$
\gamma_i : \mathcal{V}_{i1} \times \ldots \times \mathcal{V}_{iq},\; \gamma_i = log\text{-}expr(\mathcal{V}_{i1}, \ldots, \mathcal{V}_{iq}),
$$
$$
\{\mathcal{V}_{i1}, \ldots, \mathcal{V}_{iq}\} \subset \{\mathcal{V}^{z_1}, \ldots, \mathcal{V}^{z_n}\},\; \forall\, i \in [1..p],
$$

and $t_i \in \mathcal{V}_{i1} \times \ldots \times \mathcal{V}_{iq},\; \gamma_1(t_i) = true,\; \forall\, i \in [1..p]$. *Then* $t_1 \otimes \ldots \otimes t_p$ *is valid, denoted as* $valid(t_1 \otimes \ldots \otimes t_p)$.

Proof. The proof of this lemma distinguishes two cases:

Case 1: $t_1 \otimes \ldots \otimes t_p = (\ )$. The empty tuple is obviously valid;

Case 2: $t_1 \otimes \ldots \otimes t_p \ne (\ )$. Assuming that $t_1 \otimes \ldots \otimes t_p$ is not valid, according to the Definition 3.24 there exists a constraint:

$$
\gamma_h : \mathcal{V}_{h_1} \times \ldots \times \mathcal{V}_{h_q} \to boolean,
$$

such that $\gamma_h(t_h) = false$, where $t_h = \Pi_{h_1, \ldots, h_q}(t_1 \otimes \ldots \otimes t_p)$. Since $\gamma_1, \ldots, \gamma_p$ are all the constraints defined by the ZEN application, then $\gamma_h \in \{\gamma_1, \ldots, \gamma_p\}$, which contradicts one of the p constraints.

The experiment generation algorithm illustrated in pseudocode in Algorithm 1 receives as input n ZEN variables and p (value set or index domain) constraints and works according to the workflow depicted in Figure 3.7, where:

Algorithm 1. The experiment generation algorithm.

1: **function** EXPERIMENT-GENERATOR$(z_1, \ldots, z_n, \gamma_1, \ldots, \gamma_p)$

2:     $\gamma_i : \mathcal{V}_{i1} \times \ldots \times \mathcal{V}_{iq}, \; \gamma_i = \text{log-expr}(\mathcal{V}_{i1}, \ldots, \mathcal{V}_{iq}),$
        $\{\mathcal{V}_{i1}, \ldots, \mathcal{V}_{iq}\} \subset \{\mathcal{V}^{z_1}, \ldots, \mathcal{V}^{z_n}\}, \; \forall\, i \in [1..p]$ ▷ Precondition

3:     **for all** $i \in [1..p]$ **do**

4:         $I_i \leftarrow \mathcal{V}_{i1} \times \ldots \times \mathcal{V}_{iq}$

5:         $E_i \leftarrow \bigcup_{\substack{\forall\, (e_{i1}, \ldots, e_{iq}) \in \mathcal{V}_{i1} \times \ldots \times \mathcal{V}_{iq} \\ \wedge\, \gamma_i(e_{i1}, \ldots, e_{iq}) = true}} (e_{i1}, \ldots, e_{iq})$

6:     **end for**

7:     $I \leftarrow \mathcal{V}^{z_{l_1}} \times \ldots \times \mathcal{V}^{z_{l_x}}, \; \forall\, \gamma_m : \mathcal{V}^{z_{m_1}} \times \ldots \times \mathcal{V}^{z_{m_y}} \rightarrow boolean\, \wedge$
        $\wedge\, \{\mathcal{V}^{z_{l_1}}, \ldots, \mathcal{V}^{z_{l_x}}\} \cap \{\mathcal{V}^{z_{m_1}}, \ldots, \mathcal{V}^{z_{m_y}}\} = \emptyset$

8:     $\mathcal{V}(z_1, \ldots, z_n) \leftarrow \bigcup_{\substack{\forall\, (e_{11}, \ldots, e_{1q}) \in E_1 \\ \wedge \ldots \wedge \\ \forall\, (e_{p1}, \ldots, e_{pq}) \in E_p}} (e_{11}, \ldots, e_{1q}) \otimes \ldots \otimes (e_{p1}, \ldots, e_{pq})$

9:     **return** $\mathcal{V}(z_1, \ldots, z_n)$

10: **end function**

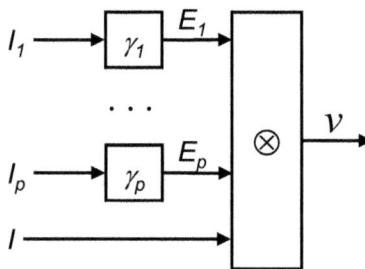

Fig. 3.7. The experiment generation algorithm data flow.

- I_i is the cross product of the value sets of the ZEN variables referred by the constraint γ_i, $\forall\, i \in [1..p]$ (line 4);
- E_i are the valid tuples that fulfil the constraint γ_i, $\forall\, i \in [1..p]$ (line 5);
- I is the multi-dimensional value set of the ZEN variables not referred by any ZEN constraint (line 7);
- $\mathcal{V}$ is the multi-dimensional value set, obtained by applying the composition operator to the valid tuple elements of the cross product $E_1 \times \ldots \times E_p \times I$ (line 8).

Based on the Lemma 3.30, the tuples belonging to the set $\mathcal{V}(z_1, \ldots, z_n)$ are valid.

Example 3.31 (Constraint evaluations).

```
!ZEN$ ASSIGN A = { 1 : 100 }
!ZEN$ ASSIGN B = { 1 : 100 }
!ZEN$ ASSIGN C = { 1 : 100 }
!ZEN$ CONSTRAINT VALUE A == B
!ZEN$ CONSTRAINT VALUE B == C
```

Example 3.31 defines three ZEN variables with the same value set:

$$\mathcal{V}^A = \mathcal{V}^B = \mathcal{V}^C = \bigcup_{i=1}^{100} i.$$

The data flow multi-dimensional value sets computed by the experiment generation algorithm according to Figure 3.7 are as follows:

$$I_1 = \mathcal{V}^A \times \mathcal{V}^B;$$
$$I_2 = \mathcal{V}^B \times \mathcal{V}^C;$$
$$I = \emptyset;$$
$$E_1 = \bigcup_{\forall a \in \mathcal{V}^A \,\wedge\, \forall b \in \mathcal{V}^B \,\wedge\, a=b} (a,b);$$
$$E_2 = \bigcup_{\forall b \in \mathcal{V}^B \,\wedge\, \forall c \in \mathcal{V}^C \,\wedge\, b=c} (b,c);$$
$$E = \bigcup_{\forall a \in \mathcal{V}^A \,\wedge\, \forall b \in \mathcal{V}^B \,\wedge\, \forall c \in \mathcal{V}^C \,\wedge\, a=b=c} (a,b,c),$$

where:

$$(a,b) \otimes (b,c) = (a,b,c),\ \forall\, a \in \mathcal{V}^A \,\wedge\, \forall\, b \in \mathcal{V}^B \,\wedge\, \forall\, c \in \mathcal{V}^C.$$

Since $|I_1| = |I_2| = 10^4$ and $|E_1| = |E_2| = 10^2$, the experiment generation algorithm evaluates $3 \cdot 10^4$ constraints. In contrast, a straight-forward algorithm, which evaluates both ZEN constraints on all the tuples of the cross product $A \times B \times C$ according to the Definition 3.24, performs $2 \cdot 10^6$ constraint evaluations that is two orders of magnitude higher.

3.2.12 Online Monitoring and Analysis

The performance and parameter study experiments described in Sections 3.2.9 and 3.2.10 assume that the performance and the output parameter data are available *post-mortem* (or *offline*) after the experiments completed. This restriction is often critical for users who need access to intermediate data from the application on-the-fly as the experiments progress. The Grid computing that defines applications running on unreliable resources is especially prone to such situations, when online data received from Grid sites unpredictably overloaded by some external users can be invaluable in taking decisive run-time steering decisions, for example for completing the application within a required or expected deadline.

Often users are interested in being notified of important *events* that are specific to their application, e.g. when a certain variable changed its value or when a specific performance metric exceeded a critical threshold. To meet such requirements, we extended the ZEN language with *event directives* for the specification and collection of online events and runtime data from running experiments. The event directives proposed in this section are part of a more general event framework which we will present in detail in Chapter 5 (see Section 5.6).

ZEN Event Directive

We introduce the *ZEN event directive* to enable the user be promptly informed of well-defined situations that occur during the runtime execution of an application. We define the ZEN event directive with the following syntax:

zen-event **is** EVENT *ident* [FILTER *bool-expr*] [SAMPLE *rate*]
ident   **is** *string*

We define three clauses as part of the ZEN event directive:

1. EVENT defines the event identifier *ident* which must be an arbitrary unique string for an application;
2. FILTER is an optional clause that filters the events to those which satisfy the associated boolean expression. The syntax of the filtering condition defined over a set of program variables is identical to the one defined by the ZEN constraint directive in Section 3.2.8. The directive defines no semantic analysis to examine whether the program variables referred by the boolean expression are valid within the runtime evaluation scope of the filtering condition. An eventual *"variable not found"* error will be produced by a subsequent ZEN file compilation;
3. SAMPLE is an optional clause which determines the directive applicability mode, as follows:
   a) *procedural mode* is selected by omitting the SAMPLE clause. Whenever the program counter reaches the directive at runtime, an event of type *ident* is generated if the filtering condition yields true. The variables involved in the filtering condition must be valid within the enclosing scope of the directive;
   b) *threaded mode* is selected by introducing the SAMPLE clause which specifies the rate (in samples per second) at which the filtering condition shall be evaluated. If the filtering condition yields true, an event of type *ident* is generated. In threaded mode, the variables involved in the filtering condition must have global scope.

Example 3.32 (ZEN event directive).

    !ZEN$ EVENT N1000 FILTER N > 1000 SAMPLE 1

Example 3.32 defines a ZEN event directive operating in the threaded mode, which generates an event of the type N1000 as soon as the program variable N is greater than 1000. The variable N must be global and is sampled every second, which defines the *accuracy* of the event.

ZEN Performance Directive

To support online performance analysis of parallel applications, we extended the ZEN performance directive introduced in Section 3.2.9 with three new clauses for expressing performance events:

> *global-perf* **is** CR *cr_mnem-list* PMETRIC *pm_mnem-list*
> [EVENT *ident*] [SAMPLE *rate*] [FILTER *bool-expr*]
> *local-perf* **is** CR *cr_mnem-list* PMETRIC *pm_mnem-list*
> [EVENT *ident*] [SAMPLE *rate*] [FILTER *bool-expr*] BEGIN
> *code-region*
> END CR

The semantics of the three additional (and also optional) clauses are as follows:

1. EVENT defines the event type;
2. SAMPLE is an event parameter which defines the rate at which the performance metrics specified by the directive are periodically sampled. No sampling is performed if this clause misses (i.e. post-mortem analysis). The measurement unit is samples per second. For each measurement, an event of type *ident* is generated if the boolean expression specified by the FILTER clause yields true (or misses). The sampling rate defines the *expiration* time of each event;
3. FILTER defines a filter as a boolean expression over the performance metric mnemonics specified by the directive. The performance mnemonics referred by the boolean expression must be present within the PMETRIC clause. An expression evaluation occurs at runtime at the rate specified by the SAMPLE clause and, if the evaluation yields true, an event of type *ident* is generated.

We implement the online clauses of the ZEN performance directive as part of the Process Manager sensor for dynamic instrumentation of running processes which we will present in Section 5.4.2.

Example 3.33 (Online ZEN performance directive).

```
!ZEN$ CR CR_P PMETRIC ODATA, WTIME EVENT comm SAMPLE 4
         FILTER ODATA > WTIME / 2
```

Example 3.33 illustrates a global ZEN performance directive which measures the execution time and the communication time of the entire program. The two metrics are sampled four times per second. An event of type comm is generated if the communication overhead ODATA dominates (i.e. is greater than half of) the wall-clock execution time WTIME.

3.3 Summary

In this section we presented a formal definition of a directive-based language called ZEN for the specification of a large number of experiments for performance and parameter studies of parallel applications. Substitute and assignment directives with arbitrary scopes allow compact specification of large value sets for arbitrary application parameters, including input problem parameters, machine sizes, software libraries, compilation options, or advanced parallelization strategies like array distributions or loop scheduling strategies. Performance directives implemented on top of a complete Fortran 90 compiler front-end allow us to request approximately 140 performance metrics for 50 different code regions types of parallel applications. Constraint directives implemented based on an efficient experiment generation algorithm generates the complete set of experiments while filtering the experiments with no useful practical meaning. In addition, we designed and implemented online event and performance directives to support runtime on-the-fly analysis of applications on dynamic Grid infrastructures. We illustrated a variety of realistic examples of employing the directives defined by the ZEN experiment specification language for performance and parameter studies of OpenMP, MPI, and HPF parallel applications.

4

ZENTURIO Experiment Management Tool

We designed ZENTURIO [140, 144] as a tool to automatically generate and conduct large number of experiments in the context of large scale performance and parameter studies on cluster and Grid architectures. ZENTURIO uses the ZEN language presented in Chapter 3 to specify a large set of performance and parameter study experiments in a compact and user friendly manner. Thereafter, it automatically generates, conducts, and analyses the performance and output data through a distributed service-oriented Grid architecture shielded from the end-user by means of a graphical User Portal. ZENTURIO systematically organises the performance and output data produced by all experiments into a well-defined Experiment Data Repository for post-mortem analysis.

4.1 User Portal Functionality

The user interacts with the ZENTURIO tool for constructing and conducting large scale performance and parameter studies through one *User Portal* consisting of four panels that export to the user the full functionality using a graphical and intuitive interface. We designed the User Portal as a small light-weight program easy to install and manage on the local machine (e.g. laptop) which shields the end-users from the complexity from the underlying Grid environment. Figure 4.1 depicts a sample snapshot of the User Portal main frame conducting a real application, which can be performed in three modes:

1. *Online Grid* is the standard mode of operating in a Grid infrastructure. The user must first authenticate using the GSI credentials (see Secure 2.4) and generate limited proxy required for secure authentication, encrypted communication, and credential delegation to the Grid middleware services. This mode uses GRAM [47] and DUROC [48] as job managers to submit experiments to the Grid sites;

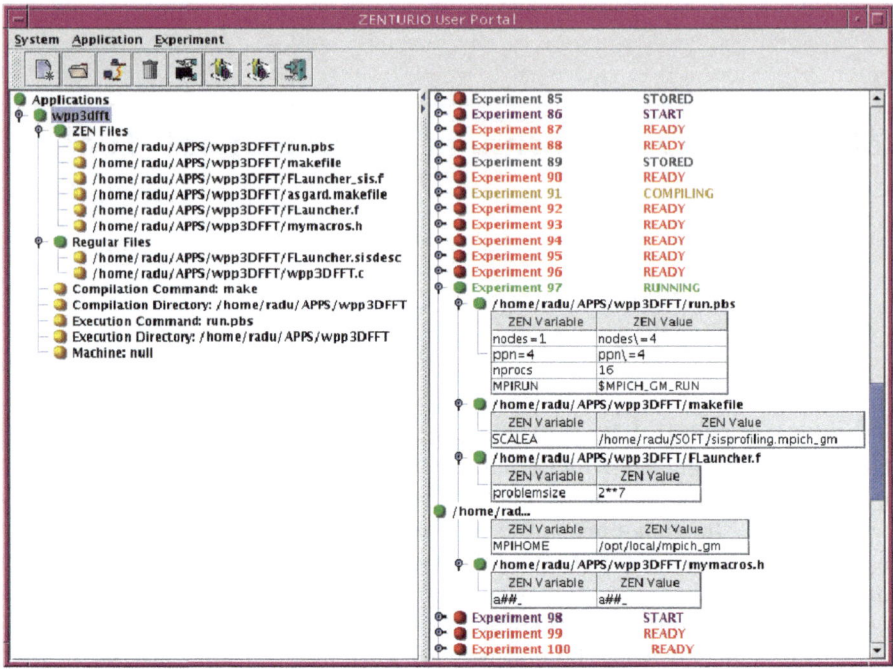

Fig. 4.1. The ZENTURIO User Portal main panel.

2. *Online Cluster* accommodates a simplified instance of the ZENTURIO infrastructure on the master front-end computer of the parallel machine. The middleware Grid services are replaced by ordinary Java objects, while the GSI security comprising user authentication is disabled. This mode uses the local job manager of the cluster (e.g. [29, 102, 123, 172, 201]) used by non-Grid users to submit, monitor, and control the experiments on the parallel machine;

3. *Offline* employs the User Portal for post-mortem analysis and visualisation of the data stored in the Experiment Data Repository previous by experiments conducted by ZENTURIO in the online mode.

4.1.1 ZEN Editor

We designed a so called *ZEN editor* to provide the user with a friendly graphical interface which facilitates the annotation of ZEN files with ZEN directives that hides all syntactic language details (e.g. escape \ characters). The local scopes of substitute, constraint, and performance directives can be easily indicated through mouse-based code region selection. An important task of the ZEN editor is to provide a centralised display summary of all the directives inserted in various ZEN files that may be difficult for a user to remember and find. Additionally, the editor provides online indication on the total number

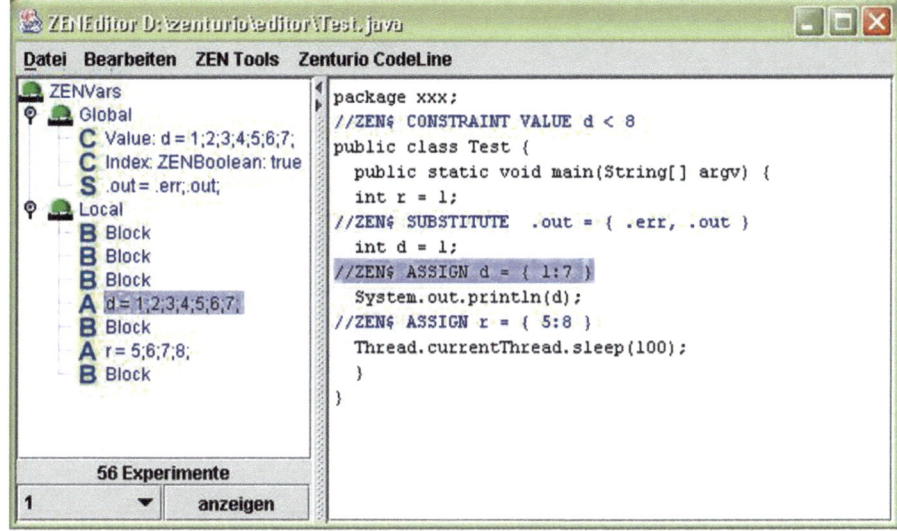

Fig. 4.2. The ZEN editor.

of experiments implied by the ZEN directives inserted, which is useful for tuning the application parameter space to a reasonable size before generating the full set of experiments. We illustrate a snapshot of the ZEN editor in Figure 4.2.

4.1.2 Experiment Preparation

The *Experiment Preparation* is a dialog-box of the User Portal depicted in Figure 4.3 that assists the user in the specification of a suite of experiments for performance or parameter study purposes through the following inputs:

1. *ZEN application* is created by selecting a list of files from arbitrary local directories, which we categorise into:
   a) *ZEN files* annotated with ZEN directives that must be processed by the ZEN Transformation System (see Section 3.1.2), which we further classify as follows:
      i. *ZEN source files* contain source code that requires separate compilation for every individual experiment. In our implementation, ZEN source files that require performance instrumentation specified through ZEN performance directives are currently limited to Fortran 90 source code files that are automatically processed by the SCALEA instrumentation engine based on the source-to-source Vienna Fortran Compiler [21];

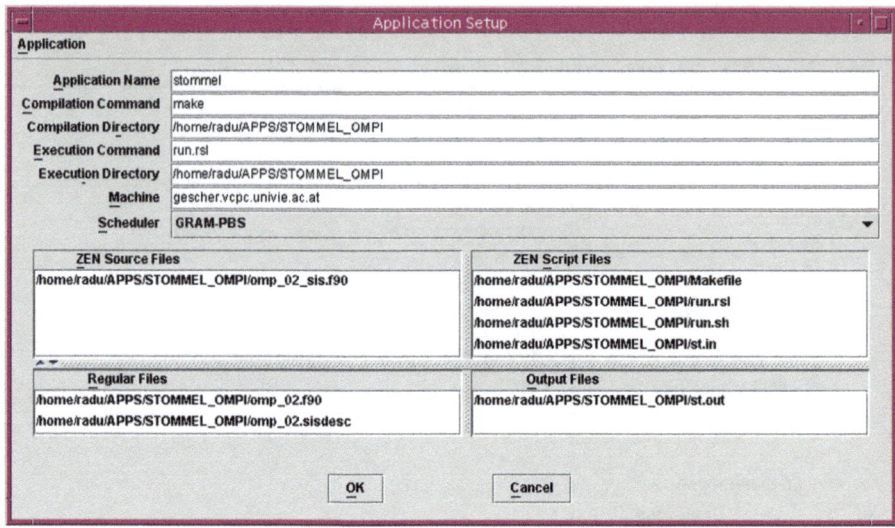

Fig. 4.3. The Experiment Preparation dialog-box.

   ii. *ZEN script files* are input files, makefiles, job submission scripts,
       or any kind of file annotated with ZEN directives that does not
       require compilation of the ZEN application instance. This infor-
       mation is used by ZENTURIO to optimise the compilation time
       of the entire experiment suite;
 b) *Regular files* that do not contain ZEN directives and therefore are
    not processed by the ZEN Transformation System and also do not
    need separate compilation for each experiment;
 Input and output file staging in online Grid mode is achieved through the
 GASS [25] functionality and is automatically handled by the GRAM [47]
 resource manager (see Section 2.5);
2. *compilation directory* and *compilation command*;
3. *execution directory* and *execution command*;
4. *Grid site* where to execute the experiments;
5. back-end local *scheduler* or job manager to use for submitting the experiments. This information is optional and can be also retrieved from
   Globus MDS introduced in Section 2.5;
6. *output files* for parameter study purposes.

After receiving all these inputs, the Experiment Preparation dialog-box automatically contacts the middleware services underneath provided by the ZEN-
TURIO distributed service-oriented architecture which will transparently generate, execute, and monitor the progress of experiments, as we will present
in detail in Section 4.4.

4.1.3 Experiment Monitor

The *Experiment Monitor* is the right panel of the main User Portal dialog-box depicted in Figure 4.1 which remotely controls and visually monitors the compilation and execution of experiments on the target Grid site. Upon selection of a ZEN application in the Experiment Preparation left panel, the corresponding set of experiments are automatically displayed in the right panel. The experiments of a ZEN application can be submitted for execution either individually, or on a collective basis. Each experiment is displayed accompanied by its status highlighted using a different colour. Upon clicking on an experiment, all the ZEN variable instantiations that describe the experiment are tabulated underneath. A *filtering* capability allows the user to select, display, or search for a subset of experiments according to specific ZEN variable instantiations.

4.1.4 Application Data Visualiser

We define in ZENTURIO two types of output data for multi-experimental post-mortem analysis:

1. *performance metrics* (e.g. execution time, synchronisation, communication) are specified through ZEN performance directives that we defined in Section 3.2.9;
2. *output parameters* are retrieved from the output files indicated by the user in the experiment preparation phase through a unique prefix string pattern (see Section 3.2.10).

We depict in Figure 4.4 a snapshot of the *Application Data Visualiser* dialog-box that we employ for automatic performance analysis across multiple experiments. The top-left panel displays the list performance metrics computed (e.g. barrier, collective communication, control of parallelism) which can be selected for analysis and visualisation. We organise the performance metrics in two different tree-based visualisation hierarchies according to the user preference:

1. *Metric-to-Region* (see Figure 4.4) displays on the first tree level the complete list of performance metrics computed. The next tree levels below the metric level display the code region hierarchy for which each parent metric holds;
2. *Region-to-Metric* displays the complete hierarchy of code regions for which performance metrics were collected. The leaves of the tree represent the performance metrics which were measured for the parent regions and subregions.

Upon mouse selection of a certain metric, the top-right panel of the Application Data Visualiser dialog-box displays the affiliated source code region,

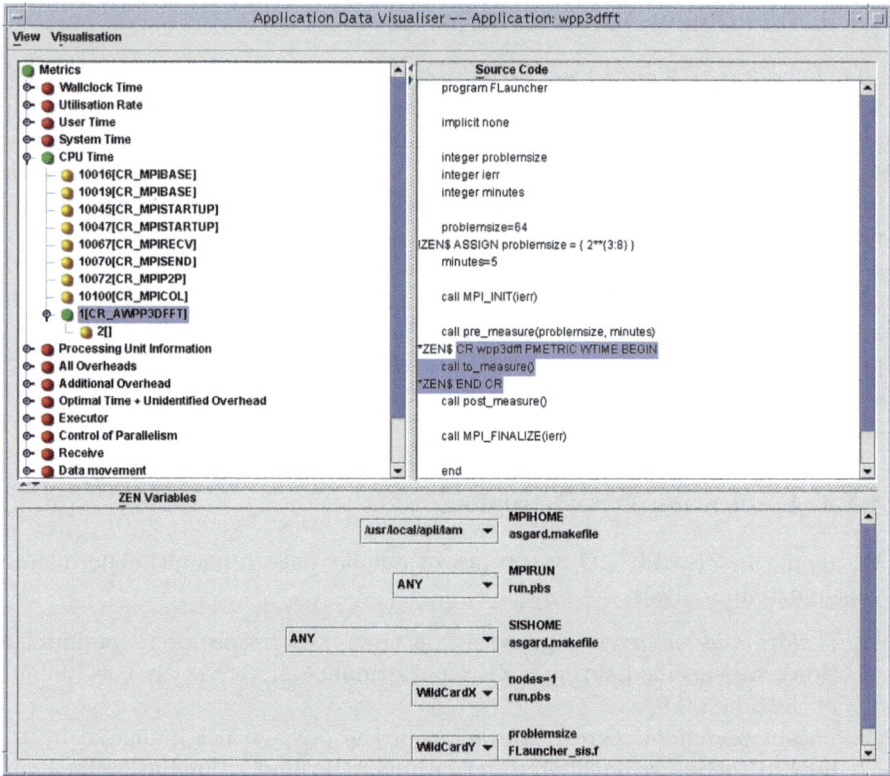

Fig. 4.4. The Application Data Visualiser for performance studies.

if this information is available from the source code compilation. The bottom panel displays the complete set of ZEN variables that annotate the ZEN application. Every ZEN variable has an associated list-box that contains its complete value set. To generate a visualisation, the user must select a subset of experiments and map ZEN variables to visualisation axes by instantiating each ZEN variable with appropriate ZEN elements. We perform the mapping of ZEN variables to visualisation axes by introducing two special ZEN elements to the value set of each ZEN variable:

1. *Wildcard* indicates that the ZEN variable is selected as a visualisation axis. The ZEN elements of the ZEN variable are displayed on the axis in the order given by the index domain function (see Definition 3.22). A number of n wildcard selections defines an $n+1$-dimensional visualisation diagram;

2. *ANY* matches any value and indicates that the ZEN variable is irrelevant for the visualisation and should be ignored. A typical case for an ANY selection is when the ZEN variable is bound via a ZEN constraint to another ZEN variable which received a wildcard.

The performance and output analysis data can be either tabulated into plain text files or graphically represented using a visualisation package that comprises linechart, barchart, piechart, and surface diagrams [67]. Our current implementation is limited to three wildcard ZEN variables which were easy to integrate and intuitive to visualise using these four types of diagrams. We predefine the X, Y, and Z axes for each visualisation diagram which can be indicated in the Application Data Visualiser through three wildcard flavours: *WildcardX*, *WildcardY*, and *WildcardZ* (i.e. the ZEN variable is displayed on the X, Y, respectively Z axis). Additionally, we allow the user to select single or multiple metric-region pairs to be represented in one visualisation. Upon single metric selection, the metric is mapped to one predefined axis in the visualisation diagram. Upon multiple metric selection, the metric visualisation axis must be indicated by the user in the dialog-box menu (i.e. *Visualisation* menu item). If no metric wildcard is indicated, only the last selected metric is visualised.

Figure 4.5 displays a similar Application Data Visualiser dialog-box for parameter study purposes to visualise the output results across multiple experiments. The performance metric panel is replaced with a list of application

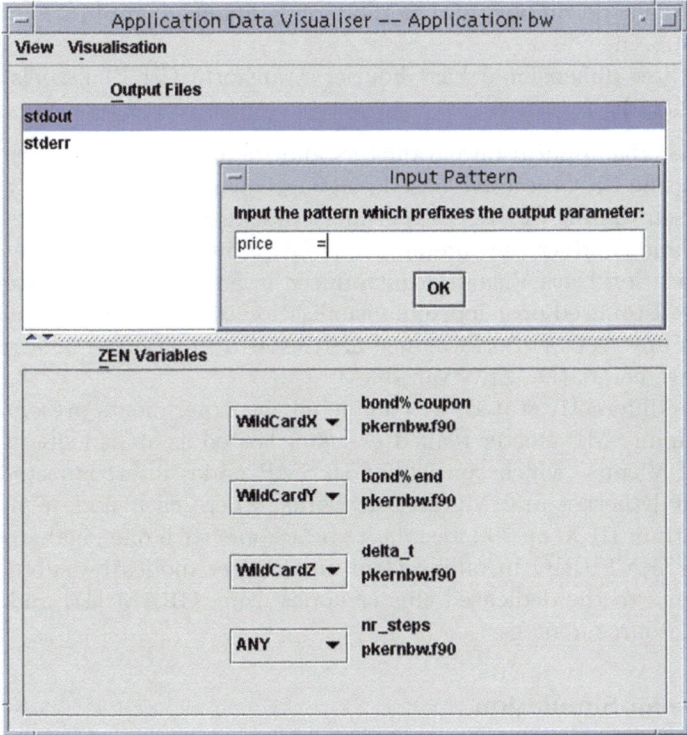

Fig. 4.5. The Application Data Visualiser for parameter studies.

output files, which includes the standard output and standard error streams. An output parameter is specified by selecting an output file and introducing a unique string pattern that prefixes the output parameter within the output file, as formally specified in Section 3.2.10. We use this pattern to extract the output parameter from the output file of each experiment involved in the visualisation.

We will give extensive examples on using the Application Data Visualiser for multi-experimental performance and parameter studies of various real-world applications in the remainder of this chapter.

4.2 Performance Studies

In this section we present a variety of multi-experimental performance studies conducted automatically using ZENTURIO experiment management tool on several real-world scientific parallel applications:

1. an ocean simulation (see Section 4.2.1);
2. a material science kernel (see Section 4.2.2);
3. a photonic application (see Section 4.2.3);
4. a benders decomposition method of a financial application (see Section 4.2.4);
5. two three-dimensional Fast Fourier Transform (FFT) kernels (see Section 4.2.5);

We defined the application parameters and the performance metrics of interest using the ZEN directive-based language specified in Chapter 3. Thereafter, we used the ZENTURIO experiment management tool to automatically generate and conduct the complete set of experiments. Finally, we employed the Application Data Visualiser introduced in Section 4.1.4 to automatically generate customised post-mortem visualisation diagrams that display the variation of any (set of) performance metrics as a function of arbitrary application parameters (i.e. ZEN variables).

Unless differently stated, we conducted the experiments presented in this section on an SMP cluster (called *gescher*) hosted as a Grid site at the University of Vienna, which consists of 16 SMP nodes interconnected through both Fast Ethernet and Myrinet networks, where each node contains four Intel Pentium III Xeon 700 megahertz processors with one gigabyte of RAM. We used ZENTURIO in online Grid and cluster modes by submitting the experiments to the dedicated cluster nodes using GRAM [47] and PBS [29] as local resource manager.

4.2.1 Ocean Simulation

The *Stommel* model [170] has been thought with the purpose of explaining the westward intensification of wind-driven ocean currents. In this section we present a performance study of a hybrid parallel Fortran 90 implementation of the Stommel model that uses OpenMP for intra-node shared memory parallelization and MPI for inter-node network communication.

We specified the following parameters for this application through ZEN directives:

1. *The machine size* consists of two dimensions:
   a) *The number of threads per SMP node* are controlled by the input parameter of the NUM_THREADS clause of the OpenMP PARALLEL directive (see Example 4.1);
   b) *The number of SMP nodes* are controlled through directives inserted in the Globus RSL script as illustrated in Example 4.3.
   We submitted each MPI experiment as a single GRAM job type which allows us to switch between various local communication libraries. We allocated one MPI process per SMP node by assigning to the count RSL parameter in Example 4.3 a value equal to the number of SMP nodes multiplied with the number of processors per node (i.e. four in our case). The shell script script.sh that we used to start the MPI application (see Example 4.2) sets the maximum number of MPI processes per node to one through the MPI_MAX_CLUSTER_SIZE environment variable. One single MPI process per SMP node leaves the intra-node parallelization to the OpenMP compiler;

2. *Two interconnection networks* (i.e. Fast Ethernet and Myrinet) were examined by linking the application with the corresponding MPI Chameleon (MPICH) library implementation [91]. We indicated the MPI implementation library locations by annotating the MPILIB variable in the application Makefile, as illustrated in Example 4.4. The constraint directive makes the correct association between the implementation specific MPI libraries and external MPIRUN ZEN variable (defined in Example 4.2) which contains the path to the mpirun script that starts the application;

3. *The problem size* was varied by changing the matrix (ocean) size and the number of iterations, as shown in Example 4.5;

4. *The performance metrics* of interest for every experiment are the execution time and the communication overhead (i.e. the mnemonics WTIME and ODATA), which we measured for the entire program and the outermost OpenMP parallel loop (i.e. the mnemonics CR_P and CR_OMPPA) expressed by the ZEN performance directive in Example 4.1.

Example 4.1 (Source code excerpt).

```
!ZEN$ CR CR_P, CR_OMPPA PMETRIC ODATA, WTIME

. . .

!ZEN$ SUBSTITUTE NUM_THREADS\(4\) = { NUM_THREADS({1:4}) }
!$OMP PARALLEL NUM_THREADS(4)
!ZEN$ END SUBSTITUTE

. . .

!$OMP END PARALLEL
```

Example 4.2 (Shell script – `script.sh`).

```
#!/bin/sh export
MPI_MAX_CLUSTER_SIZE=1
cd $PBS_O_WORKDIR
nodes = `wc -l < $PBS_NODEFILE`
MPIRUN = /opt/local/mpich/bin/mpirun
#ZEN$ ASSIGN MPIRUN = { /opt/local/mpich/bin/mpirun,
                        /opt/local/mpich_gm/bin/mpirun }
$(MPIRUN) -np $nodes -machinefile $PBS_NODEFILE omp_02_sis
```

Example 4.3 (Globus RSL script).

```
(*ZEN$ SUBSTITUTE count\=4 = { count={1:40:4} }*)
& (count=4)
  (jobtype=single)
  (directory="/home/radu/APPS/STOMMEL_OMPI")
  (executable="script.sh")
  (stdin="st.in")
  (stdout="st.out")
```

Example 4.4 (`Makefile`).

```
MPILIB = /opt/local/mpich/lib
#ZEN$ ASSIGN MPILIB = { /opt/local/mpich/lib,
                        /opt/local/mpich_gm/lib }
#ZEN$ CONSTRAINT INDEX MPILIB == script.sh:MPIRUN
. . .
$(TARGET): $(TARGET).o
     $(F90) $(TARGET).o -o $@ -L$(MPILIB) -lmpich
```

Example 4.5 (Input data file – `st.in`).

```
!ZEN$ SUBSTITUTE points = { 200, 400 }
     points points
     2000000, 40000000
     1.0e-9 2.25e-11 3.0e-6
!ZEN$ SUBSTITUTE iters = { 20000, 40000 }
     iters
!ZEN$ CONSTRAINT INDEX points == iters
```

We inserted only nine ZEN directives in three files of this application to specify a total of 160 experiments:

$$|\mathcal{V}(nodes{=}2, count{=}4, \text{MPIRUN}, \text{NUM\_THREADS}(4), \text{MPILIB}, points, iters)| = 160.$$

For a 200×200 problem size, the application does not scale with the machine size (see Figure 4.6(a)) which is explained by the excessive MPI communication (see Figure 4.6(b)). This problem size, however, scales well with the number of threads on a single SMP node. For larger number of nodes, the number of threads does not influence the overall performance due to the large MPI communication overhead that dominates the intra-node computation parallelised using OpenMP. The same problem size scales much better over the high performance Myrinet network compared to the commodity Fast Ethernet (see Figure 4.6(c)).

The 400×400 problem size shows a very reasonable scaling behaviour until four SMP nodes (see Figure 4.7(a)). Using more than four SMP nodes no longer decreases the execution time substantially because of the increased communication overhead and a decreasing ratio between the computation and the communication times (see Figure 4.7(b)). For smaller number of nodes, the computation to communication time ratio is high and, therefore, the intra-node OpenMP parallelization yields a satisfactory scaling behaviour. As expected, increasing the number of threads decreases the execution time. Similarly, this problem size scales well over the high performance Myrinet network (see Figure 4.7(c)).

We elaborated a second experiment to determine the number of nodes which produce the lowest execution time for different problem sizes over Fast Ethernet (see Figure 4.8(a)). We annotated the machine and the problem sizes as shown in the Examples 4.3 and 4.5. Employing four OpenMP parallel threads per node yields the best performance for all experiments. As expected, the optimal number of SMP nodes increases with the problem size. The flat parts of the curve are caused by imbalanced work distribution on odd number of processors.

We conducted a third experiment to examine different OpenMP loop scheduling strategies and their performance effects. We varied the scheduling strategy and the chunk size using a ZEN substitute directive, as illustrated in Example 3.14 (see Section 3.2.5, Chapter 3). We requested the execution time of the outermost OpenMP parallel loop through one ZEN performance directive, as shown in Example 4.1. Figure 4.8(b) illustrates that for the problem size examined, the STATIC scheduling performs better than the DYNAMIC and GUIDED strategies. The optimal chunk size experienced is 50. Static scheduling is superior because it implies the least runtime scheduling overhead.

4.2.2 Linearised Augmented Plane Wave

Linearised Augmented Plane Wave (LAPW) is a material science kernel, part a larger application called WIEN2k [160] (see Section 6.3.1), that calculates the potential of the Kohn-Sham eigen-value problem. This section presents a performance study of a Fortran 90 MPI implementation kernel of this method, called LAPW0.

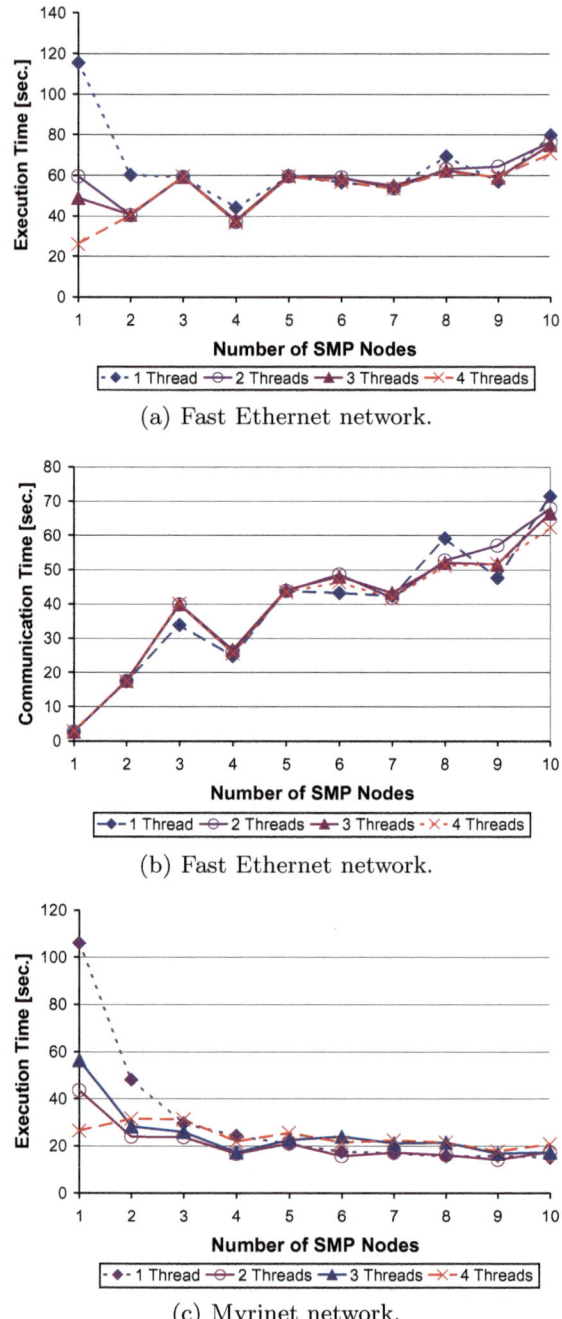

(a) Fast Ethernet network.

(b) Fast Ethernet network.

(c) Myrinet network.

Fig. 4.6. The Stommel model performance results for various intra-node and inter-node machine sizes (I), 200×200 problem size, 20000 iterations.

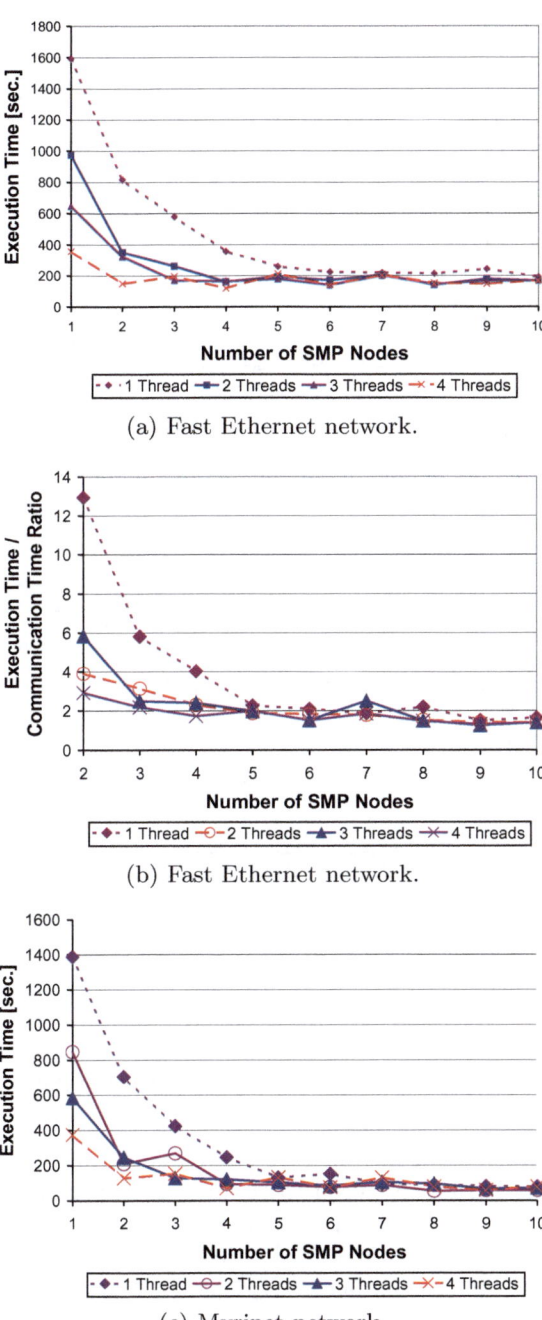

(a) Fast Ethernet network.

(b) Fast Ethernet network.

(c) Myrinet network.

Fig. 4.7. The Stommel model performance results for various intra-node and inter-node machine sizes (II), 400 × 400 problem size, 40000 iterations.

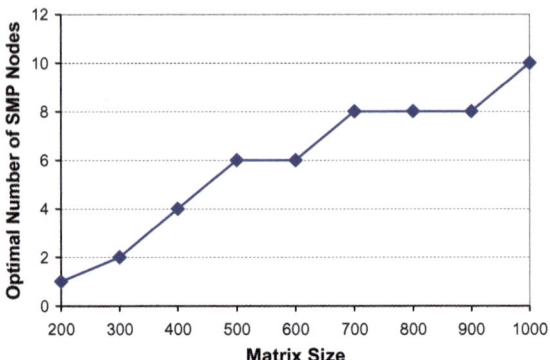

(a) Various problem sizes, four threads, 20000 iterations.

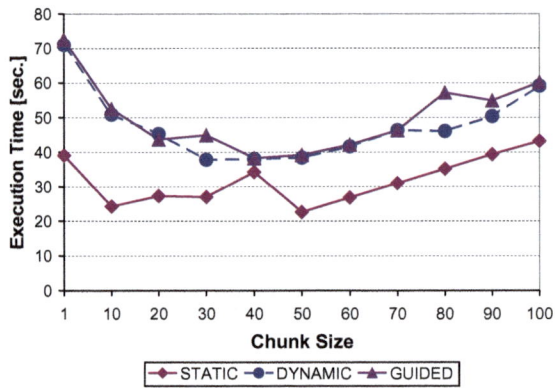

(b) Loop scheduling strategies, 200×200 problem size, 20000 iterations.

Fig. 4.8. The Stommel model performance results (III).

We annotated again a set of interesting application parameters by means of ZEN directives:

1. *The machine size* is controlled by the **nodes=1** and **no_procs** ZEN variables in the PBS script used to submit the experiments to the cluster (see Example 4.6). In this performance study we used ZENTURIO in cluster mode which bypasses GRAM (see Section 4.1). The ZEN variable **nodes=1** controls the number of SMP nodes and **no_procs** indicates the number of parallel MPI processes to execute. Each node receives four MPI processes before a new node is allocated. The constraint directive ensures that the correct amount of SMP nodes is allocated for each number of MPI processes. We could not execute a sequential version of this

application because of physical memory limitations on one SMP node. The PBS script also assigns the path of the mpirun command to the MPIRUN environment variable through one ZEN assignment directive;

2. *The interconnection network* is varied by annotating the MPILIB environment variable that specifies the path to the Fast Ethernet and Myrinet MPICH library implementations in the Makefile script used to compile and build the application (see Example 4.7). We used shared memory for MPI communication inside one SMP node. The ZEN constraint directive ensures the correct association between the network specific MPI library and the corresponding mpirun implementation script;

3. *The performance metrics* measured are the execution time (i.e. WTIME mnemonic) and the communication time (i.e. ODATA mnemonic) for the entire program (i.e. CR_P mnemonic). This is expressed by the ZEN performance directive from Example 4.8;

4. *The problem size* is expressed by pairs of .clmsum and .struct input files indicated in the lapw0.def input file (see Example 4.9). We used one ZEN substitute directive to specify the file locations that represent the problem sizes of interest which correspond to 8, 16, 32, and 64 atoms.

Example 4.6 (PBS script – run.pbs).

```
#ZEN$ SUBSTITUTE nodes\=1 = { nodes={1:40} }
#PBS -l walltime=0:29:00,nodes=1:fourproc:ppn=4
cd $PBS_O_WORKDIR
#ZEN$ ASSIGN MPIRUN = { /opt/local/mpich/bin/mpirun,
                        /opt/local/mpich_gm/bin/mpirun.ch_gm }
no_procs = 16
#ZEN$ ASSIGN no_procs = { 1:40 }
$(MPIRUN) -np $no_procs ../SRC/lapw0 lapw0.def
#ZEN$ CONSTRAINT INDEX 4 * (nodes\=1 - 1) < no_procs &&
                    no_procs <= 4*nodes\=1 && no_procs != 1
```

Example 4.7 (Makefile).

```
#ZEN$ ASSIGN MPILIB = { /opt/local/mpich/lib,
                        /opt/local/mpich_gm/lib }
#ZEN$ CONSTRAINT INDEX MPILIB == run.pbs:MPIRUN
LIBS = ... -lsismpiwrapper -L$(MPILIB) -lmpich
. . .
$(EXEC): $(OBJS)
        $(F90) -o lapw0 $(OBJS) $(LIBS)
```

Example 4.8 (Fortran source file excerpt – lapw0.F).

```
. . .
!ZEN$ CR CR_P PMETRIC WTIME, ODATA
. . .
```

Example 4.9 (Input data file – lapw0.def).

```
!ZEN$ SUBSTITUTE .125hour ={.125hour, .25hour, .5hour, 1hour}
8,'ktp_.125hour.clmsum','old','formatted',0 . . .
20,'ktp_.125hour.struct','old','formatted',0 . . .
```

We inserted eight ZEN directives into four ZEN files, based on which a total of 320 experiments were automatically generated and executed by ZEN-TURIO. Figure 4.9(a) shows the scalability of the application for all four problems sizes examined. The scalability of the algorithm improves by increasing the LAPW0 problem size (i.e. number of atoms). For a problem size of 8 atoms (i.e. .125hour), LAPW0 does not scale which is partially due to the extensive communication overhead with respect to the entire execution time. Figure 4.9(c) shows the contribution of each computed overhead to the overall execution time of each experiment. For 64 atoms (i.e. 1hour) the application scales well until 16 processes, after which the execution time becomes relatively constant.

Surprisingly, the interconnection network does not influence the communication time (see Figure 4.9(b)) because the blocking time of all message receive operations dominates the effective transfer of relatively small amount of data across MPI processes.

4.2.3 Three-Dimensional Particle-in-Cell

The *three-Dimensional Particle-In-Cell (3DPIC)* [86] is a Fortran 90 MPI application simulates the interaction of high intensity ultrashort laser pulses with plasma in three-dimensional geometry. In this section we present a 3DPIC performance study based on the following parameter annotations:

1. *The machine size* is restricted by the peculiarities of this application to 1, 4, 9, 12, 16, 25, and 36 parallel processes which we have expressed through the count argument of the GRAM RSL script shown in Example 4.10. Based on the number of processes of one experiment, GRAM allocates the correct number of dedicated SMP nodes using PBS as back-end local job manager. We set the job type to single which gave us flexibility in selecting the local interconnection network. We started the application using the shell script illustrated in Example 4.11 which assigns to the MPIRUN ZEN variable the path to the mpirun script;

2. *The interconnection network* is studied by annotating the application Makefile as already shown in Example 4.7 (see Section 4.2.2). Similarly, a constraint directive associates the implementation specific mpirun command with the correct MPI library;

3. *The performance metrics* of interest are the execution time and the communication overhead, which we specified as already shown in Example 4.8 (see Section 4.2.2).

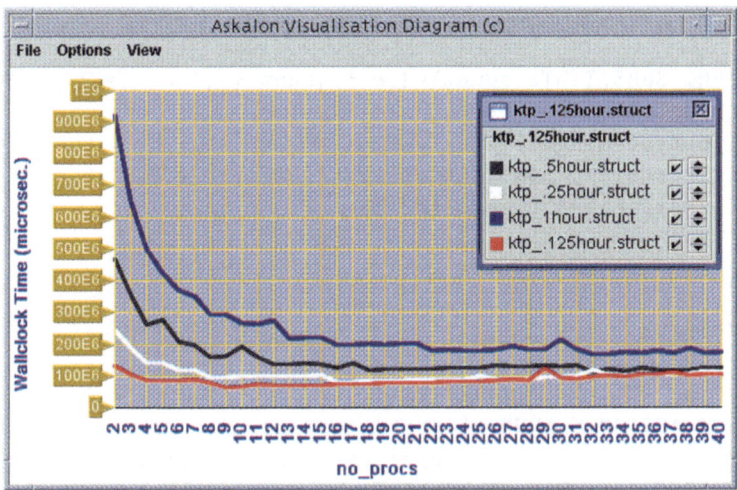

(a) Four problem sizes, Fast Ethernet network.

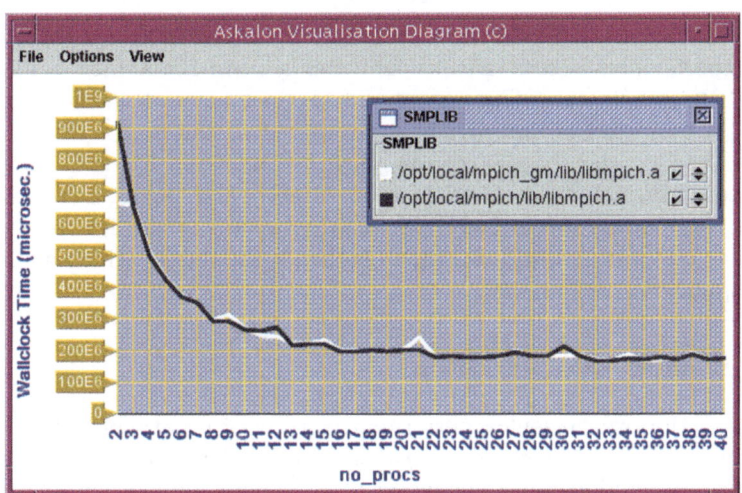

(b) Network comparison (Fast Ethernet versus Myrinet), 64 atoms problem size.

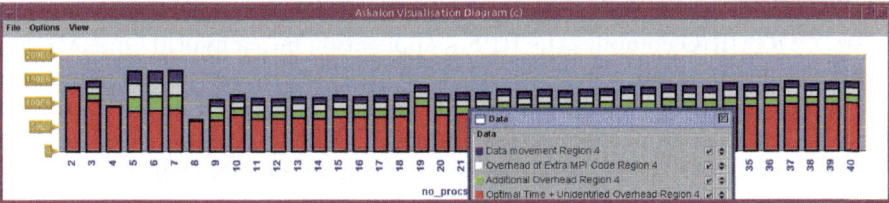

(c) Contribution of Myrinet communication overhead to the wall-clock execution time, 8 atoms problem size.

Fig. 4.9. The LAPW0 performance results for various machine sizes.

Example 4.10 (Globus RSL script – run.rsl).

```
(*ZEN$ SUBSTITUTE count\=4 = { count={1,1,3,3,4,7,9} }*)
& (count=4)
  (jobtype=single)
  (directory="/home/radu/APPS/LAPW0/znse_6")
  (executable="script.sh") )
```

Example 4.11 (Shell script – script.sh).

```
#!/bin/sh
cd $PBS_O_WORKDIR
n = 'wc -l < $PBS_NODEFILE'
#ZEN$ ASSIGN MPIRUN ={ /opt/local/mpich/bin/mpirun,
                      /opt/local/mpich_gm/bin/mpirun.ch_gm }
$(MPIRUN) -np $n -machinefile $PBS_NODEFILE lapw0
```

We inserted five ZEN directives into four files to generate a total of four-teen experiments. Figure 4.10(a) indicates a good scalability behaviour of the 3DPIC application. The use of the Myrinet network yields approxima-tely 50% performance improvement compared to the Fast Ethernet, which is explained by the reduced communication time (see Figure 4.10(b)) over the faster Myrinet network with lower latency and higher bandwidth. Fi-gure 4.10(c) shows a relatively low ratio between the application execution time (i.e. one full pie) and the MPI overheads measured, which explains the good application scalability.

4.2.4 Benders Decomposition

In this section we present a performance study of a parallel HPF+ [20] im-plementation of a *benders decomposition* method for structured stochastic optimisation employed in the context of a financial application [55] (see Sec-tion 4.3.1). HPF+ directives, which are an extension of the HPF language for SMP clusters, are used for inter-node and intra-node data distribution. As part of the performance instrumentation and experiment generation pro-cess, ZENTURIO compiles the HPF+ application into a hybrid OpenMP and MPI parallel program using the SCALEA [181] instrumentation engine built on top of the HPF+ Vienna Fortran Compiler [21]. The translated program achieves intra-node parallelization through OpenMP directives and commu-nication across the SMP nodes using MPI communication routines.

We studied the following parameters for this kernel:

1. *The machine size* consists of two dimensions:
   a) *The number of SMP nodes* is varied by the count=4 ZEN varia-ble in the Globus RSL script used to submit the experiments in

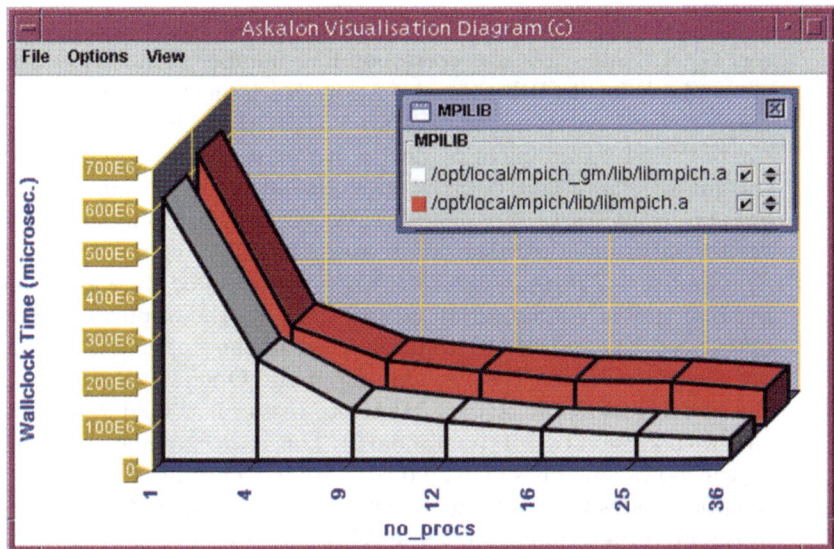

(a) Network comparison (Fast Ethernet versus Myrinet).

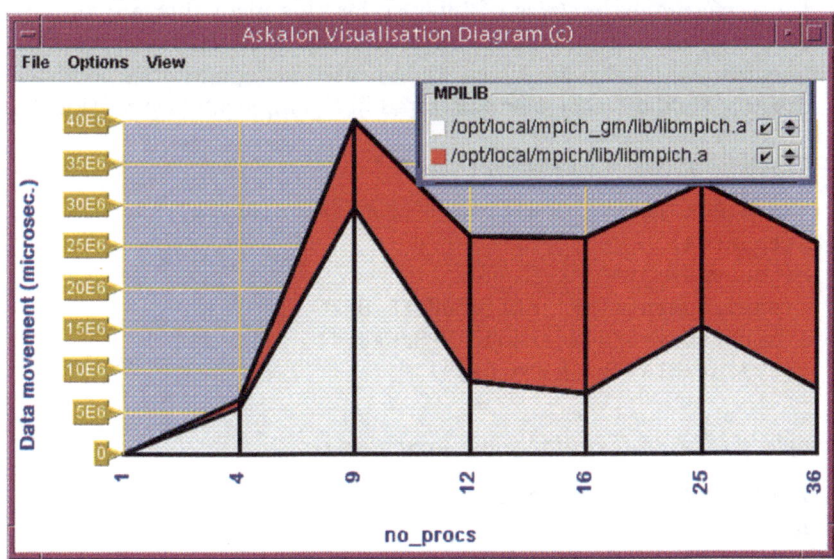

(b) Communication overhead comparison (Fast Ethernet versus Myrinet).

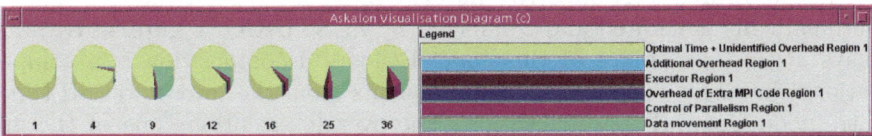

(c) Contribution of the Myrinet communication overheads to the wall-clock time.

Fig. 4.10. The 3DPIC performance results for various machine sizes.

Grid mode (see Example 4.12). Based on the count RSL parameter, GRAM allocates the corresponding number of nodes and uses an available local MPI implementation which must be defined by the user's default environment. We used MPICH in this experiment on top of the p4 communication device over Fast Ethernet. The MPICH specific MPI_MAX_CLUSTER_SIZE environment variable ensures that the mpirun script starts only one MPI process per SMP node, which leaves the intra-node parallelization to the OpenMP compiler;

b) *The number of threads per SMP node* is controlled by annotating a peculiar global configuration file designed by the application developers (see Example 4.13) which is used in the application for loop parallelization using the version one of the OpenMP standard (i.e. the NUM_THREADS clause of a PARALLEL region is available only starting with version two of the standard). This is an example of flexibility which shows how ZENTURIO deals with less elegant or outdated application codes that does not constrain the developers to learn state-of-the-art programming styles, neither forces them adapt their code to the newest specification standards;

2. *The performance metrics* of interest for this algorithm are the execution time, the MPI communication time, and the HPF+ inspector and executor overheads [20], which we indicated using one ZEN performance directive similar to the one illustrated in Example 4.8 (see Section 4.2.2).

Example 4.12 (Globus RSL script – run.rsl).

```
(*ZEN$ SUBSTITUTE count\=4 = {count={1:10}} *)
& (count=4)
  (jobtype=mpi)
  (environment=(MPI_MAX_CLUSTER_SIZE 1))
  (directory="/home/radu/APPS/HANS")
  (executable="bw_halo_sis")
```

Example 4.13 (Configuration file – bench.in).

```
!ZEN$ SUBSTITUTE threads = { 1:4 }
threads
```

We inserted three ZEN directives into two files which specify 40 experiments automatically generated and conducted by ZENTURIO. Figure 4.11(a) displays a good scalability of this code. Benders decomposition is a computational intensive code which highly benefits from the inter-node MPI and intra-node OpenMP parallelization. The overall execution time of the application significantly improves by increasing the number of nodes and the OpenMP threads per SMP node. Figure 4.11(b) displays a very high ratio between the total execution time (i.e. one full bar) and the HPF and MPI overheads which explains the good scalability behaviour. This ratio decreases for a high number of SMP nodes for which the overheads significantly degrade the overall performance.

4.2.5 Three-Dimensional FFT Benchmarks

The performance of parallel scientific applications is heavily influenced by various mathematical kernels like linear algebra software [188] that needs to be individually optimised for each particular platform to achieve acceptable high performance. In this context, we deployed ZENTURIO at the Paul Scherrer Institute, part of the Swiss Federal Institute of Technology, for automatic benchmarking of three-dimensional FFT kernels required for solving large scale partial differential simulations [138]. In this section we report experimental results produced by this international synergy effort.

Let $A(n, n, n)$ denote a three-dimensional array. A three-dimensional FFT on the array A is defined as:

$$B_{x,y,z} = \sum_{s=0}^{n-1}\sum_{t=0}^{n-1}\sum_{u=0}^{n-1} \omega^{\pm(xs+yt+zu)} A_{s,t,u}, \ \forall \ x, y, z \in [0..n-1],$$

where $n = 2^m$ and $\omega = e^{\frac{2\pi i}{n}}$ is the nth root of unity. This computation is typically parallelised by distributing the x dimension of the cube onto the set of available processors (see Figure 4.12). As a consequence, the computation over the inner y and z dimensions can be performed locally on each processor in parallel independent loops according to the following first two equations:

$$C_{s,t,z} = \sum_{u=0}^{n-1} \omega^{zu} A_{s,t,u};$$
$$D_{s,y,z} = \sum_{t=0}^{n-1} \omega^{yt} C_{s,t,z};$$
$$B_{x,y,z} = \sum_{s=0}^{n-1} \omega^{xs} D_{s,y,z}.$$

The summation on the x axis, expressed by the last equation above, requires redistribution of the matrix elements such that each processor can compute its sum locally. This is performed by rotating the cube around the z dimension in an operation called *transpose*. Finally, a second reverse transpose operation is required to rearrange the data to the original layout (see Figure 4.12).

In this section we present a comparative analysis between two three-dimensional FFT implementations:

1. *Fastest Fourier Transform in the West (FFTW)* [83] is a portable subroutine library for computing the discrete Fourier transform in one or more dimensions of arbitrary input sizes and of both real and complex data. Existing benchmarks [84] performed on a variety of platforms show that the performance of FFTW is typically superior to that of other publicly available FFT implementation and is even competitive with non-portable and highly optimised vendor codes. The power of FFTW is the ability to optimise itself to the target machine through some predefined *codelets* executed by a planner function before calling the real FFT;

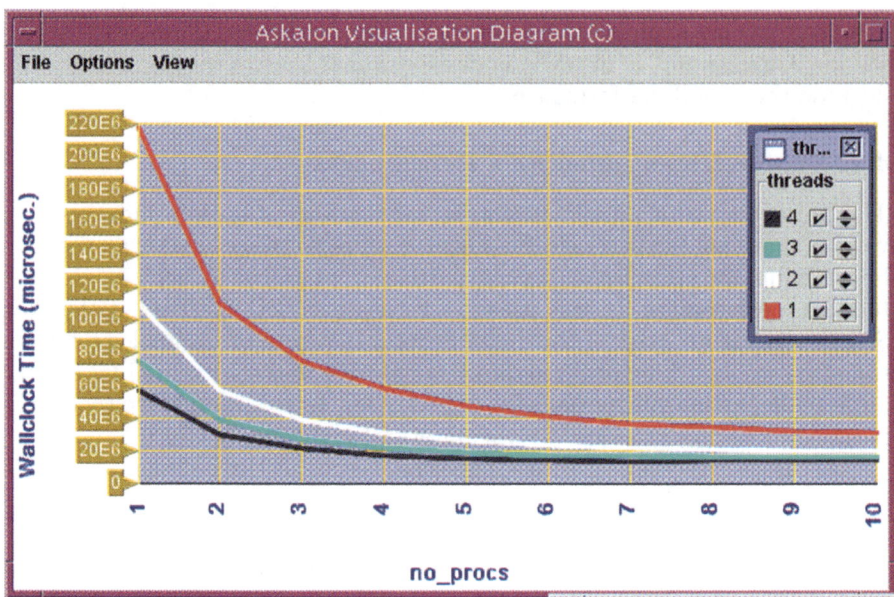

(a) Wall-clock execution time for various intra-node and inter-node machine sizes.

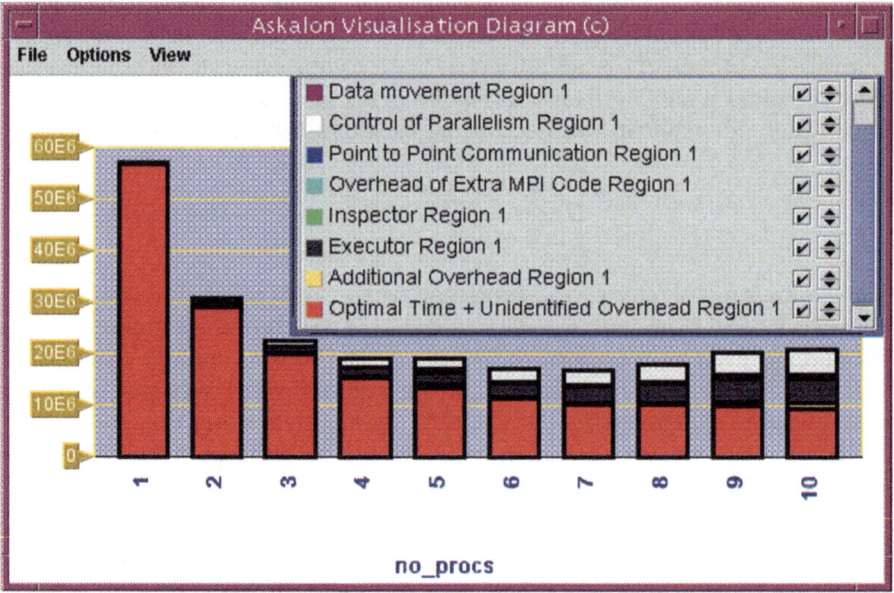

(b) Contribution of the MPI and the HPF overheads to the wall-clock execution time, for various inter-node machine sizes, four threads per SMP node.

Fig. 4.11. The benders decomposition performance results for various machine sizes.

2. *wpp3DFFT* developed at the Swiss Federal Institute of Technology Zurich uses a generic implementation of Temperton's in-place algorithm [176] for an $n = 2^m$ problem size with the particular focus of making the transpose faster. The optimised algorithm pays a flexibility price, which restricts the matrix and the machine size to powers of two.

Both applications are implemented in the C language as parallel MPI programs which we wrapped with a FORTRAN 77 front-end for the purpose of using the automatic compiler-based instrumentation provided by ZENTU-RIO. We conducted all experiments on a single SMP cluster hosted at the Paul Scherrer Institute, comprising 192 dual Pentium III SMP nodes running at 500 megahertz with one gigabyte of memory and interconnected through 100 megabit per second Fast Ethernet networks. The nodes are organised into 24 node frames interconnected through one gigabit per second optical links.

We varied the following three application parameters:

1. *The problem size* ranges from 2^3 to 2^8 which we expressed through the ZEN variable `problemsize` in Example 4.14. We could not run larger problem sizes due to memory limitations on one SMP node;
2. *The communication library* is expressed by the `MPI_HOME` ZEN variable in the application `Makefile` (see Example 4.16). The MPI implementation libraries available on the cluster which we compared are the Local Area Multicomputer (LAM) [33] and MPICH with the P4 communication device [91]. We used shared memory for communication within one SMP node;
3. *The machine size* ranges from 2^1 to 2^6 dual nodes, each node running two MPI processes. The `MPIRUN` ZEN variable refers to the implementation specific `mpirun` script which is associated with the MPI library location parameterised externally in the `Makefile` through one ZEN constraint directive. We could not run larger machine sizes because of cluster queue policy restrictions;
4. *The performance metrics* of interest are the total execution time and the transpose time which we measured using the ZEN performance directive illustrated in Example 4.14. We measured the MPI communication overheads using the SCALEA MPI wrapper library.

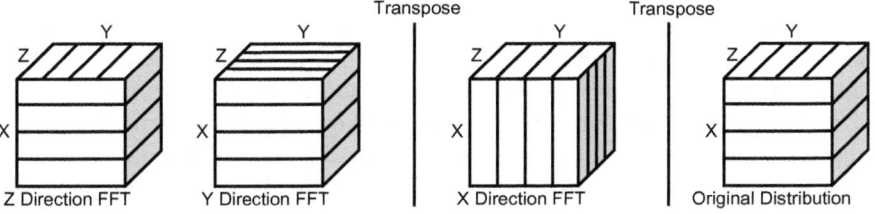

Fig. 4.12. The parallel three-dimensional FFT computation.

Example 4.14 (FFT Fortran wrapper – FLauncher.f).

```
problemsize=64
*ZEN$ ASSIGN problemsize = { 2**{3:8} }
minutes=5
call MPI_INIT(ierr)
call pre_measure(problemsize, minutes)
*ZEN$ CR wpp3dfft PMETRIC WTIME BEGIN
call to_measure()
*ZEN$ END CR
call post_measure()
call MPI_FINALIZE(ierr)
```

Example 4.15 (PBS script – run.pbs).

```
#!/bin/sh
#ZEN$ SUBSTITUTE nodes\=1 = { nodes\={2,4,8,16,32,64} }
#PBS -l walltime=3600,nodes=1:ppn=2
nproc=`wc $PBS_NODEFILE | awk '{print $1}'`
LAM_RUN="/usr/local/apli/lam/bin/mpirun -np $nproc wpp3DFFT"
MPICH_RUN="/usr/local/apli/mpich/bin/mpirun -nolocal
          -np $nproc -machinefile $PBS_NODEFILE wpp3DFFT"
/usr/local/apli/lam/bin/lamboot -v $PBS_NODEFILE
MPIRUN=$LAM_RUN
#ZEN$ ASSIGN MPIRUN = { $LAM_RUN, $MPICH_RUN }
#ZEN$ CONSTRAINT INDEX MPIRUN == Makefile:MPIHOME
$MPIRUN
```

Example 4.16 (Makefile).

```
MPI_HOME = /usr/local/apli/lam
#ZEN$ ASSIGN MPI_HOME = { /usr/local/apli/lam,
                          /usr/local/apli/mpich }
  . . .
$(EXEC): $(OBJS)
  $(MPI_HOME)/bin/mpicc -o $(EXEC) $(OBJS) $(LIBS)
```

We inserted a total of six ZEN directives into three application files to express 72 experiments automatically generated and conducted by ZENTURIO. Since small FFT problems have extremely short execution times (i.e. order of milliseconds), they are prone to perturbations coming from the operating system, instrumentation probes, or other background processes that run with low scheduling priority. To avoid such consequences, we repeated each experiment for a long enough amount of time (i.e. five minutes) and finally computed the mean of all measurements.

Figures 4.13(a) and 4.13(b) display the speedup curves of the two FFT algorithms normalised against the lowest machine size executed (i.e. two dual nodes), since we did not have a sequential implementation available. The speedup is poor for small problem sizes for which the parallelization across a large number of processors deteriorates the performance. Large problem sizes offer some speedup until a certain critical machine size. The explanation for the poor speedup curves is given by the large fraction from the overall execution time used by the transpose operation, denoted as region 2 in Figure 4.14(a), and the MPI overheads, in particular the MPI_Sendrecv_replace routine used to interchange the elements in the transpose (FFTW shows similar overhead curves). It is interesting to notice that both algorithms scale reasonably well until 16 dual nodes for a 2^8 problem size beyond which the performance degrades significantly. The reason is the fact that larger machine sizes spawn across multiple cluster frames which communicate through three bus switches, two Ethernet, and two Fast Ethernet network cards that significantly affect the transpose communication time. For small problem sizes, the execution time is basically determined by the transpose overhead that naturally increases proportional with the machine size (see Figures 4.15(a) and 4.14(b)). In contrast to wpp3dFFT, FFTW shows an interesting behaviour of keeping the transpose and the total execution time constant even for large machine sizes, which we explain in the next paragraphs through a load balance analysis.

ZENTURIO offers a series of data aggregation functions, comprising maximum, minimum, average, or sum, for metrics measured within the parallel (MPI) processes or (OpenMP) threads of an application.

Definition 4.17. *Let $\mathcal{M}_i$ denote the performance measurements of a performance metric pm_mnem for all n parallel processes or threads of a parallel application, $\forall\, i \in [1..n]$. We define the load balance aggregation function for the performance metric pm_mnem as the ratio between the average and maximum aggregation values:*

$$LB_{pm\_mnem} = \frac{\frac{\sum_{i=1}^{n} \mathcal{M}_i}{n}}{\max_{\forall\, i \in [1..n]} \{\mathcal{M}_i\}}.$$

A value of one indicates a perfect load balance while a value of zero represents the worse case of load imbalance.

The wpp3dFFT kernel shows a good load balance close to one for all the problem and machine sizes examined (see Figure 4.17(b)), while FFTW exhibits a severe load imbalance, the smaller problems are and the larger the machine sizes get (see Figure 4.17(a)). The explanation of this behaviour is the fact that FFTW in its planner function that chooses optimised codelets for a certain platform also detects that a machine size is too large for a rather small problem size to be solved. As a consequence, it decides to use only a subset of the processors for doing useful computation and transpose, while the remaining MPI processes simply exit by calling the MPI_Finalize routine. This explains the even execution time for small problem sizes in Figure 4.15(a).

Figure 4.16(a) shows a better performance of the LAM MPI implementation compared to MPICH for small problems and large machine sizes. Such experiments are characterised by a large number of small message exchanges dominated by latencies for which the LAM implementation performs better than MPICH. Large problem sizes shift the focus from message latency to network bandwidth, in which case both implementations are bound to the limited physical capabilities of the interconnection network and, therefore, perform equally well (see Figure 4.16(b)).

We performed a complementary suite of experiments on the *gescher* cluster (introduced in the beginning of Section 4.2) using the technique already presented in Example 4.7 (see Section 4.2.2) which shows that the Myrinet high performance network (not available on the Swiss cluster) gives an approximate two fold improvement in performance compared to Fast Ethernet (see Figure 4.15(b)).

A comparative analysis of the two FFT parallel algorithms shows, as expected, a better performance of wpp3DFFT compared to FFTW for large problem sizes which is due to the highly optimised wpp3DFFT transpose implementation for power of two problem sizes (see Figure 4.18(a)). For small problem sizes, FFTW performs much better due to its intelligent runtime adjustment of machine size in the planning phase (see Figure 4.18(b)). The metric in which the Swiss physicists were particularly interested is the ratio between the transpose and computation time, the latter being defined as the difference between the overall execution time and the transpose operation. We comparatively display this metric in Figures 4.19(a) and 4.19(b).

4.3 Parameter Studies

Even though our original idea when building ZENTURIO was to support multi-experimental performance studies of parallel applications, the general parameter specification approach taken by the ZEN language enabled us to perform classical parameter studies with minimal additional effort. We formally defined a parameter study experiment in Section 3.2.10.

4.3.1 Backward Pricing

The *backward pricing* kernel is a parallel implementation of the backward induction algorithm which computes the price of an interest rate dependent financial product such as a variable coupon bond. The algorithm is based on the Hull and White trinomial interest rate tree models for future developments of interest rates [55].

This application is originally encoded such that it reads its input parameters from different input data files. We performed the parameter annotations

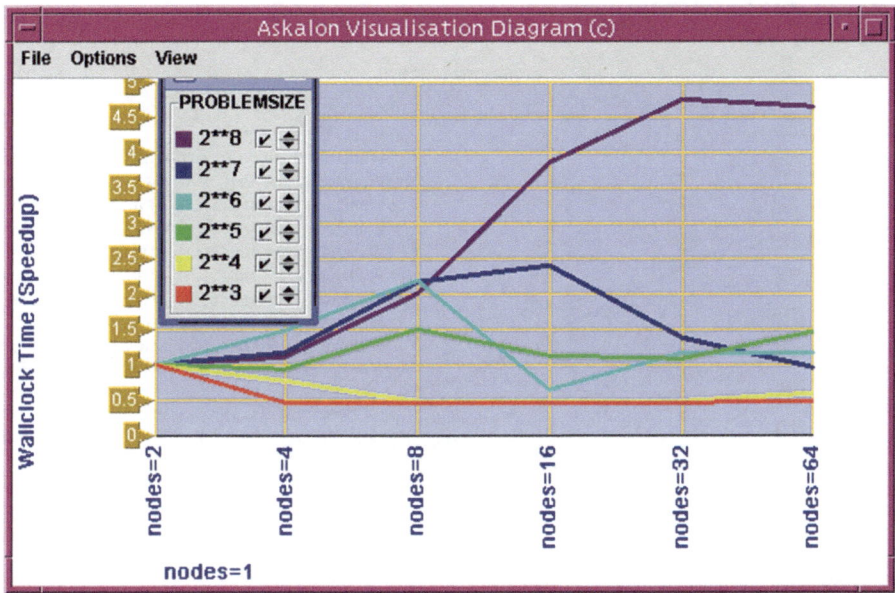

(a) FFTW speedup.

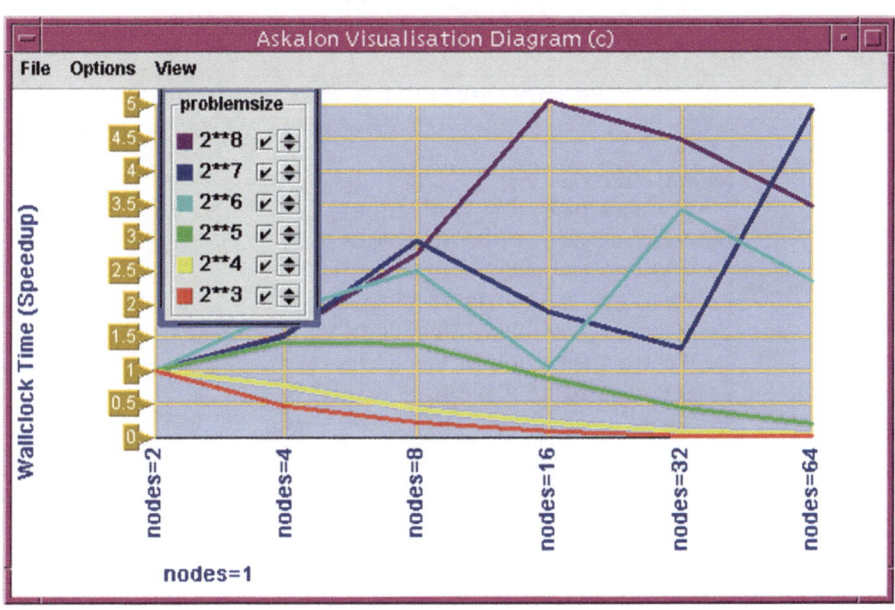

(b) wpp3DFFT speedup.

Fig. 4.13. The three-dimensional FFT benchmark results (I).

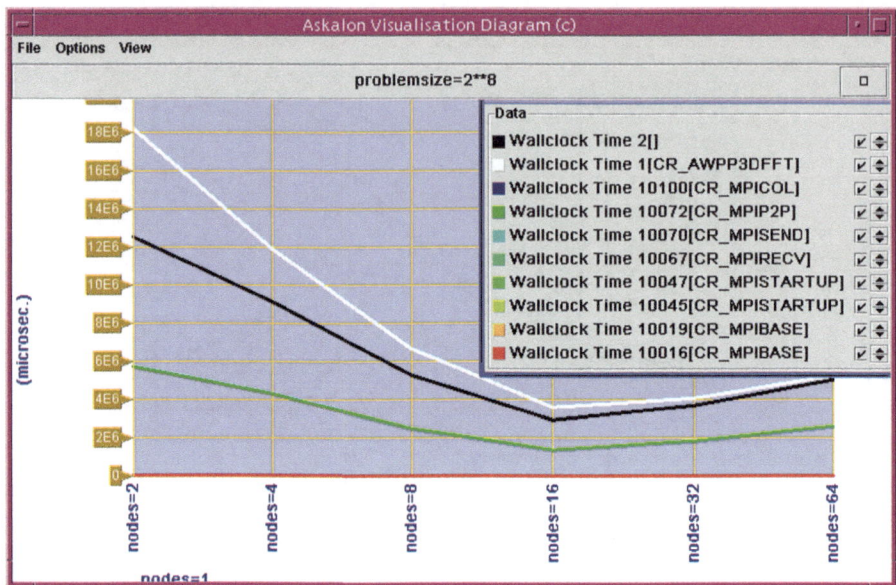

(a) wpp3DFFT overheads (2^8 problem size).

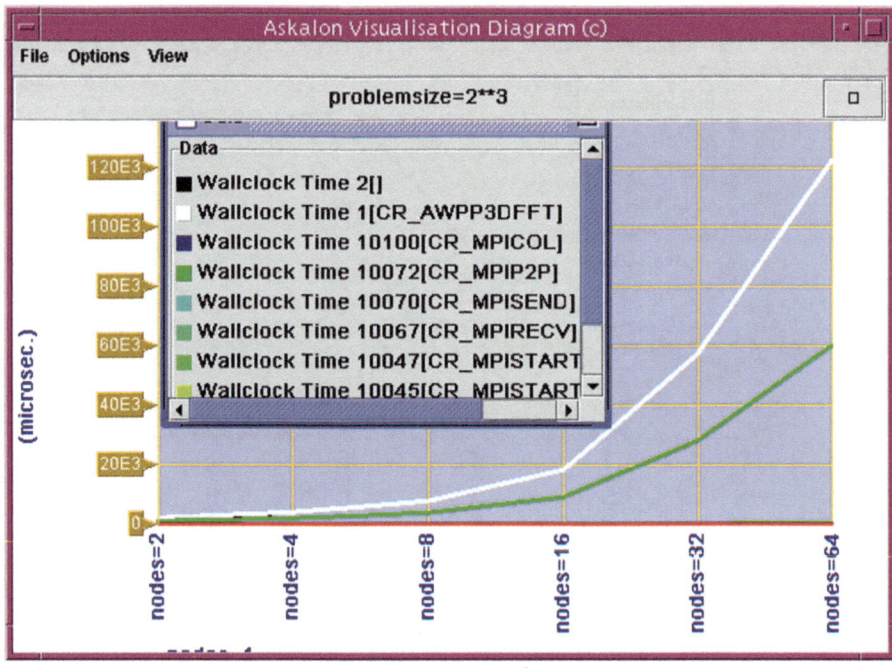

(b) wpp3DFFT overheads (2^3 problem size).

Fig. 4.14. The three-dimensional FFT benchmark results (II).

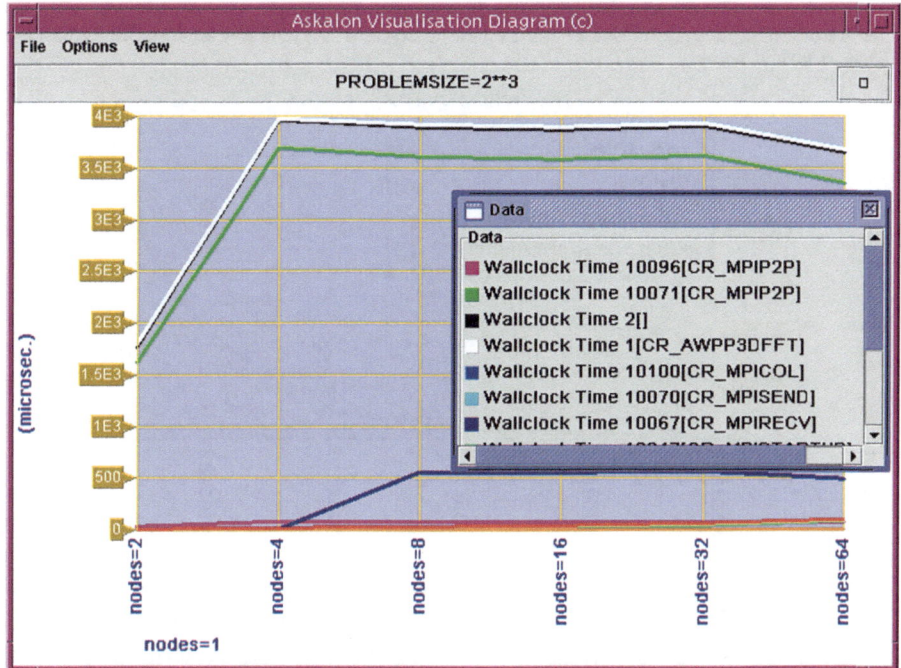

(a) FFTW overheads (2^3 problem size).

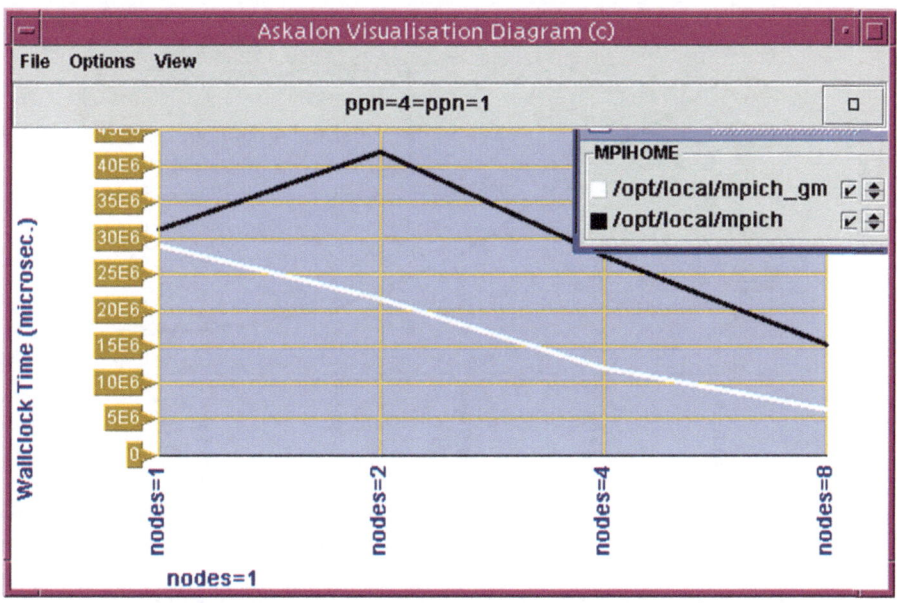

(b) wpp3DFFT network comparison (LAM versus MPICH, 2^8 problem size).

Fig. 4.15. The three-dimensional FFT benchmark results (III).

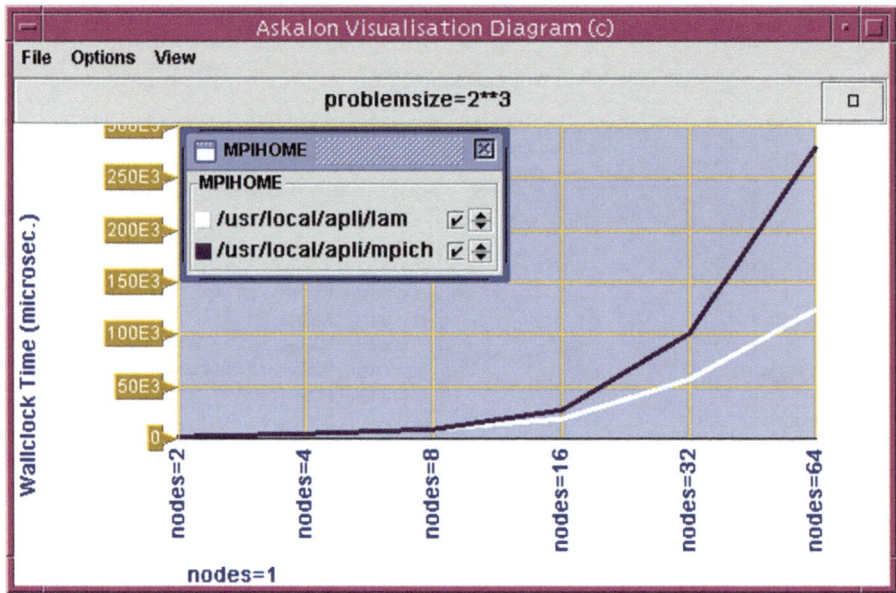

(a) wpp3DFFT network comparison (LAM versus MPICH, 2^3 problem size).

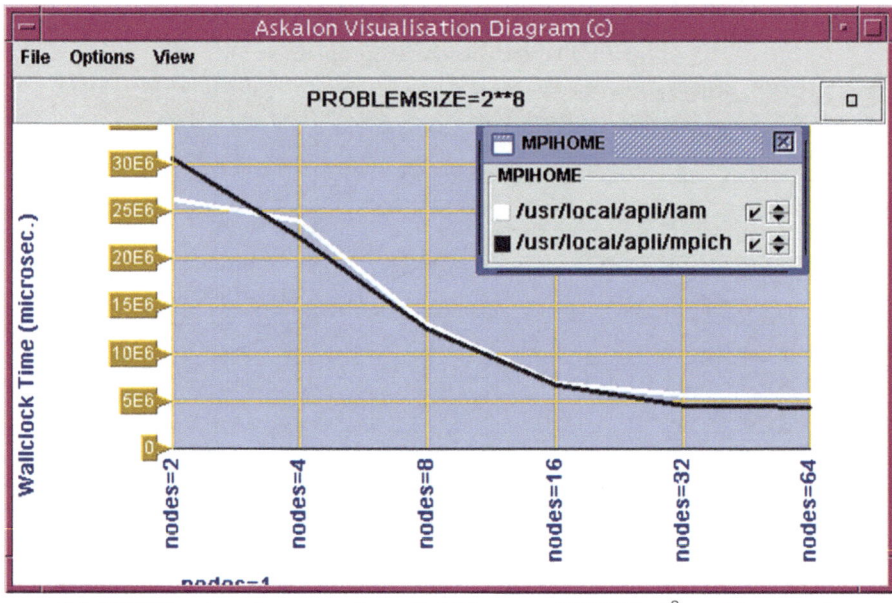

(b) FFTW network comparison (LAM versus MPICH, 2^8 problem size).

Fig. 4.16. The three-dimensional FFT benchmark results (IV).

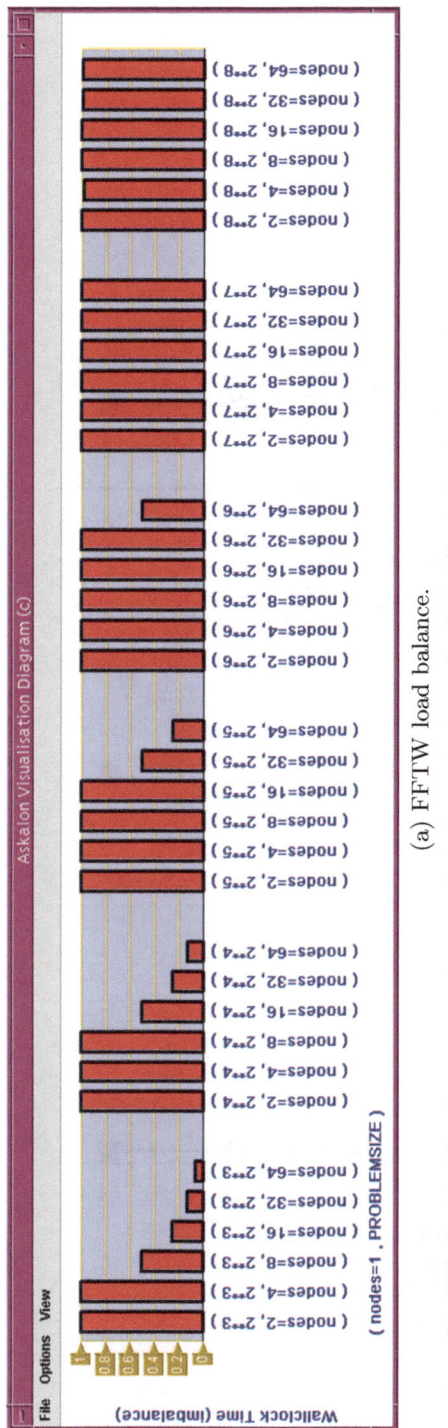

(a) FFTW load balance.

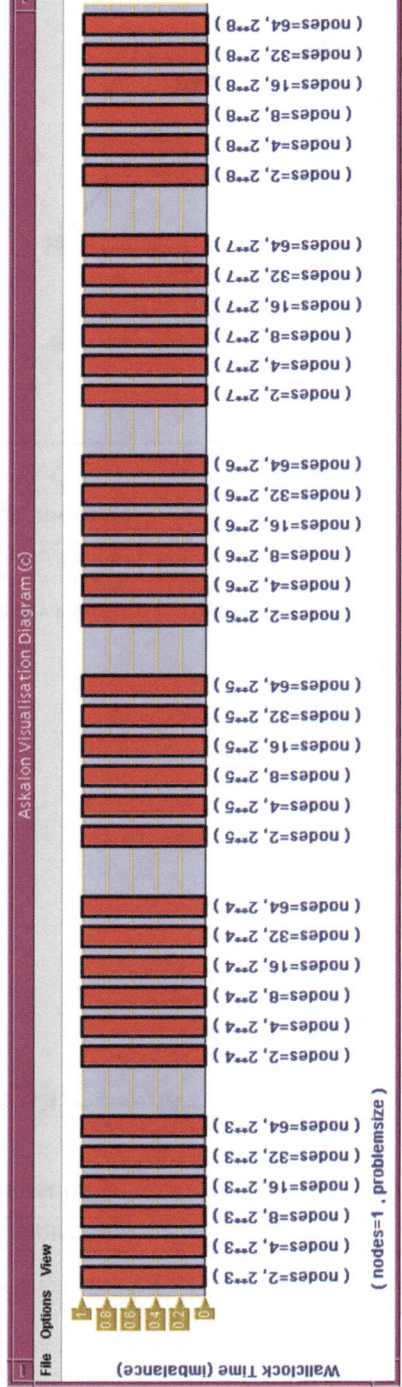

(b) wpp3DFFT load balance.

Fig. 4.17. The three-dimensional FFT benchmark results (V).

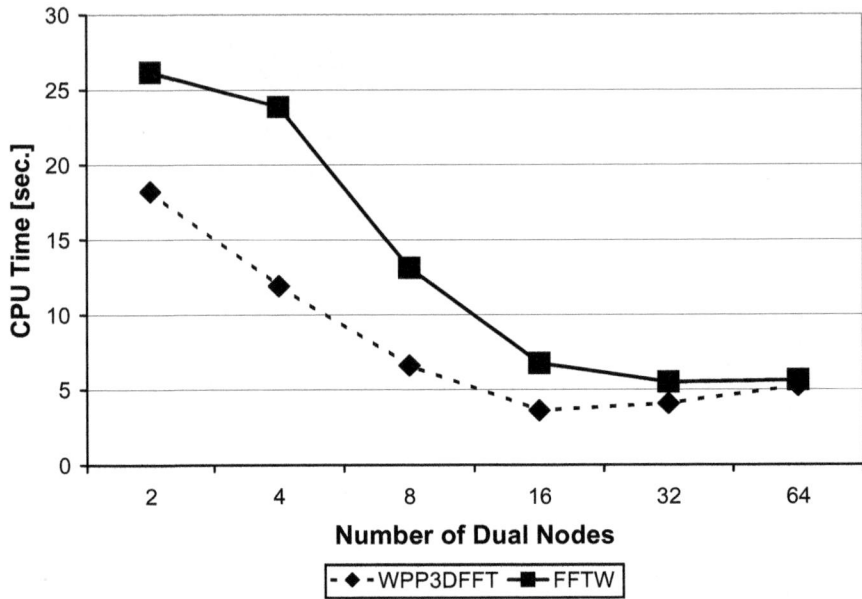

(a) wpp3DFFT versus FFTW, 2^8 problem size).

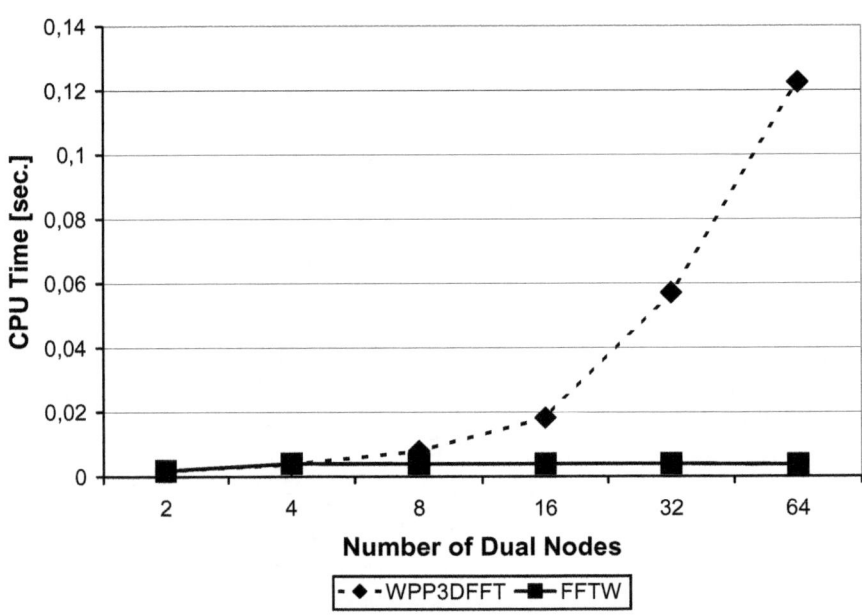

(b) wpp3DFFT versus FFTW, 2^3 problem size).

Fig. 4.18. The three-dimensional FFT benchmark results (VI).

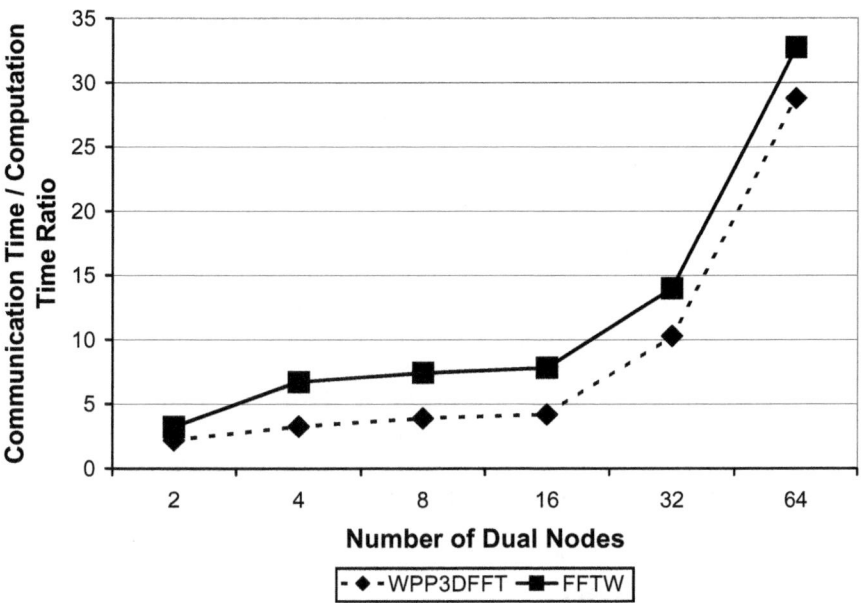

(a) wpp3DFFT versus FFTW, 2^8 problem size.

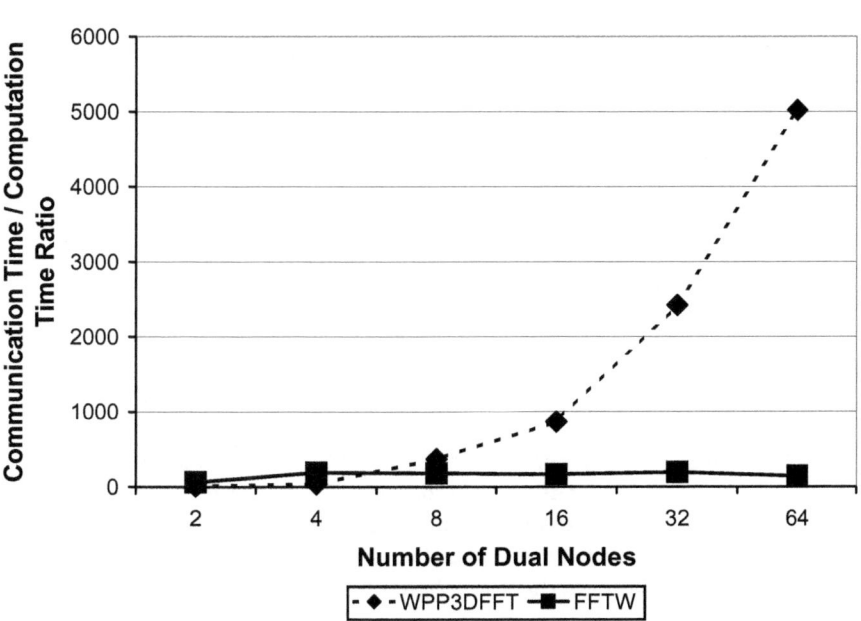

(b) wpp3DFFT versus FFTW (2^3 problem size).

Fig. 4.19. The three-dimensional FFT benchmark results (VII).

for this study by inserting ZEN assignment directives in the source code immediately after the input parameter **read** statements, as shown in Example 4.18. The **read** statements become therefore dead code and are eliminated by subsequent optimised compilation.

We varied the following four input parameters for this application:

1. *the coupon bond* denoted by the ZEN variable **coupon** (i.e. from 0.01 to 0.1 with the increment 0.001);
2. *the number of time steps* over which the price is computed, denoted by the ZEN variable **nr_steps** (i.e. from 5 to 60 with the increment 5);
3. *the coupon bond end time* denoted by the ZEN variable **bond%end**. An additional constraint directive guarantees that the coupon bond end time is identical with the number of time steps;
4. *the length of one time step* denoted by the ZEN variable **delta_t** (i.e. from 1/12 to 1 with the increment 1/12);
5. *the total price* is the output parameter of this application, whose variation as a function of the four input parameters is the subject of the study.

*Example 4.18 (Backward pricing source file excerpt – **pkernbw.f90**).*

```
read(10,*) nr_steps
!ZEN$ ASSIGN nr_steps = { 5 : 60 : 5 }
 . . .
read(10,*) delta_t
!ZEN$ ASSIGN delta_t = { 0.08, 0.17, 0.25, 0.33, 0.42, 0.5,
                         0.58, 0.67, 0.75, 0.83, 0.92, 1 }
 . . .
read(10,*) bond%end
!ZEN$ ASSIGN bond\%end = { 5 : 60 : 5 }
!ZEN$ CONSTRAINT VALUE nr_steps == bond\%end
 . . .
read(10,*) bond%coupon
!ZEN$ ASSIGN bond\%coupon = { 0.01 : 0.1 : 0.01 }
```

*Example 4.19 (Globus RSL Script – **run.rsl**).*

```
+ (&
(*ZEN$ SUBSTITUTE gescher = { pc6163-c703.uibk.ac.at,
                   gescher.vcpc.univie.ac.at/jobmanager-pbs,
                   iris.gup.uni-linz.ac.at }*)
(*ZEN$ CONSTRAINT INDEX gescher==pkernbw.f90:bond\%coupon/4*)
   (resourceManagerContact="gescher")
   (count=4)
   (jobtype=mpi)
   (directory="/home/radu/APPS/Backward/V1.0")
   (executable="pkernbw")
)
```

We inserted five ZEN directives into one single source file to specify a total of 1481 experiments that were automatically generated and conducted by ZEN-TURIO. We submitted the experiments onto the target execution Grid site using DUROC. To decrease the completion time of this rather large parameter study, we annotated the Globus RSL script with three Grid sites across which we split the full set of experiments (see Example 4.19 and Figure 4.20):

1. `pc6163-c703.uibk.ac.at` at the University of Innsbruck;
2. `gescher.vcpc.univie.ac.at` at the University of Vienna;
3. `iris.gup.uni-linz.ac.at` at the University of Linz.

By using one ZEN constraint directive, we indicated that the experiments which satisfy the condition *bond%coupon* $\leq$ 0.03 shall be scheduled on `pc6163-c703.uibk.ac.at`, the experiments for which 0.04 $\leq$ *bond%coupon* $\leq$ 0.07 shall be scheduled on `gescher.vcpc.univie.ac.at`, and the experiments having *bond%coupon* $\geq$ 0.08 shall be run on `iris.gup.uni-linz.ac.at`. By splitting the parameter study throughput onto three Grid sites, we reduced the completion time of the entire experiment suite by more than 50%. In Section 6.4 we will present an automatic throughput scheduling approach that replaces this manual scheduling method.

From the wide variety of visualisations that we automatically generated during this study, we illustrate two samples surface diagrams in Figure 4.21. The three-dimensional surface in Figure 4.21(a) shows the evolution of the total price as a function of the number of time steps and the coupon bond which has the following financial significance:

1. the price decreases with the maturity (i.e. number of time steps multiplied with the length of one time step) because the effect of discounting future payments increases (i.e. 100 Euro in 20 years are less then 100 Euro in 10 years), but only if the coupon bond is less than the interest rates (e.g. for 0.06, the coupon rate is greater than the interest rates);
2. the price increases with coupon bond because the higher the coupon rate is, the higher the future payments are;
3. for very large maturities the price linearly depends on the coupon bond only.

Figure 4.21(b) shows the total price evolution by varying the number of time steps and the length of one time step with the financial interpretation:

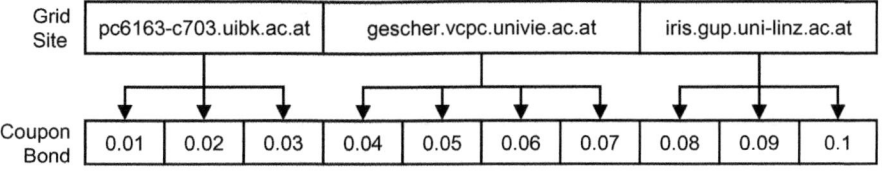

Fig. 4.20. The constraint defined in Example 4.19.

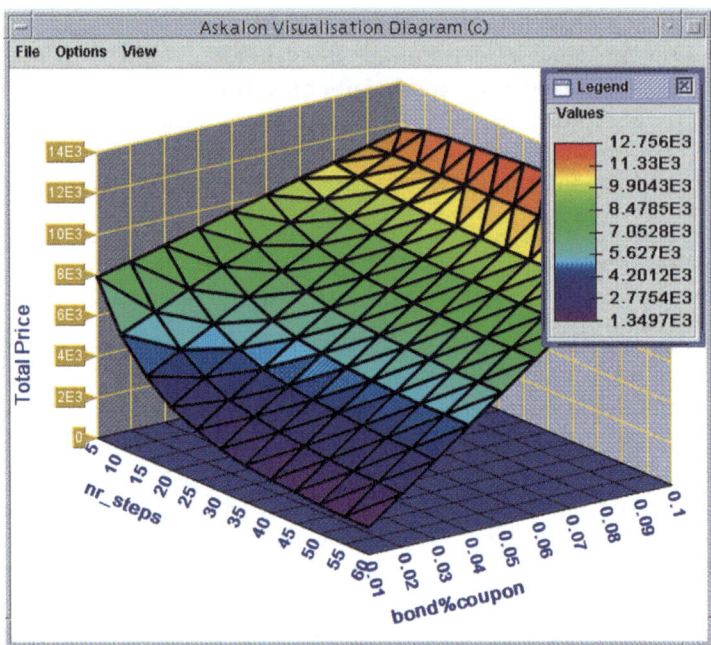

(a) Total price for delta_t = 1.0.

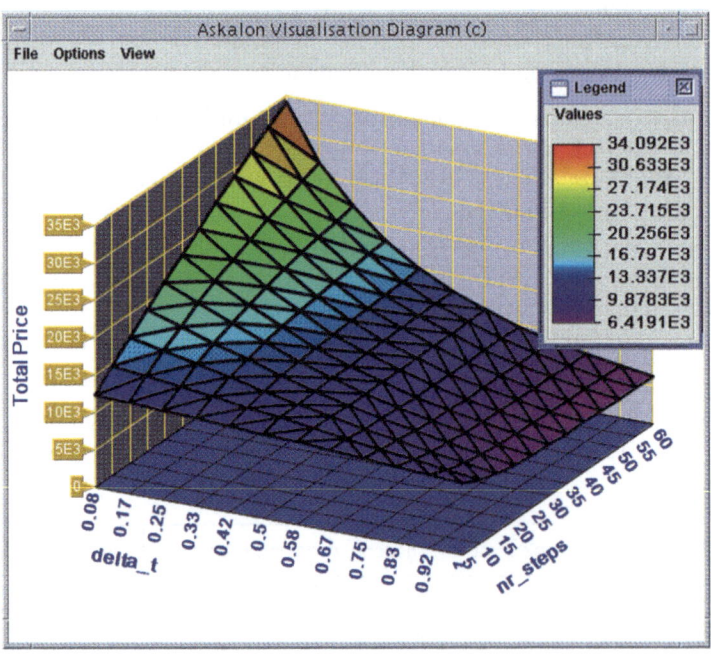

(b) Total price for coupon = 0.05.

Fig. 4.21. The backward pricing parameter study results.

1. the price decreases with the length of a time step because a smaller payment number implies less money in the future;
2. depending on the number of time steps, the price may increase or decrease with the maturity depending on how much the smaller number of payments are compensated by smaller discount effects.

4.4 Architecture

In the previous sections of this chapter we described the ZENTURIO experiment management tool for conducting large scale performance and parameter studies with particular focus on the user-oriented functionality and interface. In this section we describe the internal architectural design of ZENTURIO illustrated in Figure 4.22, which is based on a distributed service-oriented architecture compliant with the Grid infrastructure model presented in Chapter 2.

The entry point for a user is a graphical User Portal which normally resides on the local client machine (e.g. laptop) and whose functionality we described in Section 4.1. Through the portal, the user creates or loads a ZEN application annotated with ZEN directives that specify value ranges for any

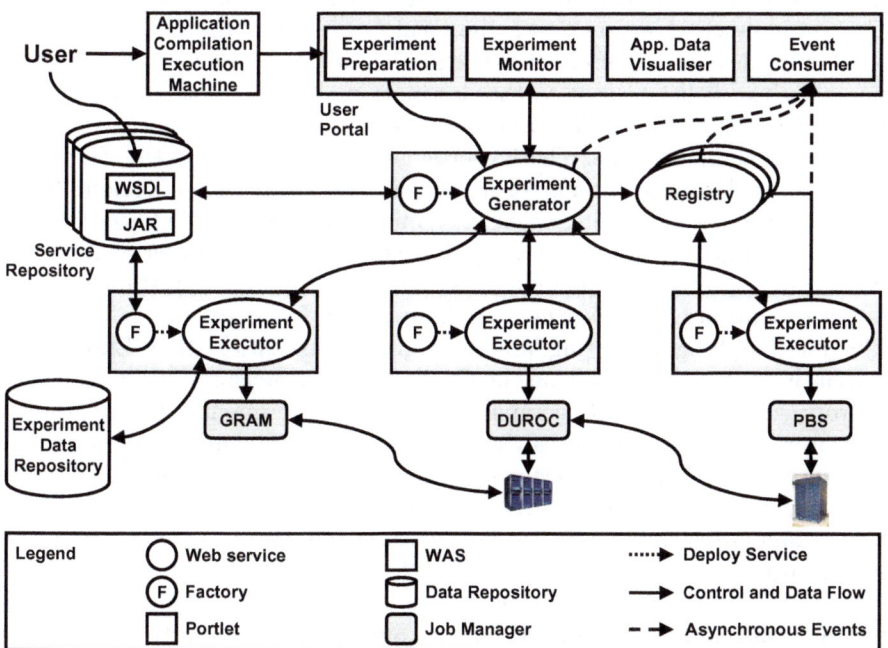

Fig. 4.22. The ZENTURIO experiment management tool architecture.

problem, system, or machine parameter, including program variables, file names, compiler options, target machines, machine sizes, scheduling strategies, or data distributions. We use the ZEN performance directives to indicate the performance metrics to be measured and computed for each experiment. The functionality of the ZENTURIO experiment management tool described in this chapter is restricted to post-mortem multi-experimental performance analysis and parameter studies.

The automatic experiment management functionality of ZENTURIO is achieved through the cooperative use of various distributed middleware services shielded from the end-user by the graphical User Portal. The *Service Repository* (see Section 5.5.2) is a database that contains persistent implementations of generic Grid services. The *Factory* (see Section 5.5.4) is a service in charge of creating service instances on arbitrary Grid sites using implementation information from the Service Repository. The *Registry* (see Section 5.5.5) manages an up-to-date list of existing transient Grid service instances and provides a variety of advanced high throughput service discovery operations. The Service Repository, the Factory, and the Registry are generic Grid services that are fundamental to the tool integration framework which we will present in Chapter 5.

After the user properly created a ZEN application, ZENTURIO automatically generates, executes, controls, and monitors the experiments on the target Grid site. The User Portal uses the Registry to locate an *Experiment Generator* service, preferably on the local Grid site. If the Experiment Generator resides on a different site, the application files are compressed into a single archive [54] and sent to the destination site using the GridFTP protocol. If no Experiment Generator service is found, an instance is created using the Factory service. The Experiment Generator parses the ZEN files, instruments the application according to the ZEN directives encountered, and generates the corresponding set of experiments as presented in Section 3.2.11 (see Algorithm 1). After generating one experiment, the Experiment Generator transfers the corresponding files (i.e. ZEN application instance) to the target execution Grid site where an *Experiment Executor* service is responsible for compiling, executing, and managing its execution. If no Experiment Executor service is available on the Grid site, an instance is created using the Factory service. Upon the completion of each experiment, the Experiment Executor automatically stores the experiment output and the performance data into a well-defined *Experiment Data Repository* (see Section 4.4.4). The users can remotely access the data stored in the repository via the User Portal or manually formulate queries for post-mortem performance analysis and visualisation.

It is usual in Grid computing that the users cannot stay online for the entire duration of their application, for example when submitting a large set of performance or parameter study experiments over night or when traveling. For this reason we designed the ZENTURIO architecture such that the

Experiment Generator is the only service with which the User Portal interacts. Once the user submitted a ZEN application, the Experiment Generator
maintains together with the Experiment Data Repository the complete information about the application and its associated experiments. This allows
the users to *disconnect* the portals from the Grid without loosing the contact information to their experiments. The users can subsequently open the
portal at any time from arbitrary Grid locations, *connect* to the Experiment
Generator, retrieve the status of the experiments, and perform the desired
performance analysis or the parameter study visualisations.

We provide both synchronous (blocking) and asynchronous (non-blocking)
flavours for all methods of the Experiment Executor and Experiment Generator services. Asynchronous methods return an asynchronous receipt, on behalf
of which synchronous methods can be invoked to poll for available results.
Such asynchronous methods, which are part of the general event framework
that we will present in Section 5.6, are crucial for implementing highly responsive clients that do not block upon calling long running synchronous
methods. All services including the Experiment Data Repository can be *accessed concurrently* by multiple clients which is a key feature for providing
scalable Grid infrastructures.

4.4.1 Experiment Generator

We designed the Experiment Generator as a Grid service in charge of generating the experiments defined by an input ZEN application as formally
specified in Chapter 3 and depicted in Figure 4.23. Each ZEN file of the ZEN
application is first parsed using the scanner and parser modules of the ZEN
Transformation System which produce an abstract syntax tree as presented
in Section 3.1.2. The abstract syntax trees of all ZEN files are then given
as input to the experiment generation algorithm which generates the set of
valid ZEN element tuples as presented in Section 3.2.11 (see Algorithm 1).
The valid ZEN element tuples determine the set of valid ZEN application
instances, whose constituent ZEN file instances are generated using the unparser module of ZEN Transformation System. A ZEN application instance
is the foundation of an experiment, as we formally defined in Definitions 3.27
and 3.28 of Chapter 3.

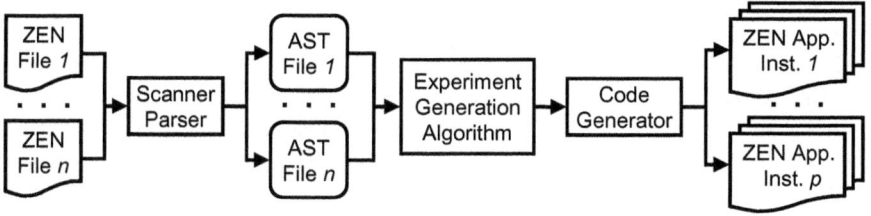

Fig. 4.23. The Experiment Generator architecture.

We use the SCALEA [181] instrumentation engine based on the Vienna Fortran Compiler [21] which provides a complete Fortran 90, OpenMP, MPI, and HPF front-end and code generator to instrument the application for performance metrics based on the ZEN performance directives. We typically run the Experiment Generator as a pre-installed Grid service that isolates several platform dependencies and proprietary components of the Vienna Fortran Compiler and serves remote experiment generation requests through a portable and platform independent interface.

Additionally, we provide an interface to logically insert ZEN directives into the abstract syntax tree of each parsed ZEN file for situations when it is not practical to insert the directives manually. We will employ this feature when modeling the Grid scheduling problem in Chapter 6 that requires a large number of ZEN variables with often large and dynamic (i.e. statically unknown) value sets.

We provide as part of the Experiment Generator service four methods for generating the experiments of a ZEN application:

1. *synchronous* by means of a single method invocation. This approach is rather primitive since the synchronous invocation can be very expensive and produces blocking (i.e. non-responsive) clients;
2. *iterative*, compliant with the pull event model (see Section 5.6), each experiment being returned by an iterator upon synchronous request;
3. *asynchronous*, compliant with the push event model (see Section 5.6), each experiment being sent to the client using an asynchronous callback as soon as it is generated;
4. *random*, by instantiating each ZEN variable (or a subset of them) with a random ZEN element. We use this method for implementing the randomised optimisation algorithms in Chapter 6.

In the case of using ZENTURIO in online Grid mode, the Experiment Generator automatically transfers the experiments to the target Grid execution site using the GridFTP protocol. In the case of using DUROC as job manager, the experiments are copied to multiple destination Grid sites which we retrieve from the RSL description of the application.

4.4.2 Experiment Executor

The Experiment Executor is a generic service with a high level interface for executing and managing experiments on target Grid execution sites. We designed the Experiment Executor as a stand-alone Grid service independent of ZENTURIO that can be deployed for experiment management purposes in other infrastructures too. The Experiment Executor assumes a properly installed application on the target execution site(s).

The Experiment Executor interacts at the back-end with a local job manager that controls the execution of experiments on the Grid site which in our current implementation can be:

1. *fork* [168] for single processor or SMP computers that host both the Experiment Executor service and the running experiments;
2. *Condor [123], Load Leveler [102], Load Sharing Facility [201], Maui, Portable Batch System (PBS) [29], and Sun Grid Engine [172]* for dedicated parallel computers. We employ this configuration in the online cluster mode of ZENTURIO, in which the Experiment Executor resides on the front-end node of the parallel computer and must receive a job submission script compliant with the local job manager used to execute the experiments on the back-end compute nodes;
3. *GRAM* [47] and *DUROC* [48] for executing remote experiments on a single, respectively multiple Grid sites. We employ this configuration in the online Grid mode of ZENTURIO, in which the Experiment Executor may reside on an arbitrary Grid site and must receive an RSL script to execute the experiments.

The Experiment Executor provides functionality to:

- add and remove experiments;
- compile experiments;
- execute experiments;
- retrieve the status of experiments;
- subscribe for experiment status change notification callbacks according to the push event model (see Section 5.6). For example, an event listener thread of the Experiment Monitor panel that we presented in Section 4.1.3 subscribes and receives notifications from the Experiment Executor about changes in the status of individual experiments. This is a light-weight and highly responsive mechanism for providing a consistent up-to-date view of the generated experiments and their status which avoids unnecessary expensive polling. This functionality is part of the more general event framework which we will present in detail in Section 5.6;
- terminate experiments;
- stage-in input data files from specific Grid sites;
- stage-out experiment output to indicated Grid sites, including standard output, standard error, output files, and performance data;
- retrieve all experiments associated with a certain application (optionally filtered to a certain state);
- set the maximum number of experiments that are concurrently executed. This feature allows the user to restrict the number of experiments simultaneously submitted to the cluster queue to a decent predefined number, or to control the number of experiments concurrently forked on one SMP computer (i.e. normally one on single processor machines);
- the number of retries in case of faulty execution of experiments. This feature is crucial for improving the fault tolerance, since often the execution of large number of experiments on cluster and Grid architectures is prone to non-deterministic failures due to unpredictable and unreliable underlying resource management support;

- store the experiment specific data including ZEN variables, ZEN elements, output files, and performance data into the Experiment Data Repository.

All the operations provided by the Experiment Executor service can be applied on individual or collective basis by providing appropriate input filters (e.g. all the experiments belonging to an application).

4.4.3 Experiment State Transition Diagram

We display in Figure 4.24 the *state transition diagram* of an experiment executed with ZENTURIO. The state diagram has one initial state *start* and two final states *stored* and *failed*. After being created by the Experiment Generator, the experiment is initialised in the *start* state. If the Experiment Executor site is different from the Experiment Generator site, the experiment goes through the optional *transfer* state during which it is copied to the target execution site. If an experiment (i.e. the associated application instance) needs compilation after being copied to the execution site, it goes through the *compiling* state. If the experiment is part of a binary (already compiled) ZEN application, it skips the *compiling* state and goes directly into the *ready* state. The *ready* state specifies that the experiment is ready for execution. From this state, the experiment can go either into the *waiting* state if the execution is postponed (e.g. through advance reservation), or into the *queued* state if the experiment is submitted to a local resource manager. If the experiment is forked, it goes directly into the *running* state. After the experiment completed its execution, the state changes to *terminate*. The final state *stored* indicates that the experiment (including the output files and the performance data) has been stored into the Experiment Data Repository. If an erroneous operation takes place (e.g. compilation or execution error) during any of the states or if the experiment is explicitly killed, the experiment goes in to the *failed* state. From the *terminated*, *stored*, and *failed* states an experiment can change to the *ready* state, if re-execution is desired (e.g. in case of casual non-deterministic faulty executions).

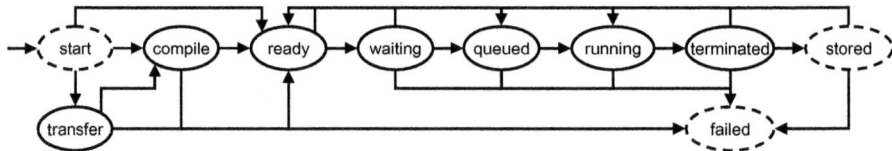

Fig. 4.24. The experiment state transition diagram.

4.4.4 Experiment Data Repository

ZENTURIO automatically stores post-mortem information about the ZEN application and the associated experiments into a common *Experiment Data*

Repository. We designed the Experiment Data Repository as a relational database implemented on top of PostgreSQL [96]. Upon the completion of each experiment, the Experiment Executor stores the descriptive information about the experiment including the ZEN variable instantiations, standard output, standard error, performance data, and output files, depending on the experiment type (i.e. performance or parameter study). In the case of large output files, we store the URL to the location of the GASS file system instead. The Experiment Data Repository enables various users and tools to interoperate by exchanging post-mortem performance and output data from previous experiments. We display in Figure 4.25 the Unified Modeling Language (UML) diagram that models the Experiment Data Repository relational schema.

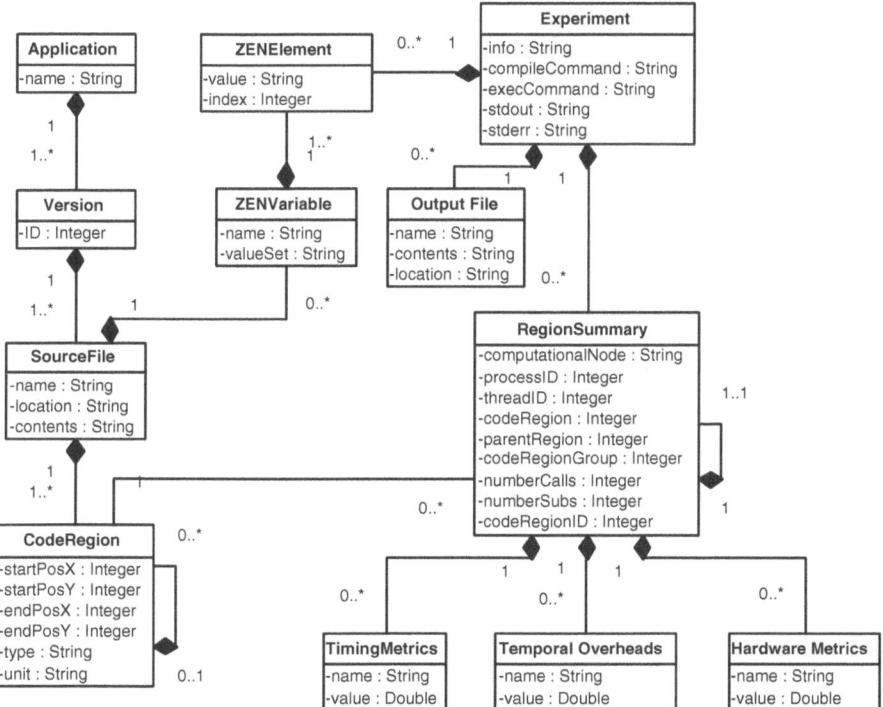

Fig. 4.25. The Experiment Data Repository schema.

4.5 Summary

In this section we presented the ZENTURIO experiment management tool for performance and parameter studies of parallel applications. We described the functionality of the tool comprising an advanced light-weight portal easy to install and manage that supports the end-users with a friendly graphical interface to create ZEN applications using the ZEN experiment specification language. Additionally, the portal assists the users to automatically generate, execute, and monitor experiments, as well to perform advanced post-mortem analysis using the performance and output data automatically organised into a shared Experiment Data Repository. We illustrated detailed experiments on using ZENTURIO for automatic multi-experimental performance and para-meter studies of six real-world parallel applications executed on several SMP cluster architectures. Finally, we presented the distributed service-oriented architecture of the tool compliant with the model presented in Section 2 and consisting of a set of generic services open for extension and interoperability.

5
Tool Integration

As applications get larger and more complex, the use of software tools becomes vital for tuning application parameters, identifying performance leaks, or detecting program defects. Extensive efforts within academia and industry over the last decade have resulted in a large collection of tools for practical application engineering. Available tools of broad interest include program source and structure browsers, editors, static program analysers, performance predictors, optimisation compilers, execution control and monitoring environments, sequential and parallel debuggers (providing deadlock detection and deterministic message replay mechanisms), data and execution visualisers, performance analysers, or various program tracers.

Despite all these huge tool development efforts to ease the parallel program development, the user acceptance in the scientific community has not been achieved. Most users still base their application development activities on manual source program instrumentation and a tedious, error-prone, and time consuming *instrumentation – compilation – link – execution – data collection – data analysis* cycle. There are two reasons for this unfortunate situation:

1. Most of the existing application tools are not available on multiple parallel platforms primarily because of their limited *portability*. When using a new parallel system the user must in most cases learn and familiarise with new tools with different functionality and user interfaces. This requires additional (often unnecessary) time and effort and can be a major deterrent against the use of more appropriate computer systems.
2. Most of the tools cannot be used cooperatively to further improve programming efficiency mainly because they are insufficiently integrated into a single coherent environment. Existing integrated tool environments [40, 191] comprising several tools do offer some degree of interoperability, however, have the disadvantage that the set of tools provided is fixed, typically decided by the initial project objectives. The resulted tools interact through internal proprietary interfaces which cannot easily be extended. The outcome is in fact not an *interoperable tool-set*, but a more complex monolithic tool which combines the functionality of the integrated tools but lacks true interoperability and extensibility.

Based on the type of analysis performed, one can distinguish between two types of software tools:

1. *Offline tools* completely separate the runtime data collection from the data analysis phase. Runtime data analysis is typically performed post-mortem after the application completed its execution. The ZENTURIO experiment management tool presented in Chapter 4 is a typical offline tool example;
2. *Online tools* collect and analyse the data on-the-fly during the execution of the application using special purpose *monitoring systems*.

There are two fundamental reasons why most of the runtime tools cannot be cooperatively used by the program developer on the same application to improve its programming productivity:

1. Runtime tools use different instrumentation techniques. While offline tools can easily solve this problem by means of standardised trace data formats [87] or common data repositories [71], online tools suffer from incompatible complex runtime monitoring systems. Most tools require special preparation of the application with specialised compilation and link flags which leads to undesired conflicts and makes the interoperability impossible;
2. At inception, tools are not considered or designed for interoperability. Most tools are designed and constructed as stand-alone applications and can only be used in isolation. Tool interoperability is a complex issue that has to be considered as a major objective when the tools are first designed and cannot simply be added as an afterthought.

We addressed the offline tool interoperability as part of the ZENTURIO experiment management tool by proposing a common Experiment Data Repository for sharing performance data which we described in Section 4.4.4. In the reminder of this chapter we will therefore focus on the online tool interoperability problem. In the next section we present a generalised extension of the ZENTURIO service-oriented architecture with new functionality and services oriented towards online tool integration and interoperability. In Section 5.2 we introduce a set of interoperable tools accompanied by a set novel interoperability scenarios in Section 5.3. Finally, we describe the internal design and implementation details of the two bottom layers of our tool integration architecture in Sections 5.4 and 5.5.

5.1 Architecture

We designed the ZENTURIO architecture presented in Chapter 4 in the context of a more general tool integration framework [110, 111, 149] depicted in Figure 5.1 which defines a three tier service-oriented architecture for interoperable tool development that instantiates the abstract Grid architectural model defined in Chapter 2.

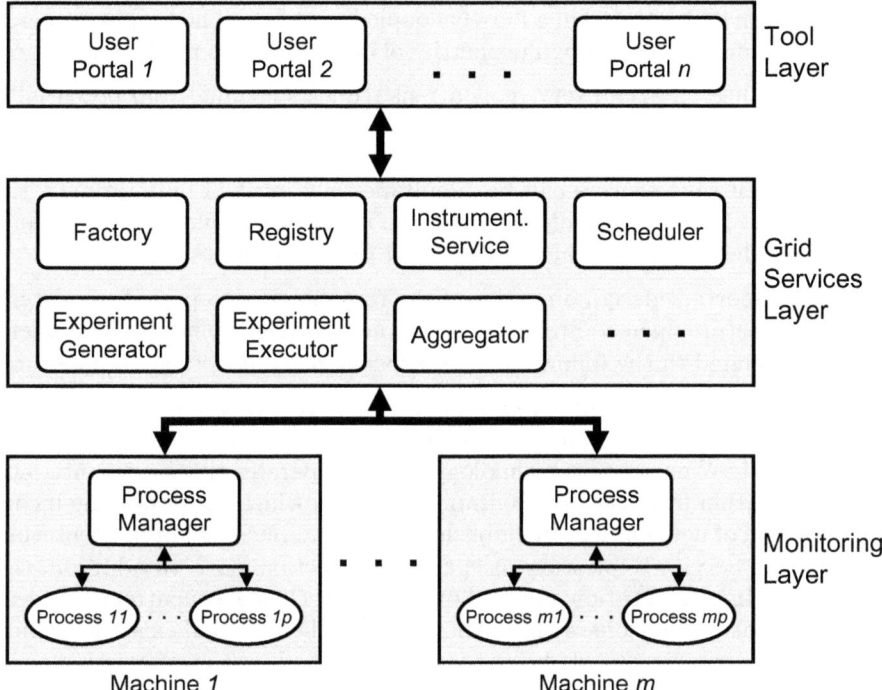

Fig. 5.1. The tool integration service-oriented architecture.

1. *Monitoring layer* represents the platform dependent part inherent to (almost) every tool implementation. This layer consists of a set of lightweight distributed sensors that build in aggregation the Grid machine layer and whose main goal in our architecture is to provide support for online tool development. The sensors typically extract and monitor low level hardware and software features specific to every platform and operating system. In designing the sensors, we focused on isolating the platform dependencies under a portable interface which reduces the effort of porting n tools onto m platforms from $n * m$ to $n + m$;
2. *Grid services layer* consists of an open set of high level portable Grid services that can be dynamically deployed and instantiated on arbitrary Grid sites, as introduced in Section 2.6.2. The Grid services facilitate the tool development and enable the interoperability through concurrent service use;
3. *Tool layer* consists of the end-user software tools, represented either by graphical user portals or by simple applications running in batch mode.

The functionality of a tool developed within this framework is no longer stored within a single monolithic front-end application acting as a black-box, but rather is exposed and distributed amongst many small and reusable Grid services often orchestrated in a loosely coupled workflow. The tool interoperability is achieved by two design properties of our service-oriented architecture:

1. the Grid services can serve concurrent requests coming from potentially different remote clients (i.e. user portals representing potentially different end-user tools);
2. the monitoring sensors can be simultaneously invoked by multiple Grid services. This allows multiple clients to concurrently monitor and manipulate the same physical processes and target machines.

Another important design objective of the framework is to provide an extensible architecture open to further integrations and developments. The extensibility is related to the following three aspects in the proposed architecture:

1. *Add new services to the environment.* This translates into the ability of incorporating new Grid services and to add new tools to the environment. The Web services technology clearly separates the service interface specification from the service implementation which facilitates the incorporation of new services by publishing their interface and implementation into the Service Repository as specified in Section 5.5.2. In addition, the service implementation must allow multiple clients concurrently access and invoke operations with no knowledge of their mutual existence which enables new client tools be naturally integrated on top of existing Grid services;
2. *Extend existing components with new functionality.* Extending existing services with specialised versions through *delegation* is not only supported but encouraged by our framework. Since the Web services technology does not adhere to the object-oriented design principles, the extensibility through *inheritance* is not possible at the WSDL service interface level, but rather at the Java class service implementation level;
3. *Implement new tools based on existing middleware services.* The tools implemented within the framework will interoperate indirectly through the common use of Grid services, as we will describe in Section 5.3.1.

5.2 Interoperable Tool Set

The ZENTURIO experiment management tool is the principal end-user tool that we built as part of the tool integration framework presented in this chapter. The ZENTURIO User Portal introduced in Section 4.1 is a thin client developed on top of high level Grid middleware services that provides transparent performance and parameter study support using a static instrumentation technology based on ZEN directives and compiler instrumentation. The offline tool interoperability is achieved through post-mortem share of data stored into the Experiment Data Repository.

In this section we describe a complementary set of interoperable prototype tools that we implemented based on a new instrumentation technology more appropriate and flexible for online on-the-fly program analysis called *dynamic instrumentation*. In contrast to the compiler-based source code instrumentation provided by ZENTURIO, dynamic instrumentation is based on runtime insertion of binary snippets into already running programs. The dynamic instrumentation is performed in our architecture by a special purpose sensor located in the monitoring layer called *Process Manager* (see Figure 5.1) that we will present in detail in Section 5.4.2. The tools operate on unmodified executable programs and can be used to monitor both user and system functions, even when there is no source code available. The tools are generic and do not depend on any compilation options, link libraries, flags, or any other preparation steps.

5.2.1 Object Code Browser

The *Object Code Browser* is a graphical browsing tool which displays the object code structure of a given process retrieved from the application binary executable file. In case of *Single Program Multiple Data (SPMD)* parallel applications (e.g. OpenMP and MPI), we retrieve the object code from one arbitrary process. For *Multiple Program Multiple Data (MPMD)* parallel applications, we display the union set of the object structures of all parallel processes. The Object Code Browser can be used in cooperation with the other tools presented in this chapter for selecting their instrumentation and analysis focus (see Section 5.3.2). The Object Code Browser receives automatic push event notifications from the Grid middleware services (i.e. Process Manager – see Section 5.4.2) upon changes in the object structure of the application that require the following display updates:

1. *fork:* show the newly created UNIX process and its object code structure;
2. *exec:* reload the modified process object code overwritten by this system call;
3. *dlopen:* add the new dynamic shared library to the list of application modules displayed;
4. *exit:* delete the terminated process from the parallel application process list;
5. *status change:* update the process execution status (i.e. running, stopped, exited).

5.2.2 Function Profiler (Z_prof)

The *Z_prof function profiler*, analogous to the UNIX tool **prof** [128], displays the call-graph profile data by timing and counting selected function calls. We implemented an MPI flavour of the tool offers functionality to:

1. *count:*
    a) the number of messages sent and received (from the MPI_Send and MPI_Recv family);
    b) the number of bytes sent and received;
    c) the number of input and output operations (based on the MPI-IO [177] specification);
    d) the number of bytes involved in input and output operations;
2. *time:*
    a) the communication routines;
    b) the synchronisation routines;
    c) the input and output routines.

Additionally, similarly to the UNIX administration tool top [23], the tool can be configured to display the first n functions in terms of number of invocations or execution time. We provide this information online as the application executes, where the refresh interval is determined by the input data sampling rate indicated during the dynamic instrumentation.

5.2.3 Function Tracer (Z_trace)

Z_trace is an online tool that traces in the style of the UNIX software tool truss [66] the functions executed by an unmodified executable binary application. The tool does not differentiate between user, system, or library calls and does not require source code information. However, in order to be able to extract the function input and return arguments from the stack, the type information is required to be present in the binary executable. Therefore, the application needs to be compiled with appropriate flags (i.e. usually -g), otherwise we only display the function name during the trace process. To manually provide the function signature to the tracer is platform dependent and is not always a feasible solution. Since the object code and the function set of most programming languages is rather large and uninteresting (e.g. the smallest C++ program has about 1500 functions, most of them located in the libc library), it is recommended that the tool be focused on an interesting subset of functions or application modules. The focus can be indicated either as an input configuration, or graphically using the Object Code Browser (see Section 5.3.2).

Since the application object code is rather large, it is impractical and inefficient to pre-instrument all the application points with tracing probes before starting the execution. Rather, we instrument the functions incrementally before being for the first time executed, as sketched by our *incremental call-graph tracing algorithm* displayed in Algorithm 2:

1. The algorithm starts by initialising the list of instrumented functions with the empty set (line 1) and starts the tracing process with the main function (line 2);

Algorithm 2. The Z_trace call-graph function tracing algorithm.
___
 1: instrFunc ← ∅
 2: Z_TRACE("main")
 3:
 4: **procedure** Z_TRACE(func)
 5:     instrFunc ← instrFunc ∪ func
 6:     TRACEPOINT(func.entry)
 7:     TRACEPOINT(func.exit)
 8:     **for all** callPoint ∈ func.callPoints **do**
 9:         **if** callPoint.calee ∉ instrFunc **then**
10:             ADDNOTIFICATION(callPoint)
11:             ADDBREAKPOINT(callPoint)
12:         **end if**
13:     **end for**
14: **end procedure**
15:
16: **procedure** NOTIFY(callPoint)
17:     Z_TRACE(callPoint)
18:     REMOVEBREAKPOINT(callPoint)
19:     RESUME
20: **end procedure**
___

2. **Z_trace** (lines 4 − 14) is the main function trace routine that inserts tracing probes at the function entry (line 6) and all the exit points (line 7) which have not yet been instrumented. Additionally, it inserts notification probes (line 10) at all the function call points to trigger notification callbacks for each new function invocation that must be traced too. Since the instrumentation is performed on-the-fly while the application is running, we have to combine each notification with a breakpoint (line 11) that stops the process and allows the tracer instrument the new function before executing it;

3. **Notify** (lines 16 − 20) is the callback triggered on behalf of the first invocation of each function (i.e. by the notification probes and the Process Manager − see Section 5.4.2). As a consequence, the tracer instruments the new function with trace probes by calling the **Z_trace** routine (line 17), removes the breakpoint (line 18), and resumes the process (line 19).

5.2.4 Function Coverager (Z_cov)

The *Z_cov* tool imitates the UNIX tool tcov to produce a test coverage analysis at function call granularity. The tool counts the number of times the program counter hits each instrumentation point which is useful in practice for detecting dead code due to, e.g. redundant conditionals or obsolete functions.

Algorithm 3. The Z_cov function coverage algorithm.

```
 1: instrFuncs ← ∅
 2: Z_COV("main")
 3:
 4: procedure Z_COV(func)
 5:     instrFuncs ← instrFuncs ∪ func
 6:     ADDCOUNTER(func.entry, rate)
 7:     ADDCOUNTER(func.exit, rate)
 8:     for all callPoint ∈ func.callPoints do
 9:         if callPoint.calee ∉ instrFuncs then
10:             ADDNOTIFICATION(callPoint)
11:             ADDBREAKPOINT(callPoint)
12:         end if
13:     end for
14: end procedure
15:
16: procedure NOTIFY(callPoint)
17:     Z_COV(callPoint.calee)
18:     REMOVEBREAKPOINT(callPoint)
19:     RESUME
20: end procedure
21:
22: procedure DATACOL(counter)
23:     if counter > 0 then
24:         DELETECOUNTER(counter)
25:         WRITE(counter.point has been hit)
26:     end if
27: end procedure
```

Similar to Z_trace, Z_cov employs an *incremental call-graph function coverage algorithm* sketched in Algorithm 3 that lazily instruments each function just-in-time before its first execution:

1. The algorithm starts by initialising the list of instrumented functions with the empty set (line 1) and starts the coverage process with the **main** function (line 2);

2. Z_cov (lines 4 − 14) is the main instrumentation routine that computes the coverage of one arbitrary function. Firstly, it inserts counters at the function entry (line 6) and all the function exit points (line 7). Similar to the incremental tracing algorithm outlined in Algorithm 2, the coverager inserts notification probes at each call point (line 10), followed by a breakpoint (line 11) that allows to instrument each function before executing it for the first time;

3. **Notify** (lines 16 − 20) is a callback from the Process Manager sensor that trapped a call to a function that has not yet been instrumented (see Section 5.4.2). As a consequence, the coverager instruments the invoked

function by calling the Z_cov routine (line 17), removes the breakpoint (line 18), and resumes the process (line 19);

4. DataCol (lines 22 − 27) is the callback routine from the Process Manager sensor that contains the count information for each instrumentation point. Each point whose counter is greater than zero was hit by the program counter and, therefore, requires no more instrumentation. As a consequence, the coverager removes this instrumentation (line 24) which reduces the intrusion in the running process.

5.2.5 Sequential Debugger (Z_debug)

Z_debug is a traditional *sequential debugging server* similar to dbx [121] or gdb [165] that provides the following functionality:

1. create a new process or attach an existing running process;
2. detach the process (i.e. disconnect and leave the process running);
3. manipulate the process state (i.e. stop, resume, terminate);
4. send a UNIX signal to the process;
5. read and write (global) variables;
6. insert and remove breakpoints at arbitrary instrumentation points;
7. insert and remove probes (i.e. counters, timers, traces, notifications) at arbitrary instrumentation points;
8. delete and replace function calls;
9. retrieve the object code information;
10. display and manipulate the process stack.

5.2.6 Memory Allocation Tool (Z_MAT)

Z_MAT is a *memory allocation tool*, inspired from Purify [95], that traces the C memory allocation functions from the malloc and free family (i.e. malloc, realloc, calloc, memalloc, valloc, free). The tool provides the following online functionality during the execution of the application:

1. display the memory allocation blocks;
2. display the totally allocated and the free heap size;
3. detect memory leaks (i.e. memory allocations with no corresponding free calls);
4. detect erroneous free memory calls that have no corresponding memory allocations (such bugs are often difficult to track and produce non-deterministic crashes);
5. display the amount of space allocated for the process data segment by instrumenting the brk and sbrk UNIX system calls.

The C++ new and delete memory allocation operators are handled differently by each compiler. Our prototype implementation supports the gcc compiler that translates these operators into __builtin_new and __builtin_delete built-in functions, which in turn invoke the `malloc` and `free` memory allocation functions followed by calls to the structure constructor, respectively destructor.

5.2.7 Resource Tracker (Z_RT^2)

Z_RT^2 is a simple tool in the style of the UNIX `icps` program that displays an online a list of the resources allocated by running processes by tracking several POSIX system calls:

1. `open` / `close` to display the open UNIX file descriptors;
2. `shmget` / `shmctl` to display the allocated UNIX shared memory segments;
3. `msgget` / `msgctl` to display the UNIX message queues;
4. `semget` / `semctl` to display the active UNIX semaphores;
5. `sigaction` to display the list of UNIX signals trapped by the process.

In addition, the tool displays a post-mortem list of warnings containing the set of resources which have been allocated and not freed by the process.

5.2.8 Deadlock Detector (`Z_deadlock`)

Z_deadlock is a tool that dynamically instruments the blocking MPI receive communication routines and checks for runtime inter-process communication cycles based on the message source process identifier.

5.3 Tool Interoperability

An important objective of the tool integration framework described in this chapter to provide an effective environment for tool interoperability. In this section we first classify the various types of tool interaction and then illustrate several examples that demonstrate how synergy can be gained through interoperable use of software tools.

5.3.1 Classification

We distinguish in our framework between two types of tool interactions:

1. *Direct Interaction* assumes direct communication between the tools and is entirely determined by the tool design and implementation. This type of interaction happens exclusively within the tool layer and is independent of the underlying framework. For example, a performance tool may provide performance data to a steering tool that checks for a specific bottleneck, or a steering tool may directly ask a debugger to execute a command in order to improve a certain metric in the program execution (see Section 5.3.3);

2. *Indirect Interaction* is a more advanced type of interaction that is transparently intermediated by the framework via the Grid services and requires no treatment or any particular knowledge from the tools. This scenario occurs in practice when the middleware Grid services interact with each other "behind the scenes" on behalf of the tools. We further classify the indirect tool interaction as follows:

   a) *Coexistence* when multiple tools operate simultaneously on different parallel applications but share the same Grid service instances or sensors (i.e. utilise the same Process Manager sensor to instrument different application processes on the same processor);

   b) *Process Share* when multiple tools attach and instrument the same application process simultaneously. This type of interoperability has the potential of creating a variety of interesting interoperability scenarios, as we will show in the next sections;

   c) *Instrumentation Share* when tools share instrumentation probes while monitoring the same application process in order to minimise their intrusion. This type of interoperability is automatically handled by the Process Manager sensor at the monitoring layer (see Section 5.4.2);

   d) *Resource Lock* when the tools require exclusive access to a specific resource, for example through the user credential. For example, a tool can ask the Process Manager sensor for a lock on a certain application resource (e.g. process, function) in order to perform some accurate timing. As a consequence, the Process Manager allows no other user to instrument that resource, though the existing timers may be reused and sampled through the instrumentation share interoperability type.

Figure 5.2 displays a live screen-shot of four of our interoperable tools instrumenting and monitoring the same *Mandelbrot* MPI application instance, i.e. clockwise from top right: Object Code Browser, Z_trace, Z_cov, and Z_prof. The tools are independently instrumenting and monitoring various functions within the same MPI process (i.e. host `cama`, pid `18462`).

5.3.2 Interaction with a Browser

A common task of most runtime tools is to display the application resource hierarchy which includes the application source or object code structure (i.e. modules, functions, and instrumentation points), processes, threads, and parallel computers that host the application. Since it a redundant effort for every tool to independently provide this functionality, we give this responsibility to a single tool like the Object Code Browser presented in Section 5.2. Apart from displaying the resource hierarchy of an application, the Object Code Browser can also be used to graphically indicate which resources are to be used when starting another interoperable tool.

The advantage of this interoperability is that tools such as Z_prof never need to manipulate the list of application resources and allow the tool

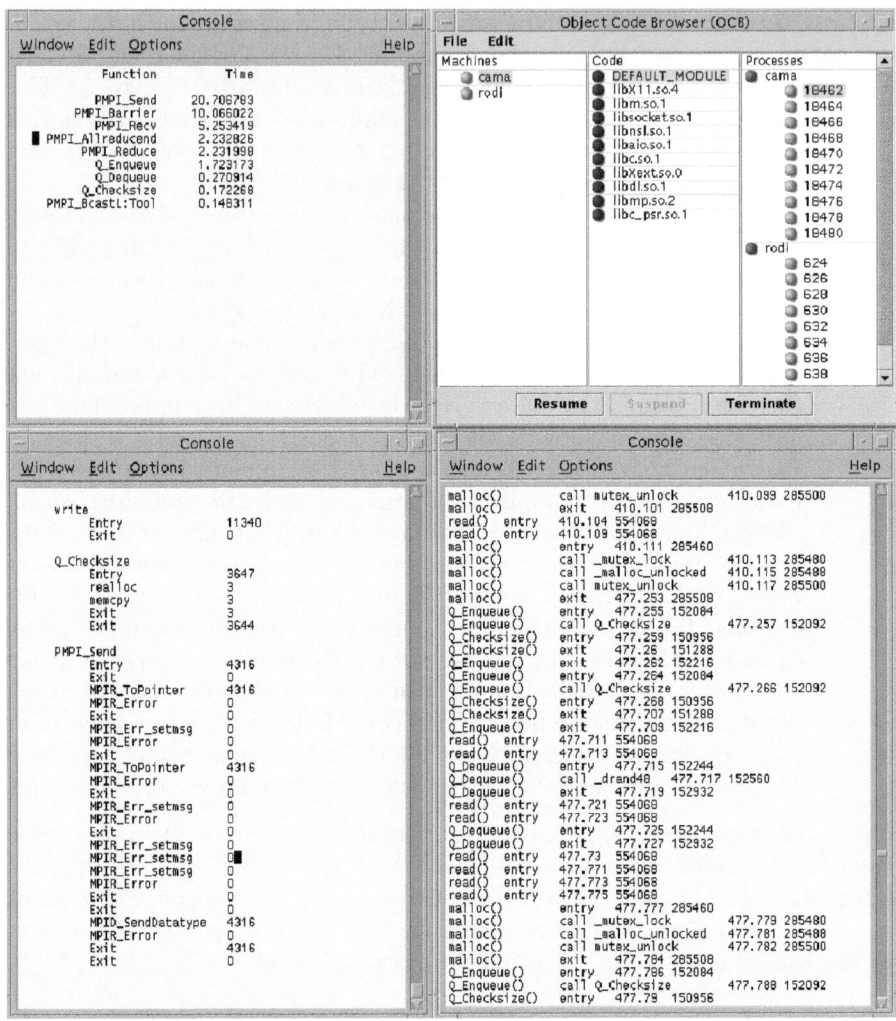

Fig. 5.2. A snapshot of interoperable online software tools.

developer concentrate on "how" to instrument, rather than "what" to instrument. By selecting a set of functions in the Object Code Browser and running Z_prof with no other arguments, the selected functions will be automatically profiled.

5.3.3 Performance Steering

Performance optimisation is a non-trivial activity that typically consists of a four phase cyclic process [116] (see Figure 5.3):

1. *performance measurement and data collection* when a performance profiler is used to collect data from the application;
2. *analysis and visualisation* when performance analysis tools are used to
   interpret the performance data. Visualisation diagrams may be optionally
   employed if the analysis process is deferred to the end-user;
3. *optimisation* when the programmers choose various options to improve
   the performance of their programs. This is the main task of the performance steering tool;
4. *modification* when the optimisations decisions taken at the previous step
   are applied to the program.

Once these four stages were completed, the performance tool again evaluates
the application performance and, if the result is still not satisfactory, the
cycle repeats.

We see two options for realising such a steering tool:

1. *static offline* targets application optimisation through repeated execution
   for various parameter instantiations. We will address this technique in
   Chapter 6;
2. *runtime online* targets application steering within one single execution.
   We approach this scenario in our framework using our interoperable tool-
   set as follows:
   a) *the performance profiler* (e.g. Z_prof) collects the performance data
      and presents it in an appropriate manner to the steering tool. Addi-
      tionally, it might also highlight sources of performance bottlenecks;
   b) *the steering tool* decides whether an optimisation is required based
      on the performance information received from the performance pro-
      filer and gives the debugger the appropriate application modification
      commands;
   c) *the debugger* (e.g. Z_debug) modifies the runtime binary code accor-
      ding to the commands received from the steering tool by inserting or
      removing binary instrumentation snippets or by tuning online varia-
      ble values using dynamic instrumentation.

We distinguish between two types of runtime online performance steering:

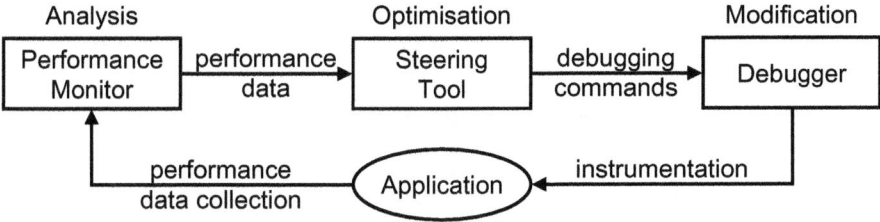

Fig. 5.3. The steering configuration.

a) *interactive* when the steering tool is replaced by the programmer who drives the execution of the performance profiler, visualises and analyses the performance data, takes optimisation decisions, and converts them into debugger commands;

b) *automatic* in which case the steering tool gives hints about the possible performance problems and generates alternatives to optimise the program.

The use of the dynamic instrumentation enables the steering process take place dynamically within one application execution without restarting it every time a modification was made. The interoperability type between the three tools is mixed. The steering tool interacts directly with the performance profiler and the debugger. The performance profiler and the debugger interact indirectly, by concurrently manipulating the same application process using the same underlying Process Manager sensor.

5.3.4 Just-in-Time Debugging

Using a traditional low level debugger to verify the correctness of a program requires to execute and repeatedly stop the program to inspect its state. If an incorrect program state is detected, all that is known is that a bug lies somewhere between the last inspection point and the current execution point (see Figure 5.4). For parallel programs, the problem gets significantly magnified due to their non-deterministic nature that leads to hardly reproducible errors. Deterministic execution tools [155], possibly in conjunction with a checkpointing tool [122, 166], may help in reproducing the error. This cyclic debugging method is, however, a time consuming process since the problem has to be repeatedly reproduced. The real bottleneck is the fact that traditional instruction level debuggers offer too low level support for spotting erroneous program states and provide no information about their real cause. Furthermore, the deterministic re-execution tools used to reproduce erroneous program executions can be very time consuming for long program executions. The *just-in-time* debugging concept attempts to eliminate the need of deterministically re-executing the program by using of an online high level bug detector to spot program defects in conjunction with a traditional low level debugger to fix the problems on-the-fly using the dynamic instrumentation. Just-in-time debugging is an example of direct tool interaction.

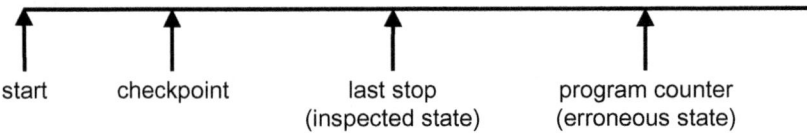

start   checkpoint   last stop   program counter
                             (inspected state)   (erroneous state)

Fig. 5.4. The cyclic debugging states.

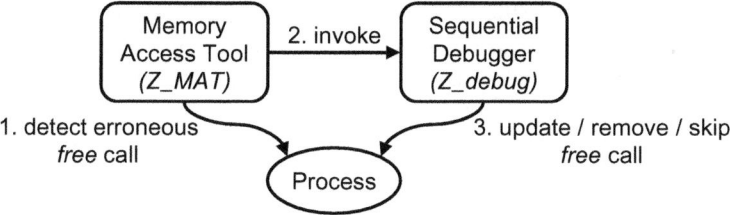

Fig. 5.5. A just-in-time debugging scenario.

In our proposed interoperability framework, the Z_MAT memory access tool can be used to detect memory access errors like an attempt to deallocate a free memory location. In the just-in-time debugging configuration depicted in Figure 5.5, Z_MAT performs additional instrumentation that stops the application at the exact location where a memory access error is detected. Additionally, Z_MAT automatically invokes the Z_debug sequential debugger on the stopped process which gives the user the opportunity to analyse the problem at the exact location where it occurred and eventually pursue online corrections. In this example, changing the memory block pointer or skipping / deleting the free instruction are crucial for avoiding a highly probable crash.

5.3.5 Interaction with a Debugger

The interaction of software tools with a runtime interactive debugger requires special care since the debugger severely interferes with the process execution. We identified the following two indirect interactions (i.e. process share) which we believe are of promising interest:

1. *Consistent Display* is an important task required by nearly any runtime tool. This issue becomes problematic when multiple tools concurrently monitor the same processes, since the display of each tool depends not only on its own activity, but also on the actions of other tools. When a visualisation tool such as the Object Code Browser interoperates with a debugger, the following sample interactions are possible:
   a) if the debugger stops the program execution, the execution visualiser needs to update its display in order to show this fact;
   b) if the debugger changes the value of a variable, the (distributed array) visualiser must update its display with the new value, for consistency;
   c) if the debugger loads a shared library in the application or replaces a call to a function, the Object Code Browser must change its code hierarchy accordingly.
2. *Accurate timing* is an important interaction that can happen between a performance tool and a debugger. For example, Z_debug could choose to stop a process while the performance tool Z_prof is profiling a function

of that process. In this situation, while the user and the system timers stop together with the process, the wall-clock time keeps running. Our underlying framework takes care of this situation through the Process Manager sensor that automatically subtracts from the wall-clock time the time during which the process was stopped by the debugger.

5.4 The Monitoring Layer

The monitoring layer of the tool integration architecture briefly introduced in Section 5.1 (see Figure 5.1) consists of an open set of sensors that run on the target Grid sites and provide low level information about the application processes and the system resources required for online tool development. The sensors can be remotely accessed through a portable platform independent interface which we developed on top of the light-weight Globus-IO library [80] and the Grid Security Infrastructure (GSI) introduced in Section 2.4.

We designed the monitoring layer motivated by the following limitations of the Vienna Fortran Compiler-based instrumentation engine used by the ZENTURIO experiment management tool:

1. the compile-time instrumentation can be applied only once prior to the application execution, which often introduces unnecessary intruding probes in the application;
2. the application needs special preparation through specific compilation and link library options which lacks flexibility required for interoperability;
3. the performance analysis is done post-mortem based on the data stored in the Experiment Data Repository;
4. in order to interoperate, all performance analysis tools will largely need to base their runtime instrumentation system on SCALEA and Vienna Fortran Compiler.

In the remainder of this section we present a general purpose instrumentation and monitoring sensor called Process Manager which aims to complement these limitations by using the dynamic instrumentation technology.

5.4.1 Dynamic Instrumentation

Dynamic instrumentation is a non-conventional instrumentation technology based on the insertion of binary code snippets at runtime into an already executing program. Dynamic instrumentation has several unique characteristics that make it suited for tool interoperability since it does not conflict with other existing instrumentation technologies:

1. it requires no advanced preparation of the application program, like special compilation options or link libraries;

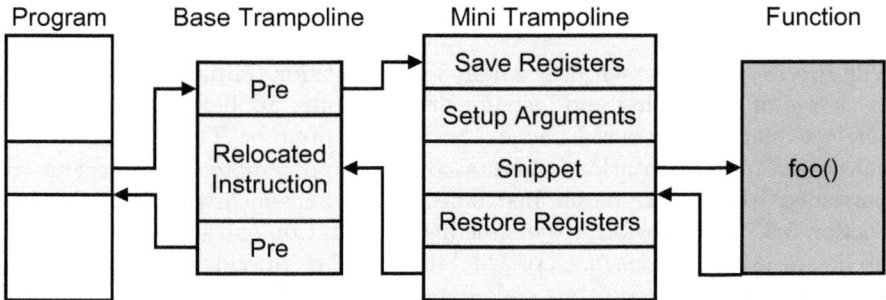

Fig. 5.6. The dynamic instrumentation control flow.

2. it allows instrumentation of binary programs compiled from any programming language, even of proprietary applications for which the source code is not available;
3. the instrumentation snippets can be inserted and removed from the code at any time which keeps the intrusion minimum.

Figure 5.6 illustrates the basic dynamic instrumentation mechanism to insert code snippets into a running process. The machine instruction code is inserted into the process by replacing an instruction located at the desired instrumentation point with a branch to a code snippet called *base trampoline*. The base trampoline saves and restores the process state before and after executing the instrumentation code. The specific instrumentation code is contained within a *mini trampoline* that can be inserted either before or after the relocated instruction. In case when the instrumentation snippet consists of function calls, additional trampoline guards ensure that the snippet is executed only if any of the functions is not on the stack.

The main limitation of dynamic instrumentation is its exclusive focus to binary executable object code. While compilation for debugging purposes (i.e. usually using the -g compilation flag) produces binary code that largely matches the source code, optimised compilation for fast execution generates highly optimised executables that can no longer be uncompiled to the original source code. The limitation becomes even more critical for high level parallel programming languages like HPF and OpenMP, for which the dynamic instrumentation cannot be used for computing high level metrics associated with specific language directives. Moreover, porting this technology to different operating systems, or even upgrading it to new system and compiler versions, is a hard challenging task that critically impacts the implementation reliability and availability.

The ZENTURIO source code instrumentation with support from the Vienna Fortran Compiler remains therefore an important asset along side the dynamic instrumentation in our tool environment.

5.4.2 The Process Manager

The *Process Manager* sensor is a light-weight daemon (implemented in C++) in charge of controlling and instrumenting running application processes on single sequential or shared memory parallel computers. The Process Manager serves instrumentation requests coming from remote Grid services (in particular from the Dynamic Instrumentor service which we will describe in Section 5.5.7) and performs dynamic instrumentation on running application processes using the *dynInst* [31] C++ library that provides a machine independent interface for runtime code patching using the (platform dependent) dynamic instrumentation technology. Typically the Process Manager sensors do not communicate with each other, however, there may be special cases when such interaction is required (see Section 5.4.3).

We provide in the Process Manager two mechanisms for connecting to an application process required to perform dynamic instrumentation:

1. *create* a process by providing the complete execution command and the input arguments;
2. *attach* to an existing process by providing the operating system process identifier.

We classify the functionality offered by the Process Manager in five categories which are implemented by four threads as shown in Figure 5.7 and described in the reminder of this section.

Information Functions

The information functions provide structural information collected from the running application processes which includes the object code structure of each process and (global) variable values. We extract this information from

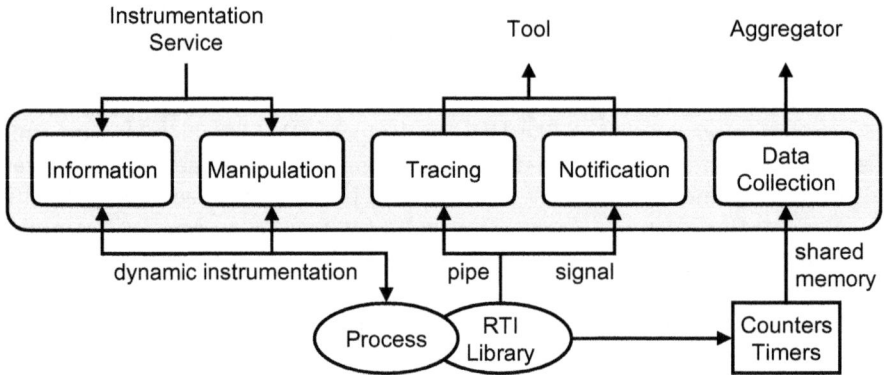

Fig. 5.7. The Process Manager architecture.

the binary executables and is complementary to the source code information, if available. Since retrieving the object code structure is a rather intrusive operation to be repeatedly invoked, the Process Manager extracts and caches the entire object structure through one single call after attaching to a running application. We refresh the cache whenever a running process issues the `exec` UNIX system call that overwrites the entire process image, or when a dynamic shared library is loaded.

The object code structure of a process largely matches the original source code if the application was compiled for debugging purposes (e.g. typically using the `-g` compiler option). In the case of highly optimised applications, however, the mapping from the binary executable to the source code becomes impossible due to complex irreversible compiler optimisation transformations.

Manipulation Functions

The manipulation functions are primarily used for dynamically injecting instrumentation probes into running application processes so that information about their execution may be gathered. We designed and implemented a *runtime instrumentation library* as a UNIX shared library [168] to facilitate the instrumentation of running application processes with high level probes, as required by the end-user tools. The library is dynamically loaded by the Process Manager into the address space of each monitored process at runtime which enables the instrumentation of unmodified binary executables. We provide as part of the runtime instrumentation library the following probe types, hierarchically depicted in Figure 5.8:

1. *Timers*, including wall-clock, user, and system time, are associated with a set of start and stop instrumentation points;
2. *Counters* are inserted before or after any set of instrumentation points. We provide two types of counter increments:
   a) *constant*, usually one in case of function call counters;
   b) *type size* used for counting the size of data structures (e.g. number of bytes passed as argument to various functions);
3. *Traces* are generated by inserting instrumentation probes that generate selective focused trace information;
4. *Notifications* insert probes that generate asynchronous events which are sent by the Notification thread to the subscribers following the push event model (see Section 5.6);
5. *Breakpoints* stop the application process whenever the program counter reaches a certain instrumentation point.

We provide in the Process Manager one instrumentation function for each probe type which is responsible for generating and inserting the appropriate binary instrumentation snippets into the running process using *dynInst*. We associate to each instrumentation probe inserted into a running process a unique handler that can be used to remove the probe if it is no longer needed.

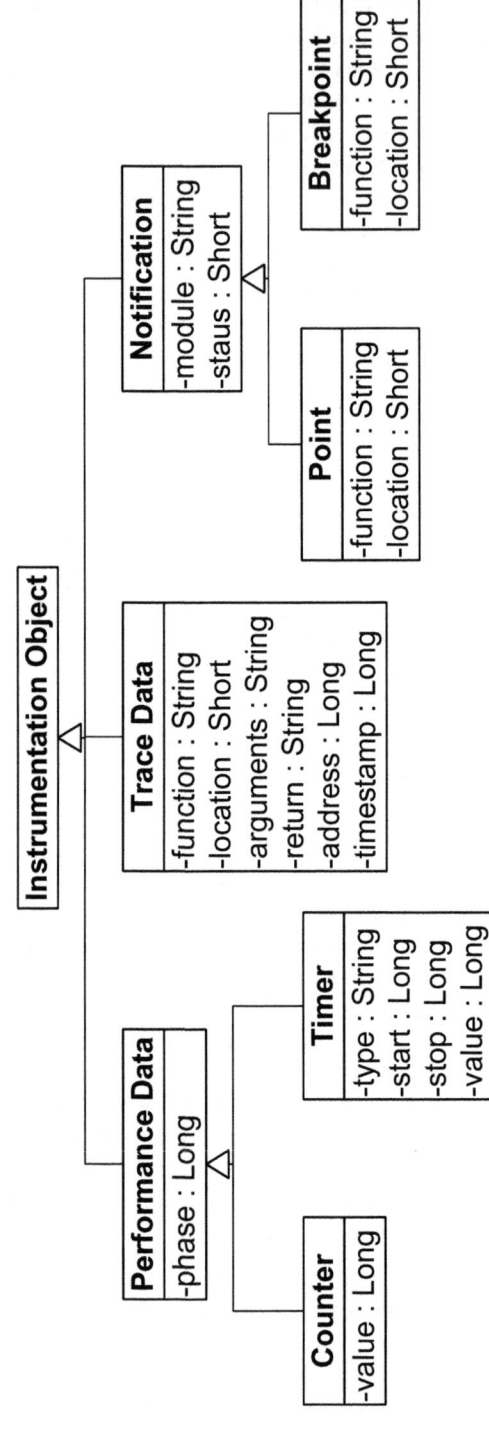

Fig. 5.8. The instrumentation probe class hierarchy.

Before instrumenting the application, the Process Manager checks whether the requested probe was previously inserted and, if so, returns the already allocated handler which avoids redundant instrumentation and minimises the intrusion.

Data Collection

We store the online performance data collected by the instrumentation probes in a memory segment that is shared between the Process Manager and the application process. From this shared memory segment, the performance data is sampled by the *data collection* thread with minimum overhead and forwarded to the tool (or to an Aggregator service – see Section 5.5.8) for online performance analysis via an asynchronous notification callback. Each performance metric has its own associated online *sampling rate* which is specified as part of the instrumentation request.

Tracing

The *tracing* thread collects selective trace information generated by the application tracing probes associated with certain instrumentation points. To simplify the implementation, we designed a simple trace data format that was sufficient for the implementation of the prototype tools that we use to validate the framework (see Section 5.2). One entry of our trace data format contains the following fields which are currently restricted to function level instrumentation granularity:

1. *function name* in which the instrumentation point is located;
2. *location* of the instrumentation point (function entry, exit, or call);
3. *argument list* of the function instance (if a function entry or a call point);
4. *return* value of the function (if a function exit or a call point);
5. *address* of the instrumentation point (needed to distinguish between different calls to the same function);
6. *timestamp* when the trace was generated.

As the trace data could get unacceptably large to be stored in the shared memory, we periodically append it to a First In First Out (FIFO) UNIX file (or pipe) [168] from where it is (albeit less efficiently than the performance data) collected by the Process Manager.

Notification

The *Notification* is a light-weight sleeping thread that is awaken through UNIX signals [168] by the notification probes when certain events happen during the process execution. As the signals can only achieve process synchronisation (not communication), we store the information that describes the occurring events in a special data structure within the shared memory segment (i.e. between the Process Manager and the executing process). The monitored application process and the Process Manager synchronise their access to this data structure by means of a UNIX semaphore [168]. This additional synchronisation is required since multiple simultaneous events may overwrite the data structure or exhaust the shared memory segment before the asynchronous notification thread manages to consume and forward the events to the requesting tool. We are currently handling there three types of notifications:

1. Arrival at instrumentation point;
2. Load or unload a shared library by trapping the **dlopen** UNIX system call [168]. This notification is used by browsing tools to provide an updated view of the application object code structure (see Section 5.2).
3. Status change (e.g. *started, stopped, running, terminated*) that allows the tools to dynamically monitor and react upon any modification in the application status. The *stopped* state is usually caused by a correctness debugger and augments the experiment state transition diagram presented in Figure 4.24 (see Chapter 4).

5.4.3 Dynamic Instrumentation of MPI Applications

We designed the Process Manager sensor for dynamic instrumentation of generic processes with no particular focus to any programming paradigm. The use of higher level parallel programming paradigms, however, require extensions to the existing functionality in order to be of convenient use to the tool developers. In this section we present a specialisation through (C++) inheritance of the Process Manager sensor to facilitate the instrumentation of MPI parallel applications

The challenge in creating an MPI application for dynamic instrumentation is to obtain the identifiers of all MPI processes which have to be created through the Process Manager on each individual processor of the parallel machine. Although MPI provides a standard interface for communicating between parallel processes, it omits to standardise the mechanism through which the parallel applications are created [164]. Currently each MPI implementation provides its own customised flavour of the **mpirun** command which starts a SPMD program on a specified number of nodes of the parallel machine[1]. The MPI-2 [92] specification aims to standardise the **mpirun** command renamed as **mpiexec**, but unfortunately it contains only advises rather than a full portable script to be adopted by all MPI implementations. The MPI Forum argues that the range of the environments is so diverse (e.g. there may not even be a command line interface to invoke **mpiexec**) that MPI cannot mandate such a universal mechanism.

---

[1] For MPMD applications, the use of the standard library call **MPI_COMM_SPAWN** defined by the MPI-2 [92] standard solves the problem in a portable manner.

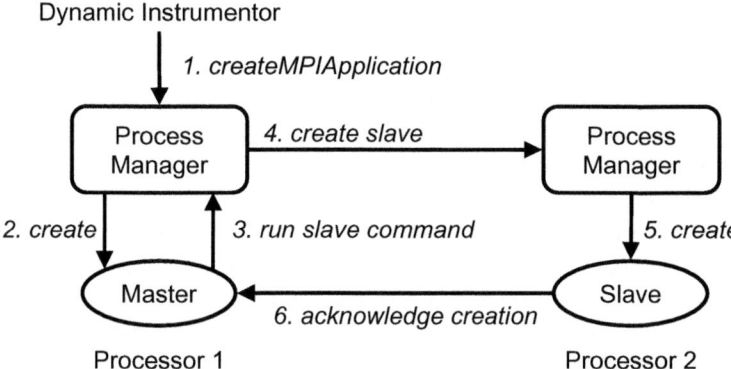

Fig. 5.9. The control flow for starting an MPI(CH) application for dynamic instrumentation.

Since we cannot achieve a generic solution, we chose the widely spread MPICH [91] for a case study implementation. We depict the technical scenario of creating an MPICH application for dynamic instrumentation in Figure 5.9. The client (i.e. the Dynamic Instrumentor service described in Section 5.5.7) requests that the Process Manager create an MPI application by invoking the (MPICH specific) `mpirun` command. The Process Manager appends the `-t` execution flag to the `mpirun` arguments that executes the command in the test mode. The result returned by the `mpirun` test command represents the list of processors of the parallel computer where the MPI processes will be started. The last entry in this list is the *master process* that has to be executed by the Process Manager on the local computer which will subsequently spawn the remaining MPI *slave processes*. The Process Manager appends the `-p4norem` flag when executing the master command, thereby preventing the master process from starting the slave processes automatically. Instead, the master process returns to the Process Manager the command required to manually start the slave processes on different processors. The Process Manager delegates this task to its counterpart running on the same processor where the slave has to be started. This is the only situation when direct communication between Process Managers is required. After being created, all MPI processes must be resumed so that the slaves can acknowledge their creation to the master within the `MPI_Init` function. As most tools require that the application be halted immediately after its creation, we insert a breakpoint at the end of the `MPI_Init` function of each process. Additionally, we insert a call to `PMPI_Comm_rank` before this breakpoint to retrieve the MPI process identifier within the `MPI_COMM_WORLD` communicator.

The implementation of this start-up mechanism raised a peculiar output buffering problem for which dynamic instrumentation as a general runtime code patching approach enables a very interesting and effective solution.

When given the `-p4norem` flag, the `MPI_Init` implementation of MPICH uses the C language `printf` command to write the master output that indicates how to start the slave processes (see Figure 5.9). Since the standard output of the master is redirected to a FIFO UNIX file (or pipe) [168] by the Process Manager, no output will be received until the output buffer is flushed. Rather than modifying the MPICH source code (which for other proprietary MPI implementations may not even be available) to explicitly flush the buffer after the offending `printf` and rebuild the whole MPICH library (thereby forcing the use of a customised library version), the Process Manager forces the flush at runtime by dynamically inserting a call to `fflush(stdout)` on-the-fly into the running master process. This enables our implementation to work with an original and unmodified MPICH library.

Dynamic instrumentation of the MPI-2 `MPI_Comm_spawn_multiple` and `MPI_Comm_spawn` routines required by the MPMD programming model allow newly spawned MPI processes be discovered at runtime and instrumented.

The dynamic instrumentation technology enables us profile MPI library calls with ease. The generic profiling and tracing operations of the Process Manager can be easily focused on the MPI library routines. The profiling interface defined by the MPI standard is of no benefit to us, since it is sufficient to apply the profiling and tracing operations to the `PMPI_`-prefixed calls directly without using the `MPI_`-prefixed wrappers. Furthermore, apart from the MPI application start-up which unfortunately is not fully standardised, all the metrics and tools developed can be applied on any (even proprietary) MPI implementation.

5.5 The Grid Services Layer

We designed the middle Grid services layer of the tool integration architecture introduced in Section 5.1 and depicted in Figure 5.1 with the following goals in mind:

1. the services shall provide a broad high level and platform independent functionality required for tool development;
2. the services can be accessed concurrently and independently by multiple clients which is essential for tool interoperability;
3. the services shall be easily instantiated on arbitrary remote Grid sites required for efficient deployment on the Grid;
4. there must be flexible and efficient means for discovering the services.

The Grid community acknowledged the Web services as the defacto ground technology for building service-oriented Grid architectures [79]. Web services, however, only mandate the use of XML documents for expressing interfaces and interactions between stateless Web services. In contrast, Grid services that model stateful Grid resources require enhancements to the basic Web

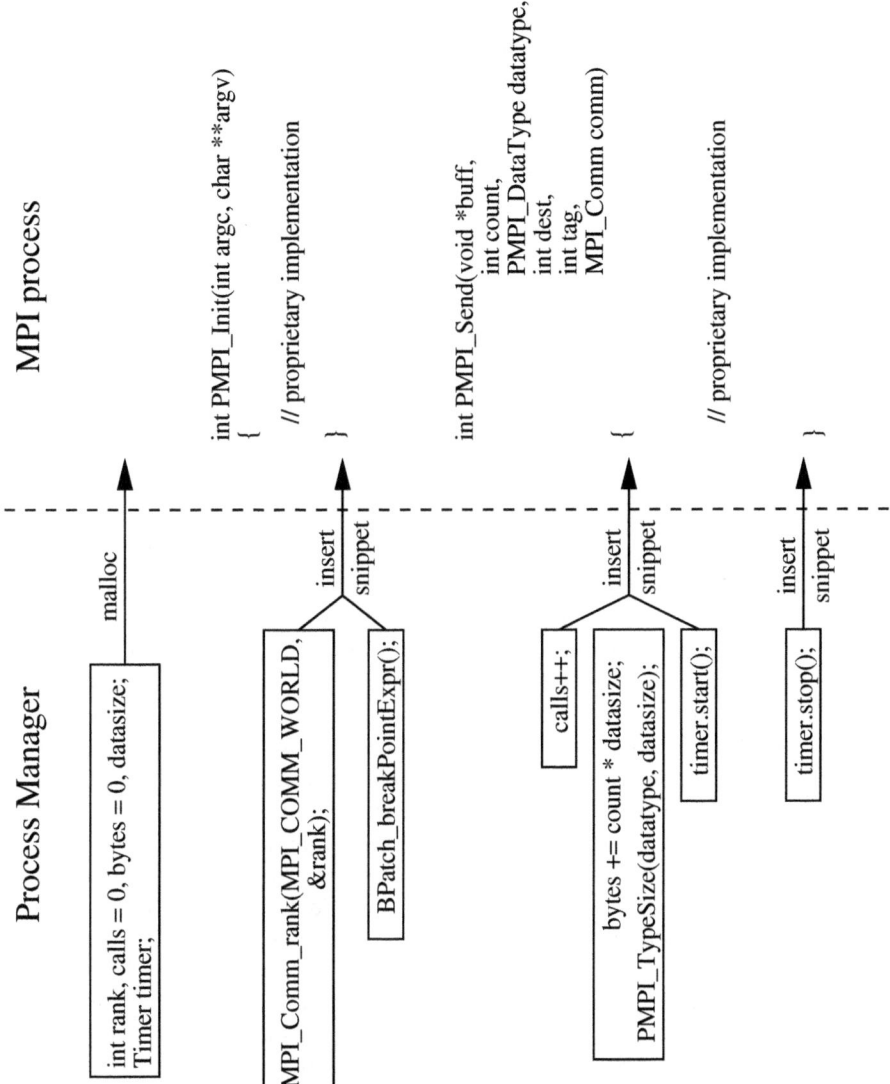

Fig. 5.10. The dynamic MPI library profiling.

services technology with functionality regarding state data (including lifecycle) and asynchronous notifications, as introduced in Section 2.6.2.

The Open Grid Services Infrastructure (OGSI) [46] standard proposed by the Global Grid Forum [37] in June 2003 failed to be acknowledged by the industry driven Web services community due to its object-oriented approach in modeling Grid services based on inheritance, lifecycle encapsulation, and service state as WSDL elements, that were not inline with the stateless Web services principles. OGSI therefore became obsolete soon and replaced by the Web Services Resource Framework [13] that is a delegation-based approach currently under standardisation within the Organisation for the Advancement of Structured Information Standards (OASIS) [135]. We carried out this work in designing the Grid services middleware layer within this this transitory period and exploited it as an opportunity to provide own contributions through the specification and implementation of several original Web services extensions for Grid computing.

5.5.1 Web Application and Services Platform (WASP)

We use the Systinet Server for Java, previously known as the Web Application and Services Platform (WASP) [129], as the Web services toolkit to implement the Grid services layer since it proved to be one of the fastest, robust, and easy to use product from a range of other implementations which we evaluated.

The WASP Web services runtime environment for Java is compliant with the Web services model described in Section 2.2. The WSDL interface of each Web service is automatically generated using WASP specific tools and is therefore implementation specific. Every Web service is designed and implemented by one Java class, deployed within, and executed by the WASP hosting environment. Upon the deployment of a Web service, a Web service instance with an associated WSDL document, whose structure we presented in Section 2.2, are automatically generated by WASP. Each automatically generated WSDL document of a Grid service deployed within the WASP hosting environment contains one service interface and one service instance section. The service interface has exactly one `portType` with the same name as the Java class that implements the service. Each Java method is mapped to one `portType` operation. The service interface is represented by exactly one `service` element which contains one `port` that defines the URL address of the SOAP `portType` network protocol binding.

Figure 5.11 depicts the state transition diagram of a Grid service deployed within the WASP hosting environment. *Offline* is the initial state and indicates that the service is not in memory, but will be loaded by the Java RPC provider (and transferred to the state *Enabled*) when a request arrives. In the *Active* state the service is processing one or more clients. The state *Stopping* indicates that a request to stop the service has been issued, but some requests are still in process. A service in the state *Stopped* remains in memory but rejects all incoming requests. *Disabled* means that the service is not in memory and cannot receive any requests. The transitions between the states are performed by the hosting environment either automatically (see the transitions marked with *italicised* text), or through explicit calls to the WASP administration service (see the transitions marked with `typewriter` style text).

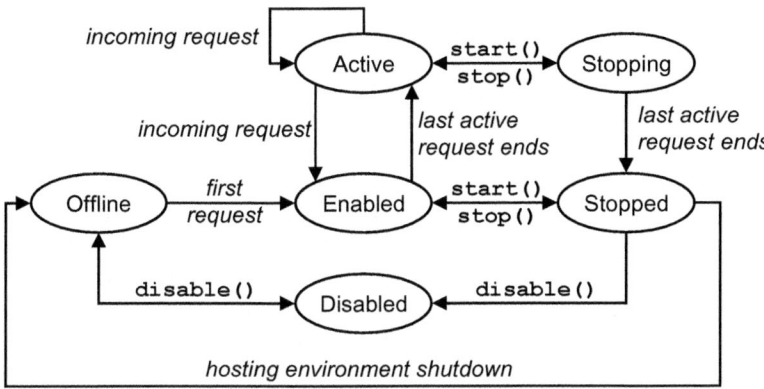

Fig. 5.11. The state transition diagram of WASP-based Web services.

5.5.2 Service Repository

The Universal Description, Discovery, and Integration (UDDI) [137] is a specification for distributed information registries of *persistent* business Web services.

One essential difference between business and Grid services, which in makes the use of UDDI in a Grid environment inappropriate, is the *service lifecycle*. While a static UDDI registry (i.e. a database) is suitable for publishing information about static and persistent business Web services, it is certainly inappropriate for storing information about *dynamic* and *transient* Grid services. In addition, publishing Grid services implementations in a Grid environment is crucial, as one cannot assume that the implementation code is available on the originally unknown remote site where the service instance would be desired. While compiled programming languages raise severe portability problems (especially due to unstandardised linkers and incompatible shared library dependencies), this issue is feasible for portable interpreted Java byte code that we use as the base implementation language for the middleware layer.

In this section we propose a new and slightly modified use of UDDI as a Service Repository for publishing *Grid service implementations* in a dynamic Grid environment (transient Grid service instances are published within a specialised Registry service that we will describe in Section 5.5.5). The UDDI best practices model that we briefly introduced Section 2.3.1 requires that the interface part of the WSDL document be published as a UDDI tModel and the instance part as a businessService element (i.e. as URLs). The businessService UDDI element is a descriptive container used to group related Web services which has one or more bindingTemplate elements that contain information for connecting and invoking a Web service. The bindingTemplate contains a pointer to a tModel element which describes the meta-data of a Web service. An `accessPoint` element is set with the SOAP address of the service (`port`). In contrast, we use the UDDI `businessService` element to publish service implementation information of transient Grid service instances. We use the `accessPoint` element of a `bindingTemplate` to store the URL to the JAR package that implements the Grid service. The WSDL service interfaces and the service implementations are manually published by the users in the UDDI Service Repository. Additionally, a notification mechanism compliant with the UDDI version three specification can be used to inform the clients when new services are registered.

The Registry (see Section 5.5.5) and the Factory (see Section 5.5.4) are the only two persistent services in our architecture for which we manually publish two entries in the UDDI repository that correspond to the service implementations and existing (arbitrary in number) service instances. The distinction between the service implementation and a persistent service instance is done based on the `accessPoint` URL syntax. Persistent Factory instances have a standardised URL derived from the Grid site name and a predefined port number (i.e. `http://hostname:port/Factory/`).

5.5.3 Abstract Grid Service

We model the Grid middleware services in a hierarchy displayed in Figure 5.12 designed using inheritance and the state encapsulation model described in Section 2.6.2. Each service is a specialisation of the *Abstract Grid Service* that defines and partially implements the most common denominator of the functionality required by all Grid services. The Abstract Grid Service implements the `Producer` and `Consumer` interfaces that describe the *push events* of the generic event framework what we will present in Section 5.6. The inheritance hierarchy is materialised, however, only at the Java implementation level since the Web services technology does not adhere to object-oriented design principles. Each automatically generated WSDL document of a WASP specific Grid service contains one single `portType` operation that merges the functionality of all the super-classes within the class hierarchy (see Section 5.5.1).

We provide the following set of generic operations as part of the Abstract Grid Service interface:

1. retrieve the URL of the WSDL file constructed using the URL of the hosting environment plus a suffix path that uniquely identifies the service instance;
2. set and control the service state within the hosting environment;
3. retrieve and set the service soft-state termination time;
4. register the service with all the available Registries (retrieved from the UDDI Service Repository) and set the leasing time (see Section 5.5.5);
5. initialise the service after the transition from the state *Offline* to the state *Enabled*;

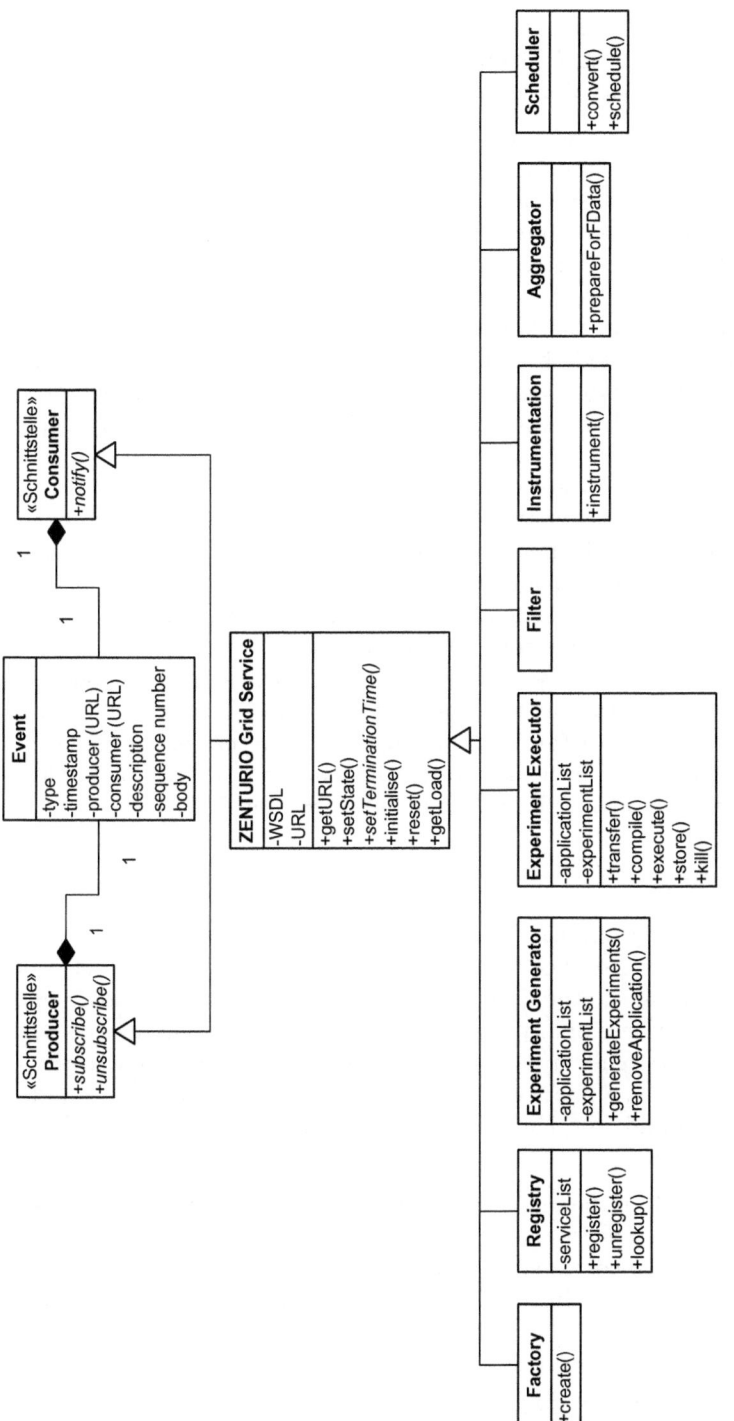

Fig. 5.12. The Grid services hierarchy.

6. reset the service by eliminating all the state information when the service is changing to the *Disabled* state;
7. retrieve the load of a service (in percentage).

The operations two and three implement the Grid service *lifecycle* based on the WASP specific interface and state transition diagram described in Section 5.5.1 and illustrated in Figure 5.11. The operations five, six, and seven describe abstract *state* information and must be specialised by each Grid service. Explicit service termination can be achieved by providing a termination time equal or prior to the current time. Destroying a Grid service requires to undeploy it from the hosting environment. We implement an additional softer destroy method that changes the service state to *Disabled* instead of undeploying it. A subsequent recreation of the service uses the existing disabled instance and changes its state to *Offline* which avoids extra deployment and undeployment overhead.

The Factory and the Registry are persistent services while the others are transient. All services in our Grid environment can be *accessed concurrently* by multiple clients which is an essential feature for achieving interoperability. Additionally, we provide for each service method a *synchronous* and an *asynchronous* version. The asynchronous version has the `Async` suffix and returns immediately an asynchronous receipt. Synchronous methods can be invoked against this receipt to verify whether the asynchronous method completed (optionally with a waiting timeout argument) or to retrieve the return result, any input or output parameter, and any exception that may have been raised. We can regard this asynchronous method invocation style as implementing the pull event model addressed in detail in Section 5.6.

5.5.4 Factory

Each hosting environment that runs on every Grid site contains by default one persistent *Factory* service which implements the *factory* abstract concept or pattern. We designed the Factory as a generic service that creates and deploys (Java) Grid services of any type which are previously packaged as JAR files. The Factory searches in the (UDDI) Service Repository for a service of a given type (i.e. as a `businessService` name – see Section 2.3.1) and, if such a service is found, the Factory creates a Grid service instance through the following steps:

1. get the URL of the service implementation (represented as an `accessPoint` element – see Section 5.5.2);
2. download the corresponding JAR package;
3. deploy the service in the same hosting environment in which the Factory resides;
4. initialise the service instance;
5. register the instance with all known Registry services (retrieved from the UDDI Service Repository);

6. set a leasing time equal to the service termination time;
7. return the URL to the WSDL file of the service instance.

The clients use this URL to retrieve the WSDL file and dynamically bind to the service through build-time generated stubs. Before searching for a service, the Factory examines within the hosting environment whether an instance of the same type was previously destroyed and disabled. If such an instance is found, the Factory changes its state to *Offline*, thus saving expensive download, package, and deployment overhead (see Figure 5.11).

5.5.5 Registry

As opposed to other distributed service technologies (e.g. Jini lookup service [64] or CORBA Naming and Trading services [120]), Web services do not provide any standard network aware means of locating transient services (we have already emphasised the limitations of UDDI in Section 5.5.2). The Web services architecture [194] introduces the concept of *discovery agent*, but leaves its design and implementation unspecified.

We designed the *Registry* as a persistent service which maintains an updated list of URLs to the WSDL files of registered Grid service instances. We organise the service URLs in special purpose hash tables for fast high throughput service discovery. There may be an arbitrary number of persistent Registries residing on any Grid site which must be registered with the UDDI Service Repository. The Registry grants *leases* to the registered services similar to the Jini [64] built-in leasing mechanism. If a service does not renew its lease before the lease expires, the Registry deletes the service from its internal service list which is an efficient mechanism to cope with dynamic transient services and network failures. A leasing time of zero seconds explicitly unregisters the service. We provide an event mechanism to inform the clients (e.g. the user tools) about new Grid services that registered with the Registry or when the lease of existing services expired. Thereby, the clients are always provided with a dynamically updated view of the Grid services-based middleware environment. The Registry is a generic service that operates on Abstract Grid Services and, therefore, can be used to register and discover services of any type in our architecture.

The *Web Services Inspection Language (WSIL)* [12] designed by IBM proposed a distributed Web services discovery method which is complementary to the UDDI centralised approach. WSIL defines an XML document that contains URL references to existing Web service instances (i.e. instance WSDL documents). We implement in the Registry service a method that generates upon request one similar WSIL document which contains references to the registered transient Grid service instances. We also associate a timestamp with the WSIL document that determines the validity of the data.

We provide as part of the Registry service three types of methods for performing lookup operations:

1. *White pages* provide service discovery based on the service URL;
2. *Yellow pages* support service discovery based on the service type compared against the `portType` of each service. As we already described in Section 5.5.1, the WSDL document of each WASP Web service contains one single `portType` with the same name as the Java class that implements the service;
3. *Green pages* perform discovery based on service functionality using the compatibility operator between two WSDL interfaces that we describe in the next section.

5.5.6 WSDL Compatibility

Functionality-based service discovery is a key feature in a Grid environment for which the Web services technology does not provide any standard support.

Definition 5.1. *We define an instance WSDL document W_1 as compatible with an instance document W_2, denoted as $W_1 \supset W_2$, if and only if:*

1. *the set of `portType` names[2] of W_1 instantiated by the `service` element is a superset of the corresponding set of W_2;*
2. *for each `portType` of W_2 instantiated by the `service` element, the set of `operation` names is a subset of the corresponding set of W_1;*
3. *two operations with the same name are identical (i.e. have identical `parameterOrder`, input, output and fault messages).*

The Grid services compatibility operator is reflexive, antisymmetric, and transitive.

5.5.7 Dynamic Instrumentor

We designed the *Dynamic Instrumentor* as a Grid service for generic dynamic runtime instrumentation of running parallel applications based on the functionality of the Process Manager sensor described in Section 5.4.2, augmented with collective operations that apply on multiple parallel processes simultaneously. The Dynamic Instrumentor provides the following four categories of operations:

1. *Information operations* are based on the Process Manager information functions which include the retrieval of the application object code or the inspection of variable values. Because it is an expensive operation at the Process Manager level, the Dynamic Instrumentor service retrieves the object code only once during the lifetime of a process (i.e. when the process is created or attached) and caches it for serving further requests;

---

[2] *qnames* in the WSDL specification and terminology [38].

2. *Performance metric operations* are based on the Process Manager manipulation functions but operate at a higher level of abstraction, e.g. count number of function calls, compute the execution time of a function, or count the size of a function parameter. On top of the generic performance metrics, we built a specialised *MPI Dynamic Instrumentor* that provides MPI specific metrics including:

   a) the number of messages sent;
   b) the number of input and output operations (based on the MPI-IO [177] standard);
   c) the time spent in communication (i.e. by timing the routines from the `MPI_Send` and `MPI_Recv` family);
   d) the time spent in input and output operations;
   e) the time spent in synchronisation (i.e. `MPI_Barrier`) ;
   f) the number of bytes sent and received in communication routines;
   g) the number of bytes involved in input and output operations;

3. *Function tracing operations* request that the entry, the exit, and the call points of a user, a system, or a library function are logged;

4. *Notification operations* request that the client (i.e. the tool) be notified (using the push event model – see Section 5.6) when certain events occur in the application (e.g. instrumentation point reached, shared library loaded, process forked or exited);

5. *Breakpoint operations* request the insertion of normal or conditional breakpoints. Since a breakpoint only stops the process when it is reached by the program counter, a typical use is in conjunction with a Notification probe that informs the client where such an breakpoint event occurred (rather than reporting only a process status change).

5.5.8 Aggregator

When dealing with parallel applications, frequently the first step in processing the collected (performance) data from all parallel processes requires a reduction step for better data understanding. We designed the *Aggregator* as a generic Grid service that receives large amounts of data and, through the use of a chosen aggregation function, reduces it to more manageable quantities. The Aggregator supports reduction over time or across processors using a variety of aggregation functions including *mean, total, variance, sum, maximum,* or *minimum*. A more specialised metric for parallel processing is the *load balance* which we defined in Section 4.2.5 (see Definition 4.17) as the ratio between the mean and the max value. A value of one indicates the perfect load balance and a value of zero indicates the worse case load balance.

The Dynamic Instrumentor provides an Aggregator service when requesting from several Process Managers to collect dynamic performance data from a parallel application. The Aggregator specialises the `Consumer` interface for receiving data from the Process Manager (upon subscription) and the `Producer` interface for sending data to the client tool. Both interfaces implement the push event model that we will describe in Section 5.6.

5.6 Event Framework

The Grid community widely acknowledged the need of an event framework for monitoringimportant events that occur in large and dynamic Grid environments [179]. Our proposed tool integration architecture adheres to this consensus by designing and implementing a generic event framework as part of its Grid service middleware layer.

Definition 5.2. *We define an* event *as a timestamped data structure generated by a sensor and sent by a producer to a consumer. An event* producer *is a Grid service that implements the* **Producer** *interface and uses sensors to generate events. An event* consumer *is a Grid service (usually a thread within the client application) that implements the* **Consumer** *interface (see Figure 5.12).*

Sensors can be stand-alone like the Process Manager or embedded inside producers. The Registry service is responsible in our architecture for maintaining up-to-date information about existing producers and consumers.

5.6.1 Representation

We model a generic event as a composite structure consisting of two parts:

1. The *event header* is the standard part of the event structure that comprises the following fields:
   a) *event type* is an identifier that refers to a category of events defined by an *event schema*;
   b) *timestamp* indicates when the event was generated. If the events are buffered, the elements in the event body may contain additional timestamp information;
   c) *event producer* (URL);
   d) *event consumer* (URL);
   e) *sequence number*;
   f) *expiration timestamp*;
2. The *event body* represents the effective information carried by the event which consists of the following four fields, where the last three are optional:
   a) *homogeneous collection* of elements where every *element* refers to a single event. The structure of an element (i.e. the type) is defined by an event schema;
   b) *element description* (textual);
   c) *measurement unit*;
   d) *accuracy.*

Our event framework depicted in Figure 5.13 supports three types of interactions between producers and consumers [179]:

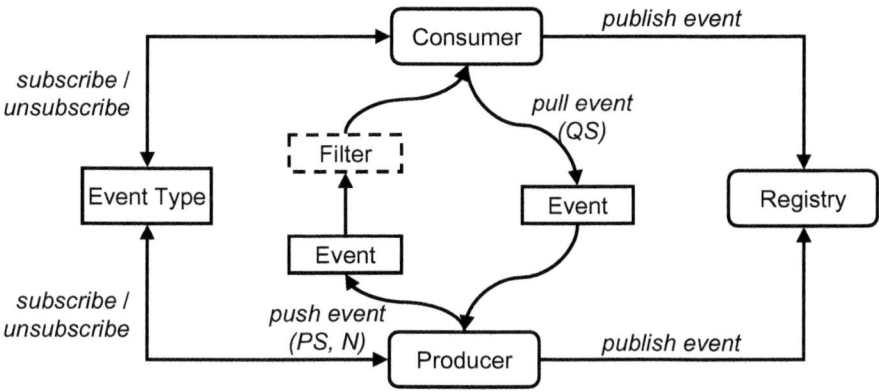

Fig. 5.13. The ZENTURIO event architecture.

1. *publish-subscribe (PS)* is a generalisation of the *push model* where the initiator can be either the producer or the consumer. The initiator searches in the Registry service for the other party (producer or consumer) and registers for (the production or the consumption of) events. The producer sends events to the consumers until the initiator unsubscribes. The consumers subscribe for events to the producers by specifying the following inputs:
   a) *event type* that uniquely identifies the category of events desired;
   b) *event consumer* (i.e. URL to the WSDL file) that specialises the Consumer interface which receives the asynchronous notifications;
   c) *event parameters* specify the properties (characteristics) of the events to be sent to the user (e.g. process identifier for which status events must be sent). The event parameters describe an event and therefore we included them as part of the event schema (i.e. as data members);
   d) *filter* specifies the conditions that must hold in order for an event to be generated (e.g. minimum value for a processor load event);
   e) *subscription expiration time*;
2. *query-response (QR)* generalises the *pull event* model. The initiator is the consumer and the event is sent in a single response any time after the event was requested;
3. *notification (N)* is a slight specialisation of the push model. The producer transfers the events to the consumer in a single notification with no preliminary subscription.

In Figure 5.14 we depict a generic classification of the events supported by our tool environment, including ZENTURIO experiment management tool, based on several event types. Table 5.1 displays the producers and the sensors for each of the event types, while Table 5.2 gives a detailed description of the event types and their use.

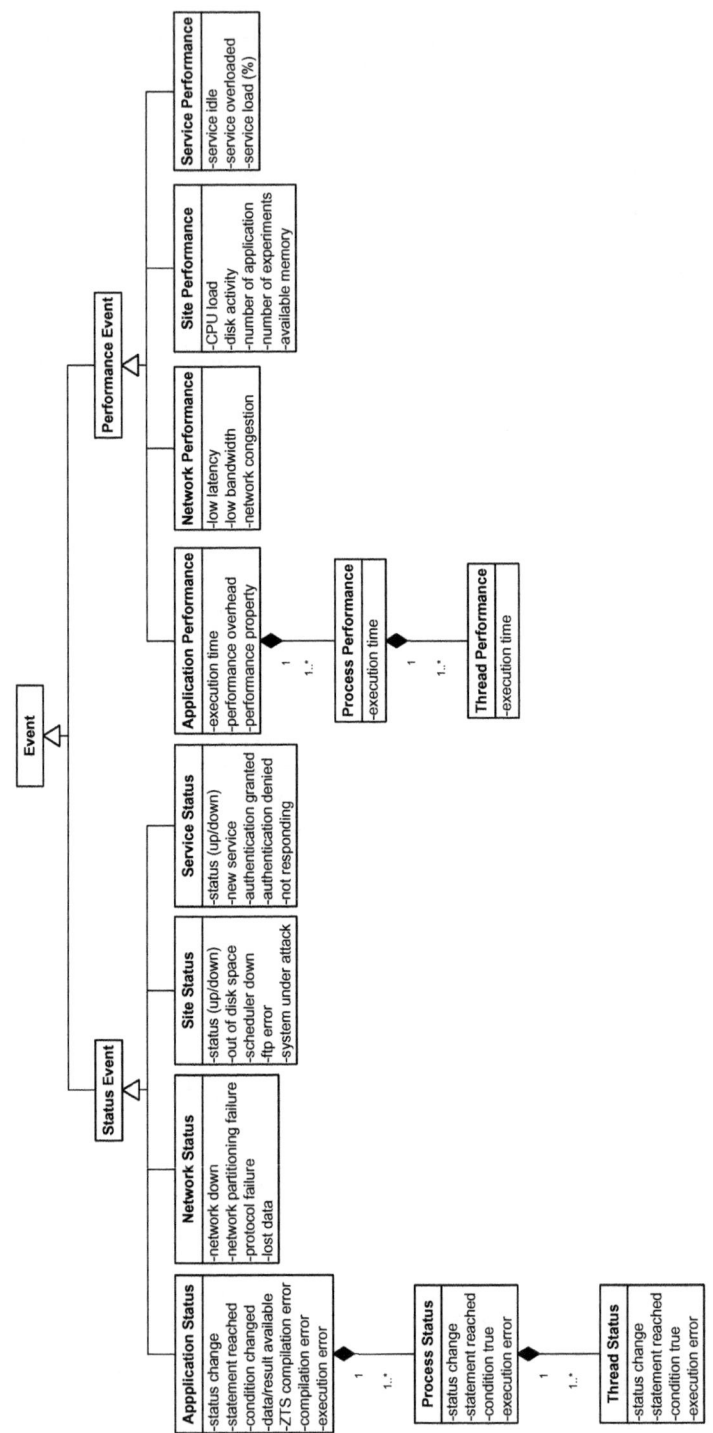

Fig. 5.14. The event hierarchy.

Table 5.1. The event implementation support.

Event Type	Producer	Sensor
Application Status	Experiment Executor Experiment Generator Dynamic Instrumentor	Experiment Executor Experiment Generator Process Manager
Process Status	Dynamic Instrumentor	Process Manager
Thread Status	Dynamic Instrumentor	Process Manager
Network Status	SCALEA-G [182]	`netstat`
Site Status	SCALEA-G	`ping`
Service Status	Abstract Grid Service Registry	Abstract Grid Service Registry
Application Performance	Aggregator Dynamic Instrumentor	Process Manager SCALEA
Process Performance	Aggregator Dynamic Instrumentor	Process Manager SCALEA
Thread Performance	Aggregator Dynamic Instrumentor	Process Manager SCALEA
Network Performance	SCALEA-G	NWS
Site Performance	SCALEA-G	NWS
Service Performance	Abstract Grid Service	Abstract Grid Service

5.6.2 Implementation

Events require support for *asynchronous messaging* which is currently standardised within OASIS through the WS-Notification standard [90], however, this specification was not supported in WASP or any other Web services toolkit by the time we carried our this work. For example, the Web services operations can be of type *one-way*, in which case no SOAP response is generated and only a HTTP notification is sent back. Moreover, WSDL version 1.1 defines operations of type *Notification* that allow an endpoint to send a message, however, it omits to define an appropriate network protocol binding.

We implement the query-response events using the WASP specific asynchronous methods with the `Async` suffix, as described in Section 5.5.3. We realise the publish-subscribe and notification interactions (flavours on the push event model) based on one-way Web services operations that reverse the roles of services and clients. The client takes the role of a service that receives one-way notification callbacks by implementing the `Consumer` WSDL interface. We base our implementation on the WASP specific *embedded server* that allows one client to start a hosting environment as a separate thread. Although the declared purpose of this WASP feature is rapid prototyping, the embedded server enables synchronous or one-way callbacks. The SOAP address of the embedded server where the callbacks are received is given to the producer service during the event subscription. This entire event implementation is, however, WASP specific and therefore not portable across other Web services toolkits.

Table 5.2. The events supported by ZENTURIO.

Event Type	Producer	Consumer	Sensor	Parameters	Filters	Event Elements	Interaction
service state	Registry	User Portal	Registry	type, site		status (up/down)	PS, QR
new service	Registry	User Portal	Registry	type, site		service type, URL	PS, QR
authentication failed	Abstract Grid Service	User Portal	Abstract Grid Service			user name	N
out of disk space	Exp. Generator, Exp. Executor	User Portal	Exp. Generator, Exp. Executor			site	N
compilation error	Exp. Generator, Exp. Executor	User Portal	Exp. Generator, Exp. Executor			ZEN file, message	N
fie transfer error	Exp. Generator, Factory	User Portal	Exp. Generator			site	N
condition true	Exp. Executor	User Portal	Exp. Generator Instrum.	identifier, app.	bool-expr		PS
application performance	Dynamic Instrumentor	User Portal	Process Manager	metric, app., sample rate	bool-expr, max, min	value	PS
new experiment	Exp. Generator	User Portal	Exp. Generator	app., ZEN vars		experiment	PS, QR
experiment status	Exp. Generator, Exp. Executor	User Portal	Exp. Generator, Exp. Executor	app., ZEN vars		experiment status	PS, QR
scheduler down	Exp. Executor	User Portal	Exp. Executor			site, scheduler	N
unknown scheduler	Exp. Executor	User Portal	Exp. Executor			site, scheduler	N
service load	Exp. Generator, Exp. Executor	User Portal	Exp. Generator, Exp. Executor	site, sample rate	max / min load	no. applications, no. experiments.	PS, QR
compilation error	Exp. Executor	User Portal	Exp. Executor			exp., message	N
execution error	Exp. Executor	User Portal	Exp. Executor			exp., message	N
repository store error	Exp. Executor	User Portal	SCALEA			experiment, message	N
repository access error	Exp. Generator, Exp. Executor	User Portal	Exp. Generator, Exp. Executor			site, message	N

5.6.3 Filters

Filters can be either encoded inside event producers (i.e. Grid services) or designed separately, as special kind of intermediaries.

Definition 5.3. *An* intermediary *is a Grid service that insinuates between a producer and a consumer during a push (i.e. publish-subscribe and notification) event notification. A* filter *is an intermediary which delivers to the consumers a subset of the messages received from the producers.*

An intermediary can be shared by multiple producers and consumers. The event subscription method of the producers can receive as input (along with the event type, consumer, and event parameters) an array of filters of the Abstract Grid Service type. The filters are chained such that the first filter receives the messages directly from the producer and the last filter delivers the output messages to the consumer. This general method of chaining filters is employed at certain latency costs (unless the deviated path through the filter has lower latency or higher bandwidth than the direct path from the producer to the consumer). We implement an abstract template filter that specialises the Abstract Grid Service and has exactly one producer and one consumer. We can therefore easily plug-in new filters by specialising this abstract class and implementing the filtering algorithm.

5.7 Firewall Management

Firewalls are a critical topic in a Grid environment where geographically distributed Grid services need to transparently communicate through message exchanges across multiple administrative domains. This section describes the pragmatic approach we took in our Grid environment for traversing firewalls, however, a proper solution that satisfies all the security constraints is beyond its scope.

The Web services hosting environment described in Section 2.3.2 offers the advantage of a *single entry point* for accessing all services through the provision of an embedded SOAP dispatcher. We associate with each Grid service two communication *ports* that have to be remotely accessible:

1. *synchronous service port* is a property of the hosting environment and therefore is common to all services hosted on a Grid site;
2. *asynchronous notification port* is a state property that must be exposed by each stateful Grid service.

All hosting environments and event consumers listening on open site ports are responsible for authenticating every request using the GSI mechanisms (see Section 2.4).

During our experience with ZENTURIO, we identified two serious obstacles in deploying large Grid infrastructures across different academic domains:

Table 5.3. The open firewall ports.

Port	Value
GLOBUS_TCP_PORT_RANGE	$40000 - 40100$
GRAM gatekeeper	2119
GridFTP server	2811
MDS GRIS	2135
MDS GIIS	2170
NWS Slapd	2112
NWS Nameserver	8090
NWS memory server	8050
NWS sensor	8060
NWS forecast	8070
Process Manager	12345
SCALEA-G	$40600 - 40625$
Hosting Environment	8080
Experiment Data Repository	5432

1. Independent (and in many cases not interacting) system administrators usually restrict the access to open ports to certain trusted administrative domains. However, various scenarios defined by the community within the Global Grid Forum often require more flexibility. One frequently mentioned requirement of the Grid users is *mobility*, i.e. the ability to connect and use the Grid from arbitrary Internet locations (e.g. during conferences), possibly from dynamic unknown IP addresses received through the Dynamic Host Configuration Protocol (DHCP) [159] which are commonly rejected by firewalls;
2. To receive events at the client sites is usually impossible, the following two scenarios being the ones we encountered most often:
   a) firewalls at foreign Internet sites outside the Grid infrastructure (e.g. where a demo is wanted) where it is impossible to ask the system administrators for any firewall changes;
   b) the use of the Network Address Translation [112] mechanism.

Table 5.3 displays the set of firewall ports that we require to be open and remotely accessible in our Grid environment. Our experience with ZENTURIO revealed that restricting the access to these open ports across n sites requires tight interaction of $C_n^2 = \frac{n \cdot (n-1)}{2}$ pairs of system administrators which is not scalable in a large Grid environment (where C_n^2 denotes combinations of n elements taken two at a time).

5.8 WASP Versus GT3 Technology Evaluation

We designed and implemented the Grid middleware services in the year 2001 based on the WASP toolkit, as described in Section 5.5.1. In the year 2003, the

Global Grid Forum finalised the Open Grid Services Infrastructure (OGSI) specification [46] that was aimed to be the standard technology for building Grid services. The extensions added by OGSI to conventional Web services comprised standard means for managing the service lifecycle (including time modeling), service data elements which exposed service state within the WSDL portTypes of each service interface, and a standard interface for light-weight notification events. The version three of the Globus toolkit (GT3) implemented the OGSI specification within the Open Grid Services Architecture (OGSA) [79] based on the Apache Axis [11] SOAP implementation.

Within this wide international effort, we ported our Grid middleware services layer to the OGSI technology using GT3 as underlying implementation platform. Even through OGSI [46] became meanwhile an obsolete standard replaced by WSRF, we report in the in the reminder of this section a comparative analysis of various aspects that were substantially different between the WASP and GT3-based implementations which we considered a useful experience and lesson learned during a timely technology evaluation effort in implementing Grid services [141, 145].

5.8.1 Stub Management

We initially developed the middleware Grid services layer based on the WASP server and SOAP engine for Java, as presented in Section 5.5.1. The transition from WASP to the OGSI-based service deployment was straightforward in accordance to the Web services principles, by using the corresponding automatic WSDL generation, packaging, and deployment tools. We encountered major difficulties when porting the clients (i.e. the tools) which was mainly due to the different stub management in the two SOAP implementations which is not standardised by the Web services technologies (see Section 2.3.2). Interoperability between WASP-based clients and GT3-based services was also not a feasible solution, since our goal was to use and validate the OGSI extensions to the Web services (e.g. notifications, service data).

The service stubs in WASP are dynamically generated at runtime during the service lookup operation and, therefore, completely transparent to the user. In contrast, the stubs of the GT3 Java clients were statically generated at compile-time using a special GSDL2Java (WSDL2Java in vanilla Axis) tool. A limitation of this tool was that it generated not only stubs for transparent remote invocation of the services, but also Java Bean implementations compatible with the Axis BeanSerializer for all the complex types that appeared as input or output arguments to the service methods. Each such bean contained the set and get methods to access the private data members, a default constructor, and additional bean (de)serialisation code. This meant that the implementation of each complex type present in a service interface must be a Java Bean which was overwritten (or generated) by the stub generator. This limitation is not imposed by WASP which allows arbitrary nontrivial implementations of the complex types that are defined in the WSDL interfaces.

The WASP serialisation is based on a `Reflection(De)Serializer` which manages the default type (de)serialisation using a Java Beans introspector that applies at runtime directly on the bean implementation class provided by the user.

Our initial WASP-based implementation of the Grid services contained nontrivial implementations of several complex types to be (de)serialised (e.g. experiment and ZEN-annotated application classes). We needed therefore to redesign the code such that the stubs physically generated by Axis do not overwrite the original implementation and remove the non Java Bean methods. We considered two solutions for solving this problem:

1. ignore the Java Bean stubs generated for the complex types and paste the serialisation code into the implementation using a macro-processing tool. This method is simple but less elegant;
2. re-engineer the implementation in a class hierarchy such that the super-class is the Java Bean that will be overwritten by the stub generator and the subclass contains the complex non Java Beans methods. We finally adopted this second solution which is neater but required a major re-engineering of the application class hierarchy.

5.8.2 Service Lifecycle

One major contribution of OGSI to conventional persistent Web services was the standardisation lifecycle management of transient Grid services. Normally each conventional Web service hosting environment implements its own state transition diagram which can be manipulated through proprietary interfaces (see Section 5.5.1). The problem is that the implementation of transient services across various service containers is not portable.

WASP provides two different instantiation models of runtime published services and automatic lifecycle management:

1. *Shared instantiation* is the usual instantiation method which shares one instance of the remote object across multiple clients. The service lifecycle is controlled through WASP specific time-to-live routines as presented in Section 5.5.1 and Figure 5.11;
2. *Per-client instantiation* is a scheme through which the WASP hosting environment automatically creates a transient instance of a persistent service for each separate client on behalf of its first service invocation. This technique is similar with the WS-Context [32] standard for implementing stateful services.

This was an interesting occasion to notice that, while following a different development path than OGSI, existing advanced Web services toolkits like WASP do provide advanced proprietary extensions for implementing transient Grid services. The OGSI specification added lifecycle as a property of Grid service instances by defining a standard interface as part of the `GridService` portType specification and by including termination time as a WSDL service data element. This solution had the key advantage of being portable across multiple OGSI compliant implementations. Moreover, the service lifecycle management is fully handled by the OGSI implementation toolkits which substantially simplifies the development of new transient Grid services.

5.8.3 UDDI-Based Service Repository

We presented in Section 5.5.2 a custom centralised repository for publishing persistent Grid services implementations based on the UDDI standard [137]. The generic WASP-based Factory service downloads the required service implementation from the UDDI Registry (if necessary) and deploys the service instance on-the-fly using the WASP runtime publishing tools. We could not implement this runtime on-the-fly service deployment technique in the GT3-based implementation that required pre-deployment of persistent services before the hosting environment was started. Transient services are purposely designed for runtime deployment, however, the corresponding byte code and WSDL interfaces needed to be pre-deployed in GT3. This limitation is very critical in a Grid environment where new services need to be deployed on new sites at runtime based on the dynamic resource availability.

5.8.4 Service Data

The OGSI most radical extension to Web services standards was the ability to expose service instance state data for query, update, and change notification. The OGSI approach introduced a serviceData child element to the WSDL portType to describe stateful Grid services. Service data was an OGSI specific feature and therefore not supported by WASP and any other traditional Web services implementation. Our WASP-based implementation exposes the Grid services state through Java Bean get and set methods which has the atomicity limitation exemplified in [46].

We enumerate the service data elements exported by our GT3-based services in Table 5.4. The service data elements of the Registry and Factory services were implemented by the GT3 distribution as part of the VORegistry respectively the FactoryServiceSkeleton implementation (the latter as an extension to OGSI). The service data elements were, however, one the major obstacles for the OGSI adoption within the Web services community due to their native object-oriented roots that conflict with the stateless Web services principles.

5.8.5 Events

Originally, OGSI defined three different WSDL portTypes that aimed to standardise the push event model which afterwards evolved into a separate

Table 5.4. The service data elements.

Service	Service Data Elements
Experiment Generator	ZEN applications
	last experiment generated
	number of experiments
	Experiment Data Repository (JDBC URL)
	notification port
Experiment Executor	ZEN applications
	number of experiments (submitted/
	queued/running/terminated/stored)
	Experiment Data Repository (JDBC URL)
	notification port
Registry	registered services
	notification port
Factory	created services
	UDDI URL
	notification port

stand-alone OASIS standard [90]: `NotificationSource`, `NotificationSink`, and `NotificationSubscription`. We presented in Section 5.6 an approach to realise push events in WASP based on embedded servers which was also adopted by GT3 in the implementation of the OGSI `NotificationSink portType`. This was another interesting occasion for us to notice that existing Web services toolkits offer solutions to implement OGSI extensions to Web services although the declared objectives and development paths were different. In addition, OGSI specified an event subscription mechanism on `serviceData` element changes like those enumerated in Table 5.4. Support for the pull event model was standardised in OGSI by means of `findServiceData` introspection on WSDL `serviceData` XML elements. This approach was completely orthogonal to the one taken by us in the WASP implementation based on asynchronous one-way methods (see Section 5.6).

5.8.6 Registry

In Section 5.5.5 we presented an advanced WASP-based Registry service for high throughput white, yellow, and green pages-based Grid service instance discovery. In order to save development time and also evaluate other implementations, we incorporated in the GT3-based implementation the so called VORegistry service provided by the GT3 distribution. The uniqueness of VORegistry was the ability to publish Grid services as service data elements with service lookup support through `findServiceData` introspections. The VORegistry published an additional service data element instantiated by WSIL [12] document containing a URL list of all services registered. The service lookup operations were based on standard XPath [39] queries against the WSIL XML document. Subscriptions on service data element changes provided support push event notifications.

We conducted an additional comparative throughput benchmark to evaluate the responsiveness of our WASP-based Registry service against the GT3 VORegistry. We performed the benchmarks automatically using ZENTURIO by running both the client and the hosting environment on a four processor 750 megahertz Sun-fire SMP computer with nine gigabytes of memory to avoid processor contention and network delays. We annotated the client application with ZEN directives as shown in Example 5.4 to specify the following benchmark parameters:

1. *the number of registered services* from 100 to 1500 with stride 100, denoted by the ZEN variable svNo;
2. *the number of concurrent clients* from 100 to 15100 with stride 1000, denoted by the ZEN variable clnts;
3. *the number of requests per second* served by the Registry were measured by manually instrumenting the client with the SCALEA instrumentation library.

These annotations specify a total of $15 \times 15 = 225$ experiments which were automatically generated and conducted by ZENTURIO as described in Chapter 4.

Example 5.4 (GT3 VORegistry benchmark client.).

```
. . .
svNo = 100;
//ZEN$ ASSIGN svNo = { 100 : 1500 : 100 }
for(int i = 0; i <= svNo; i++) {
  ((Stub) factory)._setProperty(
                    ServiceProperties.INVOCATION_ID, i);
  factory.createService(new CreationType());
}
. . .
clnts = 100;
//ZEN$ ASSIGN clnts = { 100 : 15100 : 1000 }
for(int j = 0; j < clnts.length; j++) {
  new Thread() { public void run() {
    ExtensibilityType queryResult = registry.
      findServiceData(QueryHelper.getXPathQuery(
                "GridServiceRegistryWSInnspection
                XPathExpr, namespaces));
  }.start();
}
```

Our WASP-based Registry offers an excellent throughput of approximately 600 requests per second for around 300 concurrent requests (see Figure 5.15(a)). As expected, the performance decreases to about 300 requests

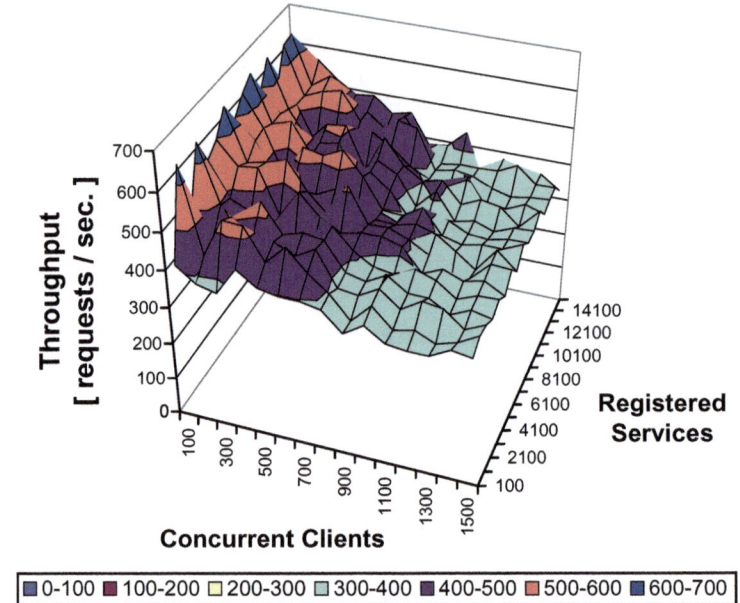

(a) WASP-based Registry.

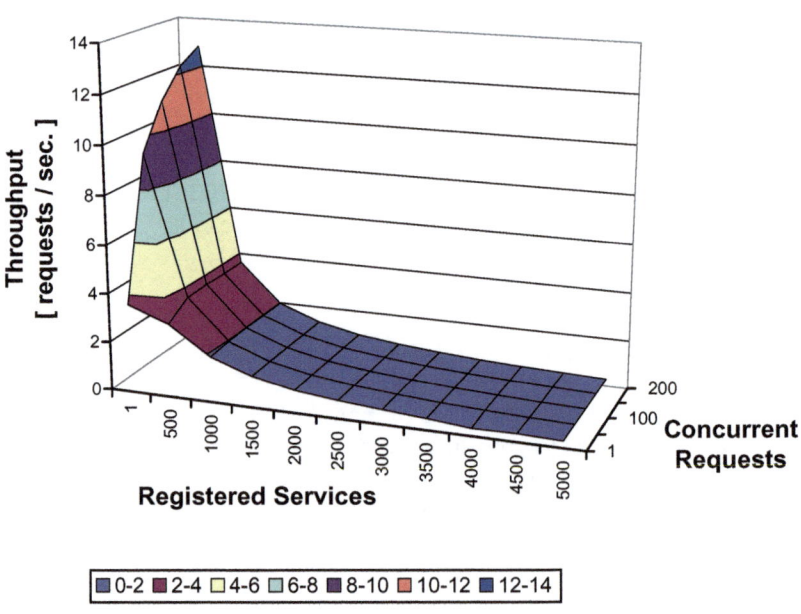

(b) GT3-based VORegistry.

Fig. 5.15. The Registry throughput results.

per second in the case of 1500 concurrent clients. The number of registered services does not influence the overall performance due to the hash table-based organisation of services in our implementation. The various peaks in the graph are due to the Java Virtual Machine management of this memory intensive application and the occasional garbage collection invocations. We expect to see the same sustained performance for higher number of services until the memory limits are reached and the Registry starts swapping.

For the GT3 VORegistry, the throughput of the service lookup operations based on findServiceData XPath queries rapidly decreases with the number of registered services (see Figure 5.15(b)). The reason is the sequential organisation of the service data elements into a single XML document which is clearly not a scalable approach for high throughput discovery.

5.8.7 Security

We represent the user identity using the GSI standard (see Section 2.4) based on a private and public key pair plus an X.509 certificate. We realise the secure communication across Grid services based on message level WS-Security [131] standard that describes enhancements to SOAP for message integrity through XML digital signatures, message confidentiality through XML encryption, and single message authentication. Our GT3-based implementation includes complete GSI support comprising proxy delegation from the client to the Grid services, which is the main limitation of the WASP PKI-based security across pure Web services. This limitation is critical in using ZENTURIO experiment management tool in several situations, for example in the following typical use scenarios:

1. The WASP-based Grid services employ the real user private (and public) key for mutual authentication which may be a crucial security flow;
2. When the Factory (running potentially with administration permissions) creates a new Grid service, it is often natural to give to the newly created instance the identity of the end-user that requested it. This requires that the remote service instance have access to the user private key which is an unacceptable security risk. Through the GSI delegation mechanism, the Factory delivers a limited proxy to the service instance that impersonates the user for a limited time interval that significantly reduces the security risks;
3. Similarly, it is natural to generate and execute the experiments of a performance or parameter study on the target Grid site using the identity of the client that requested them, rather than some neutral identity of the Experiment Generator and Experiment Executor services;
4. When multiple Grid services are chained in a workflow, they often need act on behalf on the end-user. Similarly to the Factory case, the proxy delegation achieves this goal with less security risks than propagating the user private key on all Grid sites that host the services from the workflow chain.

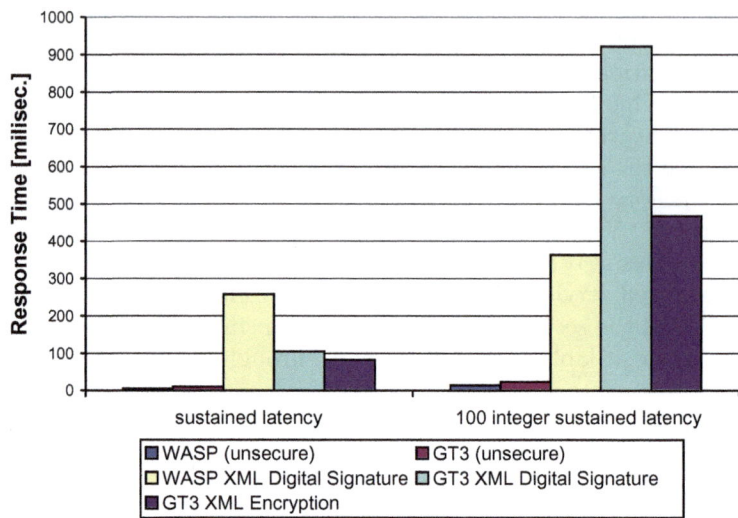

Fig. 5.16. The secure versus insecure response time comparison.

We employ GSI in the WASP implementation too when interacting with the Globus infrastructure services like GASS, GRAM, and GridFTP.

The XML message-based security provides a significantly higher degree of security than the SSL transport-based security protocols (i.e. it is easier to read a credit card number from an XML message than from a network packet), however at a higher latency price. We performed a small test for both WASP and GT3-based implementations that shows an increase in latency of about two orders of magnitude with each authenticated call, as opposed to the non-secure version (see Figure 5.16). This high overhead is due to the additional message exchanges between the client and the Grid service needed for performing the mutual authentication.

5.8.8 Grid Service Throughput

During the testing phase of the GT3-based prototype of ZENTURIO on various performance and parameter studies, we experienced a severe decrease in the responsiveness of the overall Grid middleware services layer compared to the WASP-based version. The performance was particularly poor in two situations:

1. when the Experiment Generator service generates experiments at a high rate and delivers them immediately to the Experiment Executor service for execution;
2. when many notification events are sent to the User Portal at the same time as a result of multiple experiments changing state simultaneously.

We therefore conducted a small automatic benchmark test using ZENTURIO that compares the WASP and GT3 service throughput. The purpose was not to perform a fair benchmark between the two SOAP implementations, nor to debug their internal source code to detect the real cause of the performance bottleneck, but rather to highlight an existing GT3 performance bug. We measured the service throughput in requests per second for the following three different SOAP invocations:

1. an array of 100 elements;
2. a string of 100 characters;
3. an array of 100 strings of 100 characters each.

We included no input argument to the requests (i.e not an echo test) because we expect most of the real-world Grid applications to send small requests most of the time. We performed all experiments on a four processor 750 megahertz SMP Sun-fire parallel computer with nine gigabytes of memory to avoid network delays and processor contention between the client and the hosting environment. We used the default serialisers and SOAP encodings of each (i.e. WASP and Axis) SOAP engine. We pre-built the array and the string structures on the server as static data members and configured a start-up period of 100 transactions to ignore service loading and other optimisation settings specific to each hosting environment. We used the default hosting environments provided by WASP and GT3 distributions, plus an additional test where both SOAP platforms are deployed within the Tomcat [119] hosting environment for fairness reasons. We performed the same test also for vanilla Apache Axis deployed in Tomcat. We properly configured all hosting environments to accommodate the full amount of concurrent requests needed. We automatically conducted the experiments with ZENTURIO using a benchmark client similar to the one shown in Example 5.4 (i.e. ZEN variable clnts).

Our results depicted in Figure 5.17 show that WASP is doubling the throughput offered by the GT3 implementation. The object size and the memory consumption are similar in both implementations (though WASP has an overall memory usage slightly larger). The performance differences are due to a more mature streaming architecture offered by WASP which includes interception, XML parsing, and SOAP message processing. As expected, GT3 displays similar performance with vanilla Apache Axis, since it does not add any overhead on top of the JAX-RPC serialisation. The Tomcat deployment does not influence the results significantly, though for WASP it introduces a slight overhead. The poor performance of the GT3-alpha release (which was the initial implementation platform that motivated our entire benchmark) on manipulating arrays was due to a serialisation performance problem in the underlying Axis 1.1 Release Candidate 2 used.

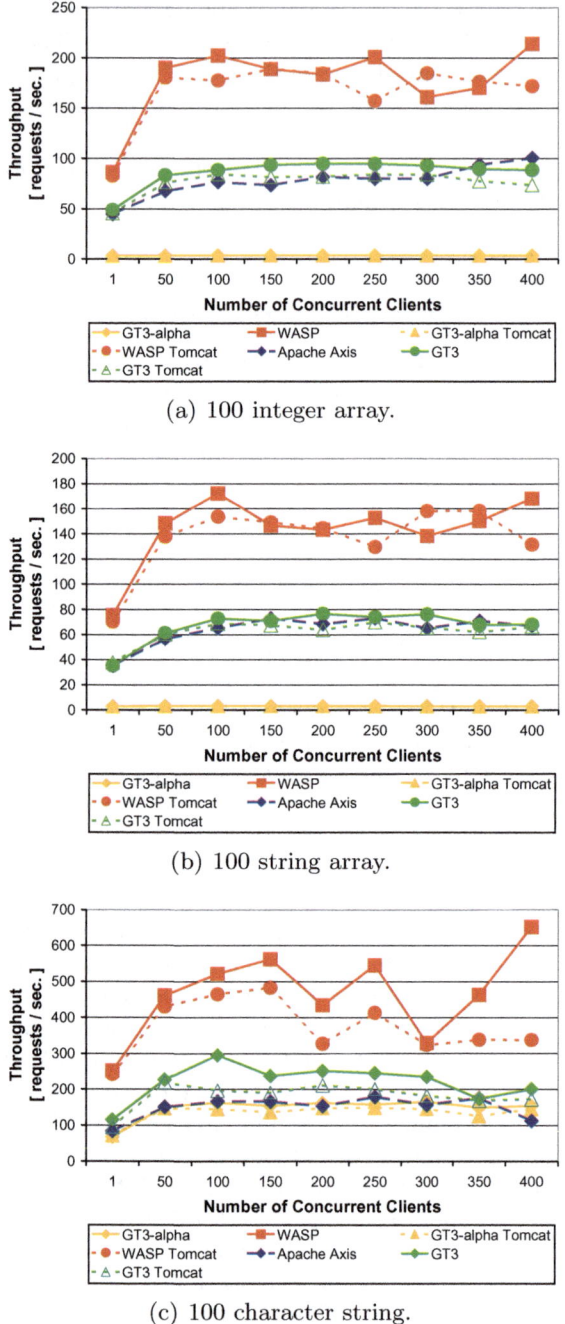

(a) 100 integer array.

(b) 100 string array.

(c) 100 character string.

Fig. 5.17. The throughput results of WASP, GT3, and vanilla Axis services.

Table 5.5. The comparative analysis of WASP versus GT3-based Grid services.

Functionality	ZENTURIO WASP	ZENTURIO GT3
WSDL interface	single `portType`	OGSI compliant
Grid service	Abstract Grid Service	`GridService` interface
Registry	yes	yes (VORegistry)
Factory	yes	yes
service creation	dynamic, on-the-fly	static, pre-installed
service lifecycle	WASP proprietary	OGSI compliant
events	WASP proprietary Producer-Consumer	OGSI compliant `NotificationSource-Sink`
pull events	asynchronous methods	Service data queries
service state	Java Bean access methods	WSDL `findServiceData` introspection
Service Repository	custom UDDI-based	no
security	SOAP XML message, no delegation	SOAP XML message, GSI delegation
stubs	runtime, dynamic	static, compile-time
input structures	arbitrarily complex	Java Beans only
service throughput	200 req./sec., 100 int array 400 req./sec., 100 char string	100 req./sec., 100 int array 200 req./sec., 100 char string
registry throughput	Registry service $700 - 300$ req./sec.	VORegistry service $50 - 0.1$ requests/second
WSIF support	no	yes

5.8.9 Comparison

We present in Table 5.5 a summary of the various features that we comparatively analysed in the WASP and GT3-based implementations.

Despite the portability limitation, there are some clear advantages in our WASP-based implementation compared to the GT3-based prototype:

1. WASP generates stubs to remote services dynamically at runtime which avoids unnecessary compilation steps. GT3 Apache Axis generates stubs statically at compile-time which restricts the implementation of WSDL complex structures to Java Beans;
2. The WASP-based Factory allows runtime on-the-fly service creation and deployment. We could not achieve this feature in the GT3-based prototype which restricts the transient service creation to pre-deployed services. This is a severe limitation in a Grid environment where creating services dynamically on unknown remote sites is a mandatory requirement;
3. We define a novel use of the UDDI standard for storing implementations of transient Grid services;
4. Our WASP-based services provide a better throughput which is important in a heavily used Grid environment with multiple concurrent clients;

5. Our WASP-based Registry service provides a much better throughput than the GT3 VORegistry, the reason being the hash table-based organisation or the registered services, as opposed to the sequential XML-based service data document provided by the VORegistry.

5.9 Summary

We presented in this comprehensive section a distributed service-oriented environment for interoperable tool development consisting of three layers compliant with the abstract Grid architectural model introduced in Chapter 2. We described a set of online performance and debugging software tools that make use of dynamic instrumentation technology to instrument and perform on-the-fly runtime analysis of running applications. We classified the tool interoperability and presented a variety of scenarios how cooperative use of tools can improve the effectiveness in the software engineering process of applications. Finally, we presented the individual services that we designed as part of our architecture, including generic Factory, Registry, Aggregator, Dynamic Instrumentor, UDDI Service Repository, and an event framework based on the XML Web services technology that ensures interoperability in a Grid environment. We introduced new custom solutions for modeling state and lifecycle using a toolkit implementing standard Web services technologies and compare our approach against other standardisation efforts under way in the Grid computing field at the time we carried out the work.

6

Optimisation Framework

We introduced in Chapter 4 the ZENTURIO experiment management tool for multi-experimental performance and parameter studies of parallel applications. To achieve this goal, ZENTURIO performs an automatic *exhaustive sweep* of the entire parameter space defined using the ZEN directive-based experiment specification language described in Chapter 3.

With the emergence of Grid computing that aggregates a potentially unbounded number of resources, new classes of applications such as workflows and parameter studies are of increasing interest to the scientists. The parameter space of such large scale Grid applications can easily achieve rather huge dimensions for which the exhaustive parameter sweep performed by ZENTURIO is no longer a feasible solution. In general, a complete parameter sweep gives useful detailed insight on the application behaviour but also produces vast amounts of data that are irrelevant for further studies. Often the user's ultimate goal is to find parameter combinations that *optimise* a certain application behaviour, such as a performance metric or an output result. Such optimisation problems are known as *NP-complete* [85] and require advanced heuristics to find approximate or reasonably good solutions.

In this chapter we extend ZENTURIO with a generic optimisation framework [145] sketched in Figure 6.1 that employs general purpose (meta-) heuristics for solving NP-complete performance and parameter optimisation problems for parallel and Grid applications. The input to the optimisation framework consists of a ZEN application and an objective function. The ZEN application defines through ZEN directives a large parameter space impossible to be exhaustively explored. The ZEN application represents the input to a heuristic-based *search engine* that attempts to find a ZEN application instance which maximises the optimisation function. For the realisation of the search engine we consider general purpose meta-heuristics like genetic algorithms.

Definition 6.1. *Let $\mathcal{A}$ denote a ZEN application and $\mathcal{V}^{\mathcal{A}}$ its value set defined in Chapter 3 (see Definition 3.19) representing the complete set of possible experiments which defines a search space of size $\left| \mathcal{V}^{\mathcal{A}} \right|$ (i.e. the cardinality*

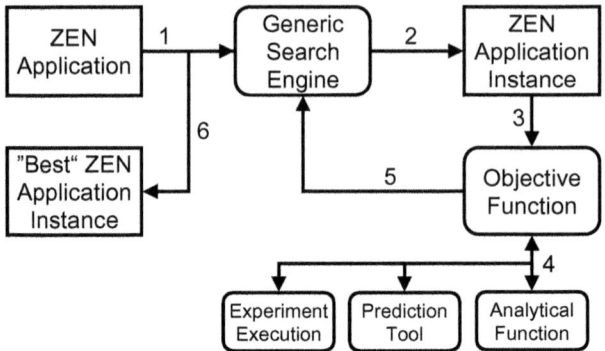

Fig. 6.1. The ZENTURIO optimisation framework design.

of the value set). We define the objective function *to be maximised by the optimisation framework with the following problem independent signature:*

$$\mathcal{F} : \mathcal{V}^{\mathcal{A}} \to \mathbb{R}.$$

The objective function is the only module whose implementation depends on the target application which must be supplied for each particular optimisation problem separately. In case of performance tuning of parallel applications, the objective function is a performance metric defined through ZEN performance directives as defined in Section 3.2.9 and evaluated through *experiment execution* (see Definition 3.27). In case of scheduling problems, the objective function can be implemented by a *performance prediction tool* [68], or approximated through an application specific *analytical function*. We provide in our framework a generic objective function interface that hides its internal problem dependencies, thus keeping the search engine entirely generic (see Definition 6.1).

To support optimisation scenarios in ZENTURIO, we replace the exhaustive experiment generation algorithm presented in Section 3.2.11 and encoded as part of the Experiment Generator service (see Section 4.4.1 and Figure 4.23) with the heuristic-based search engine that we applied on three concrete problems:

1. scheduling of single Grid workflow applications in Section 6.1;
2. scheduling of large sets of independent activities (e.g. parameter studies) for high throughput on the Grid in Section 6.4;
3. optimisation of parallel applications, with particular focus on data distribution on heterogeneous Grid resources in Section 6.5.

For the realisation of the problem independent search engine we address a genetic algorithm in Section 6.2 and plan to study new general purpose heuristics like subdivision, simplex methods, or simulated annealing in future work.

6.1 Workflow Scheduling

Workflow modeling is a well established area in computer science that was strongly influenced by business process modeling work [187]. Recently, the Grid community generally acknowledged that orchestrating existing applications in large scale workflows represents a promising paradigm for programming wide area Grid environments [1, 7, 10, 26, 65, 106, 114, 127].

On computational Grids, we see two distinct aspects related to the general workflow scheduling problem:

1. *static scheduling* targets mapping of an entire workflow application onto a fixed set of resources that optimises a certain performance metric. We address this problem in this section as an instantiation of the ZENTURIO optimisation framework using genetic algorithms;
2. *runtime rescheduling* is a steering problem that adaptively changes the workflow schedule to the dynamic availability of Grid resources which we will addressed in Chapter 7 (see Section 7.3.5).

Scheduling a workflow of n activities onto m computational Grid resources is a well known NP-complete optimisation problem of $\mathcal{O}(m^n)$ (exponential) complexity [183]. In this section we formally instantiate the workflow scheduling problem within the ZENTURIO optimisation framework using the workflow model introduced in Chapter 2 (see Section 2.6.3).

Definition 6.2. *A ZEN variable z is an application parameter that represents an abstract machine which can be a sequential processor or a parallel computer (see Section 2.6.1). A ZEN application $\mathcal{A}(z_1, \ldots, z_n) = (Nodes, C\text{-}edges)$ implements a workflow as defined in Definition 2.7, where:*

1. $\forall \; CA(z) \in Nodes \implies z \in \{z_1, \ldots, z_n\};$
2. $\forall \; DA(z, z') \in Nodes \implies \{z, z'\} \subset \{z_1, \ldots, z_n\}.$

The value set $\mathcal{V}^{z_i}$ of a ZEN variable z_i represents the entire set of concrete processors of all Grid sites available. A workflow schedule is a mapping:

$$\mathcal{S}_\mathcal{A} = \mathcal{S}\left(\mathcal{A}(z_1, \ldots, z_n)\right) = \mathcal{AI}(e_1, \ldots, e_n), \; \forall \; e_i \in \mathcal{V}^{z_i}, \; \forall \; i \in [1..n].$$

Within $\mathcal{AI}$, a computational activity schedule is a mapping:

$$\mathcal{S}_{CA(z_j)} = e_j, \; e_j \in \mathcal{V}^{z_j}$$

and a data transfer schedule is a mapping:

$$\mathcal{S}_{DA(z_k, z_l)} = (e_k, e_l), \; e_k \in \mathcal{V}^{z_k} \; \wedge \; e_l \in \mathcal{V}^{z_l}.$$

Finding the workflow schedule that maximises the objective function is the (static) workflow scheduling problem.

Example 6.3 (Java CoG-based workflow).

```
//ZEN$ SUBSTITUTE z1 = { e{1:100} }
//ZEN$ SUBSTITUTE z2 = { e{1:100} }
//ZEN$ SUBSTITUTE z3 = { e{1:100} }
//ZEN$ SUBSTITUTE z4 = { e{1:100} }
//ZEN$ SUBSTITUTE z5 = { e{1:100} }

Task ca1 = createCA("z1");
Task ca2 = createCA("z2");
Task ca3 = createCA("z3");
Task da4 = createDA("z1", "z4");
Task ca5 = createCA("z4");
Task da6 = createDA("z4", "z1");
Task ca7 = createCA("z5");
Task ca8 = createCA("z1");

TaskGraph taskGraph = new TaskGraphImpl();
taskGraph.add(ca1);
taskGraph.add(ca2);
taskGraph.add(ca3);
taskGraph.add(da4);
taskGraph.add(ca5);
taskGraph.add(da6);
taskGraph.add(ca7);
taskGraph.add(ca8);

Dependency dependency = new DependencyImpl();
dependency.add(ca1, ca2);
dependency.add(ca1, ca3);
dependency.add(ca1, da4);
dependency.add(ca2, ca5);
dependency.add(ca3, ca5);
dependency.add(da4, ca5);
dependency.add(ca5, da6);
dependency.add(ca5, ca7);
dependency.add(da6, ca8);
dependency.add(ca7, ca8);
taskGraph.setDependency(dependency);
```

We base our proof of concept implementation on the a low level workflow package provided by the Java CoG kit [9]. Example 6.3 sketches an implementation of the workflow depicted in Figure 6.5 annotated as a ZEN application denoted as $\mathcal{A}(z_1, z_2, z_3, z_4, z_5)$, where z_1, z_2, z_3, z_4, and z_5 are the abstract machines where the workflow activities need to be scheduled. The

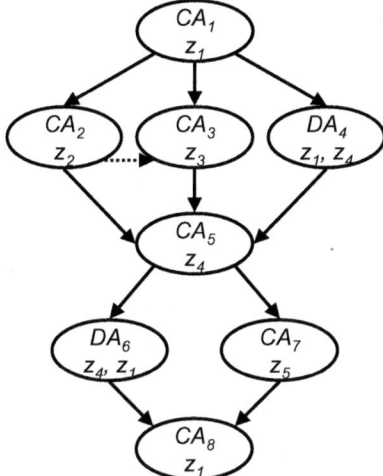

Fig. 6.2. A sample workflow application.

ZEN directive annotations define the aggregated set of processors of all Grid sites available (with cardinality 100 in our example) that instantiate each abstract machine within a workflow schedule. The search space in this example contains $100^5 = 10^7$ points.

Since Grid workflows can often consist of hundreds to thousands of activities running in dynamic infrastructures, it is inconvenient for the user to manually annotate the application as illustrated in Example 6.3. We use instead the instrumentation interface provided by the Experiment Generator service that we described in Section 4.4.1 for dynamic runtime annotation of the application with ZEN directives. We instantiate the value set of each ZEN variable with Grid site information based on the actual availability obtained by querying the Globus MDS information service.

6.1.1 Schedule Dependencies

Definition 6.4. *If the same ZEN variable or abstract machine appears in the definition of two distinct activities (see Definition 2.7), it defines a* static *schedule dependency.*

A typical example is the abstract machine z_4 in the sample workflow depicted in Figure 6.2, where the activity CA_5 (z_4) stages in its input file from the machine z_1 through the activity DA_4 (z_1, z_4) and stages out its output file to the machine z_1 through the activity DA_6 (z_4, z_1). Static schedule dependencies can also be set between CA activities. In Figure 6.2 for example, the activities CA_1 (z_1) and CA_8 (z_1) define a static schedule dependence that restricts their schedule to the same concrete machine, i.e. $\mathcal{S}_{CA_1(z_1)} = \mathcal{S}_{CA_8(z_1)}$.

Definition 6.5. *Let* $CA_1, \ldots, CA_m$ *be a set of independent computational activities such that* $\mathcal{S}_{CA_1} = \ldots = \mathcal{S}_{CA_m}$. *A valid workflow schedule is obtained by augmenting the original workflow application with* runtime schedule dependencies *that prohibit two independent computational activities run on the same processor concurrently:*

$$C\text{-}edges' = C\text{-}edges \bigcup_{\substack{\forall\, i \in [1..m-1]\, \wedge \\ \mathcal{S}_{CA_i} = \mathcal{S}_{CA_{i+1}}}} (CA_i, CA_{i+1}).$$

The reason for introducing runtime schedule dependencies is the fact that executing two computational intensive processes in sequence on the same processor is faster than competing for processor cycles or other resources. However, we do not define runtime schedule dependency constraints on data transfers since multiple streams over the same high performance network are likely to increase the overall bandwidth utilisation due to limitations of the TCP protocol caused by limited window and buffer sizes, slow recovery upon packet loss, or slow restart after idle connections.

We illustrate in Figure 6.2 such a runtime schedule dependency between the activities CA_2 and CA_3 assuming that $\mathcal{S}_{CA_2} = \mathcal{S}_{CA_3}$, which adds a new element to the set of workflow control flow dependencies:

$$C\text{-}edges' = C\text{-}edges \cup \{(CA_2, CA_3)\}.$$

If a runtime schedule dependency involves m independent activities, there are $m!$ possible runtime schedule dependencies that must be evaluated. We expect in practice that this number m be relatively low or irrelevant (i.e. involving similar activities for which the execution order does not matter) and, therefore, does not add an extra complexity to our scheduling problem.

6.1.2 Objective Function

The objective function for the scheduling problem is represented by a performance metric to be optimised. The computation of workflow performance metrics for scheduling purposes relies on *prediction* techniques for each individual activity which is a difficult research topic [68] that goes beyond the scheduling work that we target in this chapter. We adopt in the following a simple general prediction model that we successfully applied for some of the real-world applications that we used to validate our work (see Section 6.3.1).

Definition 6.6. *Let* N *be an arbitrary activity with the schedule* $\mathcal{S}_N$. *We approximate the* predicted execution time *of activity* N *onto* $\mathcal{S}_N$ *is as:*

$$T_N^{\mathcal{S}_N} = \mathcal{L} + \frac{W_N}{v_{\mathcal{S}_N}},$$

where $\mathcal{L}$ *denotes the latency required to start the activity,* W_N *denotes for the* work *of activity* N, *and* $v_{\mathcal{S}_N}$ *the speed of* $\mathcal{S}_N$ *with the following semantics:*

1. $\mathcal{L}$ is the latency usually dominated by the GSI-based mutual authentication to the Grid services (e.g. GRAM and GridFTP), as well as queuing and polling for termination time when interacting with local resource managers;
2. W_{CA} represents the total number of floating point operations of activity CA;
3. $v_{\mathcal{S}_{CA}}$ represents the performance rate of the machine $\mathcal{S}_{CA}$ in floating point operations per second, e.g. as measured using the LINPACK benchmark [56];
4. W_{DA} approximates the size of the file to be transferred;
5. $v_{\mathcal{S}_{DA}}$ is the bandwidth of a single TCP stream between e_1 and e_2, where $\mathcal{S}_{DA} = (e_1, e_2)$.

Definition 6.7. Let $\mathcal{A} = (Nodes, C\text{-}edges)$ denote a workflow application. We evaluate a workflow schedule $\mathcal{S}$ by constructing the Gantt chart that simulates the workflow execution. The end timestamp of each workflow activity $N \in Nodes$ is recursively defined by the following function:

$$end : Nodes \longrightarrow \mathbb{R}_+^*,$$

$$end(N) = \begin{cases} T_N^{\mathcal{S}_N}, & pred(N) = \emptyset; \\ \max_{(N', N) \in C\text{-}edges} \left\{ end\left(N'\right) \right\} + T_N^{\mathcal{S}_N}, & pred(N) \neq \emptyset, \end{cases}$$

where $\mathbb{R}_+^*$ denotes the set of real positive non-zero numbers and $\emptyset$ the empty set.

Figure 6.3 illustrates a sample Gantt chart for the workflow depicted in Figure 6.5, assuming the runtime schedule dependency (CA_2, CA_3) (i.e. $\mathcal{S}_{CA_2} = \mathcal{S}_{CA_3}$), where:

$$end(CA_1) = T_{CA_1}^{e_1};$$
$$end(CA_2) = end(CA_1) + T_{CA_2}^{e_2};$$
$$end(CA_3) = end(CA_2) + T_{CA_3}^{e_3};$$
$$end(DA_4) = end(CA_1) + T_{CA_3}^{(e_1, e_4)};$$
$$end(CA_5) = \max\left\{ end(CA_2), end(CA_3), end(DA_4) \right\} + T_{CA_5}^{e_4};$$
$$end(DA_6) = end(CA_5) + T_{DA_6}^{(e_4, e_1)};$$
$$end(CA_7) = end(CA_5) + T_{CA_7}^{e_5};$$
$$end(CA_8) = \max\left\{ end(DA_6), end(CA_7) \right\} + T_{CA_8}^{e_1}.$$

Definition 6.8. Let $\rho = \{N_1, \ldots, N_p\}$ denote a workflow execution path, i.e. $pred(N_1) = \emptyset \wedge succ(N_p) = \emptyset \wedge (N_i, N_{i+1}) \in C\text{-}edges, \forall i \in [1..p-1]$. If N_p is the activity with the maximum end time and ρ is the shortest path to N_p then ρ is called the critical schedule path:

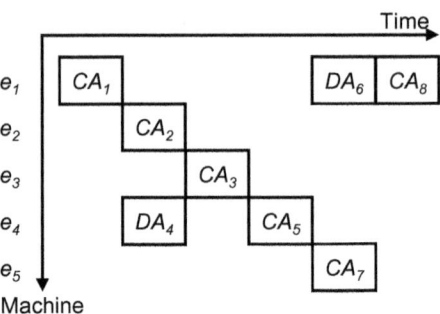

Fig. 6.3. A sample Gantt chart for the workflow depicted in Figure 6.2, assuming that $e_2 = e_3$ (i.e. $\mathcal{S}_{CA_2} = \mathcal{S}_{CA_3}$).

1. $end\left(N_p\right) = \max\limits_{\forall\, N \in Nodes\, \wedge\, succ(N)=\emptyset} \{end(N)\};$

2. $\sum_{\forall\, N \in \rho} T_N^{\mathcal{S}_N} \leq \sum_{\forall\, N' \in \rho'} T_{N'}^{\mathcal{S}_{N'}}, \; \forall\, \rho' = \left\{N_1', \ldots, N_q'\right\}$ a workflow execution path (i.e. $pred\left(N_1'\right) = \emptyset \;\wedge\; succ\left(N_q'\right) = \emptyset \;\wedge\; \left(N_i', N_{i+1}'\right) \in$ C-edges, $\forall\, i \in [1..q-1]$), such that $end\left(N_p\right) = end\left(N_q'\right).$

Let $\mathcal{A} = \left(Nodes = Nodes^{CA} \cup Nodes^{DA},\, C\text{-edges}\right)$ denote a workflow application and $\mathcal{AI}\left(e_1, \ldots, e_n\right)$ a workflow schedule. In the following, we give a range of sample *workflow performance metrics* representing useful objective functions that can be simply plugged-in to the optimisation framework. Since we designed the framework to solve maximum problems, we need to subtract some of the workflow metrics that require minimisation from a large enough constant $\mathcal{C}$.

- *Execution time* (or makespan):

$$\mathcal{F}(\mathcal{AI}) = \mathcal{C} - T_{\mathcal{AI}},$$
$$T_{\mathcal{AI}} = end\left(N_p\right),$$

  where $\{N_1, \ldots, N_p\}$ is the critical schedule path;
- *Speedup* uses the sequential execution time on the fastest machine as the reference execution time:

$$\mathcal{F}(\mathcal{AI}) = S_{\mathcal{AI}},$$
$$S_{\mathcal{AI}} = \frac{T_{\mathcal{AI}}^{seq}}{T_{\mathcal{AI}(e_1, \ldots, e_n)}},$$
$$T_{\mathcal{AI}}^{seq} = \min\limits_{\forall\, i \in [1..n]} \left\{ T_{\mathcal{AI}(e_i, \ldots, e_i)} \right\},$$
$$T_{\mathcal{AI}(e_i, \ldots, e_i)} = \sum\limits_{\forall\, CA \in Nodes^{CA}} T_{CA}^{e_i},$$

  where $\mathcal{AI}\left(e_i, \ldots, e_i\right)$ is the sequential workflow schedule on machine e_i;

- *Efficiency* normalises the speedup against the sum of all the processors where each individual activity is scheduled, where each processor is weighted with its relative speed in computing the workflow sequentially:

$$\mathcal{F}(\mathcal{AI}) = E_{\mathcal{AI}},$$

$$E_{\mathcal{AI}} = \frac{S_{\mathcal{AI}}}{\sum_{i=1}^{n} \frac{T_{\mathcal{AI}}^{seq}}{T_{\mathcal{AI}(e_i,\ldots,e_i)}}} = \frac{T_{\mathcal{AI}(e_1,\ldots,e_n)}^{-1}}{\sum_{i=1}^{n} T_{\mathcal{AI}(e_i,\ldots,e_i)}^{-1}}.$$

Maximising the efficiency combined with minimisation of the execution time is a good metric for high *throughput scheduling* in the context of multiple workflows or parameter studies;
- *Communication* due to file transfer activities on the critical path:

$$\mathcal{F}(\mathcal{AI}) = \mathcal{C} - COM_{\mathcal{AI}},$$

$$COM_{\mathcal{AI}} = \sum_{\forall N \in \rho \cap Nodes^{DA}} T_N^{\mathcal{S}_N},$$

where ρ is the critical schedule path;
- *Synchronisation* due to activity dependencies on the critical schedule path:

$$\mathcal{F}(\mathcal{AI}) = \mathcal{C} - SYN_{\mathcal{AI}},$$

$$SYN_{\mathcal{AI}} = T_{\mathcal{AI}} - \sum_{\forall N \in \rho} T_N^{\mathcal{S}_N},$$

where ρ is the critical schedule path;
- *Load balance* due to uneven work distribution:

$$\mathcal{F}(\mathcal{AI}) = LB_{\mathcal{AI}},$$

$$LB_{\mathcal{AI}} = \frac{\underset{\forall e \in \bigcup_{i=1}^{n} e_i}{avg} \left\{ \sum_{\forall CA \in Nodes^{CA} \wedge S_{CA}=e} T_{CA}^e \right\}}{\underset{\forall e \in \bigcup_{i=1}^{n} e_i}{max} \left\{ \sum_{\forall CA \in Nodes^{CA} \wedge S_{CA}=e} T_{CA}^e \right\}}.$$

$LB_{\mathcal{AI}} = 1$ indicates the perfect load balance and $LB_{\mathcal{AI}} = 0$ the worst case load balance;
- *Total overhead* is defined by the Amdahl's law [8]:

$$\mathcal{F}(\mathcal{AI}) = \mathcal{C} - O_{\mathcal{AI}},$$

$$O_{\mathcal{AI}} = T_{\mathcal{AI}} - \frac{T_{\mathcal{AI}}^{seq}}{\sum_{i=1}^{n} \frac{T_{\mathcal{AI}}^{seq}}{T_{\mathcal{AI}(e_i,\ldots,e_i)}}} =$$

$$= \sum_{\forall N \in \rho \cap Nodes^{CA}} T_N^{\mathcal{S}_N} + COM_{\mathcal{AI}} + SYN_{\mathcal{AI}} - \frac{1}{\sum_{i=1}^{n} T_{\mathcal{AI}(e_i,\ldots,e_i)}^{-1}};$$

- *Loss of parallelism* due to heterogeneity and activity dependencies on the critical path:

$$\mathcal{F}(\mathcal{AI}) = \mathcal{C} - LP_{\mathcal{AI}},$$

$$LP_{\mathcal{AI}} = O_{\mathcal{AI}} - COM_{\mathcal{AI}} - SYN_{\mathcal{AI}} =$$

$$= \sum_{\forall N \in \rho \cap Nodes^{CA}} T_N^{S_N} - \frac{1}{\sum_{i=1}^{n} T_{\mathcal{AI}(e_i,\dots,e_i)}^{-1}};$$

We instantiate these metrics for the workflow defined in Example 6.3 and depicted in Figure 6.2 as follows:

- $T_{\mathcal{AI}} = end(CA_8);$

- $S_{\mathcal{AI}} = \dfrac{\min\limits_{\forall\, i \in [1..5]}\left\{ T_{\mathcal{AI}(e_i,\dots,e_i)} \right\}}{end(CA_8)}$, where $T_{\mathcal{AI}(e_i,\dots,e_i)} = T_{CA_1}^{e_i} + T_{CA_2}^{e_i} + T_{CA_3}^{e_i} + T_{CA_5}^{e_i} + T_{CA_7}^{e_i} + T_{CA_8}^{e_i};$

- $E_{\mathcal{AI}} = \dfrac{end(CA_8)^{-1}}{\sum_{i=1}^{5} T_{\mathcal{AI}(e_i,\dots,e_i)}^{-1}};$

- $COM_{\mathcal{AI}} = T_{DA_4}^{(e_1,e_4)} + T_{DA_6}^{(e_4,e_1)};$

- $SYN_{\mathcal{AI}} = T_{\mathcal{AI}} - T_{CA_1}^{e_1} - T_{CA_2}^{e_2} - T_{CA_5}^{e_4} - T_{DA_6}^{(e_4,e_1)} - T_{CA_8}^{e_1}$, where the workflow path $(CA_1, CA_2, CA_5, DA_6, CA_8)$ is the critical schedule path, which assumes that the following conditions hold:

$$T_{CA_1}^{e_1} + T_{CA_2}^{e_2} + T_{CA_5}^{e_4} + T_{DA_6}^{(e_4,e_1)} + T_{CA_8}^{e_1} \leq T_{CA_1}^{e_1} + T_{CA_3}^{e_3} + T_{CA_5}^{e_4} + T_{DA_6}^{(e_4,e_1)} + T_{CA_8}^{e_1};$$

$$T_{CA_1}^{e_1} + T_{CA_2}^{e_2} + T_{CA_5}^{e_4} + T_{DA_6}^{(e_4,e_1)} + T_{CA_8}^{e_1} \leq T_{CA_1}^{e_1} + T_{DA_4}^{(e_1,e_4)} + T_{CA_5}^{e_4} + T_{DA_6}^{(e_4,e_1)} + T_{CA_8}^{e_1};$$

$$T_{CA_1}^{e_1} + T_{CA_2}^{e_2} + T_{CA_5}^{e_4} + T_{DA_6}^{(e_4,e_1)} + T_{CA_8}^{e_1} \leq T_{CA_1}^{e_1} + T_{CA_2}^{e_2} + T_{CA_5}^{e_4} + T_{CA_7}^{e_5} + T_{CA_8}^{e_1};$$

$$T_{CA_1}^{e_1} + T_{CA_2}^{e_2} + T_{CA_5}^{e_4} + T_{DA_6}^{(e_4,e_1)} + T_{CA_8}^{e_1} \leq T_{CA_1}^{e_1} + T_{CA_3}^{e_3} + T_{CA_5}^{e_4} + T_{CA_7}^{e_5} + T_{CA_8}^{e_1};$$

$$T_{CA_1}^{e_1} + T_{CA_2}^{e_2} + T_{CA_5}^{e_4} + T_{DA_6}^{(e_4,e_1)} + T_{CA_8}^{e_1} \leq T_{CA_1}^{e_1} + T_{DA_4}^{(e_1,e_4)} + T_{CA_5}^{e_4} + T_{CA_7}^{e_5} + T_{CA_8}^{e_1};$$

- $LB_{\mathcal{AI}} = \dfrac{avg\left\{ T_{CA_1}^{e_1} + T_{CA_8}^{e_1}, T_{CA_3}^{e_3}, T_{CA_5}^{e_4}, T_{CA_7}^{e_5} \right\}}{max\left\{ T_{CA_1}^{e_1} + T_{CA_8}^{e_1}, T_{CA_3}^{e_3}, T_{CA_5}^{e_4}, T_{CA_7}^{e_5} \right\}}.$

The two remaining metrics (i.e. total overhead and loss of parallelism) derive from these five presented.

6.2 Genetic Search Engine

Genetic algorithms [88] are a class of randomised optimisation programs which mimic the natural evolution of *individuals* in a *population*. Genetic algorithms use a vocabulary borrowed from natural genetics. Often individuals are called *chromosomes* which are made of units called *genes* arranged in linear succession. Genes are located at certain places in the chromosome called *loci*. The value of a gene which determines one character of an individual (such as hair colour) is called *allele*. The genetic algorithms are iterative algorithms that start from an initial population and use natural evolution operators on the population individuals. The *selection* operator selects some better fit individuals from the population according to a *fitness function*. The selected individuals then qualify for *reproduction, crossover*, and *mutation* with certain probabilities and, as a result, produce a new population of more superior individuals. The iterative process continues on the newly formed population until a convergence criterion is fulfilled.

In this section we present a sample instantiation of the generic search engine provided by the ZENTURIO optimisation framework based on a classical generational genetic algorithm. Our algorithm is independent of the objective function and therefore can be applied to arbitrary optimisation problems provided that an appropriate search space and objective function are properly defined. For the workflow scheduling problem, we define the search space through ZEN directives as presented in Section 6.1, while the objective function is instantiated by the performance metrics that we formally defined in Section 6.1.2.

Definition 6.9. *Let* $\mathcal{A}(z_1, \ldots, z_n)$ *denote a ZEN application, where* z_i *are ZEN variables,* $\forall\, i \in [1..n]$ *and let* $\mathcal{V}^{z_i}$ *denote the value set of a ZEN variable* z_i. *A* gene *is a ZEN variable* z_i. *An* allele *is a gene instantiation, i.e. a ZEN element* $e_i \in \mathcal{V}^{z_i}$. *The totally ordered set* $\{z_1, \ldots, z_n\}$ *of all ZEN variables of* $\mathcal{A}$ *is a* chromosome. *The* locus i *of a gene* z_i *is given by its index within the totally ordered set chromosome. An* individual *is a ZEN application instance* $\mathcal{AI}(e_1, \ldots, e_n)$, *where* $e_i \in \mathcal{V}^{z_i}$, $\forall\, i \in [1..n]$. *We defined the* objective function, *called in genetic terms* fitness function, *in Definition 6.1.*

Based on this definition, we illustrate in the following the generic encoding of the genetic algorithm sketched in Algorithm 4.

6.2.1 Initial Population

We build the *initial population* of individuals of fixed size p by generating a random set of ZEN application instances by assigning random ZEN elements from the value set to ZEN variables (line 2):

$$POP = \bigcup_{i=1}^{p} \mathcal{AI}_i(e_1, \ldots, e_n),\ e_j \in \mathcal{V}^{z_j},\ \forall\, j \in [1..n].$$

Usually, the appropriate population size p needs to be experimentally determined for each particular problem. We provide an additional interface for manually inserting ZEN application instances, that are known to be good solution candidates, in the initial population which can significantly improve the performance of the genetic algorithm since the search starts from a population of higher quality individuals.

Algorithm 4. The generational genetic search algorithm.

1: **function** GENETIC-SEARCH-ENGINE$(\mathcal{A}(z_1, \ldots, z_n), \mathcal{F}, p, Pr_c, Pr_m, max\_gen, T)$
2: $\quad POP \leftarrow \bigcup_{i=1}^{p} \mathcal{AI}(\text{RAND}(z_1), \ldots, \text{RAND}(z_n))$ ▷ First population (size p)
3: $\quad \mathcal{F} \ \mathcal{AI}_B^0 \ = \ \max_{\forall i \in [1..p]} \{\mathcal{F}(\mathcal{AI}_i)\}$ ▷ Best individual
4: $\quad gen \leftarrow 1$
5: $\quad$ **repeat**
6: $\qquad \overline{\mathcal{F}} \leftarrow \frac{\sum_{i=1}^{p} \mathcal{F}(\mathcal{AI}_i)}{p}$ ▷ Average fitness
7: $\qquad POP' \leftarrow \bigcup_{i=1}^{p} \bigcup_{j=1}^{\frac{\mathcal{F}(\mathcal{AI}_i)}{\overline{\mathcal{F}}}} \text{CLONE}(\mathcal{AI}_i)$ ▷ Selection
8: $\qquad$ **while** $|POP'| < |POP|$ **do**
9: $\qquad\quad$ **for all** $j \in [1..p]$ **do**
10:
11: $\qquad\qquad$ **if** $\dfrac{\sum_{k=1}^{j-1} \frac{\mathcal{F}(\mathcal{AI}_k)}{\overline{\mathcal{F}}}}{\sum_{k=1}^{p} \frac{\mathcal{F}(\mathcal{AI}_k)}{\overline{\mathcal{F}}}} < \text{RAND}(0,1) \leq \dfrac{\sum_{k=1}^{j} \frac{\mathcal{F}(\mathcal{AI}_k)}{\overline{\mathcal{F}}}}{\sum_{k=1}^{p} \frac{\mathcal{F}(\mathcal{AI}_k)}{\overline{\mathcal{F}}}}$ **then**
12: $\qquad\qquad\quad POP' \leftarrow POP' \cup \text{CLONE}(\mathcal{AI}_j)$
13: $\qquad\qquad$ **end if**
14: $\qquad\quad$ **end for**
15: $\qquad$ **end while**
16: $\qquad POP_c \leftarrow \emptyset$
17: $\qquad$ **for all** $i \in [1..p]$ **do**
18: $\qquad\quad$ **if** $\text{RAND}(0,1) \leq Pr_c$ **then** ▷ Pr_c = crossover probability
19: $\qquad\qquad POP_c \leftarrow POP_c \cup \mathcal{AI}_i$ ▷ Select for crossover
20: $\qquad\quad$ **end if**
21: $\qquad$ **end for**
22: $\qquad POP \leftarrow POP' \setminus POP_c$
23: $\qquad$ **for all** $\{\mathcal{AI}_1(e_1, \ldots, e_n), \mathcal{AI}_2(e_1', \ldots, e_n')\} \subset POP_c$ **do** ▷ Random pair
24: $\qquad\quad r \leftarrow \text{RAND}(1, n-1)$
25: $\qquad\quad POP \leftarrow POP \cup \{\mathcal{AI}_1'(e_1, \ldots, e_r, e_{r+1}', \ldots, e_n')\}$ ▷ Crossover
26: $\qquad\quad POP \leftarrow POP \cup \{\mathcal{AI}_2'(e_1', \ldots, e_r', e_{r+1}, \ldots, e_n)\}$
27: $\qquad\quad POP_c \leftarrow POP_c \setminus \{\mathcal{AI}_1, \mathcal{AI}_2\}$
28: $\qquad$ **end for**
29: $\qquad$ **for all** $\mathcal{AI}(e_1, \ldots, e_n) \in POP$ **do**
30: $\qquad\quad$ **for all** $i \in [1..n]$ **do**
31: $\qquad\qquad$ **if** $\text{RAND}(0,1) \leq Pr_m$ **then** ▷ Pr_m = mutation probability
32: $\qquad\qquad\quad e_i \leftarrow \text{RAND}(z_i)$ ▷ Mutation
33: $\qquad\qquad$ **end if**
34: $\qquad\quad$ **end for**
35: $\qquad$ **end for**
36: $\qquad \mathcal{F}(\mathcal{AI}_B^{gen}) = \max_{\forall i \in [1..p]} \{\mathcal{F}(\mathcal{AI}_i)\}$ ▷ Elitist model
37: $\qquad$ **if** $\mathcal{F}(\mathcal{AI}_B^{gen}) < \mathcal{F} \ \mathcal{AI}_B^{gen-1}$ **then** ▷ Lost best individual
38: $\qquad\quad POP \leftarrow POP \setminus \mathcal{AI} \cup \mathcal{AI}_B^{gen-1}, \ \mathcal{AI} \in POP$ ▷ Preserve the best
39: $\qquad$ **end if**
40: $\qquad gen \leftarrow gen + 1$ ▷ Next generation
41: $\quad$ **until** $gen > max\_gen \vee \mathcal{AI}_B^{gen-1} \geq T$ ▷ Maximum generation or
threshold
42: $\quad$ **return** $\mathcal{AI}_B^{gen-1}$ ▷ Return best individual
43: **end function**

6.2.2 Selection

The *selection* operator (lines $6 - 15$) creates a new population by choosing the best ZEN application instances for *reproduction*. Let POP denote a population of cardinality p and $\overline{\mathcal{F}}$ its average fitness:

$$\overline{\mathcal{F}} = \frac{\sum_{i=1}^{p} \mathcal{F}(\mathcal{AI}_i)}{p}.$$

We employ the *reminder stochastic sampling with replacement* [88] selection model that creates a new population:

$$POP' = POP_1 \cup POP_2$$

in two steps, as follows:

1. $POP_1 = \bigcup_{i=1}^{p} \bigcup_{j=1}^{\left\lfloor \frac{\mathcal{F}(\mathcal{AI}_i)}{\overline{\mathcal{F}}} \right\rfloor} clone\,(\mathcal{AI}_i)$, where $\lfloor x \rfloor$ denotes the integer part of the real number $x \in \mathbb{R}$. This step is called *expected value model* because it selects each application instance proportional with its fitness value and eliminates stochastic sampling errors (line 7);

2. $POP_2 = \bigcup_{i=1}^{s} clone\,(\mathcal{AI}_j)$, where $s = |POP| - |POP_1|$, $r_i \in [0,1]$ is a random number such that:

$$\frac{\sum_{k=1}^{j-1} \left\{ \frac{\mathcal{F}(\mathcal{AI}_k)}{\overline{\mathcal{F}}} \right\}}{\sum_{k=1}^{p} \left\{ \frac{\mathcal{F}(\mathcal{AI}_k)}{\overline{\mathcal{F}}} \right\}} < r_i \leq \frac{\sum_{k=1}^{j} \left\{ \frac{\mathcal{F}(\mathcal{AI}_k)}{\overline{\mathcal{F}}} \right\}}{\sum_{k=1}^{p} \left\{ \frac{\mathcal{F}(\mathcal{AI}_k)}{\overline{\mathcal{F}}} \right\}},$$

where $\{x\}$ denotes the fractional part of real number $x \in \mathbb{R}$ (i.e. $\{x\} = x - \lfloor x \rfloor$) and $|POP|$ denotes the cardinality of the set POP (lines $8-15$). Informally, the population places that remained empty in the first step are filled by simulating a roulette wheel with slots proportional with the fractional part of each individual fitness normalised against the average population fitness.

6.2.3 Crossover

The *crossover* operator (lines $16 - 28$) is used in genetic algorithms for performing quick searches for local maxima. We employ in our algorithm a *single point crossover operator* defined by the random function (lines $23 - 28$):

$$\oplus_r : \mathcal{V}^{\mathcal{A}} \times \mathcal{V}^{\mathcal{A}} \rightarrow \mathcal{V}^{\mathcal{A}} \times \mathcal{V}^{\mathcal{A}},$$

$$\mathcal{AI}_1\,(e_1, \ldots, e_n) \oplus \mathcal{AI}_2\,(e'_1, \ldots, e'_n) = \left(\mathcal{AI}'_1, \mathcal{AI}'_2 \right),$$

where:

$$\mathcal{AI}'_1 = \mathcal{AI}'_1 \left(e_1, \ldots, e_r, e'_{r+1}, \ldots, e'_n\right),$$
$$\mathcal{AI}'_2 = \mathcal{AI}'_2 \left(e'_1, \ldots, e'_r, e_{r+1}, \ldots, e_n\right),$$

and $r \in [1, n-1]$ is a random number (see Figure 6.4(a)).

Let $POP = \{\mathcal{AI}_1, \ldots, \mathcal{AI}_p\}$ denote a population of ZEN application instances and let Pr_c be the probability of crossover that has to be experimentally determined for each individual problem. We calculate the subset of ZEN application instances which undergo crossover as follows:

$$POP_c = \bigcup_{i=1}^{p} \mathcal{AI}'_i,$$

where:

$$\mathcal{AI}'_i = \begin{cases} \mathcal{AI}_i, & r_i < Pr_c; \\ \emptyset, & r_i \geq Pr_c, \end{cases}$$

and $r_i \in [0, 1]$ is a random number, $\forall\, i \in [1..p]$. We randomly select the crossover pairs from POP_c (lines $16 - 21$).

6.2.4 Mutation

The *mutation* operator (lines $29 - 35$) enables the algorithm to jump to another search space region which avoids local stagnation stages of the population. We employ a *mutation* operator that applies gene-wise on ZEN application instances, according to the function (line 33):

$$\ominus : \mathcal{V}^{\mathcal{A}} \to \mathcal{V}^{\mathcal{A}}, \quad \ominus \left(\mathcal{AI}\left(e_1, \ldots, e_n\right)\right) = \mathcal{AI}' \left(e'_1, \ldots, e'_n\right),$$

where:

$$e'_i = \begin{cases} e''_i, & r_i < Pr_m; \\ e_i, & r_i \geq Pr_m, \end{cases}$$

Pr_m is the (experimentally tuned) probability of mutation for a gene, $r_i \in [0, 1]$ is a random number, and $e''_i \in \mathcal{V}^{z_i}$ is a randomly selected allele, $\forall\, i \in [1..n]$. We illustrate a sample chromosome which undergoes a single gene mutation in Figure 6.4(b).

6.2.5 Elitist Model

Repeated crossover and mutation may lead to the elimination of the best individual which could have negative impacts on the final solution. Let POP_{gen} denote a population at some generation gen, $\mathcal{AI}_B^{gen} \in POP_{gen}$ the current best ZEN application instance, i.e. $\mathcal{F}\left(\mathcal{AI}_B^{gen}\right) \geq \mathcal{F}\left(\mathcal{AI}\right)$, $\forall\, \mathcal{AI} \in POP_{gen}$, and POP_{gen+1} the next generation. We employ the so called *elitist model* (lines $36 - 39$) that forces the best ZEN application instance be preserved across generations:

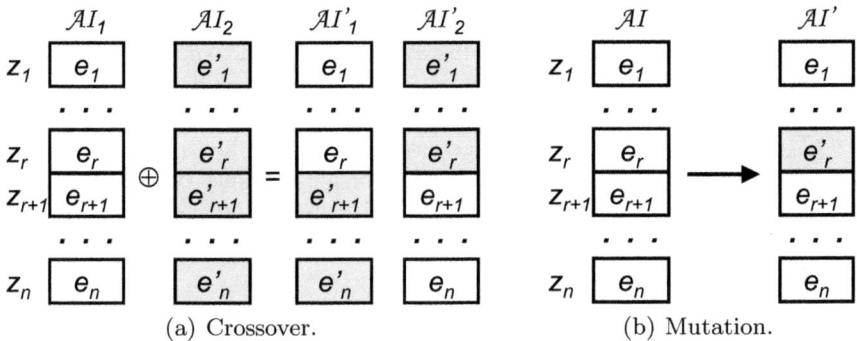

(a) Crossover.   (b) Mutation.

Fig. 6.4. The genetic operators.

$$POP'_{gen+1} = \begin{cases} POP_{gen+1}, & \mathcal{AI}_B^{gen+1} \geq \mathcal{AI}_B^{gen}; \\ POP_{gen+1} - \mathcal{AI} \ \cup \ \mathcal{AI}_B^{gen}, & \mathcal{AI}_B^{gen+1} < \mathcal{AI}_B^{gen}, \end{cases}$$

where $\mathcal{AI} \in POP_{gen+1}$ is a randomly eliminated individual. The elitist model may lead to premature convergence of the algorithm if not carefully applied.

6.2.6 Fitness Scaling

There are two problems with our selection method that we described in Section 6.2.2:

1. at the start of the algorithm, it is common to have several super-individuals (but globally average) that would dominate the later generations and lead to fast premature convergence of the algorithm;
2. late in the run, the population average fitness often gets close to the best fitness. In this case, average and best members get equally represented in the future generations and the survival of the fittest chromosome necessary for improvement becomes a random walk among the mediocre.

Let $\overline{\mathcal{F}}$ denote the average population fitness. We define *linear fitness scaling* as a new scaled fitness function for one ZEN application instance:

$$\mathcal{F}' = a \cdot \mathcal{F} + b,$$

where a and b are determined by solving the following system of equations:

$$\begin{cases} a \cdot \overline{\mathcal{F}} + b = \overline{\mathcal{F}} \\ a \cdot \mathcal{F}_{\max} + b = C_{mult} \cdot \overline{\mathcal{F}}. \end{cases}$$

These two equations ensure two crucial aspects for proper genetic algorithm convergence:

1. the average scaled fitness $\overline{\mathcal{F}'}$ is equal to the average raw fitness $\mathcal{F}$ because each average ZEN application instance is expected to contribute with one offspring to the next generation;
2. the best ZEN application instance $\mathcal{F}_{\max}$ is expected to contribute with C_{mult} offsprings to the next generation. This reduces the gap between super and average individuals in initial generations (which avoids premature convergence) and increases this gap in late generations (which ensures strong competition necessary for continuous healthy survival and improvement).

6.2.7 Convergence Criterion

For flexibility reasons, we define three *convergence criteria* for the algorithm defines which can be freely combined:

1. when the objective function exceeds a user defined *threshold* (line 42);
2. after a predefined *maximum number of generations* (line 41);
3. when a *steady state* stagnation is achieved and no further improvements are made in new generations. We check the steady state by examining the fitness function of the best individual within a sliding window of a predefined number of generations (i.e. percentage from the maximum generation number).

6.3 Genetic Workflow Scheduling

In this section, we instantiate the genetic algorithm described in the previous section for the workflow scheduling problem introduced in Section 6.1.

Definition 6.10. *Let $\mathcal{A}(z_1, \ldots, z_n)$ denote a ZEN application that represents a workflow application as defined in Definition 6.2. A gene z is a ZEN variable that represents an abstract Grid machine. An allele $e_i \in \mathcal{V}^{z_i}$ is a concrete Grid machine, $\forall\, i \in [1..n]$. The totally ordered set $(\{z_1, \ldots, z_n\}, \prec_c)$ builds a* chromosome, *where the total order $\prec_c$ of genes in a chromosome (i.e. loci) is fixed and respects the (partial) node topological order:*

$$N_i \prec_c N_j \implies N_i \notin succ^p(N_j).$$

We depict in Figure 6.5 two sample crossover and mutation operations for the workflow application illustrated previously in Example 6.3 and Figure 6.2.

6.3.1 WIEN2k

We use as pilot application for our scheduling work the *WIEN2k* [160] program package for performing electronic structure calculations of solids using

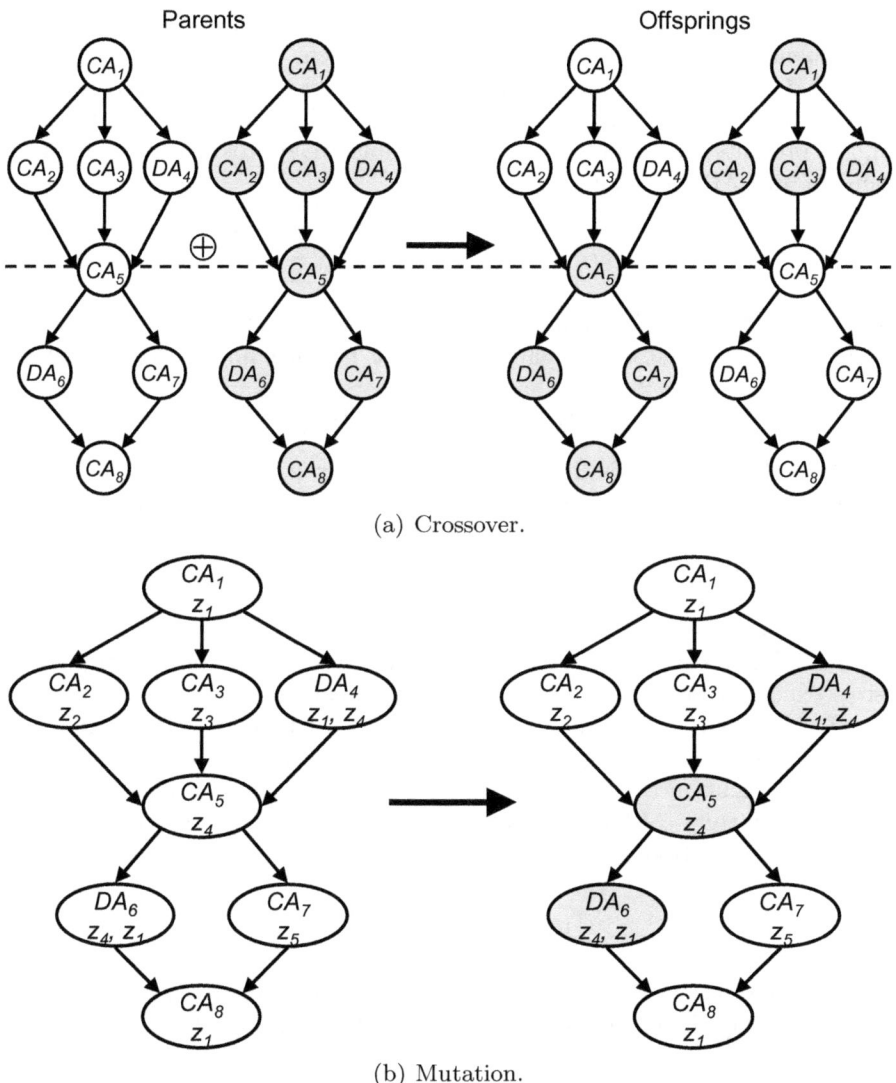

(a) Crossover.

(b) Mutation.

Fig. 6.5. The workflow genetic operators.

density functional theory based on the full potential (linearised) augmented plane wave ((L)APW) and local orbital (lo) method. We first ported the application onto the Grid by splitting the monolithic code into several course grain activities coordinated in a workflow as illustrated in Figure 6.6. The LAPW1 and LAPW2 activities can be solved in parallel by a fixed number of so called *k-points*. A final activity called *Converged* applied on several output files tests whether the problem convergence criterion is fulfilled. The number of sequential loop iterations is statically unknown.

We developed together with the WIEN2k physicists reasonably accurate prediction functions for the most critical workflow activities following the model presented in Definition 6.6. For example, we approximate the execution time of an LAPW1 k-point as:

$$T_{LAPW1} = \frac{W_{LAPW1}}{v} = \frac{7 \cdot A \cdot N^2 + N^3}{v},$$

where A represents the number of atoms, N represents the matrix size, 7 is a scaling factor, and v is a quantification for the machine speed. Similarly,

$$T_{LAPW2} = 10\% \cdot T_{LAPW1}.$$

For LAPW0 we use existing measurements from a previous exhaustive scalability study that we conducted using the ZENTURIO experiment management tool, as presented in Section 4.2.2. We generate regression functions of various types (i.e. linear, polynomial, exponential, power) to approximate the prediction results on space points that were not measured and choose the one with the best regression coefficient (i.e. closest to one). Figure 6.7(a) displays the scalability regression functions for four representative LAPW0 problem sizes executed on the homogeneous *gescher* cluster that we introduced in Section 4.2. Similarly, Figure 6.7(b) calculates the regression function for the work expressed in floating point operations which we use to approximate the LAPW0 execution time on different Grid sites. We approximate the largest file transfer time (of file `case.vector`) between two LAPW1 and LAPW2 k-point computations as:

$$T_{12} = \frac{W_{12}}{v_{12}} = \frac{200 \cdot N \cdot A}{v_{12}},$$

where v_{12} represents the network bandwidth between the source and the destination machines measured using the NWS sensor [192].

Example 6.11 (WIEN2k Java CoG excerpt).

```
//ZEN$ SUBSTITUTE lapw0_host = { machine{1:200} }
//ZEN$ SUBSTITUTE lapw1_host1 = { machine{1:200} }
//ZEN$ SUBSTITUTE lapw1_host2 = { machine{1:200} }
. . .
Task lapw0 = createCA("lapw0_host", "lapw0");
Task lapw1_1 = createCA("lapw1_host1", "lapw1 2");
Task lapw1_2 = createCA("lapw1_host2", "lapw1 1");
Task k1 = createDA("k1","lapw0_host","lapw1_host1");
Task k2 = createDA("k2","lapw0_host","lapw1_host2");
. . .
```

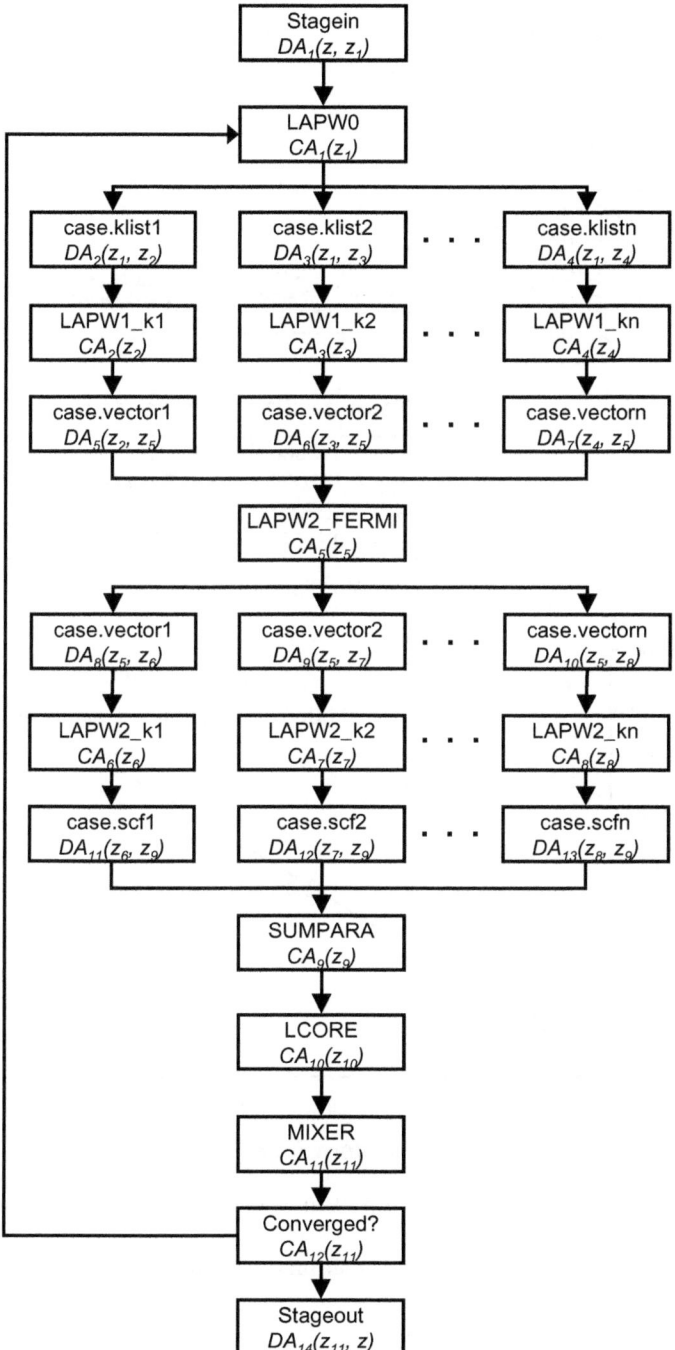

Fig. 6.6. A simplified WIEN2k workflow.

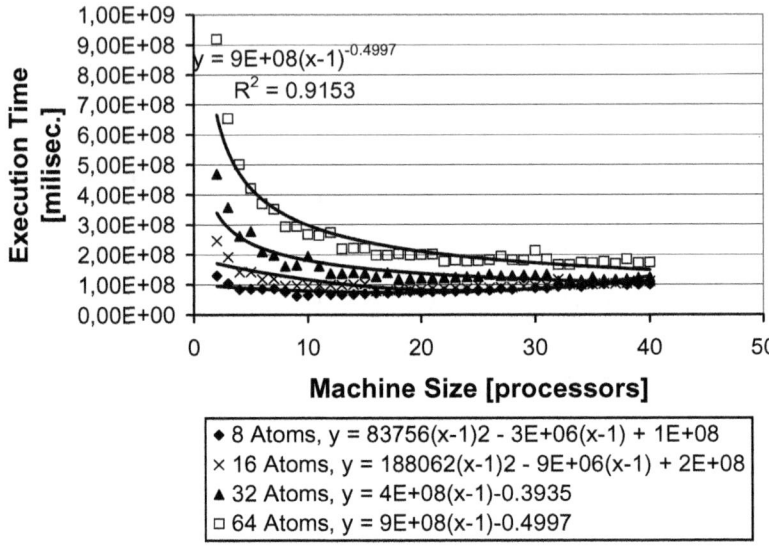

(a) LAPW0 scalability.

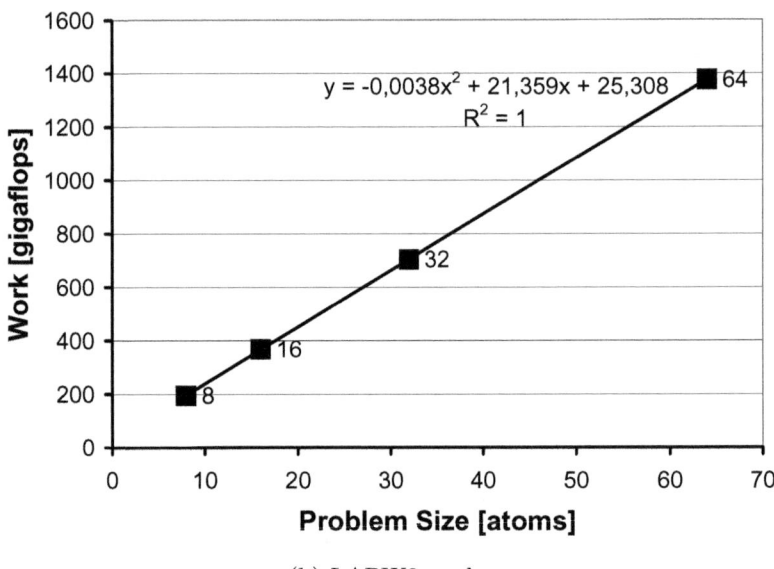

(b) LAPW0 work.

Fig. 6.7. The regression functions for LAPW0.

```
TaskGraph activityGraph = new ActivityGraphImpl();
activityGraph.add(lapw0);
taskGraph.add(lapw1_k1);
activityGraph.add(lapw1_k2);
taskGraph.add(k1);
activityGraph.add(k2);
. . .
Dependency dependency = new DependencyImpl();
dependency.add(lapw0.getId(), k1.getId());
dependency.add(lapw0.getId(), k2.getId());
dependency.add(k1.getId(), lapw1_k1.getId());
dependency.add(k2.getId(), lapw1_k2.getId());
. . .
taskGraph.setDependency(dependency);
```

Example 6.11 illustrates a sample Java CoG program [9] that implements a fragment of the WIEN2k workflow application. The *CA* workflow activities lapw0, lapw1_k1, and lapw1_k2 run on the abstract machines (genetic algorithm genes) lapw0_host, lapw1_host1, respectively lapw1_host2. The *DA* activities k1 and k2 transfer the output files of LAPW0 from lapw0_host to the abstract machines lapw1_host1 and lapw1_host2 where the LAPW1 k-points execute through static schedule dependencies (see Section 6.1.1). The ZEN directives illustrated in Example 6.11 specify the possible instantiation values of each abstract machine that annotates the workflow which we retrieve at runtime from the MDS information service. The parameter space defined by the ZEN directives is the scope of the scheduling search engine based on the genetic algorithm.

We conduct the experiments in subset testbed of a national Grid infrastructure [2] consisting of 200 processors. To achieve a more effective evaluation of the scheduling algorithm under difficult external conditions, we introduced artificial perturbations to the processor and network data provided by MDS and NWS at random time intervals. As a consequence, the performance of the processor and network resources in our Grid testbed follows an exponential distribution with overloaded resources outnumbering the idle high performance ones (which we expect to be the case in future large scale world wide Grid infrastructures).

Figure 6.8 depicts the generational evolution of the best population individual (i.e. workflow makespan) for several instantiations of the genetic algorithm applied on various WIEN2k problem size configurations. Even though the algorithm exhibits a steady smooth improvement across generations (i.e. convergence to local minima through crossover and steep escapes from local minima through mutation), the quality of the resulting solutions is heavily influenced by several input parameters:

1. the population size;
2. the crossover probability;
3. the mutation probability;
4. the maximum generation number;
5. the steady state generation percentage;
6. the fitness scaling factor;
7. the use of the elitist model.

A correct tuning of these parameters is crucial for the algorithm to quickly convergence to high quality solutions. In a conventional approach, this requires extensive manual experimental testing.

Example 6.12 (Genetic algorithm parameter tuning – PBS script).

```
#!/bin/sh
#PBS -l walltime=00:10:00:nodes=1
#PBS -N scheduler
size = 150
#ZEN$ ASSIGN size = { 50 : 200 : 50 }
crossover = 0.9
#ZEN$ ASSIGN crossover = { 0.4 : 1 : 0.2 }
mutation = 0.001
#ZEN$ ASSIGN mutation = { 0.001, 0.01, 0.1 }
generations = 500
#ZEN$ ASSIGN generations = { 100 : 500 : 100 }
convergence = 0.2
#ZEN$ ASSIGN convergence = { 0.1, 0.2 }
scaling = 2
```

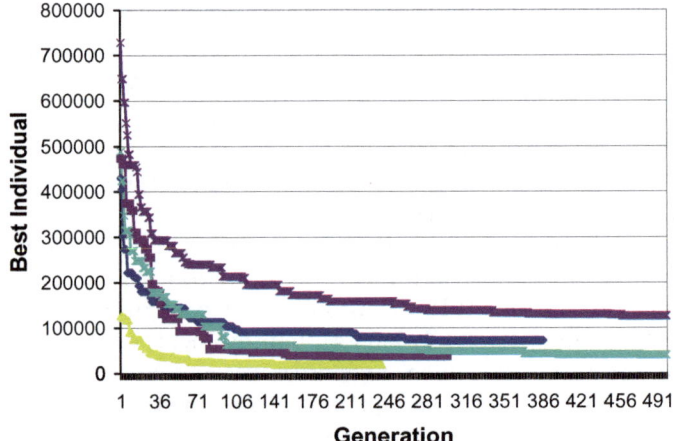

Fig. 6.8. The best individual evolution for various application instances.

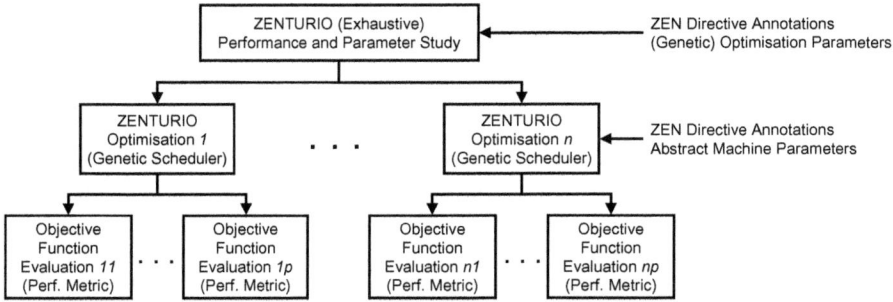

Fig. 6.9. The experimental setup for genetic static scheduler tuning.

```
#ZEN$ ASSIGN scaling = { 1, 1.5, 2 }
elitist = T
#ZEN$ ASSIGN elitist = { T, F }
${JAVA} -DSIZE=${size} -DCROSSOVER=${crossover} ...
```

We tuned the genetic algorithm parameters by conducting an aggressive exhaustive performance study using ZENTURIO in cluster mode, as presented in Chapter 4. We inserted seven ZEN directives (see Example 6.12) that specify total of 2880 experiments in the PBS script used by ZENTURIO to automatically generate and submit the experiments on the *gescher* cluster introduced in Section 4.2. We chose for this experiment a workflow of average size of about 55 activities (i.e. 10 parallel k-points). Every experiment represents an instance of the scheduling algorithm configured using a different genetic parameter combination. Each scheduling experiment annotates the application with ZEN directives that define the possible instantiations of each abstract machine, as already illustrated in Example 6.11. All experiments use the Grid resource information retrieved from MDS at the same time instance (i.e. Grid snapshot). We illustrate in Figure 6.9 this particular hierarchical experimental setup that applies ZENTURIO (exhaustive) performance study tool on ZENTURIO optimisation search engine (instantiated for the scheduling problem).

We instantiated the objective (fitness) function with the predicted workflow makespan which raises the maximum optimisation difficulty since it considers all workflow activities in the evaluation process. For the purpose of evaluating the quality of the solutions produced by the algorithm, we premeasured the workflow execution time offline on a set of idle (unperturbed) high performance Grid resources which we regard as *optimal fitness* $\mathcal{F}_o$. We computed three metrics for each experiment that characterise the performance of the genetic algorithm:

1. *precision* P of the best individual $\mathcal{F}_b$ compared to the artificial optimum $\mathcal{F}_o$, defined as:

$$P = \frac{\mathcal{F}_o - \mathcal{F}_b}{C - \mathcal{F}_o} \cdot 100;$$

2. *visited points* representing the total set of individuals (i.e. schedules) which were evaluated by the algorithm during the search process;

3. *improvement* I in the fitness $\mathcal{F}_b$ of the last generation best schedule compared to the first generation best schedule $\mathcal{F}_f$:

$$I = \frac{\mathcal{F}_b - \mathcal{F}_f}{C - \mathcal{F}_b} \cdot 100.$$

To attenuate the stochastic errors to which randomised algorithms are bound, we repeated each scheduling experiment for 30 times and report the arithmetic mean of the results measured in each run.

Due to the large search space (i.e. 10^{25} points) and difficult external Grid conditions (i.e. exponential resource load distribution), large populations above 50 individuals are required in this scenario for converging to good solutions (see Figure 6.10(a)). As expected, the precision improves with the number of generations. Lower population sizes (e.g. 50) do not ensure enough variety in the genes and converge prematurely. Larger populations (e.g. 200) converge to good solutions in fewer generations, however, the number of visited points may be unnecessarily large which increases the algorithm duration. The number of visited points (i.e. the schedules computed) required for converging to good solutions is of the order of 10^4 which represents a fraction from the total search space size of 10^{25} points (see Figure 6.10(b)). The improvement in the best individual is remarkable of up to 700% over 500 generations for large populations (see Figure 6.10(c)). A value of 20% from the maximum generation number is a good effective estimate for checking whether the algorithm reached a steady state (see Figure 6.11(a)). The higher the crossover probability, the faster the algorithm converges to local maxima (see Figure 6.11(b)). A correct low mutation probability is crucial for escaping from local maxima and for obtaining good solutions (see Figure 6.11(c)). In this experiment the mutation probability had to be surprisingly low (i.e. 0.001%) due to the rather large population sizes and genes per individual (i.e. 45). Higher mutation probabilities produce too much instability in the population and chaotic jumps in the search space that do not allow the algorithm to converge to local maxima through crossover. Fitness scaling is crucial for smooth steady improvement over large number of generations (see Figure 6.12(a)) and produces about 10 fold improvement in solution. The use of the elitist model (see Figure 6.12(b)) is beneficial due to the high heterogeneity of the search space and delivers in average 33% better solutions.

As a consequence of this performance tuning experiment, we currently use the following parameter configuration to run the genetic algorithm within this Grid testbed:

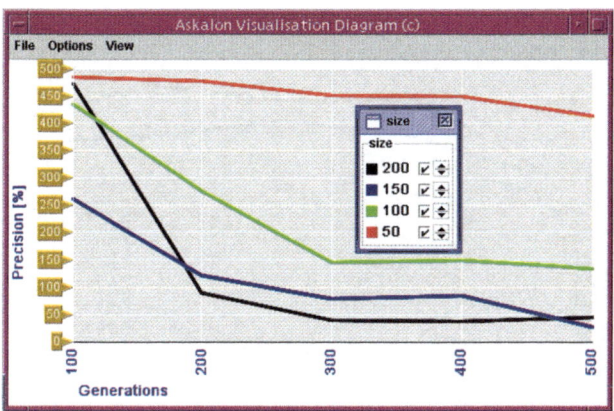

(a) Population size.

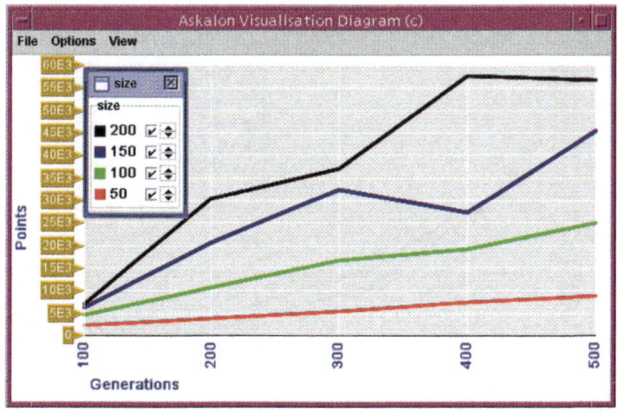

(b) Visited points.

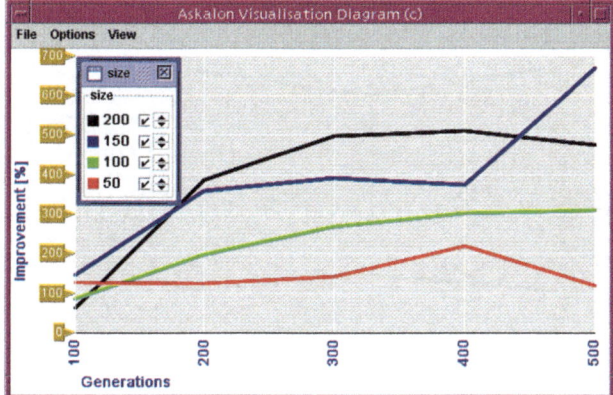

(c) Best individual improvement.

Fig. 6.10. The genetic scheduler tuning results (I).

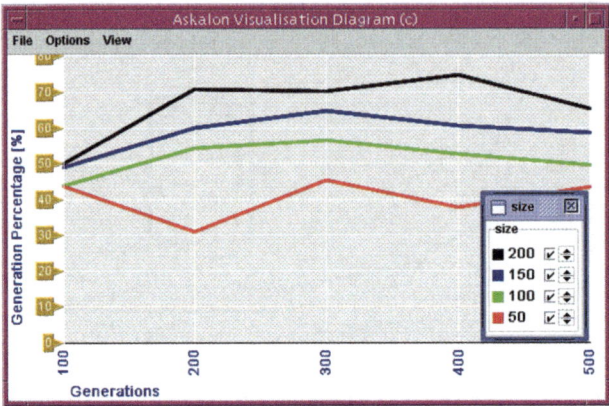

(a) Generation percentage.

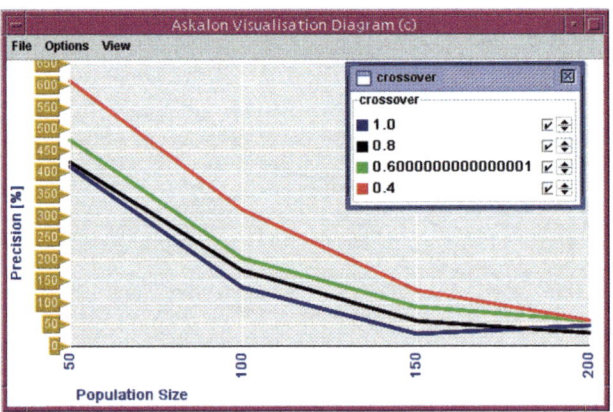

(b) Crossover probability.

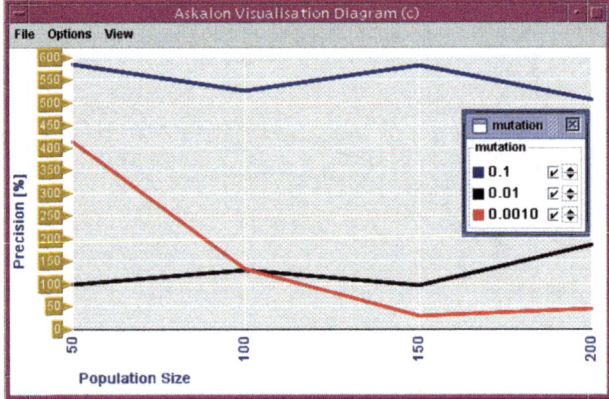

(c) Mutation probability.

Fig. 6.11. The genetic scheduler tuning results (II).

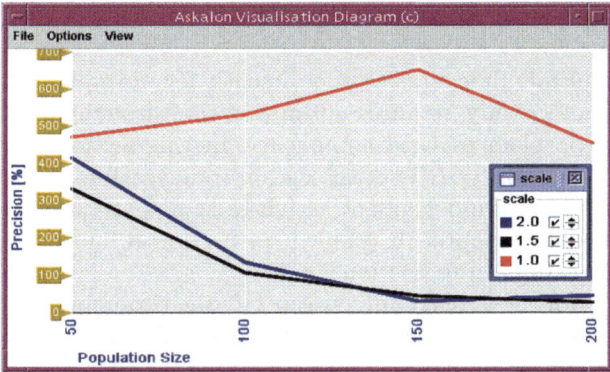

(a) Fitness scaling factor.

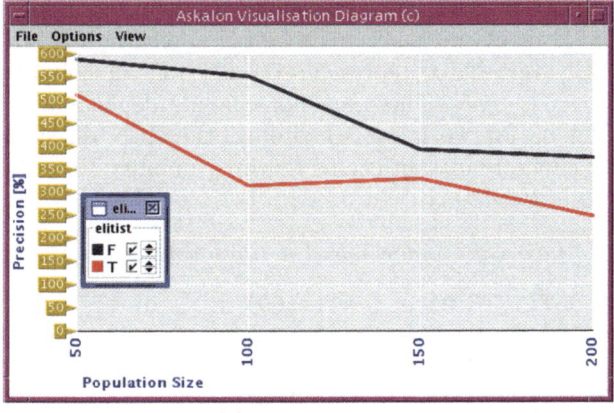

(b) Elitist model.

Fig. 6.12. The genetic scheduler tuning results (III).

1. population size: 150;
2. crossover probability: 0.9;
3. mutation probability: 0.001;
4. maximum generation: 500;
5. steady state generation percentage: 20%;
6. fitness scaling factor: 2;
7. elitist model: yes.

In this configuration, the algorithm constantly delivers 25% precision and a remarkable 700% improvement in solution by visiting a fraction (i.e. $5 \cdot 10^4$) of the entire search space points. The most sensitive parameter that needs be tuned to the workflow characteristics is the mutation probability (i.e. inversely proportional with the population size multiplied with the workflow size). The other parameter values have to be tuned to the Grid resource characteristics and are less dependent on the particular workflow.

6.4 Throughput Scheduling

Scheduling multiple independent experiments, for example in the context of a large parameter study, requires optimising the throughput that is another NP-complete problem in Grid computing. In this section we illustrate an instantiation the ZENTURIO optimisation framework for throughput scheduling of large sets of independent activities as a specialisation of the static workflow scheduling approach problem in Section 6.1 using the parameter study model introduced in Section 2.6.3.

Similar to workflow scheduling, we specify the throughput scheduling problem by defining the parameter space through ZEN directive annotation of each activity and by supplying appropriate objective (fitness) functions based on prediction models for each independent activity using the method described in Definition 6.6. Example 6.13 defines a set of five independent activities using the Java CoG kit package as a ZEN application $\mathcal{A}(z_1, z_2, z_3, z_4, z_5)$, where each ZEN variable z_i represents the abstract machine that hosts the activity $CA_i, \forall\ i \in [1..5]$. There are no schedule dependencies between activities. Similar as for workflow scheduling, the ZEN directives define the set of possible concrete instantiations (with cardinality 100) of each abstract machine parameter.

Example 6.13 (Java CoG independent activity set).

```
//ZEN$ SUBSTITUTE z1 = { e{1:100} }
//ZEN$ SUBSTITUTE z2 = { e{1:100} }
//ZEN$ SUBSTITUTE z3 = { e{1:100} }
//ZEN$ SUBSTITUTE z4 = { e{1:100} }
//ZEN$ SUBSTITUTE z5 = { e{1:100} }
. . .
Task CA1 = createCA("z1");
Task CA2 = createCA("z2");
Task CA3 = createCA("z3");
Task CA4 = createCA("z4");
Task CA5 = createCA("z5");
. . .
TaskGraph activitySet = new ActivityGraphImpl();
activitySet.add(CA1);
activitySet.add(CA2);
activitySet.add(CA3);
activitySet.add(CA4);
activitySet.add(CA5);
activitySet.setDependency(new DependencyImpl());
```

We specify through the following definition the generic instantiation of the ZENTURIO optimisation framework and the genetic search engine for the throughput scheduling problem.

Definition 6.14. *A* ZEN *application is a set of n independent activities: $\mathcal{A}(z_1, \ldots, z_n) = (Nodes, \text{C-edges})$, where $Nodes = \{CA_1(z_1), \ldots, CA_n(z_n)\}$, and $\text{C-edges} = \emptyset$. A* ZEN *variable (gene) z_i is a parameter that represents an abstract Grid machine where the activity CA_i executes. The value set $\mathcal{V}^{z_i}$ of a* ZEN *variable z_i represents the entire set of concrete Grid machines. An allele $e_i \in \mathcal{V}^{z_i}$ is a concrete machine in the Grid, $\forall\, i \in [1..n]$. An activity schedule is a function that maps each activity onto a concrete machine from the Grid:*

$$\mathcal{S} : Nodes \rightarrow \mathcal{V}^{z_i}.$$

An individual *is a* ZEN *application instance $\mathcal{AI}(e_1, \ldots, e_n)$, where $\mathcal{S}(CA_i) = e_i$ and $e_i \in \mathcal{V}^{z_i}$, $\forall\, i \in [1..n]$.*

The crossover and mutation operators for independent activities can be graphically represented as in Figure 6.4.

Definition 6.15. *Let $\mathcal{V}^z$ denote the full set of machines in the Grid, N_{par} a set of independent activities, and $\mathcal{S} : N_{par} \rightarrow \mathcal{V}^z$ the activity schedule function. We define the* Gantt chart *of N_{par} as a function:*

$$\mathcal{G} : \mathcal{V}^z \rightarrow \mathcal{P}(N_{par}), \;\; \mathcal{G}(e) = \bigcup_{\forall\, \mathcal{S}(CA)=e} CA,$$

where $\mathcal{P}$ denotes the power set. We define the throughput fitness function *as:*

$$\mathcal{F} : \mathcal{V}^{\mathcal{A}} \rightarrow \mathbb{R}_+, \;\; \mathcal{F}(\mathcal{AI}(e_1, \ldots, e_n)) = \mathcal{C} - \max_{\forall\, e \in \{e_1, \ldots, e_n\}} \left\{ \sum_{\forall\, CA \in \mathcal{G}(e)} T^e_{CA} \right\},$$

where $\mathcal{C}$ is a large enough constant. Maximising the throughput fitness function is the throughput scheduling problem.

Informally, with each individual we associate a Gantt chart that maps each activity onto one Grid machine. The activities scheduled onto the same machine are executed sequentially in irrelevant order. The machine with the maximum execution time determines the schedule makespan that needs to be minimised. We define the fitness function as the makespan subtracted from a large enough constant $\mathcal{C}$ since our framework solves maximisation problems. For example, the throughput fitness function or the makespan of the five activities defined in Example 6.13 can be expressed as:

$$\mathcal{F}(\mathcal{AI}(e_1, e_2, e_3, e_1, e_1)) = \mathcal{C} - \max\left\{ T^{e_1}_{CA_1} + T^{e_1}_{CA_4} + T^{e_1}_{CA_5}, T^{e_2}_{CA_2}, T^{e_3}_{CA_3} \right\},$$

assuming the Gantt chart depicted in Figure 6.13 :

$$\mathcal{S}(CA_1) = \mathcal{S}(CA_4) = \mathcal{S}(CA_5) = e_1;$$
$$\mathcal{S}(CA_2) = e_2;$$
$$\mathcal{S}(CA_3) = e_3.$$

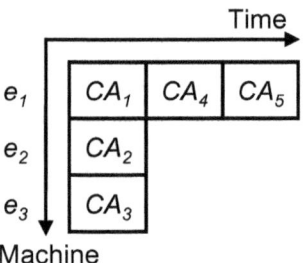

Fig. 6.13. A sample Gantt chart for the activity set defined in Example 6.13.

6.5 Performance Tuning of Parallel Applications

Finding appropriate parameter combinations, often representing paralleliza-tion options, that optimise a certain performance metric (usually minimise the execution time) is known as *performance tuning* that is another NP-complete problem. We employ the ZENTURIO optimisation framework for performance tuning of parallel applications by specifying the application pa-rameters through ZEN substitute, assignment, and constraint directives and indicating the objective function as a performance metric of interest (or an arithmetical combination of multiple performance metrics) using the ZEN performance directive, as formally specified in Chapter 3.

Definition 6.16. *Let $\mathcal{A}$ denote a ZEN application, $\mathcal{M}$ a performance mea-surement as defined in Section 3.2.9 (see Definition 3.25), and M a target Grid site. We define the* objective function *for performance tuning of parallel applications as follows:*

$$\mathcal{F} : \mathcal{V}^{\mathcal{A}} \to \mathbb{R}, \ \mathcal{F}(\mathcal{AI}) = \delta_M(\mathcal{M}, \mathcal{AI}),$$

where δ_M is the performance data defined in Definition 3.27.

Let $\mathcal{CR}$ denote the outermost code region of a ZEN application (i.e. the entire application) as introduced in Definition 3.25 and M a Grid site (i.e. a parallel computer to execute the application). We define in the following a few repre-sentative performance metrics that can be plugged-in as objective functions to be automatically tuned using ZENTURIO optimisation framework. Since some of the metrics require minimisation, we had to subtract them from a large enough constant $\mathcal{C}$.

- *Execution Time:*
$$\mathcal{F}(\mathcal{AI}) = \mathcal{C} - \delta_M(\mathcal{M}, \mathcal{AI}),$$

  where $\mathcal{M} = (\texttt{WTIME}, \mathcal{CR})$ and WTIME denotes the wall-clock time metric (see Definition 3.25);

- *Communication Time:*

$$\mathcal{F}(\mathcal{AI}) = \mathcal{C} - \delta_M(\mathcal{M}, \mathcal{AI}),$$

where $\mathcal{M} = (\text{COMM}, \mathcal{CR})$ and COMM denotes the communication time metric;

- *Speedup:*

$$\mathcal{F}(\mathcal{AI}(e)) = \frac{\delta_M(\mathcal{M}, \mathcal{AI}(e_0))}{\delta_M(\mathcal{M}, \mathcal{AI}(e))},$$

where $\mathcal{M} = (\text{WTIME}, \mathcal{CR})$, z is a ZEN variable that represents the application machine size, $e, e_0 \in \mathcal{V}^z$, and $\mathcal{AI}(e_0)$ represents the sequential version of $\mathcal{A}$;

- *Efficiency:*

$$\mathcal{F}(\mathcal{AI}(e)) = \frac{\delta_M(\mathcal{M}, \mathcal{AI}(e))}{\vartheta^{-1}(e) \cdot \delta_M(\mathcal{AI}(\mathcal{M}, e_0))},$$

where $\mathcal{M} = (\text{WTIME}, \mathcal{CR})$, z is a ZEN variable that represents the application machine size, $\vartheta^{-1}(e)$ is the machine size, $e, e_0 \in \mathcal{V}^z$, and $\mathcal{AI}(e_0)$ represents the sequential version of $\mathcal{A}$;

- *Speed:* [171]

$$\mathcal{F}(\mathcal{AI}) = \frac{\delta_M(\mathcal{M}_2, \mathcal{AI})}{\delta_M(\mathcal{M}_1, \mathcal{AI})},$$

where $\mathcal{M}_1 = (\text{WTIME}, \mathcal{CR})$, $\mathcal{M}_2 = (\text{FPIS}, \mathcal{CR})$, and FPIS denotes the floating point instructions per second metric;

- *Average Speed:* [171]

$$\mathcal{F}(\mathcal{AI}(e)) = \frac{\delta_M(\mathcal{M}_2, \mathcal{AI})}{\delta_M(\mathcal{M}_1, \mathcal{AI}) \cdot \vartheta^{-1}(e)},$$

where $\mathcal{M}_1 = (\text{WTIME}, \mathcal{CR})$, $\mathcal{M}_2 = (\text{FPIS}, \mathcal{CR})$, z is a ZEN variable that represents the machine size of $\mathcal{A}$, $e \in \mathcal{V}^z$, and $\vartheta^{-1}(e)$ is the machine size;

- *Scalability:* [171]

$$\mathcal{F}(\mathcal{AI}(e_1, e_2)) = \frac{\vartheta^{-1}(e_1', e_2') \cdot \delta_M(\mathcal{M}, \mathcal{AI})}{\vartheta^{-1}(e_1, e_2) \cdot \delta_M(\mathcal{M}, \mathcal{AI}')},$$

where $\mathcal{M} = (\text{FPIS}, \mathcal{CR})$, z_1 and z_2 are ZEN variables that represent the problem size, respectively the machine size of $\mathcal{A}$, $e_2, e_2' \in \mathcal{V}^{z_2}$, $\vartheta^{-1}(e_2)$ and $\vartheta^{-1}(e_2')$ are the machine sizes of $\mathcal{AI}$ and $\mathcal{AI}'$, and $\mathcal{AI}'(e_1', e_2')$ is a reference problem and machine size.

6.5.1 Parallel Applications on the Grid

MPI is currently the most successful standard for writing parallel applications especially for distributed memory parallel computers (but not only) based on a low level message exchange paradigm. Even though the existing MPI implementations do not provide appropriate support for Grid computing, for example with respect to security, job and firewall management, or fault tolerance, this low level message passing model has been successfully employed in the Grid community as an easy and immediate solution for gaining early experiences in executing existing parallel applications in Grid environments.

The MPICH-G library [75] extends the modular design of MPICH [91] with a new `globus` communication device that enables transparent GridFTP-based communication between MPI processes running on different Grid sites, while using a local optimised (potentially native) MPI installation for communication between processes on the same site. The MPI application is submitted to multiple Grid sites using the DUROC [48] co-allocator provided by the Globus toolkit. This approach enables therefore straightforward transparent execution of existing parallel MPI applications in a Grid environment by simply relinking the compiled parallel application with the new Grid-enabled counterpart. In this context, optimising MPI applications for a heterogeneous set of Grid resources raises complex data distributions and load balancing problems which are difficult to address due to the low level of abstraction of the message passing paradigm (i.e. often called fragmented programming).

High Performance Fortran (HPF) [98] was an attempt in the late 1990s to alleviate the MPI fragmented programming model by providing high level abstractions for distributing arrays across the distributed memory of parallel computers, while offering the programmer a single program view which is not fragmented by low level message passing library routines. Special purpose source-to-source HPF compilers, like the Vienna Fortran Compiler [21], have been developed by the community to translate a high level HPF application into an MPI equivalent. In Section 3.1.5 we presented the `BLOCK` and `CYCLIC` array distributions that are the fundamental HPF distribution patterns used for regular problems on homogeneous parallel computers. In this section we propose a new case study of applying the ZENTURIO optimisation framework for distributing (i.e. scheduling) parallel applications on the Grid using irregular array distributions that were introduced in the HPF-2 standard for parallelising irregular problems. We restrict our presentation to two-dimensional arrays for clarity reasons without loosing any generality in our approach.

General Block Distribution

The general block distribution is a generalisation of the regular HPF `BLOCK` distribution indicated through a vector representing the individual sizes of all contiguous distribution blocks, rather than one single homogeneous size for all blocks.

Definition 6.17. *Let* $MAT(m, n)$ *denote a two-dimensional matrix and let* $GRID(p, q)$ *denote a two-dimensional processor array. Let* $Bx(p)$ *and* $By(q)$

denote two one-dimensional distribution arrays, such that: $\sum_{i=1}^{p} Bx_i \geq m$ *and* $\sum_{i=1}^{q} By_i \geq n$. *The* general block data distribution *of MAT is defined by the function:*

$$DISTR : [1..m] \times [1..n] \rightarrow [1..p] \times [1..q], \ DISTR(x, y) = (z, w),$$

where:

$$\sum_{i=1}^{z-1} Bx_i < x \leq \sum_{i=1}^{z} Bx_i, \ \forall \ x \in [1..p];$$
$$\sum_{i=1}^{w-1} By_i < y \leq \sum_{i=1}^{w} By_i, \ \forall \ y \in [1..q].$$

The partition:

$$MAT_{GRID_{i,j}} = \bigcup_{\substack{DISTR(k,l)=(i,j) \ \wedge \\ \forall \ k \in [1..m] \wedge \forall \ l \in [1..n]}} MAT_{k,l}$$

is called the distribution *of MAT onto the processor GRID$_{ij}$. Each distribution array element Bx_i and By_j, $\forall \ i \in [1..p]$, $\forall \ j \in [1..q]$, is a ZEN variable annotated to specify the complete set of possible general block distributions.*

Example 6.18 defines the matrix MAT(m, n) which has both dimensions distributed over the processor array GRID(p, q) using the HPF general block mapping arrays $Bx(p)$ and $By(q)$, as specified by the directive **d7** (see Figure 6.14). The elements of the mapping arrays $Bx(p)$ and $By(q)$ are program constants which are annotated with the ZEN substitute directives **d2–d6** that specify the complete set of general block distribution possibilities. A distribution of size zero on one processor controls the machine size, since that processor will not take part in the computation. The constraint directives **d8** and **d9** ensure that the sum of the general block mapping elements is equal to the matrix size in each dimension (see Definition 6.17). These ZEN annotations define a search space of possible array distributions of size $(m + 1)^{p-1} \cdot (n + 1)^{q-1}$, where two orders of magnitude are eliminated by the two constraints. The HPF and MPI execution models consider the Grid as a single parallel computer. The HPF **PROCESSORS** directive **d1** in this approach represents the complete set of processors available on the Grid (i.e. of cardinality $p \cdot q$) organised into a two-dimensional array GRID(p, q).

Example 6.18 (HPF general block array distribution).

```
        INTEGER, PARAMETER m = 4
        INTEGER, PARAMETER n = 8
        INTEGER, PARAMETER p = 2
        INTEGER, PARAMETER q = 3
        REAL MAT(m, n)
d1: !HPF$ PROCESSOR GRID(p, q)
        INTEGER, PARAMETER :: x1 = 3
        INTEGER, PARAMETER :: x2 = 1
        INTEGER, PARAMETER :: y1 = 2
        INTEGER, PARAMETER :: y2 = 2
```

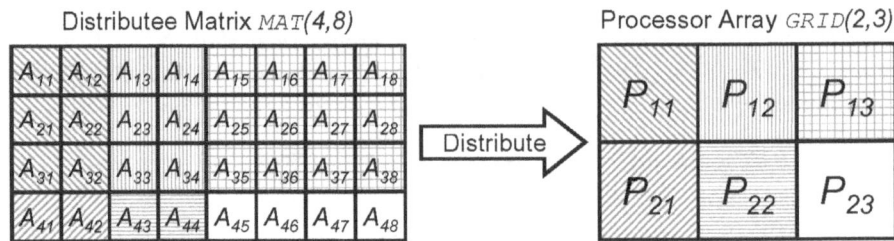

Fig. 6.14. The default general block array distribution defined in Example 6.18.

```
              INTEGER, PARAMETER :: y3 = 4
d2:  !ZEN$ SUBSTITUTE x1 = { 0 : 4 } BEGIN
d3:  !ZEN$ SUBSTITUTE x2 = { 0 : 4 } BEGIN
d4:  !ZEN$ SUBSTITUTE y1 = { 0 : 8 } BEGIN
d5:  !ZEN$ SUBSTITUTE y2 = { 0 : 8 } BEGIN
d6:  !ZEN$ SUBSTITUTE y3 = { 0 : 8 } BEGIN
              INTEGER, PARAMETER :: Bx(p) = (/ x1, x2 /)
              INTEGER, PARAMETER :: By(q) = (/ y1, y2, y3 /)
d6:  !ZEN$ END SUBSTITUTE
      . . .
d7:  !HPF$ DISTRIBUTE MAT(GEN_BLOCK(Bx), GEN_BLOCK(By))
                                              ONTO GRID
d8:  !ZEN$ CONSTRAINT VALUE x1 + x2 == 4
d9:  !ZEN$ CONSTRAINT VALUE y1 + y2 + y3 == 8
```

A ZEN application annotated as specified in Definition 6.17 (and exemplified in Example 6.18) represents the input to the ZENTURIO optimisation framework. The realisation of the search engine is, e.g. as described in Section 6.2 using a genetic algorithm which requires no further attention for this new problem. The only missing item is the instantiation of the objective function which we base on a simple primitive performance prediction model for parallel applications, since a more comprehensive approach is a difficult research topic on its own that goes beyond our present scheduling and optimisation work [68].

Definition 6.19. *Let $\mathcal{A}$ denote a ZEN application (e.g. as sketched in Example 6.18), $\mathcal{CR}$ the outermost code region (i.e. entire program), $\mathcal{M}_1 = (COMP, \mathcal{CR})$ the computation time measurement, $\mathcal{M}_2 = (COMM, \mathcal{CR})$ the communication time measurement (see Definition 3.25), and $GRID(p, q)$ a collection of Grid sites acting as a single parallel computer organised in a two-dimensional array of processors. We approximate the objective function that predicts the execution time of application $\mathcal{A}$ on the parallel computer $GRID$ using the (general block) distribution DISTR as:*

$$\mathcal{F}\left(\mathcal{AI}\right) = \max_{\forall\,(i,j)\in[1..p]\times[1..q]} \left\{\delta_{GRID}\left(\mathcal{M}_1, \mathcal{AI}\left(GRID_{i,j}, DISTR\right)\right) + \right.$$

$$\left. \delta_{GRID}\left(\mathcal{M}_2, \mathcal{AI}\left(GRID_{i,j}, DISTR\right)\right)\right\},$$

where $\mathcal{AI}\left(GRID_{i,j}, DISTR\right)$ denotes the partition of $\mathcal{AI}$ hosted by the machine $GRID_{i,j}$ according to the distribution $DISTR$.

We use again application specific analytical prediction models to estimate the computation and the communication performance data, denoted as $\delta_{GRID}\left(\mathcal{M}_1, \mathcal{AI}\left(GRID_{i,j}, DISTR\right)\right)$ and $\delta_{GRID}\left(\mathcal{M}_2, \mathcal{AI}\left(GRID_{i,j}, DISTR\right)\right)$, respectively. For example, a parallel implementation of the *Jacobi relaxation* method performs the same computation repeatedly on all matrix elements, while the communication requires exchanging the boundary elements with all the neighbouring processors. In case of the general block array distribution, we can analytically approximate these two metrics as follows:

$$\delta_{\texttt{GRID}}\left(\mathcal{M}_1, \quad \mathcal{AI}\left(\texttt{GRID}_{i,j}, DISTR\right)\right) = Bx_i \cdot By_j \cdot \frac{W_e}{v_{\texttt{GRID}_{i,j}}} \cdot I;$$

$$\delta_{\texttt{GRID}}\left(\mathcal{M}_2, \quad \mathcal{AI}\left(\texttt{GRID}_{i,j}, DISTR\right)\right) = \overline{\mathcal{L}\left(\texttt{GRID}_{i,j}\right)} +$$
$$+ Bx_i \cdot S_e \cdot \left(\frac{1}{\mathcal{B}(\texttt{GRID}_{i,j}, \texttt{GRID}_{i-1,j})} + \frac{1}{\mathcal{B}(\texttt{GRID}_{i,j}, \texttt{GRID}_{i+1,j})}\right) +$$
$$+ By_j \cdot S_e \cdot \left(\frac{1}{\mathcal{B}(\texttt{GRID}_{i,j}, \texttt{GRID}_{i,j-1})} + \frac{1}{\mathcal{B}(\texttt{GRID}_{i,j}, \texttt{GRID}_{i,j+1})}\right),$$

$\forall\, i \in [1..p]$, $\forall\, j \in [1..q]$, where:

- $W_e = \delta_{\texttt{GRID}}(\texttt{FP\_INST}, \mathcal{CR})$ is the work required to compute one matrix element expressed in floating point operations;
- $v_{\texttt{GRID}_{i,j}}$ is the speed of the processor $\texttt{GRID}_{i,j}$ that computes the matrix element expressed in floating point operations per second (e.g. measured using the LINPACK benchmark [56]);
- I is the number of iterations performed;
- S_e is the size in bytes of a matrix element, i.e. $S_e = sizeof(e)$;
- $\overline{\mathcal{L}\left(\texttt{GRID}_{i,j}\right)}$ is the total latency of the communication with the four neighbouring matrix elements:

$$\overline{\mathcal{L}\left(\texttt{GRID}_{i,j}\right)} = \mathcal{L}\left(\texttt{GRID}_{i,j}, \texttt{GRID}_{i-1,j}\right) + \mathcal{L}\left(\texttt{GRID}_{i,j}, \texttt{GRID}_{i+1,j}\right) +$$
$$+ \mathcal{L}\left(\texttt{GRID}_{i,j}, \texttt{GRID}_{i,j-1}\right) + \mathcal{L}\left(\texttt{GRID}_{i,j}, \texttt{GRID}_{i,j+1}\right);$$

- $\mathcal{L}\left(\texttt{GRID}_{i,j}, \texttt{GRID}_{k,l}\right)$ is the latency between the processors $\texttt{GRID}_{i,j}$ and $\texttt{GRID}_{k,l}$;
- $\mathcal{B}\left(\texttt{GRID}_{i,j}, \texttt{GRID}_{k,l}\right)$ is the bandwidth between the processors $\texttt{GRID}_{i,j}$ and $\texttt{GRID}_{k,l}$.

Indirect Distribution

The indirect distribution allows arbitrarily complex array distributions which are no longer restricted to contiguous blocks, by specifying the processor mapping for every individual array element separately. We apply the same parametrisation technique presented in the previous section on this more general kind of distribution.

Definition 6.20. *Let* $MAT(m, n)$ *denote a two-dimensional matrix and let* $GRID(p, q)$ *denote a two-dimensional processor array. Let* $I(p, q)$ *denote a one-dimensional distribution array, such that* $I(i, j) \leq p \cdot q$, $\forall\, i \in [1..m]$, $\forall\, j \in [1..n]$. *The* indirect data distribution *of* MAT *is a function:*

$$DISTR : [1..m] \times [1..n] \rightarrow [1..p] \times [1..q],$$

$$DISTR(x, y) = \left(I(x, y) \; mod \; p, \; \left\lfloor \frac{I(x, y)}{p} \right\rfloor \right).$$

We define each distribution array element $I(x, y)$, $\forall\, x \in [1..p]$, $\forall\, j \in [1..q]$, *as a ZEN variable annotated to specify the complete set of possible indirect array distributions.*

Example 6.21 defines the matrix $MAT(m, n)$ which has the elements indirectly distributed across the processor array $GRID(p, q)$ according to the mapping array $I(m, n)$ as specified by the HPF directive d18 (see Figure 6.15). The elements of the mapping array $I(m, n)$ are program constants which are annotated with the ZEN substitute directives d2–d17 that specify the complete set of possible indirect distributions. These ZEN annotations define a search space of $(p \cdot q)^{mn}$ possible array mappings. The HPF PROCESSOR directive d1 in this approach represents the complete set processors available on the Grid (i.e. of cardinality $p \cdot q$) organised into a two-dimensional array $GRID(p, q)$. Since it is clearly impractical to manually annotate the application as shown in Example 6.21, we insert the ZEN directives at runtime with support from the ZENTURIO Experiment Generator service (see Section 4.4.1) with actual Grid site availability retrieved from the MDS information service.

We express the objective function similarly as in the context of the general block distribution (see Definition 6.19) using application specific analytical functions. For the Jacobi relaxation application with an irregular array distribution, we approximate the computation and the communication performance data as follows:

$$\delta_{\texttt{GRID}} \left(\mathcal{M}_1, \; \mathcal{AI} \left(\texttt{GRID}_{i,j}, \texttt{DISTR} \right) \right) = \left| \texttt{MAT}_{\texttt{GRID}_{i,j}} \right| \cdot \frac{W_e}{v_{\texttt{GRID}_{i,j}}};$$

$$\delta_{\texttt{GRID}} \left(\mathcal{M}_2, \; \mathcal{AI} \left(\texttt{GRID}_{i,j}, \texttt{DISTR} \right) \right) = \sum_{\forall\, (k,l) \in \texttt{MAT}_{\texttt{GRID}_{i,j}}} S_e \cdot$$

$$\cdot \left(\frac{1}{\mathcal{B}\left(\texttt{GRID}_{i,j}, \texttt{GRID}_{\texttt{DISTR}(k-1,l)} \right)} + \frac{1}{\mathcal{B}\left(\texttt{GRID}_{i,j}, \texttt{GRID}_{\texttt{DISTR}(k+1,l)} \right)} + \right.$$

$$\left. + \frac{1}{\mathcal{B}\left(\texttt{GRID}_{i,j}, \texttt{GRID}_{\texttt{DISTR}(k,l-1)} \right)} + \frac{1}{\mathcal{B}\left(\texttt{GRID}_{i,j}, \texttt{GRID}_{\texttt{DISTR}(k,l+1)} \right)} \right),$$

where $\left| \texttt{MAT}_{\texttt{GRID}_{i,j}} \right|$ is the cardinality (i.e. number of matrix elements) of the distribution of MAT onto the processor $\texttt{GRID}_{i,j}$. We ignore the less critical latencies for brevity reasons.

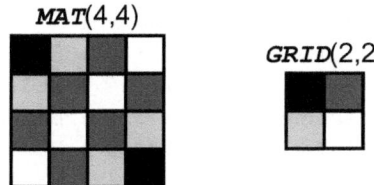

Fig. 6.15. The default indirect array distribution defined in Example 6.21.

6.6 Summary

In this section we presented a generic framework for optimising parallel and Grid applications in heterogeneous Grid environments. The framework accepts as input generic ZEN application that defines a huge parameter space impossible to be exhaustively explored and uses general purpose meta-heuristics to search for a ZEN application instance that maximises a certain input objective function. We implemented a generic search engine based on a generational genetic algorithm that can be applied to any optimisation problem which is simply instantiated by the implementation of the objective function. We illustrated instantiations of the framework for three important Grid computing problems: Grid workflow scheduling, Grid throughput scheduling, and performance tuning of parallel application on the Grid.

Example 6.21 (HPF indirect array distribution).

```
          INTEGER, PARAMETER m = 4
          INTEGER, PARAMETER n = 4
          INTEGER, PARAMETER p = 2
          INTEGER, PARAMETER q = 2
          DIMENSION MAT(m,n)
d1:  !HPF$ PROCESSOR GRID(p,q)
          INTEGER, PARAMETER M11 = 1
          INTEGER, PARAMETER M12 = 2
          INTEGER, PARAMETER M13 = 3
          INTEGER, PARAMETER M14 = 4
          INTEGER, PARAMETER M21 = 2
          INTEGER, PARAMETER M22 = 3
          INTEGER, PARAMETER M23 = 4
          INTEGER, PARAMETER M24 = 2
          INTEGER, PARAMETER M31 = 3
          INTEGER, PARAMETER M32 = 4
          INTEGER, PARAMETER M33 = 3
          INTEGER, PARAMETER M34 = 2
          INTEGER, PARAMETER M41 = 4
          INTEGER, PARAMETER M42 = 3
          INTEGER, PARAMETER M43 = 2
```

```
                  INTEGER, PARAMETER M44 = 1
 d2:   !ZEN$ SUBSTITUTE M11 = { 1 : 4 } BEGIN
 d3:   !ZEN$ SUBSTITUTE M12 = { 1 : 4 } BEGIN
 d4:   !ZEN$ SUBSTITUTE M13 = { 1 : 4 } BEGIN
 d5:   !ZEN$ SUBSTITUTE M14 = { 1 : 4 } BEGIN
 d6:   !ZEN$ SUBSTITUTE M21 = { 1 : 4 } BEGIN
 d7:   !ZEN$ SUBSTITUTE M22 = { 1 : 4 } BEGIN
 d8:   !ZEN$ SUBSTITUTE M23 = { 1 : 4 } BEGIN
 d9:   !ZEN$ SUBSTITUTE M24 = { 1 : 4 } BEGIN
 d10:  !ZEN$ SUBSTITUTE M31 = { 1 : 4 } BEGIN
 d11:  !ZEN$ SUBSTITUTE M32 = { 1 : 4 } BEGIN
 d12:  !ZEN$ SUBSTITUTE M33 = { 1 : 4 } BEGIN
 d13:  !ZEN$ SUBSTITUTE M34 = { 1 : 4 } BEGIN
 d14:  !ZEN$ SUBSTITUTE M41 = { 1 : 4 } BEGIN
 d15:  !ZEN$ SUBSTITUTE M42 = { 1 : 4 } BEGIN
 d16:  !ZEN$ SUBSTITUTE M43 = { 1 : 4 } BEGIN
 d17:  !ZEN$ SUBSTITUTE M44 = { 1 : 4 } BEGIN
                  INTEGER I(m,n) = (/ (/ M11, M12, M13, M14 /),
                                      (/ M21, M22, M23, M24 /),
                                      (/ M31, M32, M33, M34 /),
                                      (/ M41, M42, M43, M44 /) /)
 d17:  !ZEN$ END SUBSTITUTE
 d16:  !ZEN$ END SUBSTITUTE
 d15:  !ZEN$ END SUBSTITUTE
 d14:  !ZEN$ END SUBSTITUTE
 d13:  !ZEN$ END SUBSTITUTE
 d12:  !ZEN$ END SUBSTITUTE
 d11:  !ZEN$ END SUBSTITUTE
 d10:  !ZEN$ END SUBSTITUTE
 d9:   !ZEN$ END SUBSTITUTE
 d8:   !ZEN$ END SUBSTITUTE
 d7:   !ZEN$ END SUBSTITUTE
 d6:   !ZEN$ END SUBSTITUTE
 d5:   !ZEN$ END SUBSTITUTE
 d4:   !ZEN$ END SUBSTITUTE
 d3:   !ZEN$ END SUBSTITUTE
 d2:   !ZEN$ END SUBSTITUTE
 d18:  !HPF$ DISTRIBUTE MAT(INDIRECT(I)) ONTO GRID
```

7
Scientific Grid Workflows

Workflow modeling is a well established area in computer science that was strongly influenced by business process modeling work [187]. Recently, the Grid community has generally acknowledged that orchestrating existing software applications implemented as Grid services in course grain workflows represents an important class of applications that matches the loosely coupled Grid model and, therefore, can benefit from being executed in distributed Grid infrastructures. Similarly, in order to efficiently harness the computational resources provided by the Grid, existing monolithic scientific applications are currently being re-engineered and decomposed in a set of atomic activities orchestrated in a loosely coupled scientific workflow [58, 133].

Despite their similarities with the workflows originating from the business world, scientific workflows to be executed in Grid infrastructures present fundamental differences that make them rather unique and, therefore, impose specific requirements to support them:

- large number of activity instances (i.e. hundreds to thousands) which are difficult or impossible to express individually;
- computationally intensive activities with long and often unpredictable execution times;
- complex data dependencies of various sizes ranging from few bytes to several gigabytes;
- sequential loops that transform workflows into complex DG-based structures, as opposed to simpler DAGs characteristic to the business world;
- dynamic control and data flow structure, often unknown before the execution, that may change at runtime depending on the input workflow parameters or on the output results produced by the workflow activities;
- unreliable execution resources that raise complex fault tolerant issues.

There is currently a large amount of research in the Grid community devoted to the specification of scientific workflow applications that range from low level scripting languages [1, 53, 114, 127, 161], to high level abstract XML representations [7, 10, 45, 63, 70, 101, 106, 115], and user friendly graphical interfaces [26, 35, 65, 151]. Still, a common consensus on the fundamental structural and runtime characteristics of scientific Grid workflows is missing. In this chapter we aim to complement these efforts by introducing a formal model for expressing scientific workflows and a runtime environment for reliable and scalable execution in dynamic Grid infrastructures.

7.1 Workflow Model

In Section 2.6.3 we introduced a simple workflow model that represents the final runtime representation of the application scheduled on heterogeneous Grid resources using the ZENTURIO optimisation framework. Such a representation, however, is clearly not friendly for describing scientific workflows at the user level assuming the characteristics listed at the beginning of this chapter, like large sets of activities whose precise number is statically unknown before the execution of the workflow.

In this section we present a generic abstract model for formally representing large scale and complex scientific workflows in Grid environments. Our representation is generic and independent of any language or grammar as underlying implementation platform. For example, we implemented our model through the XML-based Abstract Grid Workflow Language (AGWL) that we described in [70].

Definition 7.1. *We define a* scientific workflow application *as a DAG:* $W = (Nodes, C\text{-}edges, D\text{-}edges, IN\text{-}ports, OUT\text{-}ports)$, *where:*

1. *Nodes is the set of workflow activities;*
2. *C-edges* $= \bigcup_{N_s, N_d \in Nodes} (N_s, N_d)$ *is the set of* control flow dependencies;
3. *D-edges* $= \bigcup_{N_s, N_d \in Nodes} (N_s, N_d, D\text{-}port)$ *is the set of* data flow dependencies;
4. *IN-ports is the set of workflow* input data ports;
5. *OUT-ports is the set of workflow* output data ports.

An activity $N \in Nodes$ *is a mapping from a set of input data ports IN-ports^N to a set of output data ports OUT-ports^N:*

$$N: IN\text{-}ports^N \to OUT\text{-}ports^N.$$

A data port $D\text{-}port \in IN\text{-}ports^N \times OUT\text{-}ports^N$ *is an an association between a* unique *identifier (within the workflow representation) and a well-defined type:*

$$D\text{-}port = (identifier, \ type).$$

The type of a data port is instantiated by the type system supported by the underlying implementation language, e.g. the XML schema. The most important data type according to our experience that shall be supported for Grid workflows is *file* along side other basic types such as integer, float, or string.

An activity $N \in Nodes$ can be of several kinds:

1. *computational activity* or *atomic activity* represents an atomic unit of computation such as a legacy sequential or parallel application following the model that we defined in Section 2.6.3;
2. *composite activity* is a generic term for an activity that aggregates multiple (atomic and composite) activities according to one of the following four patterns:
   a) *parallel loop activity* allows the user to express large scale workflows consisting of a large number (i.e. hundreds to thousands) of atomic activities in a compact manner;
   b) *sequential loop activity* defines iterative recursive computations with possibly unknown number of iterations determined by dynamic convergence criteria that depend on the runtime output data port values computed within one iteration;
   c) *conditional activity* models `if` and `switch`-like statements that activate one from its multiple successor activities based on the evaluation of a boolean condition;
   d) *workflow activity* is introduced for modularity and reuse purposes, and is recursively defined according to Definition 7.1.

Definition 7.2. *Our workflow model is therefore based on a hierarchical representation, in which an activity N is called the* child *of the parent composite activity $N_p = Parent(N)$ to which it belongs: $N \in N_p$. We denote as $Parent^n(N)$ the ancestor of degree n of the activity N, where: $N \in Parent(N) \in \ldots \in Parent^{n-1}(N) \in Parent^n(N)$. We call the workflow that models the entire scientific application according to Definition 7.1 as* root workflow.

7.1.1 Computational Activity

A *computational activity* defines an atomic unit of work instantiated at runtime by a computational job running on a remote Grid site according to the model defined in Section 2.6.3. A computational activity has a unique *type* that defines the computation performed by any underlying implementation such as matrix multiplication, LAPW material science calculation (see Section 4.2.2), 3DPIC photonic application (see Section 4.2.3), benders decomposition method (see Section 4.2.4), or three-dimensional FFT (see Section 4.2.5). An activity type has a well-defined interface described by the type of its input and output data ports.

Definition 7.3. *A computational activity deployment is a mapping from an activity type to a URL that indicates the Grid location where an implementation of the activity type exists:*

$$AD : type \rightarrow URL.$$

Similarly, a computational activity instance *is a mapping from an activity deployment to an URL that defines the Grid location where the activity deployment is executing. We express the* data port runtime value *of an activity instance N using an evaluation function:*

$$\omega_N : \textit{IN-ports}^N \cup \textit{OUT-ports}^N \rightarrow \textit{type}.$$

In our model, the activity deployment URL uses the `gsi` GridFTP protocol, while the activity instance URL is accessible through a Web service-enabled GRAM server using the `http` protocol (see Section 2.6.3). Activity types and activity deployments are typically published within a Grid information service like Globus MDS.

7.1.2 Control Flow Dependencies

Definition 7.4. *The set of* control flow dependencies *C-edges of a workflow introduced in Definition 7.1 defines a* control precedence relation, *denoted as $\prec_c$ which is a partial order over the activity set Nodes:*

$$\prec_c: \textit{Nodes} \times \textit{Nodes} \rightarrow \textit{boolean}, \ N_1 \prec_c N_n \iff$$
$$\iff \exists \, \rho = \{N_1, \ldots, N_n\} \subset \textit{Nodes} \ \wedge \ (N_i, N_{i+1}) \in \textit{C-edges},$$
$$\forall \, i \in [1..n-1] \ \wedge \ \nexists \, (N_j, N_k) \in \rho \ \wedge \ 1 \leq k < j \leq n.$$

We call N_1 the *source* and N_n the *sink* of the control flow dependency (N_1, N_n), with the execution semantics indicating that N_1 cannot start before N_n completes its execution.

The control precedence relation between two activities $N_1 \prec_c N_n$ can be of two kinds:

1. *direct* $\iff (N_1, N_n) \in \textit{C-edges}$;
2. *indirect* $\iff (N_1, N_n) \notin \textit{C-edges}$.

Similar to Definition 2.7 in Chapter 2, we define the set of *predecessors* of a workflow activity N as the set:

$$pred(N) = \bigcup_{\forall \, (N_{pred}, N) \in \textit{C-edges}} N_{pred},$$

and the set of *successors* of a workflow activity N as the set:

$$succ(N) = \bigcup_{\forall \, (N, N_{succ}) \in \textit{C-edges}} N_{succ}.$$

7.1.3 Data Flow Dependencies

Definition 7.5. *The* data flow dependency *elements of the D-edges set define a* data precedence relation, *denoted as* $\prec_d$, *over the set of the activities Nodes of a workflow:*

$$\prec_d: Nodes \times Nodes \rightarrow boolean,$$
$$N_s \prec_d N_d \iff (N_s, N_d, D\text{-}port) \in D\text{-}edges.$$

A data flow dependency between two activities is *consistent* if and only if it connects one input port of the source activity N_1 with one output port of the sink activity N_2:

$$(N_1, N_2, D\text{-}port) \in D\text{-}edges \iff$$
$$\iff D\text{-}port \in OUT\text{-}ports^{N_1} \wedge D\text{-}port \in IN\text{-}ports^{N_2}.$$

The semantics of the dependency is that the sink activity N_2 requires as input one output data of the source activity N_1, denoted as *D-port*.

In our current execution model, the data precedence is a stronger relationship which implies a control flow precedence too:

$$N_1 \prec_d N_2 \implies N_1 \prec_c N_2.$$

The semantics for the workflow enactment is that the output data of activity N_1 is considered as completed and can be sent to N_2 only after N_1 finished its execution. We are planning in future work to eliminate this constraint through other communication patterns such as data streams or pipelines.

7.1.4 Conditional Activity

Conditional activities model `if` or `switch`-like conditional statements whose purpose is to select (enact) only one activity from a set of successor activities (rather than fork all of them in parallel as in the case of DAGs or parallel loops).

Definition 7.6. *We represent a* conditional activity *of a scientific workflow as a tuple:* $N_{if} = (if, Branches, IN\text{-}ports^{N_{if}}, OUT\text{-}ports^{N_{if}})$ *where (see Figure 7.1(a)):*

1. *Branches* $= \bigcup_{\forall i \in [1..n]} N_i$ *is a set of so called* branch activities *that can be atomic or composite activities, as introduced in Definition 7.1;*
2. *if is a surjective function that selects (enacts) one of the n branch activities* $N_i \in Branches$ *based on its evaluation result:*

$$if : D\text{-}port_1 \times \ldots \times D\text{-}port_n \rightarrow Branches,$$

where $IN\text{-}ports^{N_{if}} = \bigcup_{i=1}^{n} D\text{-}port_i;$

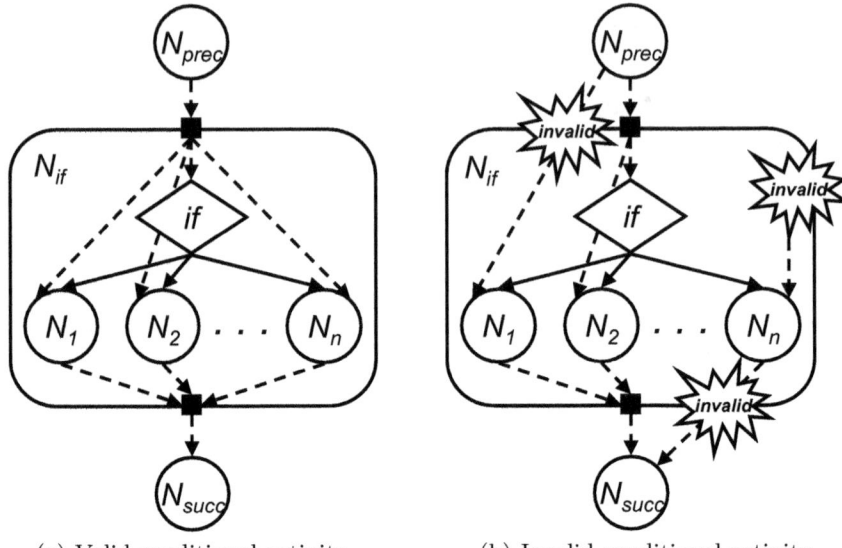

(a) Valid conditional activity.   (b) Invalid conditional activity.

Fig. 7.1. A valid and an invalid conditional activity example.

3. *each input data port of the each branch activity must be consistently connected to one input data port of the conditional activity:*

$$IN\text{-}ports^{N_i} \subseteq IN\text{-}ports^{N_{if}}, \ \forall \ i \in [1..n].$$

This constraint ensures that no input data port of any branch activity remains not instantiated or connected outside the conditional activity (see Figure 7.1(b));

4. *each output data port of the conditional activity must be consistently connected to exactly one output port of each branch activity:*

$$OUT\text{-}ports^{N_{if}} \subset \bigcup_{i=1}^{n} OUT\text{-}ports^{N_i}.$$

This constraint ensures that no conditional branch leaves any of the output data ports of the conditional activity not instantiated (see Figure 7.1(b)). All the remaining output ports of the branch activities from the set $\bigcup_{i=1}^{n} OUT\text{-}ports^{N_i} \setminus OUT\text{-}ports^{N_{if}}$ are ignored.

7.1.5 Parallel Loop Activity

A common characteristic of scientific workflows is a large number of activities instances of the same type with no dependencies in between which can be executed in parallel on different Grid processors or sites. We therefore introduce the parallel loop as a special type of composite activity which provides a powerful mechanism for expressing such large scale workflow constructs in a compact and user friendly manner.

Definition 7.7. *We represent a parallel loop activity as a tuple:* $N_{par} = \left(N_{body}, \text{IN-ports}^{N_{par}}, \text{OUT-ports}^{N_{par}} \right)$, *where:*

1. $\exists \ (D\text{-}port_{card}, integer) \in \text{IN-ports}^{N_{par}}$ *a predefined cardinality input port of type integer that defines the runtime cardinality of the parallel loop, denotes as* $|N_{par}|$:

$$\omega_{N_{par}} (D\text{-}port_{card}) = |N_{par}| \, ;$$

2. N_{body} *is an atomic or composite activity representing the parallel loop body of which* $|N_{par}|$ *independent instances are executed.*

The cardinality port can be instantiated either statically before the workflow execution or at runtime during workflow execution, for example from one output port of a predecessor activity through a data flow dependency.

Obviously, it is often the case that such large parallel activities involve a high number of data dependencies that are inconvenient to be individually expressed, especially since for parallel loops they often follow certain regular pattern. To meet this requirement and support expressive communication patterns involving parallel activities of high cardinality, we introduce a new composite data port type called collection.

Definition 7.8. *A* collection *is a composite data port* $D\text{-}port_{COL}$ *that consists of a homogeneous set of atomic data ports (of the same* type*) of cardinality* $|D\text{-}port_{COL}| = card$ *and an additional field called* pattern *that defines various types of collective communication, as illustrated in Figure 7.2:*

$$D\text{-}port_{COL} = (identifier, \ type, \ card, \ pattern).$$

1. *broadcast* (see Figure 7.2(a)) distributes the collection $D\text{-}port_{COL}$ produced by one atomic activity A to each atomic activity of the successor parallel activity according to the constant function:

$$\texttt{DISTR}_{\texttt{BCAST}} : A \ \times \ N_{par} \to D\text{-}port_{COL}, \ \texttt{DISTR}_{\texttt{BCAST}} (A, N) = D\text{-}port_{COL},$$

that generates the following set of data dependencies:

$$D\text{-}edges^{N_{par}} = A \ \times \ N_{par} \times \texttt{DISTR}_{\texttt{BCAST}} (A, N_{par}) =$$
$$= \bigcup_{\forall \, N \in N_{par}} (A, N, D\text{-}port_{COL}),$$

where $\times$ denotes the cross product operator between two sets;

2. *scatter* (see Figure 7.2(b)) distributes every i^{th} element of the collection $D\text{-}port_{\text{COL}}$ produced by the atomic activity A to the ith element of the successor parallel activity N_{par} according to the bijective function:

$$\text{DISTR}_{\text{SG}} : A \times N_{par} \rightarrow D\text{-}port_{\text{COL}}, \ \text{DISTR}_{\text{SG}}\left(A, N_{par}[i]\right) = D\text{-}port_{\text{COL}}[i],$$

that generates the following set of data dependencies:

$$D\text{-}edges^{N_{par}} = A \times N_{par} \times \text{DISTR}_{\text{SG}}\left(A, N_{par}\right) =$$
$$= \bigcup_{\forall\, N \in N_{par}} \left(A, N, \text{DISTR}_{\text{SG}}\left(A, N\right)\right).$$

The cardinality of the collection is equal with the cardinality input port $D\text{-}port_{card}$ of the parallel activity N_{par}:

$$|D\text{-}port_{\text{COL}}| = \omega_{N_{par}}\left(D\text{-}port_{card}\right);$$

3. *gather* (see Figure 7.2(c)) is the opposite of scatter and collects the output of every i^{th} atomic activity of the parallel activity N_{par} into the ith element of the input data port collection $D\text{-}port_{\text{COL}}$ of the successor atomic activity A that generates the following set of data dependencies:

$$D\text{-}edges^{N_{par}} = N_{par} \times A \times \text{DISTR}_{\text{SG}}\left(N_{par}, A\right) =$$
$$= \bigcup_{\forall\, N \in N_{par}} \left(N, A, \text{DISTR}_{\text{SG}}\left(N, A\right)\right),$$

where DISTR_{SG} is a bijection function defined equally as for the scatter communication. Similarly, the cardinality of the collection is equal with the cardinality input port of the parallel activity N_{par}:

$$|D\text{-}port_{\text{COL}}| = \omega_{N_{par}}\left(D\text{-}port_{card}\right);$$

4. *parallel* (see Figure 7.2(d)) distributes the ith collection element produced by the parallel activity AN_{par} to the ith activity of the successor parallel activity BN_{par} according to the function:

$$\text{DISTR}_{\text{PAR}} : AN_{par} \times BN_{par} \rightarrow D\text{-}port_{\text{COL}},$$
$$\text{DISTR}_{\text{PAR}}\left(AN[i], BN[j]\right) = \begin{cases} D\text{-}port_{\text{COL}}[i], & i = j; \\ \emptyset, & i \neq j, \end{cases}$$

where $\emptyset$ denotes the empty set which expresses that no data dependency between the two activities exists. This produces the following set of data dependencies:

$$D\text{-}edges^{N_{par}} = AN_{par} \times BN_{par} \times \text{DISTR}_{\text{PAR}}\left(AN_{par}, BN_{par}\right) =$$
$$= \bigcup_{\forall\, (N_1, N_2) \in AN_{par} \times BN_{par}} \left(N_1, N_2, \text{DISTR}_{\text{PAR}}\left(N_1, N_2\right)\right).$$

The cardinality of the collection is equal with the cardinality input ports $D\text{-}port_{card}^{AN_{par}}$ and $D\text{-}port_{card}^{BN_{par}}$ of the two parallel activities AN_{par}, respectively BN_{par}:

$$|D\text{-}port_{\text{COL}}| = \omega_{AN_{par}}\left(D\text{-}port_{card}^{AN_{par}}\right) = \omega_{BN_{par}}\left(D\text{-}port_{card}^{BN_{par}}\right);$$

5. *parallel broadcast* (see Figure 7.2(e)) distributes the entire collection $D\text{-}port_{\text{COL}}$ produced by one parallel activity AN_{par} to all atomic activities of the successor parallel activity BN_{par} according to the constant function:

$$\text{DISTR}_{\text{PBCAST}} : AN_{par} \times BN_{par} \rightarrow D\text{-}port_{\text{COL}},$$

$$\text{DISTR}_{\text{PBCAST}}\left(N_1, N_2\right) = D\text{-}port_{\text{COL}},$$

which generates the following set of data flow dependencies:

$$D\text{-}edges^{N_{par}} = AN_{par} \times BN_{par} \times \text{DISTR}_{\text{PBCAST}}\left(AN_{par}, BN_{par}\right) =$$

$$= \bigcup_{\forall\,(N_1, N_2) \in AN_{par} \times BN_{par}} \left(N_1, N_2, D\text{-}port_{\text{COL}}\right).$$

The cardinality of the collection is equal with the cardinality input port of the input parallel activity AN_{par}:

$$|D\text{-}port_{\text{COL}}| = \omega_{AN_{par}}\left(D\text{-}port_{card}\right).$$

7.1.6 Sequential Loop Activity

Sequential loops typically model a series of repetitive (recursive) computations possibly with a statically unknown number of iterations using a control flow dependency that violates the control precedence relation (see Section 7.1.2, Definition 7.4).

Definition 7.9. *We define a sequential loop activity of a scientific workflow as a tuple:* $N_{loop} = \left(if, N_{body}, IN\text{-}ports^{N_{loop}}, OUT\text{-}ports^{N_{loop}}\right)$, *where (see Figure 7.3):*

1. N_{body} *is a composite or atomic activity that represents the loop body whose input ports are a subset of the sequential loop activity input ports for modularity reasons:*

$$IN\text{-}ports^{N_{body}} \subseteq IN\text{-}ports^{N_{loop}};$$

2. *if is a boolean function that decides upon true evaluation whether a new iteration of the loop body N_{body} must be executed:*

$$if : IN\text{-}ports^{N_{loop}} \rightarrow boolean;$$

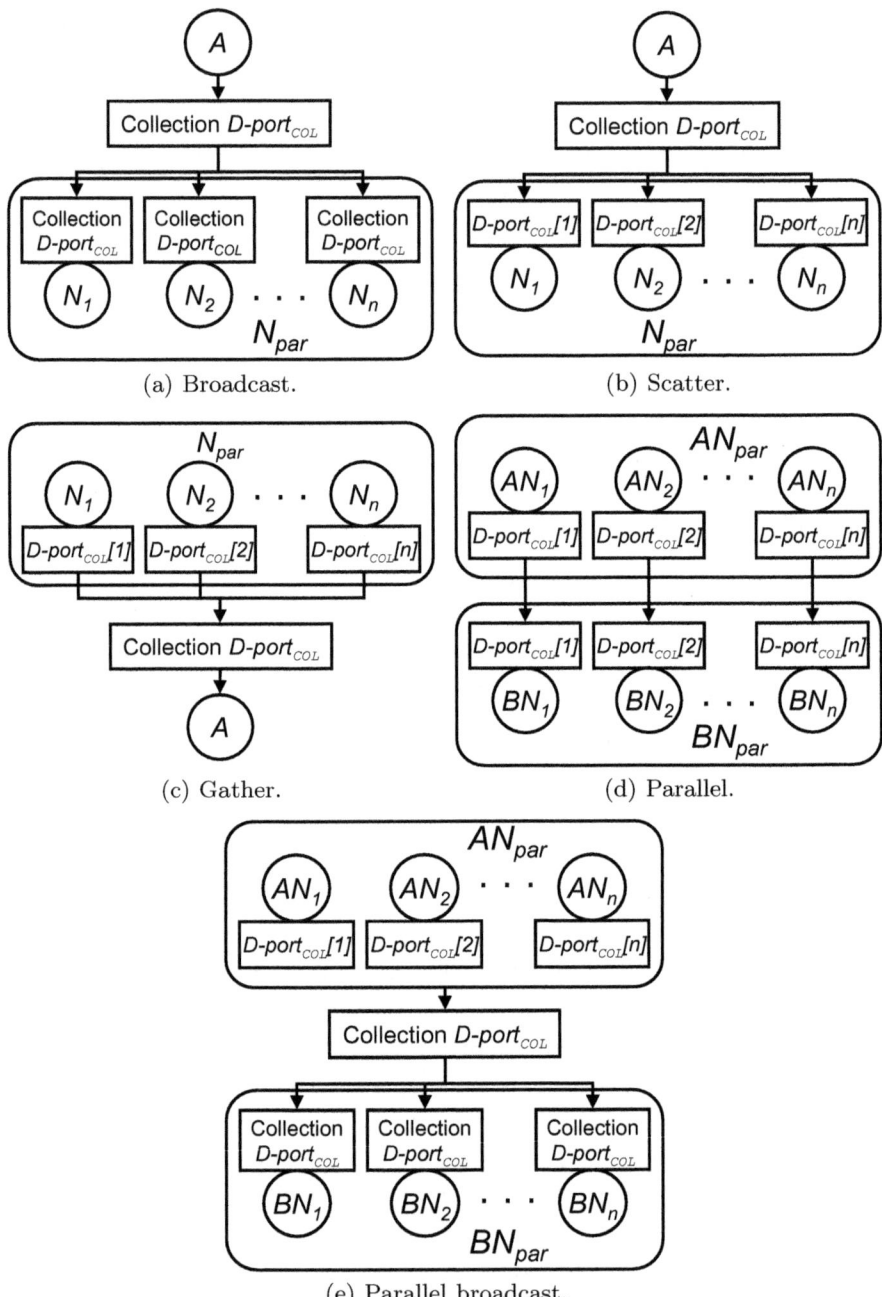

(a) Broadcast.

(b) Scatter.

(c) Gather.

(d) Parallel.

(e) Parallel broadcast.

Fig. 7.2. The collection transfer patterns.

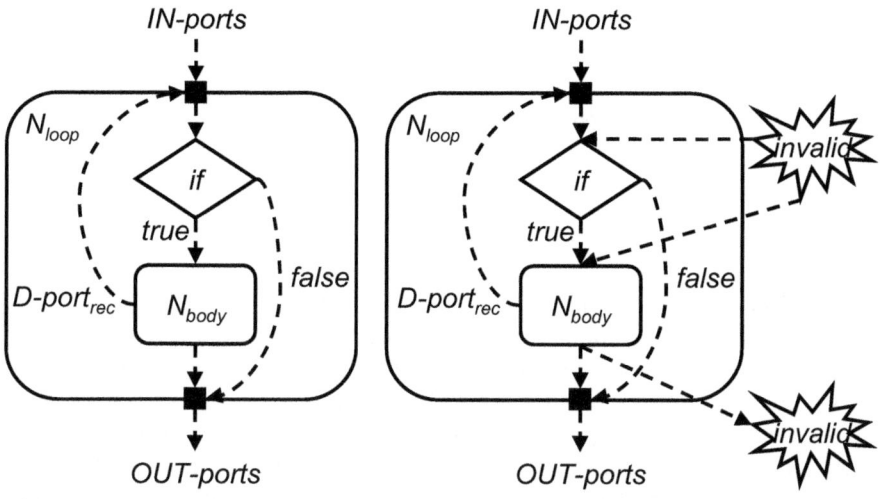

(a) Valid sequential loop activity.   (b) Invalid sequential loop activity.

Fig. 7.3. A valid and an invalid sequential loop activity.

3. *the conditional and the body activities share a subset of so called* recursive ports *that dynamically influence condition evaluation and, therefore, number of loop iterations:*

$$D\text{-}port_{rec} = IN\text{-}ports^{N_{loop}} \cap OUT\text{-}ports^{N_{body}} \neq \emptyset;$$

4. *the output ports OUT-ports of the sequential loop must belong to the output ports of the body activity N_{body} or replicate the input ports $IN\text{-}ports^{N_{loop}}$ for consistency and modularity reasons:*

$$OUT\text{-}ports^{N_{loop}} \subseteq IN\text{-}ports^{N_{loop}} \cup OUT\text{-}ports^{N_{body}}.$$

7.1.7 Workflow Activity

Workflow activities isolate composite functionality of scientific workflows for modularity and reuse purposes.

Definition 7.10. *We define a* workflow activity *of as a tuple compliant with the scientific workflow introduced in Definition 7.1, where: $\mathcal{W}_{sub} = (Nodes_{sub}, C\text{-}edges_{sub}, D\text{-}edges_{sub}, IN\text{-}ports_{sub}, OUT\text{-}ports_{sub})$, where*

1. *every input data ports of the workflow activity must be consistently connected to one input port of its underlying activities:*

$$IN\text{-}ports^{\mathcal{W}_{sub}} \subseteq \bigcup_{\forall N \in Nodes_{sub}} IN\text{-}ports^{N};$$

2. *each workflow output data port must be consistently connected to one output port of one underlying activity:*

$$OUT\text{-}ports^{\mathcal{W}_{sub}} \subseteq \bigcup_{\forall N \in Nodes_{sub}} OUT\text{-}ports^N.$$

7.2 Scheduler

The *Scheduler* [189, 190] is a best effort service in our tool integration architecture whose goal is to find good mappings of entire workflows onto available Grid resources. In Chapter 6 we presented an implementation of the Scheduler within the generic ZENTURIO optimisation framework using a primitive intermediate workflow representation and a modular architecture open to different plug-and-play algorithms and objective functions. In this section, we extend our service with two modular components to incorporate the high level scientific workflow model described in the previous section:

1. *workflow converter* (see Section 7.2.1) for transforming compact hierarchical scientific workflows into flat DAGs compliant with the model presented in Section 2.6.3 that can be given as input to the optimisation framework described in Chapter 6;
2. *scheduling engine* (see Section 7.2.2) which includes a specialised graph-based algorithm that aims to reduce the complexity of the genetic algorithm for finding good workflow schedules, as we will demonstrate in Sections 7.2.4 and 7.2.5.

7.2.1 Workflow Converter

A peculiarity of the workflow scheduling heuristics, such as our optimisation approach presented in Chapter 6, is that they are based on the DAG model for two main reasons:

1. static DAGs allow objective functions be precisely evaluated for the entire workflow. This clearly cannot be achieved for our scientific workflow model that contains loops with unknown number of iterations or undecidable conditional activities (see Section 7.1);
2. scheduling complete workflows in advance has the potential of producing better mappings optimised for the particular workflow structure, as we will demonstrate in the experimental part of this section.

The purpose of the *workflow converter* is therefore to transform hierarchical DG-based scientific workflows into plain DAGs, compliant with the model introduced in Section 2.6.3, that can be subject to heuristic algorithms for optimised scheduling on the Grid such as the genetic algorithm presented in Chapter 6. There are four constructs corresponding to the four composite activities described in Section 7.1 which need to be handled by the converter for transforming hierarchical scientific workflows into static DAGs of atomic activities: conditional activities, sequential loops, parallel loops, and sub-workflows. These transformations usually require additional prediction information such as the probability of execution of each branch in conditional activities or the number of iterations within sequential and parallel loops, which we compute from historical data stored in the Experiment Data Repository. Transformations based on correct assumptions can imply substantial performance benefits, while incorrect assumptions require appropriate runtime adjustments such as undoing existing optimisations or rescheduling based on the new information available.

Algorithm 5 depicts the pseudocode of the workflow conversion algorithm implemented by the `wf-converter` function that inlines a composite activity N into the root workflow $\mathcal{W}$. The algorithm invokes a custom conversion function based on the type of composite activity (see lines 3, 5, 7, and 9) that, as an outcome, is inlined into the original root workflow. The algorithm is first called using the original root workflow $\mathcal{W}$ as composite activity. i.e.

$$\texttt{wf-converter}\,(\mathcal{W}, \mathcal{W})$$

which is transformed into a DAG as a result of the function evaluation. We present in the following subsections the custom conversion function for each particular composite activity.

Branch Expansion

Let $N_{if} = \left(if, Branches, IN\text{-}ports^{N_{if}}, OUT\text{-}ports^{N_{if}}\right)$ denote a conditional activity. The *branch expansion* transformation uses prediction information about the probability of execution of each alternative branch activity defined by the following function:

$$Pr : Branches \rightarrow [0,1], \quad \sum_{\forall\, N \in Branches} Pr(N) = 1.$$

As an outcome, this transformation replaces the conditional activity with the complete set of branch activities, as follows (see Figure 7.4 and Algorithm 5):

1. add the branch activities to the set of activities of the root workflow (line 17);
2. replace the control and data flow dependencies involving the conditional activity with control and data flow dependencies to, respectively from, the branch activities (lines 18 and 19), depending on the data port type;
3. eliminate the conditional activity together with the incoming and outgoing control and data flow dependencies (line 20);
4. recursively apply the workflow conversion algorithm on all the composite branch activities (lines 21 − 23).

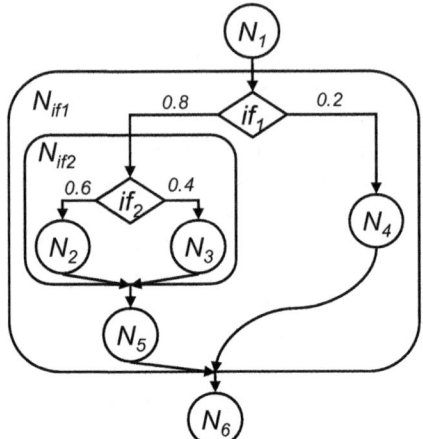

(a) Original workflow.

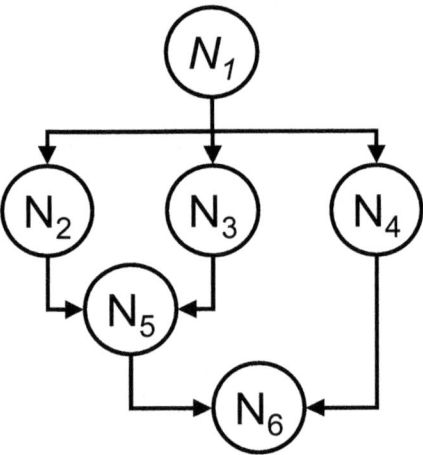

(b) Workflow after branch expansion.

Fig. 7.4. A sample workflow with two nested conditional activities.

Definition 7.11. *Let N denote an arbitrary workflow activity and T_N its predicted execution time. We calculate the probabilistic predicted time of N by weighting it with its probability of execution $Pr(N)$:*

$$\overline{T_N} = Pr(N) \cdot T_N.$$

The probability of execution of an arbitrary activity N with respect to the entire root workflow $\mathcal{W}_{root} = Parent^n(N)$ is the probability of execution $Pr(N)$ weighted with the execution probabilities all parent activities:

$$Pr_{root}(N) = Pr(N) \cdot \prod_{i=1}^{n} Pr\big(Parent^i(N)\big).$$

Obviously, $Pr(\mathcal{W}_{root}) = 1.$

We employ the probabilistic predicted time (rather than predicted execution time) of each individual activity when calculating the makespan objective function during the scheduling algorithm (see Section 6.1.2).

For example, Figure 7.4(a) displays a workflow containing two conditional activities N_{if1} and N_{if2} and the corresponding probabilities of executing the branch activities, where:

$$
\begin{aligned}
N_{if1} \quad &= Parent(N_{if2}) = Parent^2(N_2) = Parent^2(N_3) = \\
&= Parent(N_4) = Parent(N_5)\,; \\
N_{if2} \quad &= Parent(N_2) = Parent(N_3)\,; \\
Pr_{root}(N_1) \quad &= Pr(N_{if1}) = Pr(N_6) = 1; \\
Pr_{root}(N_{if2}) \quad &= 1 \cdot Pr(N_{if1}) = 0.8; \\
Pr_{root}(N_2) \quad &= Pr(N_2) \cdot Pr(N_{if2}) \cdot Pr(N_{if1}) = 0.6 \cdot 0.8 \cdot 1 = 0.48; \\
Pr_{root}(N_3) \quad &= Pr(N_3) \cdot Pr(N_{if2}) \cdot Pr(N_{if1}) = 0.4 \cdot 0.8 \cdot 1 = 0.32; \\
Pr_{root}(N_4) \quad &= Pr(N_4) \cdot Pr(N_{if1}) = 0.2 \cdot 1 = 0.2; \\
Pr_{root}(N_5) \quad &= Pr(N_5) \cdot Pr(N_{if1}) = 0.8 \cdot 1 = 0.8.
\end{aligned}
$$

Parallel Loop Unrolling

Parallel loop unrolling uses prediction information about the number of atomic activities in a composite parallel loop activity which instantiates the cardinality port:

$$\omega_{N_{par}} : \textit{IN-ports}^{N_{par}} \cup \textit{OUT-ports}^{N_{par}} \rightarrow \textit{integer},$$

$$\omega_{N_{par}}(\textit{D-port}_{card}) = |N_{par}|.$$

As an outcome, this transformation eliminates the parallel loop and generates a larger graph of atomic activities suitable for optimisation scheduling heuristics, as follows (see Algorithm 5):

1. unroll the parallel loop by adding a number of activity body clones (i.e. identical copies) to the root workflow activity set equal to the runtime value of the cardinality port (lines 37 and 38);
2. replace the control flow dependencies involving the composite parallel loop activity with control and data flow dependencies to, respectively from, all activity body clones representing the unrolled loop iterations (line 39);
3. replace the data flow dependencies to / from the parallel loop activity with data flow dependencies to / from all activity body clones according to the collection transfer patterns presented in Section 7.1.5 (line 40);

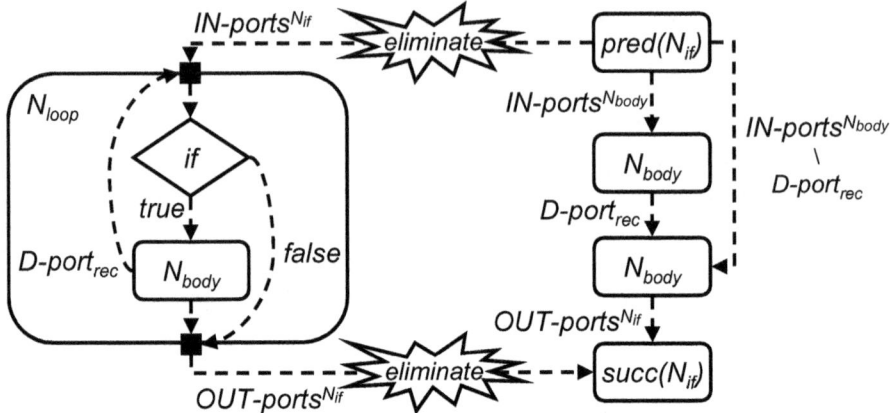

Fig. 7.5. The two iteration sequential loop unrolling.

4. eliminate the parallel loop activity together with the incoming and outgoing control and data flow dependencies (line 41);
5. recursively convert the unrolled activity body clones in case they are composite activities (line 42).

For example, Figure 7.7(a) in Section 7.2.4 illustrates a compact representation of the WIEN2k workflow (originally introduced in Section 6.3.1), while Figure 7.7(b) displays the new workflow after unrolling the two parallel loops LAPW1 and LAPW2.

Sequential Loop Unrolling

Sequential loop unrolling uses forecast information about the number of iterations to be executed in sequential loops. As an outcome, the converter unrolls the loops which eliminates the recursive cycles in scientific workflows that, as a consequence, are transformed from DG-based structures into DAGs. This transformation is particularly useful in cases when the resources and execution time required by the workflow activities depend on the iteration number. The Scheduler can therefore achieve better mappings by considering multiple iterations in advance.

The unrolling of one loop iteration is performed in several steps, as follows (see Algorithm 6):

1. add a clone of the sequential loop body to the set of activities of the root workflow (lines 53 − 54);
2. insert the body activity in the root workflow by adding the appropriate control flow and data flow dependencies, as depicted in Figure 7.5 (lines 55 − 56);
3. recursively inline the loop body in the root workflow by recursively applying the workflow conversion function (line 57);

4. connect the control and data flow of the last unrolled loop iteration body with the successors of the conditional activity (lines 60 − 61);

5. finally, eliminate the sequential loop activity from the workflow (line 62);

For example, Figure 7.7(a) in Section 7.2.4 illustrates a compact representation of the WIEN2k workflow (originally introduced in Section 6.3.1) using a UML-based modeling tool [151]. The left window displays the sequential loop composite activity, while the right window models the loop body. Figure 7.7(b) displays the new DAG-based workflow after unrolling *one* iteration of the sequential loop body (and also the parallel loops as presented in the previous section).

Workflow Inlining

The *workflow inlining* transformation expands sub-workflows, defined for modularity and reuse purposes as composite activities, into the root workflow for optimised mapping of large flat workflow structures using heuristic-based optimisation algorithms. A sub-workflow is inlined into the parent workflow through the following steps (see Algorithm 6):

1. add the activities of the sub-workflow to the activity list of the root workflow (line 68);

2. add the control flow and data flow dependencies of the sub-workflow to the control flow, respectively data flow dependencies of the root workflow (see lines 69 and 70);

3. replace the control and data flow dependencies to / from the sub-workflow with control and data flow dependencies to / from the sub-workflow nodes with no predecessors / successors (line 71);

4. replace the data flow dependencies to / from the sub-workflow with data flow dependencies to / from the sub-workflow nodes with the same input / output data ports (line 72);

5. eliminate the sub-workflow composite activity together with the incoming and outgoing control flow and data flow dependencies (line 73);

6. recursively apply the workflow conversion algorithm to all the composite sub-workflow activities (line 74 − 76).

Data Port Elimination

Data port elimination does one last cosmetic change to the workflow by converting each data flow dependency into one data transfer activity connected through control flow dependencies to the source, respectively the sink of the eliminated data dependency (see Algorithm 7, lines 81 − 84). Additionally, the input and output ports of the workflow are transformed into data transfer activities that perform input and output file staging (see lines 85 − 88, respectively 89 − 92). The purpose of this transformation is to make the workflow compliant with the internal representation introduced in Section 2.6.3 which we used for optimisation in Chapter 6.

Algorithm 5. The workflow conversion algorithm (I).

1: **function** WF-CONVERTER($\mathcal{W}_{root}, N$)
2:     **if** N is a N_{if} **then**
3:         $\mathcal{W}_{root} \leftarrow$ BRANCH-EXPANSION($\mathcal{W}_{root}, N$)
4:     **else if** N is a N_{loop} **then**
5:         $\mathcal{W}_{root} \leftarrow$ SEQ-LOOP-UNROLLING($\mathcal{W}_{root}, N$)
6:     **else if** N is a N_{par} **then**
7:         $\mathcal{W}_{root} \leftarrow$ PAR-LOOP-UNROLLING($\mathcal{W}_{root}, N$)
8:     **else if** N is a $\mathcal{W}$ **then**
9:         $\mathcal{W}_{root} \leftarrow$ WF-INLINING($\mathcal{W}_{root}, N$)
10:     **end if**
11:     **return** $\mathcal{W}_{root}$
12: **end function**
13:
14: **function** BRANCH-EXPANSION($\mathcal{W}, N_{if}$)
15:     $\mathcal{W} = Nodes, C\text{-}edges, D\text{-}edges, IN\text{-}ports^{\mathcal{W}}, OUT\text{-}ports^{\mathcal{W}}$
16:     $N_{if} = if, Branches, IN\text{-}ports^{N_{if}}, OUT\text{-}ports^{N_{if}}$ ▷ **Preconditions**
17:     $Nodes \leftarrow Nodes \cup Branches$
18:     $C\text{-}edges \leftarrow C\text{-}edges \cup (pred(N_{if}) \times Branches) \cup (Branches \times succ(N_{if}))$

19:     $D\text{-}edges \leftarrow D\text{-}edges \bigcup_{\forall (N_{pred}, N_{if}, D\text{-}port) \in D\text{-}edges \wedge} (N_{pred}, N, D\text{-}port) \cup$
            $\phantom{D\text{-}edges \leftarrow} \scriptstyle \forall N \in Branches \wedge D\text{-}port \in IN\text{-}ports^{N}$
            $\phantom{D\text{-}edges \leftarrow} \bigcup_{\forall (N_{if}, N_{succ}, D\text{-}port) \in D\text{-}edges \wedge} (N, N_{succ}, D\text{-}port)$
            $\phantom{D\text{-}edges \leftarrow} \scriptstyle \forall N \in Branches \wedge D\text{-}port \in IN\text{-}ports^{N}$

20:     $\mathcal{W} \leftarrow$ ACTIVITY-ELIMINATION($\mathcal{W}, N_{if}$)   ▷ **Eliminate composite activity**
21:     **for all** $N \in Branches$ **do**
22:         $\mathcal{W} \leftarrow$ WF-CONVERTER($\mathcal{W}, N$)   ▷ **Convert the branch activities**
23:     **end for**
24:     **return** $\mathcal{W}$
25: **end function**
26:
27: **function** ACTIVITY-ELIMINATION($\mathcal{W}, N$)
28:     $\mathcal{W} = (Nodes, C\text{-}edges, D\text{-}edges, IN\text{-}ports, OUT\text{-}ports)$ ▷ **Precondition**
29:     $Nodes \leftarrow Nodes \setminus N$
30:     $C\text{-}edges \leftarrow C\text{-}edges \setminus (pred(N) \times N) \setminus (N \times succ(N))$

31:     $D\text{-}edges \leftarrow D\text{-}edges \setminus pred(N) \times N \times IN\text{-}ports^{N} \setminus$
            $\phantom{D\text{-}edges \leftarrow D\text{-}edges} \setminus N \times succ(N) \times OUT\text{-}ports^{N}$

32:     **return** $\mathcal{W}$
33: **end function**

7.2.2 Scheduling Engine

The *scheduling engine* is responsible for the actual mapping of a workflow application converted into a DAG onto the Grid resources. We designed the engine as an independent module on top of the optimisation framework presented in Chapter 6, which allows different DAG-based scheduling heuristics be plugged-in with no external modifications. The algorithms with varying

Algorithm 6. The workflow conversion algorithm (II).

34: **function** PAR-LOOP-UNROLLING$(\mathcal{W}, N_{par})$
35:    $\mathcal{W} = $ Nodes, C-edges, D-edges, IN-ports$^{\mathcal{W}}$, OUT-ports$^{\mathcal{W}}$
36:    $N_{par} = N_{body}$, IN-ports$^{N_{par}}$, OUT-ports$^{N_{par}}$ ▷ **Preconditions**
37:    $PN \leftarrow \bigcup_{i=1}^{|N_{par}|}$ CLONE(N)
38:    $Nodes \leftarrow Nodes \cup PN$
39:    $C\text{-}edges \leftarrow C\text{-}edges \cup (pred(N_{par}) \times PN) \cup (PN \times succ(N_{par}))$
40:    $D\text{-}edges \leftarrow D\text{-}edges \bigcup_{\forall (N, N_{par}, D\text{-}port) \in D\text{-}edges} D\text{-}edges^{N_{par}}$ ▷ **D-edges**$^{N_{par}}$ **was**
      $\forall (N_{par}, N, D\text{-}port) \in D\text{-}edges$
   defined in Section 7.1.5
41:    $\mathcal{W} \leftarrow$ ACTIVITY-ELIMINATION$(\mathcal{W}, N_{par})$ ▷ **Eliminate composite activity**
42:    **for all** $N \in N_{par}$ **do**
43:       $\mathcal{W} \leftarrow$ WF-CONVERTER$(\mathcal{W}, N)$ ▷ **Convert the loop body**
44:    **end for**
45:    **return** DATA-PORT-ELIMINATION$(\mathcal{W})$
46: **end function**
47:
48: **function** SEQ-LOOP-UNROLLING$(\mathcal{W}, N_{loop}, n)$ ▷ **Unroll** n **iterations**
49:    $\mathcal{W} = $ Nodes, C-edges, D-edges, IN-ports$^{\mathcal{W}}$, OUT-ports$^{\mathcal{W}}$
50:    $N_{loop} = if, N_{body}$, IN-ports$^{N_{loop}}$, OUT-ports$^{N_{loop}}$ ▷ **Preconditions**
51:    $N_{pred} \leftarrow pred(N_{loop})$
52:    **for all** $i \in [1..n]$ **do**   ▷ **Unroll the loop body**
53:       $CN_{body} \leftarrow$ CLONE(N_{body})
54:       $Nodes \leftarrow Nodes \cup CN_{body}$
55:       $C\text{-}edges \leftarrow C\text{-}edges \cup (N_{pred} \times CN_{body})$
       $D\text{-}edges \leftarrow D\text{-}edges \bigcup_{\forall (N, N_{loop}, D\text{-}port) \in D\text{-}edges \wedge} (N, CN_{body}, D\text{-}port) \cup$
56:       $\phantom{D\text{-}edges \leftarrow} {}_{D\text{-}port \in IN\text{-}ports^{N_{body}} \setminus D\text{-}port_{rec}}$
       $\bigcup_{\forall (N, N_{loop}, D\text{-}port) \in D\text{-}edges} (N_{pred}, CN_{body}, D\text{-}port)$
       $ {}_{\wedge\ D\text{-}port \in D\text{-}port_{rec}}$
    ▷ **D-port$_{rec}$ was defined in Section 7.1.6**
57:       $\mathcal{W} \leftarrow$ WF-CONVERTER$(\mathcal{W}, CN_{body})$ ▷ **Convert the loop body**
58:       $N_{pred} \leftarrow CN_{body}$
59:    **end for**
60:    $C\text{-}edges \leftarrow C\text{-}edges \cup (CN_{body} \times succ(N_{loop}))$
61:    $D\text{-}edges \leftarrow \bigcup_{\forall (N_{loop}, N_{succ}, D\text{-}port) \in D\text{-}edges} (CN_{body}, N_{succ}, D\text{-}port)$
62:    $\mathcal{W} \leftarrow$ ACTIVITY-ELIMINATION$(\mathcal{W}, N_{loop})$ ▷ **Eliminate composite activity**
63:    **return** $\mathcal{W}$
64: **end function**

Algorithm 7. The workflow conversion algorithm (III).

65: **function** WF-INLINING$(\mathcal{W}, \mathcal{W}_{sub})$

66:     $\mathcal{W} = \langle Nodes, C\text{-}edges, D\text{-}edges, IN\text{-}ports^{\mathcal{W}}, OUT\text{-}ports^{\mathcal{W}} \rangle$ ▷ **Preconditions**

67:     $\mathcal{W}_{sub} = \langle Nodes_{sub}, C\text{-}edges_{sub}, D\text{-}edges_{sub}, IN\text{-}ports^{\mathcal{W}_{sub}}, OUT\text{-}ports^{\mathcal{W}_{sub}} \rangle$

68:     $Nodes \leftarrow Nodes \cup Nodes_{sub}$

69:     $C\text{-}edges \leftarrow C\text{-}edges \cup C\text{-}edges_{sub}$

70:     $D\text{-}edges \leftarrow D\text{-}edges \cup D\text{-}edges_{sub}$

71:
$$C\text{-}edges \leftarrow C\text{-}edges \cup \left(pred(\mathcal{W}_{sub}) \times \bigcup_{\substack{\forall N \in Nodes_{sub} \\ \wedge\, pred(N)=\emptyset}} N \right) \cup$$
$$\cup \bigcup_{\substack{\forall N \in Nodes_{sub} \\ \wedge\, succ(N)=\emptyset}} N \times succ(\mathcal{W}_{sub})$$

72:
$$D\text{-}edges \leftarrow \bigcup_{\forall (N, \mathcal{W}_{sub}, D\text{-}port) \in D\text{-}edges} \left(N \times \bigcup_{\substack{\forall N' \in Nodes_{sub}\, \wedge \\ D\text{-}port \in IN\text{-}ports^{N'}}} N' \times D\text{-}port \right) \cup$$
$$\bigcup_{\forall (\mathcal{W}_{sub}, N, D\text{-}port) \in D\text{-}edges} \left(\bigcup_{\substack{\forall N' \in Nodes_{sub}\, \wedge \\ D\text{-}port \in OUT\text{-}ports^{N'}}} N' \times N \times D\text{-}port \right)$$

73:     $\mathcal{W} \leftarrow$ ACTIVITY-ELIMINATION$(\mathcal{W}, \mathcal{W}_{sub})$ ▷ **Eliminate composite activity**

74:     **for all** $N \in Nodes_{sub}$ **do**

75:         $\mathcal{W} \leftarrow$ WF-CONVERTER$(\mathcal{W}, N)$ ▷ **Convert all composite activities**

76:     **end for**

77:     **return** $\mathcal{W}$

78: **end function**

79:

80: **function** DATA-PORT-ELIMINATION$(\mathcal{W})$

81:     **for all** $(CA_1(z_1), CA_2(z_2), D\text{-}port) \in D\text{-}edges$ **do**

82:         $Nodes \leftarrow Nodes \cup DA_{D\text{-}port}(z_1, z_2)$

83:         $C\text{-}edges \leftarrow C\text{-}edges \cup (CA_1, DA_{D\text{-}port}) \cup (DA_{D\text{-}port}, CA_2)$

84:     **end for**

85:     **for all** $D\text{-}port \in IN\text{-}ports^{\mathcal{W}}$ **do**

86:         $Nodes \leftarrow Nodes \bigcup_{\substack{\forall CA(z) \in Nodes\, \wedge \\ D\text{-}port \in IN\text{-}ports^{CA}}} DA(z_{D\text{-}port}, z)$

87:         $C\text{-}edges \leftarrow C\text{-}edges \bigcup_{\substack{\forall CA(z) \in Nodes\, \wedge \\ D\text{-}port \in IN\text{-}ports^{CA}}} (DA(z_{D\text{-}port}, z), CA(z))$

88:     **end for**

89:     **for all** $D\text{-}port \in OUT\text{-}ports^{\mathcal{W}}$ **do**

90:         $Nodes \leftarrow Nodes \bigcup_{\substack{\forall CA(z) \in Nodes\, \leftarrow \\ D\text{-}port \in OUT\text{-}ports^{CA}}} DA(z, z_{D\text{-}port})$

91:         $C\text{-}edges \leftarrow C\text{-}edges \bigcup_{\substack{\forall CA(z) \in Nodes\, \wedge \\ D\text{-}port \in OUT\text{-}ports^{CA}}} (CA(z), DA(z, z_{D\text{-}port}))$

92:     **end for**

93:     **return** $(Nodes, C\text{-}edges)$

94: **end function**

accuracy and complexity are based on different metrics as optimisation goals, as already presented in Section 6.1.2 (see Chapter 6).

In this section we present two additional heuristics that we use to implement the scheduling engine along side the genetic algorithm presented in Section 6.1:

1. *Heterogeneous Earliest Finish Time (HEFT)* [200] algorithm that is a list scheduling heuristic purposely tuned for scheduling complex DAGs in heterogeneous environments;
2. a *myopic* just-in-time algorithm acting like an opportunistic resource broker, similar to the Condor matchmaking mechanism used by DAGMan.

Heterogeneous Earliest Finish Time Algorithm (HEFT)

Let $\mathcal{A} = (\textit{Nodes}, \textit{C-edges})$ denote a workflow application, where *Nodes* represents the set of activities, and *C-edges* the set of control flow dependencies. The HEFT algorithm, illustrated in pseudocode in Algorithm 8, is an extension of the classical list scheduling algorithm for heterogeneous environments which consists of three distinct phases:

1. the *weighting phase* (lines $3 - 8$);
2. the *ranking phase* (lines $9 - 19$);
3. the *mapping phase* (lines $20 - 22$).

We explain in the following these three phases through a concrete example depicted in Figure 7.6.

Weighting

During the weighting phase (lines $3 - 8$) adjusted for heterogeneous Grid environments, we assign weights to the workflow activities equal to their probabilistic predicted time that we defined in Section 7.2.1 (see Definition 7.11). We estimate the predicted time of individual computational and data transfer activities based on historical data or application specific analytical models using techniques that we described in Section 6.1.2 and 6.3.1. Afterwards, we calculate the weight associated to a computational activity $CA \in \textit{Nodes}$ as the average value of the predicted execution times $T_{CA}^{\texttt{PROC}}$ on every individual processor $\texttt{PROC}$ available on the Grid (lines $3 - 5$):

$$\overline{w}_{CA} = \underset{\forall\, \texttt{PROC} \in \texttt{GRID}}{avg} \left\{ T_{CA}^{\texttt{PROC}} \right\}, \ \forall\ CA \in \textit{Nodes}.$$

Similarly, we compute the weight associated to a data transfer activity as the average of the predicted transfer times across all pairs of Grid sites (rather than all Grid processors – lines $6 - 8$).

$$\overline{w}_{DA} = \underset{\forall\, (M_1, M_2) \in \texttt{GRID}}{avg} \left\{ T_{DA}^{(M_1, M_2)} \right\}, \ \forall\ DA \in \textit{Nodes}.$$

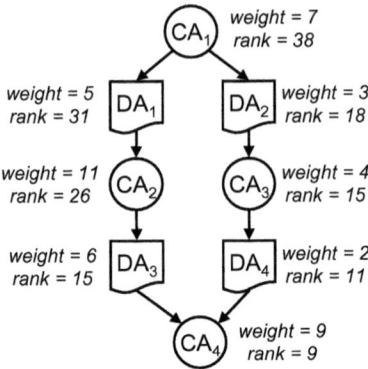

Fig. 7.6. The HEFT weights and ranks for a sample workflow.

In the example depicted in Figure 7.6, the Grid consists of three processors PROC_1, PROC_2, and PROC_3, therefore, the weight of activity N_1 is calculated as follows:

$$\overline{w}_{CA_1} = \frac{T_{CA_1}^{\text{PROC}_1} + T_{CA_1}^{\text{PROC}_2} + T_{CA_1}^{\text{PROC}_3}}{3} = \frac{5 + 8 + 8}{3} = 7,$$

and similarly:

$$\overline{w}_{DA_1} = \frac{T_{DA_1}^{(\text{PROC}_1, \text{PROC}_2)} + T_{DA_1}^{(\text{PROC}_1, \text{PROC}_3)} + T_{DA_1}^{(\text{PROC}_2, \text{PROC}_3)}}{3} = \frac{6 + 4 + 5}{3} = 5.$$

Table 7.1 displays the weights of all workflow activities calculated using the same formulas.

Table 7.1. The HEFT weight and rank calculations for the sample workflow depicted in Figure 7.6.

(a) Computational activity ranks.

	PROC_1	PROC_2	PROC_3	$\overline{w}$
CA_1	5	8	8	7
CA_2	9	13	11	11
CA_3	3	4	5	4
CA_4	7	10	10	9

(b) Data transfer activity ranks.

	$(\text{PROC}_1, \text{PROC}_2)$	$(\text{PROC}_1, \text{PROC}_3)$	$(\text{PROC}_2, \text{PROC}_3)$	$\overline{w}$
DA_1	6	4	5	5
DA_2	4	2	3	3
DA_3	7	4	7	6
DA_4	1	1	4	2

Algorithm 8. The HEFT algorithm.

1: **function** HEFT($\mathcal{W}$, GRID)
2:     $\mathcal{W} = (Nodes, C\text{-}edges)$ ▷ Precondition
3:     **for all** $CA \in Nodes$ **do**   ▷ Weighting phase
4:         $\overline{w}_{CA} \leftarrow \frac{\sum_{\forall \text{ PROC} \in \text{GRID}} T_{CA}^{\text{PROC}}}{|\text{GRID}|}$ ▷ |GRID| = no. of processors in GRID
5:     **end for**
6:     **for all** $DA \in Nodes$ **do**
7:         $\overline{w}_{DA} \leftarrow \frac{\sum_{\forall \text{ PROC}_1 \neq \text{PROC}_2 \in \text{GRID}} T_{DA}^{(\text{PROC}_1, \text{PROC}_2)}}{C_{|\text{GRID}|}^2}$ ▷ $C_{|\text{GRID}|}^2$ = combination of |GRID|
   elements taken 2 at a time
8:     **end for**
9:     $List_{C\text{-}edges} \leftarrow C\text{-}edges$ ▷ Ranking phase
10:     $List_{Nodes} \leftarrow Nodes$
11:     **while** $List_{C\text{-}edges} \neq \emptyset$ **do**
12:         **for all** $N \in List_{Nodes} \wedge (succ(N) \cap List_{C\text{-}edges} = \emptyset)$ **do**
13:             $\overline{R}_N \leftarrow \overline{w}_N + \max_{\forall N_{succ} \in succ(N)} \{\overline{w}_{Nsucc}\}$
14:             $List_{C\text{-}edges} \leftarrow List_{C\text{-}edges} \setminus (pred(N) \times N)$
15:
16:             $List_{Nodes} \leftarrow List_{Nodes} \setminus N$
17:         **end for**
18:     **end while**
19:     $RL \leftarrow \text{SORT}(Nodes, \overline{R}_N)$ ▷ Sort the activities based on ranks
20:     **for all** $i \in [1..|RL|]$ **do**   ▷ Mapping phase
21:         $N \leftarrow RL_i$
22:         $\mathcal{S}_N \leftarrow \text{PROC}$, where $end(N, \text{PROC}) = \min_{\forall P \in \text{GRID}} \{end(N, P)\}$ ▷ end function
   was defined in Section 6.1.2 (see Definition 6.7)
23:     **end for**
24:     **return** $\mathcal{S}_{\mathcal{W}}$ ▷ Workflow schedule
25: **end function**

Ranking

The ranking phase (lines $9 - 19$) is performed by traversing the workflow graph upwards and assigning a rank value to each activity. The rank value of an activity is equal to the weight of the activity plus the maximum rank value of all the successors (line 13):

$$\overline{R}_N = \max_{\forall N_{succ} \in succ(N)} \left\{\overline{w}_N + \overline{R}_{N_{succ}}\right\}.$$

For example, the rank of the activity CA_1 is calculated as:

$$\overline{R}_{CA_1} = \max \left\{\overline{w}_{CA_1} + \overline{R}_{DA_1}, \overline{w}_{CA_1} + \overline{R}_{DA_2}\right\} = \max \{7 + 31, 7 + 18\} = 38.$$

The list of workflow activities is then sorted in a descending order according to their ranks (line 19), i.e. CA_1, DA_1, CA_2, DA_2, CA_3, DA_3, DA_4, and CA_4.

Mapping

Finally in the mapping phase (lines $20 - 22$), the ranked activities are mapped onto the processors that deliver the earliest completion time according to the Definition 6.7 in Section 6.1.2, i.e.:

$$end(CA_1) = \min\{5, 8, 8\} = 5 \qquad\qquad \Rightarrow \mathcal{S}(CA_1) = \text{PROC}_1;$$
$$end(CA_2) = \min\{5 + 0 + 9, 5 + 6 + 13, 5 + 4 + 11\} = 14 \Rightarrow \mathcal{S}(CA_2) = \text{PROC}_1;$$
$$end(CA_3) = \min\{14 + 0 + 3, 5 + 4 + 4, 5 + 2 + 5\} = 12 \quad \Rightarrow \mathcal{S}(CA_3) = \text{PROC}_3;$$
$$end(CA_4) = \min\{\max\{14 + 0, 12 + 1\} + 7,$$
$$\max\{14 + 7, 12 + 4\} + 10,$$
$$\max\{14 + 4, 12 + 0\} + 10\} = 21 \qquad \Rightarrow \mathcal{S}(CA_4) = \text{PROC}_1.$$

Myopic Algorithm

To compare the two heuristic-based scheduling algorithms addressed so far (i.e. HEFT and genetic algorithm), we developed a simple and inexpensive heuristic which makes the mapping based on local optimal decisions similar to the matchmaking mechanism performed by a resource broker like Condor DAGMan [1] (see Algorithm 9). The algorithm traverses the workflow in the top-down direction (lines 5 and 6), analysis every activity separately, and assigns it to the processor which delivers the earliest completion time (line 7).

7.2.3 Layered Partitioning

We designed two alternative approaches for applying the scheduling algorithms to better cope with various workflow topology structures:

Algorithm 9. The myopic scheduling algorithm.

1: **function** MYOPIC($\mathcal{W}$, GRID)
2:    $\mathcal{W} = (Nodes, C\text{-}edges)$ ▷ Precondition
3:    $List_{Nodes} \leftarrow Nodes$
4:    $List_{C\text{-}edges} \leftarrow C\text{-}edges$
5:    **while** $List_{Nodes} \neq \emptyset$ **do**
6:        **for all** $N \in List_{Nodes} \wedge (pred(N) \cap List_{C\text{-}edges} = \emptyset)$ **do**
7:            $\mathcal{S}_N \leftarrow$ PROC, where $end(N, \text{PROC}) = \min\limits_{\forall P \in \text{GRID}} \{end(N, P)\}$ ▷ *end*
    function was defined in Section 6.1.2 (see Definition 6.7)
8:            $List_{Nodes} \leftarrow List_{Nodes} \setminus N$
9:            $List_{C\text{-}edges} \leftarrow List_{C\text{-}edges} \setminus (N \times succ(N))$
10:       **end for**
11:    **end while**
12:    **return** $\mathcal{S}_{\mathcal{W}}$ ▷ Workflow schedule
13: **end function**

---

1. *full-ahead scheduling* considers the entire workflow as part of the conversion and optimisation processes and is more suitable for workflows with irregular (imbalanced) structures (see Section 7.2.5);
2. *layered partitioning* considers as input to the conversion algorithm only a sub-workflow of a given depth of n atomic activities, calculated for a workflow $\mathcal{W} = \left(Nodes,\, C\text{-}edges,\, D\text{-}edges,\, IN\text{-}ports^{\mathcal{W}},\, OUT\text{-}ports^{\mathcal{W}} \right)$, as follows:

$$\mathcal{W}_n = \left(Nodes_n,\, C\text{-}edges_n,\, D\text{-}edges_n,\, IN\text{-}ports^{\mathcal{W}_n},\, OUT\text{-}ports^{\mathcal{W}_n} \right),$$

where:

- $Nodes_n \subseteq Nodes$;
- $succ^m(N) \in Nodes_n,\ \forall\, N \in Nodes_n\ \wedge\ pred(N) = \emptyset\ \wedge\ \forall\, m \in [1..n]$;
- $succ^{n+1}(N) \notin Nodes_n,\ \forall\, N \in Nodes_n\ \wedge\ pred(N) = \emptyset$;
- $D\text{-}edges_n = \bigcup_{\substack{\forall\,(N_1, N_2, D\text{-}port) \in D\text{-}edges \\ \wedge\ N_1, N_2 \in Nodes_n}} (N_1, N_2, D\text{-}port)$;
- $IN\text{-}ports^{\mathcal{W}_n} = IN\text{-}ports^{\mathcal{W}}$;
- $OUT\text{-}ports^{\mathcal{W}_n} = \bigcup_{\substack{\forall\, N \in Nodes_n\ \wedge \\ succ(N) \notin Nodes_n}} OUT\text{-}ports^{N}$.

This method is more suitable for workflows with regular structures and large number of activities, since it needs less scheduling time to compute optimised mappings of smaller sub-workflows (especially for the genetic algorithm described in Section 6.2) while preserving the overall quality of the solution (see Section 7.2.4)

7.2.4 WIEN2k

The first real application that we use for the scheduling experiments is the WIEN2k material science application that we already introduced in Section 6.3.1. In the first step, we modeled the application in a compact and intuitive manner according to the scientific workflow model described in Section 7.1 using a graphical UML modeling portal [151]. The hierarchical UML representation of WIEN2k consists of one outermost sequential loop composite activity called *whileConv* depicted in the left window of Figure 7.7(a). The right window displays the content of the sequential loop body (one iteration) which consists of five serialised activities interconnected through control and data flow dependencies, where LAPW1 and LAPW2 are composite parallel loops while the others are atomic activities. We automatically translate this graphical representation into an XML format [70] that is given as input to the middleware services for scheduling followed by execution in a Grid environment.

One peculiarity of the WIEN2k workflow is that the cardinality of parallel LAPW1 and LAPW2 activities (see Section 7.1.5) is unknown until the first activity LAPW0 completes its execution. Since this number is statically unknown, the Scheduler instantiates the cardinality port of type integer with a default value which assumes *one* single serial activity in each case. As a

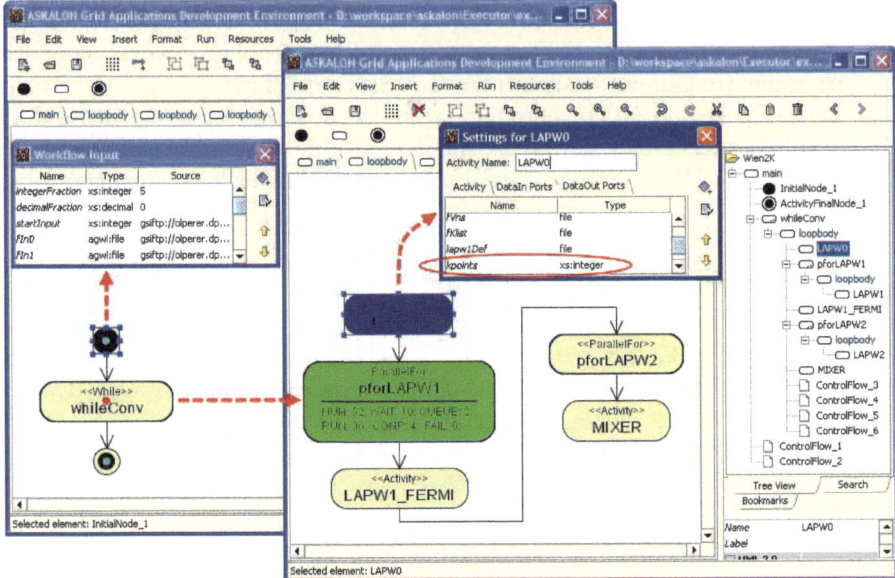

(a) The WIEN2k hierarchical UML model.

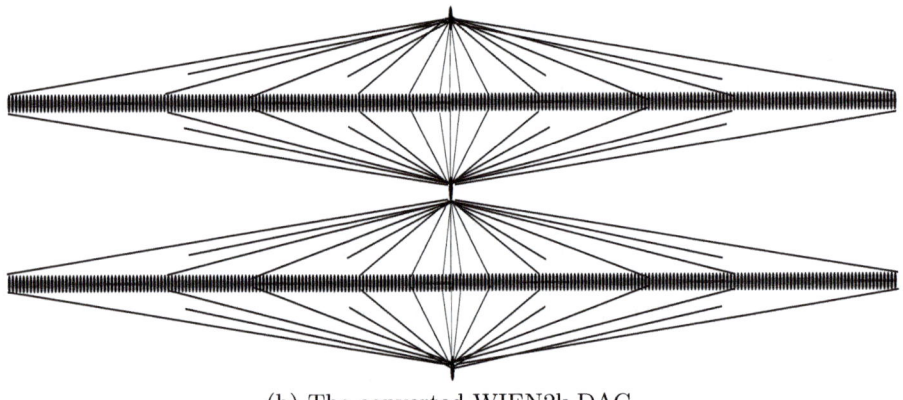

(b) The converted WIEN2k DAG.

Fig. 7.7. The WIEN2k workflow representation.

consequence, the workflow is converted into a DAG which has a total of only nine serialised activities that the Scheduler easily maps onto the same Grid site that delivers the lowest makespan. Figure 7.8(a) displays the graphical representation of the Gantt chart produced by the Scheduler after this initial step, which we implemented based on a customised version of the Jumpshot tool [199] for postmortem visualisation of MPI(CH) execution traces.

After the LAPW0 activity completes its execution, the Enactment Engine (which we will present in detail in Section 7.3) reads the LAPW1 cardinality

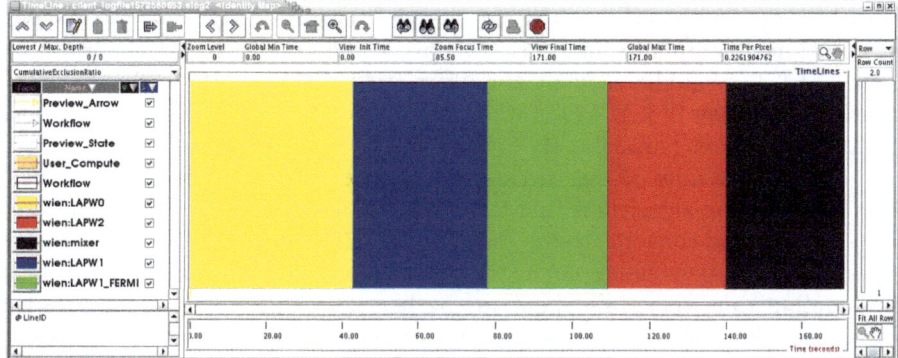

(a) Initial Gantt chart.

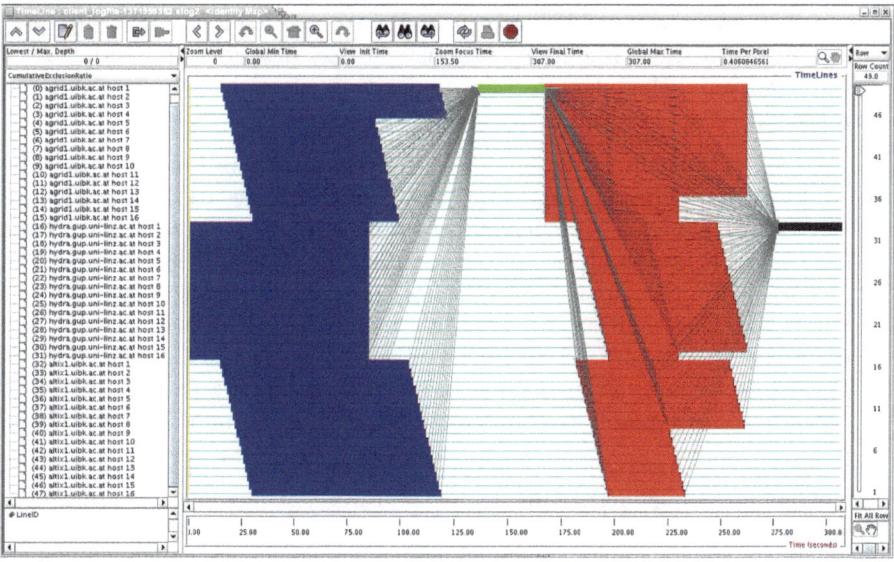

(b) Gantt chart after rescheduling.

Fig. 7.8. The scheduling Gantt charts.

port that indicates the number of activities in the parallel loop (i.e. 250 in this experiment) and issues an event that sends the workflow back to the Scheduler for rescheduling. The Scheduler uses this new runtime information to convert the scientific workflow into a new larger DAG consisting of 250 activities in each LAPW1 and LAPW2 parallel loop, plus one enclosing sequential loop iteration. After this second workflow conversion operation, the Scheduler applies one of the heuristic-based algorithms on the large DAG depicted in Figure 7.7(b) for optimised mapping onto the Grid. Figure 7.8(b) illustrates the updated Gantt chart of the new workflow after rescheduling, in which one can clearly see the two parallel activities LAPW1 and LAPW2, whose inner computational activities are distributed across the Grid sites available. The middle sequential activity LAPW2_FERMI synchronises the parallel activities of LAPW1, gathers the collection data, and scatters it once again in the next parallel activity LAPW2.

In the remainder of this section, we comparatively analyse the three heuristic scheduling algorithms that we developed applied on the DAG generated after the second conversion step (see Figure 7.7(b)) based on two metrics: the predicted workflow makespan as the optimisation objective function, and the scheduling time (i.e. time spent in the heuristic algorithm to compute the schedule). We applied the genetic algorithm on a population of 100 chromosomes transformed in 20 generations, which was enough to converge to good results in a reasonable scheduling time. We fixed the probability of crossover to 0.25 and the mutation rate to 0.01. We also compare the full-ahead scheduling with the layered partitioning strategy described in Section 7.2.3. We applied our Scheduler and the underlying algorithms in two different scenarios:

1. *without performance prediction* meaning that we do not provide the Scheduler with any predictions about the execution times of the workflow activities. In this case, the Scheduler assumes that all activities have equal execution times on all computer architectures available in our Grid;

2. *with performance prediction* meaning that we provide the Scheduler with prediction information, for example using the techniques that we presented in Sections 6.1.2 and 6.3.1. The predictions are provided to the Scheduler in a two-dimensional array containing the execution time of each activity type on each processor architecture available in our Grid.

We performed the experiments on seven heterogeneous Grid sites of the Austrian Grid [2] infrastructure illustrated in Table 7.2, aggregating 116 processors in total.

Figure 7.9(a) shows that the results when using performance prediction are in the best case nearly twice better than those achieved without performance prediction. Performance estimates are clearly important in heterogeneous Grid environments, even if they are not highly accurate. Further, we

Table 7.2. The Austrian Grid testbed for scheduling experiments.

Site	Architecture	Size	Processor	Gigahertz	Location
agrid	NOW, Fast Ethernet	20	Pentium 4	1.8	Innsbruck
hydra	COW, Fast Ethernet	16	AMD 2000	1.6	Linz
agrid1	NOW, Fast Ethernet,	16	Pentium 4	1.8	Innsbruck
altix1.jku	ccNUMA SGI Altix 3000	Itanium 2	1.6	16	Innsbruck
altix1.uibk	ccNUMA, SGI Altix 350	16	Itanium 2	1.6	Linz
schafberg	ccNUMA, SGI Altix 350	16	Itanium 2	1.6	Salzburg
gescher	COW, Gigabit Ethernet	16	Pentium 4	3	Vienna

can notice that the HEFT algorithm produces better results than the other algorithms. More precisely, the predicted makespan of the workflow is 17% shorter than the one produced by the genetic algorithm and 21% shorter than the myopic one. The simple matchmaking solution applied by the myopic algorithm appears to be insufficient for large and complex workflows and produces the worst results. The genetic algorithm needs two orders of magnitude longer time to converge to good solutions, however, this is still negligible compared to the execution time of real-world workflow problem cases. In case of scheduling without performance guidance, the search space has a more regular shape and the genetic algorithm performs equally good (or even better) than the other two algorithms. Additionally, we performed a three-layer partitioning of the workflow and incrementally scheduled each partition using the HEFT algorithm. The results obtained using this method were almost identical as for the entire workflow scheduling strategy due to the symmetry in the workflow structure while the overhead of the scheduling heuristic is lower.

7.2.5 Invmod

Invmod [178] is a hydrological application designed at the University of Innsbruck for calibration of parameters of the WaSiM tool developed at the Swiss Federal Institute of Technology Zurich. Invmod uses the Levenberg-Marquardt algorithm to minimise the least squares of the differences between the measured and the simulated runoff for a determined time period. We re-engineered the monolithic Invmod application into a Grid-enabled scientific workflow consisting of two levels of parallelism as depicted Figure 7.10(a):

1. the calibration of parameters is calculated separately for each value using multiple, so called, *parallel random runs* modeled as workflow (outermost) parallel loos;
2. for each optimisation step represented by an inner sequential loop iteration, all parameters are simultaneously changed using a nested parallel loop construct and the goal function is separately calculated.

The number of inner loop iterations is variable and depends on the actual convergence of the optimisation process, however, it is usually equal to the input maximum iteration number.

   The Invmod workflow is a common case of strongly imbalanced workflows in which one of the outermost parallel loop iterations is significantly longer than the others due to the fact that the number of inner sequential loop iterations significantly differs. In our case, the converted DAG consists of 100 parallel iterations, one of which contains 20 sequential iterations of the inner optimisation loop, while the other 99 iterations only contain 10 optimisation iterations each (see Figure 7.10(b)). This means that one parallel iteration needs approximately approximately twice the execution time of the others. We performed the scheduling experiments on the same Grid testbed depicted

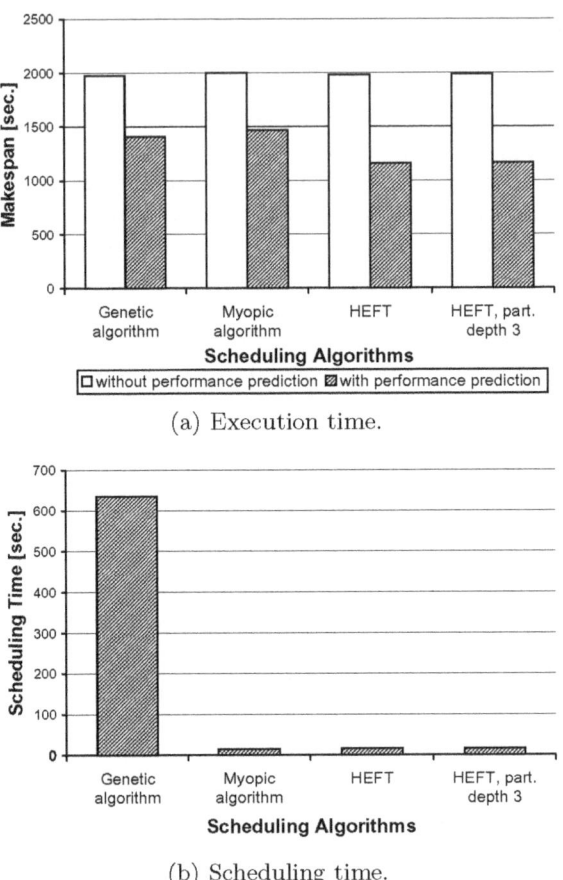

(a) Execution time.

(b) Scheduling time.

Fig. 7.9. The WIEN2k scheduling results.

in Table 7.2, with and without performance prediction information as for the WIEN2k workflow.

The experimental results for the Invmod workflow illustrated in Figure 7.11(a) explain how each of the three algorithms deals with such strongly imbalanced workflow structures. As expected, the myopic algorithm provides the worst results which are approximately 32% worse than HEFT. The genetic algorithm produces quite good results, however, worse than HEFT since it does not consider in the optimisation process the execution order of parallel activities scheduled on same processor. In addition, we applied incremental scheduling using with 10, 20, and 30 partitioning layers and compared the results against the full-ahead workflow scheduling consisting of 44 layers. For such strongly imbalanced workflows, the activities belonging to workflow execution paths that are much longer than the critical schedule path (see De-

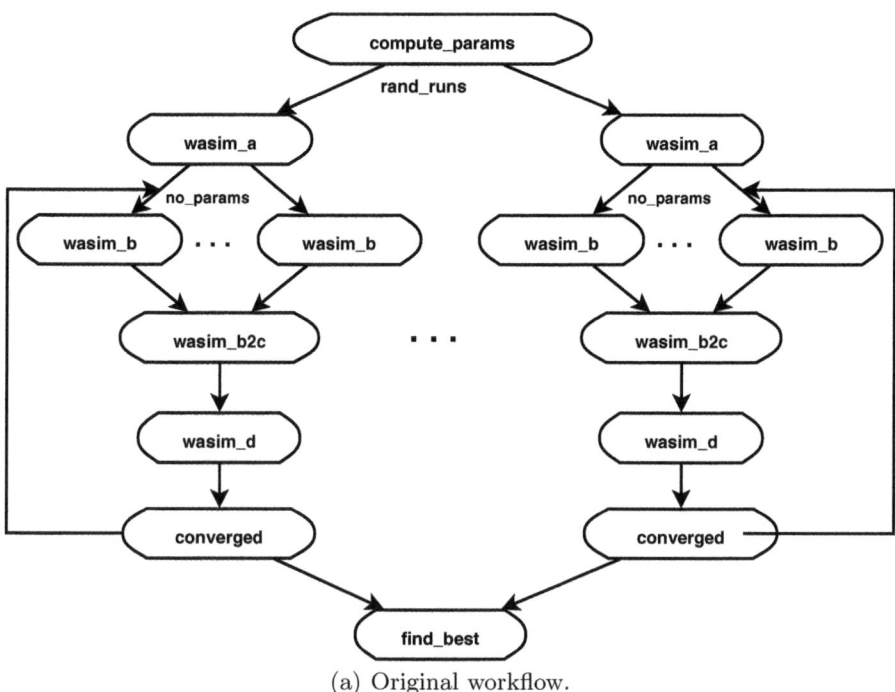

(a) Original workflow.

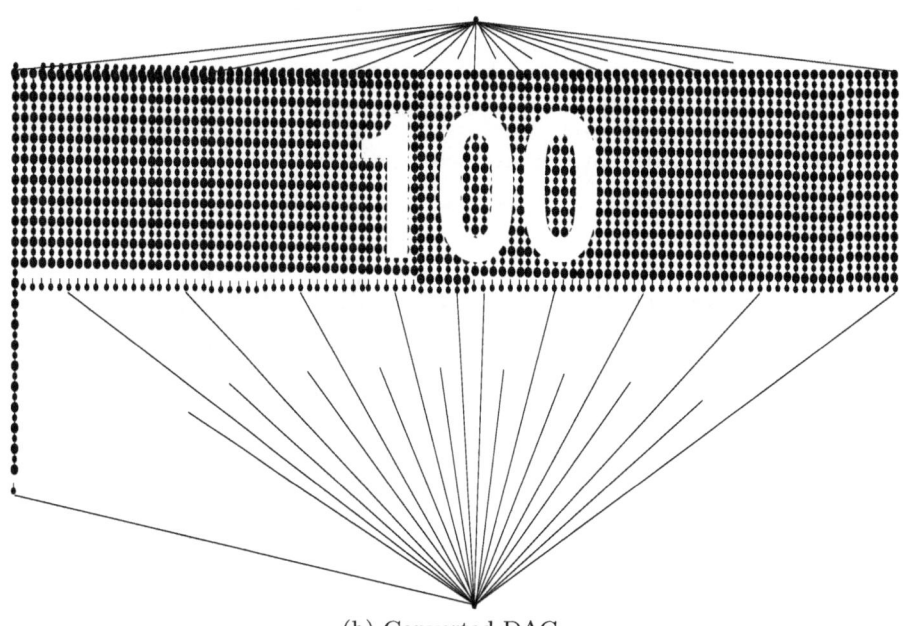

(b) Converted DAG.

Fig. 7.10. The Invmod scientific workflow.

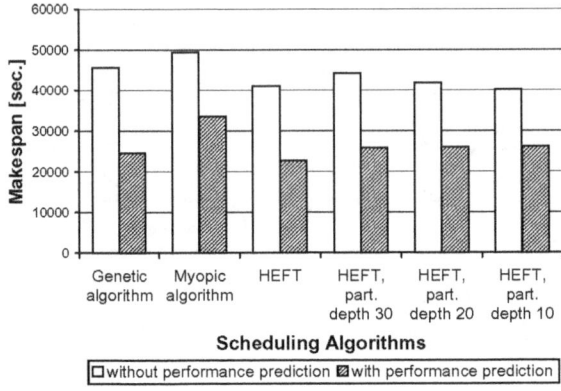

(a) Execution time in heterogeneous environment.

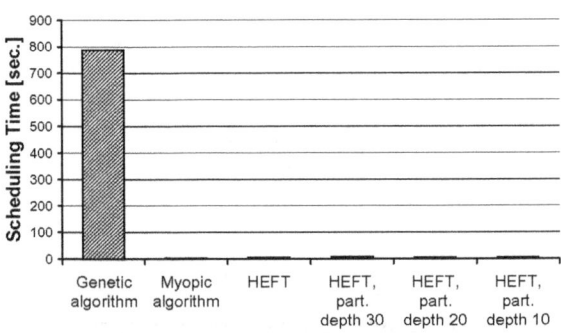

(b) Scheduling time in heterogeneous environment.

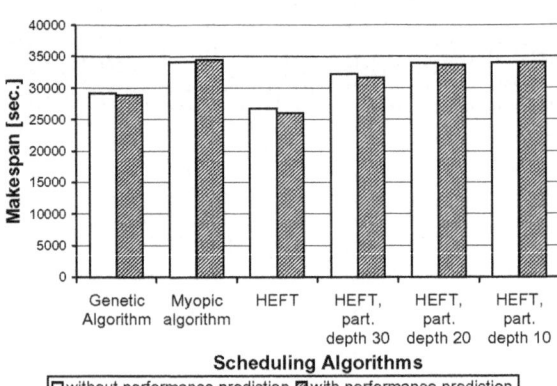

(c) Execution time in homogeneous environment.

Fig. 7.11. The Invmod scheduling results.

finition 6.8 in Section 6.1.2) should be given priority which is well handled by the entire workflow scheduling strategy based on optimisation heuristics like HEFT and genetic algorithm. Therefore, scheduling strategies based workflow partitioning deliver worse results than those based on full workflow analysis, although their results are still better than the one found by the myopic algorithm. The genetic algorithm requires again two orders of magnitude longer than the others to converge to good solutions (see Figure 7.11(b)). Performance prediction is again extremely beneficial for achieving good schedules in heterogeneous Grid environments. Figure 7.11(c) presents the execution results of the Invmod workflow in a homogeneous environment consisting of three nearly identical Grid sites. As expected, in this case there is almost no difference between scheduling with and without performance prediction since the execution on each cluster needs relatively the same amount of time. Again, the HEFT algorithm produces the best results which are 24% better than the myopic one.

7.3 Enactment Engine

In order to support reliable and high performance execution of scientific workflows in dynamic Grid environments, we developed an *Enactment Engine* service [59, 60, 61] based on a distributed service-oriented architecture organised in a master-slave communication model which includes three types of services:

1. one *master engine* receives the workflow representation compliant with the model described in Section 7.1 and interacts with the Scheduler for appropriate mapping onto the available Grid resources. The master engine monitors the execution of the entire workflow and the state of the slave engines;
2. several *slave engines*, usually one for each Grid site, monitor the execution of individual workflow partitions and report to the master whenever individual activities change their state or when the partitions produce some intermediate output data relevant to other partitions or to the overall execution;
3. if the master engine crashes, a random *backup engine* (chosen by the master beforehand) becomes the master and immediately selects another backup slave randomly.

Such a distributed architecture increases the fault tolerance of the engine and offers improved scalability through decentralised orchestration of large numbers of activities characteristic to scientific workflows. Every engine consists of the following modules:

1. *workflow partitioning* module (see Section 7.3.1) resides within the master engine and distributes the workflow into smaller partitions that can be

executed more efficiently and with smaller overheads by individual slave engines, usually one for each Grid site;

2. *control flow management* module executes the workflow activities according to the control precedence relation;

3. *data flow management* module manages the efficient transfer of complex data dependencies between activities and partitions according to the data precedence relation, including advanced collection management and optimisations through archiving and compression of multiple files;

4. *fault management* module resides in both master and slave engines and handles different runtime failures through appropriate recovery strategies like retry, checkpointing, or replication;

5. *steering* module [146] provides support within the slave engines for workflow runtime adaptations to cope with situations when the execution no longer follows the original optimised plan computed by the Scheduler. Additionally, it also handles the case of special workflows whose structure is statically unknown or may change during the execution.

We perform the optimised and fault tolerant execution of a workflow in a four phase procedure, as follows:

1. in the first step, the (XML-based) workflow representation is delivered to the Scheduler for appropriate mapping onto the Grid resources;

2. once the concrete workflow schedule is received, the master engine starts partitioning the workflow, then performs control and data flow optimisations which transform and simplify the workflow for a light-weight execution with reduced latencies and data transfer overheads;

3. after all these optimisations are performed, the master engine sends each partition to a slave engine for execution;

4. during runtime, the workflow execution is dynamically improved by the steering module.

7.3.1 Workflow Partitioning

The basis in our approach for distributed execution of scientific workflow is the *workflow partitioning* which needs to be performed such that the communication between the master and the slave engines that coordinate the individual partitions is minimised. Determining the number of partitions of a set of n numbers is a classical problem of combinatorial mathematics called the *n-th Bell number* which is an NP-complete problem. Some related partitioning approaches were already proposed to solve this problem although their algorithms have different goals [15, 53].

Definition 7.12. *We define a* workflow partition *as the largest sub-workflow* $\mathcal{W}_P = (Nodes_P, C\text{-}edges_P, D\text{-}edges_P)$ *with the following properties:*

1. all activities are scheduled on the same Grid site:

$$\mathcal{S}(N_1) = \mathcal{S}(N_2), \ \forall \ N, N_2 \in Nodes_P;$$

2. there must be no control flow and data flow dependencies to / from activities that have predecessors / successors within the partition:

$$pred(N) = \emptyset \ \vee \ pred(N) \in Nodes_P, \ \forall \ N \in Nodes_P.$$

The goal of the partitioning algorithm presented in this section is to generate a partitioned workflow $\mathcal{W}_P = (Nodes_P, C\text{-}edges_P, D\text{-}edges_P)$ from a workflow $\mathcal{W} = (Nodes, C\text{-}edges, D\text{-}edges)$, where:

$$Nodes_P = \{P_1, \ldots, P_n\}$$

is the set of partitions that fulfil Definition 7.12, and:

$$\bigcap_{i=1}^{n} P_i = \emptyset \ \wedge \ \bigcup_{i=1}^{n} P_i = Nodes,$$

and n is minimum. We base our partitioning algorithm on graph transformation theory [16] as the formal background to rigourously express it. We define several rules for defining valid workflow partitions that aim to decrease the complexity of the algorithm (to polynomial) and create the set of cooperating workflow partitions.

Let $(\mathcal{W}, \mathcal{R})$ denote a workflow transformation system, where $\mathcal{R}$ denotes the set of graph transformation rules. We approach the workflow partitioning problem using a four step transformation sequence:

$$\left(\mathcal{W} \overset{\mathcal{R}_{CF}}{\Longrightarrow} \mathcal{W}_{CF}, \ \mathcal{W} \overset{\mathcal{R}_{DF}}{\Longrightarrow} \mathcal{W}_{DF} \right) \overset{\mathcal{R}_{M1}}{\Longrightarrow} \mathcal{W}' \overset{\mathcal{R}_{M2}}{\Longrightarrow} \mathcal{W}_P,$$

where:

$$\begin{aligned}
\mathcal{W}_{CF} &= \left(Nodes_{CF}, C\text{-}edges_{CF}, D\text{-}edges_{CF} \right), \\
\mathcal{W}_{DF} &= \left(Nodes_{DF}, C\text{-}edges_{DF}, D\text{-}edges_{DF} \right), \\
\mathcal{W}' &= \left(Nodes', C\text{-}edges', D\text{-}edges' \right),
\end{aligned}$$

and $\mathcal{W}_P$ are partition sets generated using different transformation rules that preserve the control and data flow dependencies of the original workflow $\mathcal{W}$. We omit the workflow input and output data ports for clarity reasons since they are irrelevant to our partitioning algorithm.

Step 1: $\mathcal{W} \overset{\mathcal{R}_{CF}}{\Longrightarrow} \mathcal{W}_{CF}$.

Partition the original workflow according to three control flow dependency rules $\mathcal{R}_{CF}$:

1. every activity of the workflow must belong to exactly one partition:

$$\forall \ N \in Nodes, \ \exists \ P \in Nodes_{CF} \ \wedge \ N \in P \ \wedge \ N \notin P' \ \wedge \ \forall \ P' \in Nodes_{CF} \setminus P;$$

2. every partition is one composite or atomic activity. Currently we perform this step by using additional information provided by the user in the XML-based workflow representation [70] and mapping one composite activity (e.g. parallel activity consisting of a set of independent atomic activities) to one partition;

3. no control flow dependencies between intermediate activities in different partitions are allowed:

$$\forall \ N_1 \in P_1 \in Nodes_{CF} \ \wedge \ (pred(N_1) \in P_1 \ \vee \ succ(N_1) \in P_1) \ \wedge$$
$$(\nexists \ (N_1, N_2) \in C\text{-}edges_{CF} \ \wedge \ \nexists \ (N_2, N_1) \in C\text{-}edges_{CF},$$
$$\forall \ N_2 \in P_2 \in Nodes_{CF}),$$

where $pred$ and $succ$ denote the predecessor, respectively the successor of an activity in the workflow;

4. the number of activities inside one composite activity must be more than the average processor number on one Grid site. We introduce this rule to avoid too fine grained partitions in the workflow that would start slave engines on sites with little workload.

For example, in Figure 7.12(a) we partition all atomic activities of the composite activities N_{if}, N_{par}, and N_{seq} into one partition, respectively, which produces the following control flow partitioning:

$$Nodes_{CF} = \{\{N_1\}, \{N_2\}, \{N_3, \ldots, N_6\}, \{N_7, \ldots, N_{10}\}, \{N_{11}\}, \{N_{12}, N_{13}\}\}.$$

Step 2: $\mathcal{W} \overset{\mathcal{R}_{DF}}{\Longrightarrow} \mathcal{W}_{DF}.$

Partition the original workflow according to three data flow dependency rules $\mathcal{R}_{DF}$:

1. each activity of the workflow must belong to exactly one partition:

$$\forall \ N \in Nodes, \ \exists \ P \in Nodes_{DF} \ \wedge \ N \in P \ \wedge \ N \notin P', \ \forall \ P' \in Nodes_{DF} \setminus P;$$

2. the data dependencies between activities scheduled on the same Grid site are eliminated:

$$D\text{-}edges_{DF} = D\text{-}edges \setminus (N_1, N_2, D\text{-}port), \ \forall \ N_1, N_2 \in Nodes \ \wedge \ \mathcal{S}_{N_1} = \mathcal{S}_{N_2};$$

3. activities scheduled on the same Grid site belong to the same partition:

$$\forall \ N_1 \in P \in \mathcal{W}_{DF} \ \wedge \ \forall \ N_2 \in P \ \wedge \ \mathcal{S}_{N_1} = \mathcal{S}_{N_2}.$$

Figure 7.12(b) displays the result of the data flow partitioning according to the schedule of the workflow activities:

$$Nodes_{DF} = \{\{N_1, N_2\}, \{N_3, \ldots, N_6, N_{13}\}, \{N_7, \ldots, N_{11}, N_{12}\}\}.$$

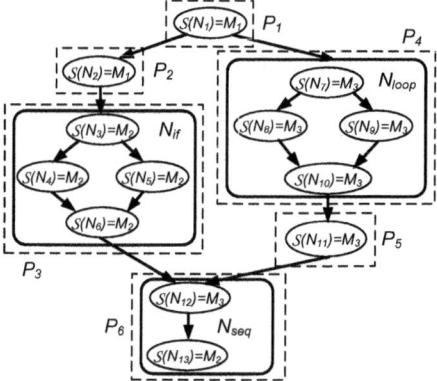

(a) Control flow partitioning ($\mathcal{R}_{CF}$).

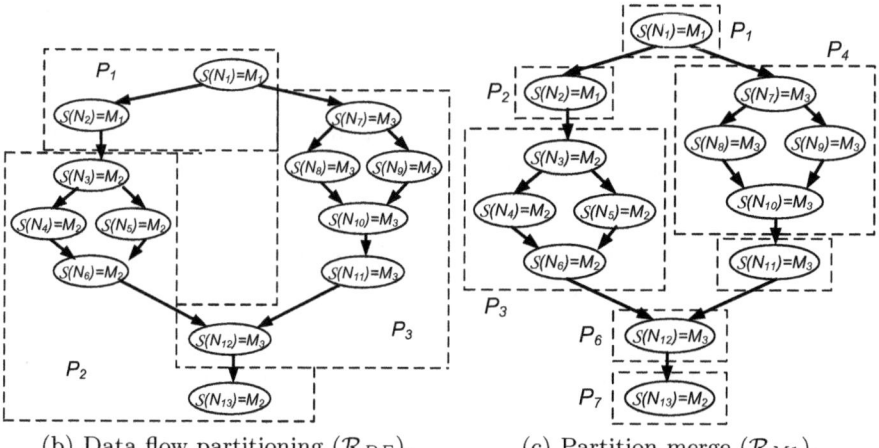

(b) Data flow partitioning ($\mathcal{R}_{DF}$).   (c) Partition merge ($\mathcal{R}_{M1}$).

(d) Partitioned workflow ($\mathcal{R}_{M2}$).

Fig. 7.12. A workflow partitioning example.

Step 3: $(\mathcal{W}_{CF}, \mathcal{W}_{DF}) \overset{\mathcal{R}_{M1}}{\Longrightarrow} \mathcal{W}'$.

Merge the two sets $Nodes_{CF}$ and $Nodes_{DF}$ of control and data flow-based partitions computed in the previous two steps into one partition set, as follows:

$$\mathcal{W}' = \bigcup_{\substack{\forall\, Nodes_1 \in Nodes_{CF} \\ \forall\, Nodes_2 \in Nodes_{DF}}} \{Nodes_1 \cap Nodes_2\},$$

while preserving the control and data flow dependencies and the partitioning goals formally described in the beginning. For our example in Figure 7.12(c) we obtain:

$$Nodes' = \{\{N_1\}, \{N_2\}, \{N_3, \dots, N_6\}, \{N_7, \dots, N_{10}\}, \{N_{11}\}, \{N_{12}\}, \{N_{13}\}\}.$$

Step 4: $\mathcal{W}' \overset{\mathcal{R}_{M2}}{\Longrightarrow} \mathcal{W}_P$.

Since the partitioning may have been done too fine grain, we merge the partitions connected through control flow dependencies using the following two merge rules:

1. merge the partitions that are connected through control flow dependencies but have no data flow dependencies (i.e. they are scheduled on the same site):

$$Nodes_P = \bigcup_{\forall\, P_i \neq P_j \in \mathcal{W}'} \{\{P_i \cup P_j\} \setminus \{P_i\} \setminus \{P_j\} \mid \forall\, N_1 \in P_i \,\wedge$$

$$\forall\, N_2 \in P_j \,\wedge\, \nexists\, (N_1, N_2, D\text{-}port) \in D\text{-}edges \,\wedge\, (P_i, P_j) \in C\text{-}edges'\} \,;$$

2. in the final partition, there must be no control and data flow dependencies to / from activities that have predecessors / successors within the partitions. This is achieved by iteratively applying the following formula within fixed point algorithm until nothing changes anymore and the largest partitions are achieved:

$$Nodes_P = \bigcup_{\forall\, P_i \neq P_j \in \mathcal{W}'} \{\{P_i \cup P_j\} \setminus \{P_i\} \setminus \{P_j\} \mid$$

$$\neg\big((P_i, P_j, D\text{-}port) \in D\text{-}edges'\big) \,\wedge\, \big((P_i, P_j) \in C\text{-}edges'\big) \,\wedge$$

$$\big((\nexists\, P_x \neq P_j \in \mathcal{W}' \mid ((P_i, P_x) \in C\text{-}edges')\big) \,\wedge$$

$$\big(\nexists\, P_x \neq P_i \in \mathcal{W}' \mid ((P_x, P_j) \in C\text{-}edges')\big)\big)\}.$$

Therefore,

$$Nodes_P = \{\{N_1\}, \{N_2\}, \{N_3, \dots, N_6\}, \{N_7, \dots, N_{11}\}, \{N_{12}\}, \{N_{13}\}\}.$$

This partitioning of a workflow helps the slave engines execute the workflow partitions independently with little asynchronous communication among themselves. The workflow partitioning also contributes to the reduction of the latency and coordination overheads of large numbers of activities characteristic to our scientific workflows.

7.3.2 Control Flow Management

Our experience in running real-world applications in the Austrian Grid environment revealed that executing one computational activity on a remote Grid site according to the model that we introduced in Section 2.6.3 contains in average about $10-20$ seconds of overhead mainly due to mutual authentication latency and polling for job termination. This overhead may be significantly larger if the access to Grid sites is performed through local job management systems and, therefore, becomes critical for large scientific workflows comprising hundreds to thousands of activities. The objective of the control flow management module is to simplify and reduce the workflow structure and size by merging atomic activities into larger aggregate ones that can be executed as one single remote job submission on a Grid site, which reduces the overall latencies and decreases the complexity of large and complex workflows.

The control flow management module receives a workflow partition P and performs a transformation that produces a new partition P_{CF} that merges the activities linked through control flow dependencies but with no data dependencies (i.e. since they are scheduled on the same Grid site) into composite activities that can be executed as an atomic unit of work (i.e. remote GRAM job submission):

$$P_{CF} = \{CN_1, \ldots, CN_n\},$$

where:

$$
\begin{aligned}
CN_i = \{N\} \ &\vee \ (\forall \ N_1 \in CN_i, \ \exists \ N_2 \in CN_i \ \wedge \\
&((N_1, N_2) \in \textit{C-edges}_P \ \vee \ (N_2, N_1) \in \textit{C-edges}_P) \ \wedge \\
&\nexists \ N_3 \in CN_i \ \wedge \ ((N_1, N_3, \textit{D-port}) \in \textit{D-edges}_P \ \vee \\
&\qquad (N_3, N_1, \textit{D-port}) \in \textit{D-edges}_P)), \ \forall \ i \in [1..n].
\end{aligned}
$$

Figure 7.13(a) illustrates one typical static control flow optimisation in a workflow consisting of activities $A_1, \ldots, A_n$ and $B_1, \ldots, B_n$, where A_i and

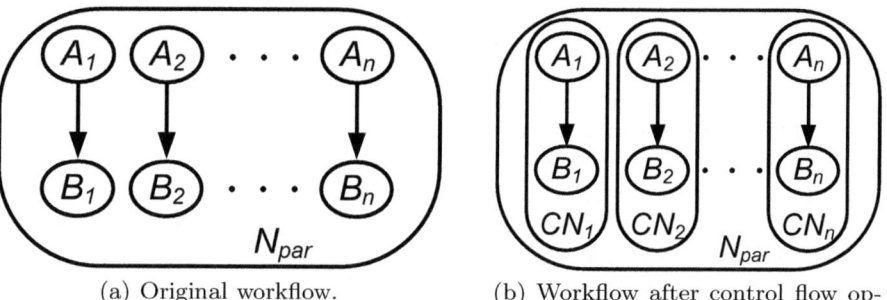

(a) Original workflow.   (b) Workflow after control flow optimisation.

Fig. 7.13. A control flow optimisation example.

B_i are linked through a direct control flow dependency and were scheduled on the same Grid site, which means that any eventual data dependency was eliminated in the second step of the partitioning algorithm. Figure 7.13(b) displays the analysis of the control flow optimisation which groups activities A_i and B_i in one single composite activity that simplifies the workflow and, therefore, reduces the job submission latencies to half in this particular example.

7.3.3 Data Flow Management

An important task of the Enactment Engine is to automatically track and resolve dynamic and statically unknown data dependencies between activities. Depending on their type, data ports may map at runtime either to data files referred through (GridFTP or GASS-based) URLs, or to objects corresponding to abstract data types like integer, float, or string. Additionally, the Enactment Engine transparently supports all five collection communication patterns introduced in Section 7.1.5 which we did not encounter in related workflow management systems [10, 65, 136, 1, 184].

Similar to remote job submissions, GridFTP-based authenticated file transfers in Grid environments exhibit latencies of about $5-10$ seconds which is rather critical in case of a large number of small files produced by the real-world applications that we use as case study. To address this problem, the data flow management module reorganises first the input and output of the partitions and composite activities, analyses the data dependencies between all activities, groups them according to all dependencies involving the same source and destination Grid sites, and generates a file transfer activity of a single compressed archive whenever the source and destination sites are different:

$$D\text{-}edges_P = \bigcup_{\forall\, P_1, P_2 \in Nodes_P} \{(P_1, P_2, D\text{-}port_{archive})\}\,,$$

where:

$$D\text{-}port_{archive} = \bigcup_{\substack{\forall\, (N_1, N_2, D\text{-}port) \in D\text{-}edges \\ \wedge\, N_1 \in P_1 \wedge N_2 \in P_2}} \{D\text{-}port\}$$

is a compressed archive of all data dependencies between partitions P_1 and P_2 (typically instantiated during execution by files).

Figure 7.14(a) presents a typical example in which activity B collects the output data from a large number of parallel activities $A_1, \ldots, A_n$. First of all, the data flow analysis packages the data output ports of all activities belonging to the same partition (i.e. scheduled on the same site – see Figure 7.14(b)). Afterwards, one single (GridFTP-based) file transfer activity is generated between the partitions that are scheduled on different sites which reduces the number of file transfers from n to $k-1$ in this example, where $k \ll n$ (see Figure 7.14(c)).

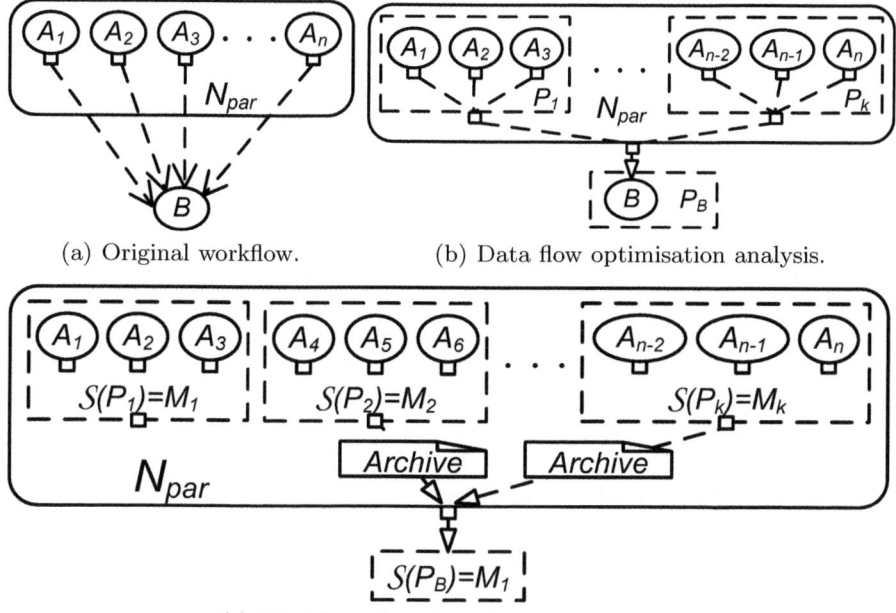

(a) Original workflow.   (b) Data flow optimisation analysis.

(c) Workflow after data flow optimisation.

Fig. 7.14. A data flow optimisation example.

7.3.4 Virtual Single Execution Environment

Certain scientific workflow applications are characterised by a large (hundreds to thousands) number of activities with complex data dependencies which are relatively small in size. In such cases, the overhead of communication is dominated by latencies for sending individual small files where the effective data transfer is negligible. To handle this situation, we propose a new data flow optimisation technique called *Virtual Single Execution Environment* (VSEE) which replaces the data dependencies between activities with the full data environment, recursively defined for a partition P as follows:

$$V_P = \bigcup_{\forall\, (P',P,D\text{-}port)\in D\text{-}edges_P} V_{P'} \quad \bigcup_{\forall\, (P,P'',D\text{-}port)\in D\text{-}edges_P} \{D\text{-}port\}\,.$$

Clearly, the following property holds:

$$\exists\, \left(P',P,D\text{-}port\right) \in D\text{-}edges_P \iff V_{P'} \subset V_P.$$

Upon executing a workflow partition on a Grid site, each slave engine automatically creates and removes one working directory that represents its execution environment. The VSEE mechanism transforms complex data dependencies between activities into one environment dependency between partitions that is packaged and transferred at runtime as one single data transfer activity. VSEE, therefore, noticeably reduces the latency and the number of data transfers for compute intensive Grid applications that have large amounts of small sized data dependencies. The VSEE mechanism can also reduce the overhead of activity migration upon workflow steering that we will formally describe in Section 7.3.5 and practically experiment in Section 7.3.7. Another benefit of using VSEE is the fact that specifying large amounts (tens to hundreds) of input and output data ports between activities (which is often the case for scientific workflows) can be painful and error prone for the end-user. With this technique, the users can assume that activities have one single aggregated data dependency to their predecessors which eliminates the need to specify all fine grained logical data ports explicitly. This simplification shields the user from the complexity of the workflow definition and it gives to the scientists from other areas a more friendly interface to Grid computing.

Figure 7.15 illustrates the WIEN2k workflow that we introduced in Section 6.3.1 scheduled on three Grid sites $\{M_1, M_2, M_3\}$. First of all, the workflow is split into seven partitions:

$$Nodes_P = \bigcup_{i=1}^{7} P_i,$$

based on the algorithm presented in Section 7.3.1 (see Figure 7.15(a)). Then, the data flow between partitions is optimised according to the VSEE-based relationships depicted in Table 7.3(a). For example, transferring data between partitions only according to the data flow dependencies requires P_6 receive the data from:

$$V_{in} \cup V_1 \cup V_2 \cup V_3 \cup V_4 = V_4,$$

since $V_{in} \subset V_1 \subset V_2 \subset V_3 \subset V_4$. Table 7.3(b) displays the final result of this VSEE data flow optimisation process. For certain compute intensive applications characterised by large numbers of small data dependencies like WIEN2k, the VSEE mechanism can drastically decrease the number of file transfers (up to orders of magnitude) as we will experimentally illustrate in Section 7.3.7.

7.3.5 Workflow Steering

There may occur many external factors that affect the execution of large workflows in dynamic Grid environments which no longer follows the original plan computed by the Scheduler. Such unpredictable factors may include unpredictable queuing times, external load on processors (e.g. on Grid sites that also serve as student workstation laboratories in our real Grid environment), unpredictable availability of processors on workstation networks (e.g. if a student shuts down a machine or reboots it in Windows operating system mode), jobs belonging to other users on parallel machines, congested

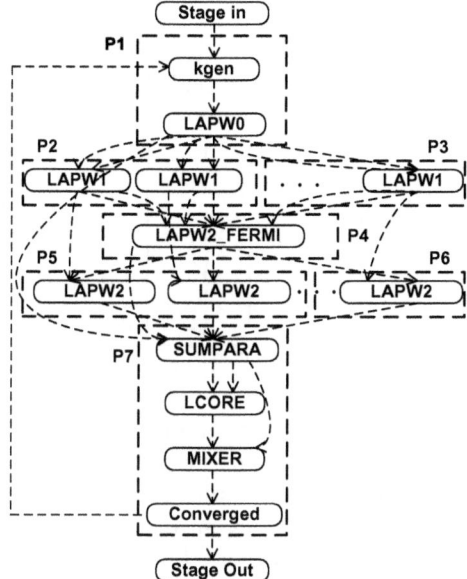

(a) Original partitioned data flow.

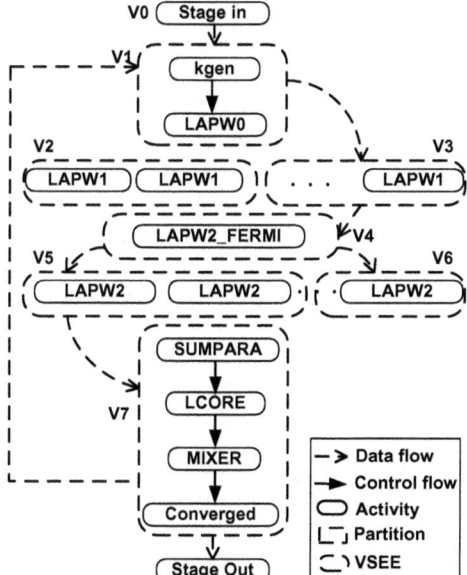

(b) Optimised VSEE data flow.

Fig. 7.15. A VSEE example.

Table 7.3. The VSEE results for the WIEN2k workflow.

(a) VSEE relationships.

$\mathcal{R}_V$	V_1	V_2	V_3	V_4	V_5	V_6	V_7	V_{out}
V_{in}	$\subset$	$\subset$	$\subset$	$\subset$	$\subset$	$\subset$		
V_1	$-$	$\subseteq$	$\subset$	$\subseteq$	$\subset$	$\subset$	$\subset$	
V_2		$-$	$\subseteq$	$\subset$	$\subset$			
V_3			$-$	$\subset$	$\subseteq$	$\subset$		
V_4				$-$	$\subset$	$\subset$	$\subset$	
V_5					$-$		$\subset$	
V_6						$-$	$\subseteq$	
V_7	$\subset$						$-$	$\supset$

(b) Minimum VSEE transfer set.

$Transfer$	P_1	P_2	P_3	P_4	P_5	P_6	P_7	$Output$
V_{in}	✓							
V_1		✓						
V_2								
V_3			✓					
V_4				✓	✓			
V_5						✓		
V_6								
V_7	✓							✓

networks, or simply inaccurate prediction information. Moreover, we often encountered in our real Grid environment sites that offer a reduced capacity for certain resources, for example small number of input and output nodes that only allow a limited number of concurrent file transfers, otherwise generate a denial of service attack. The *steering* module of the Enactment Engine aims to minimise the losses upon to such unpredictable situations that violate the optimised static mapping computed by the Scheduler through appropriate rescheduling techniques.

For example, executing such large numbers of parallel activities in dynamic Grid environments often produces a load imbalance that leaves some of the Grid sites idle, while others are overloaded with activities waiting in the queue. To handle this situation, the Enactment Engine regularly checks the load of available Grid sites based on the number of activities queued and, if an uneven distribution is detected (using predicted execution time information), it selects some of the queued activities for migration and replicates them to the less loaded sites (e.g. with free processors). Additionally, the engine must also replicate the necessary input files as part of a data flow optimisation process.

Rescheduling Events

The steering module of the Enactment Engine continuously monitors the workflow execution and triggers appropriate *rescheduling events* whenever any of the following situations occur:

- *cardinality port value change* which implies modifications in the workflow shape, in particular in the size of parallel loops (see Section 7.1.5 for the formal definition and Section 7.2.4 for a real-world example);
- *prediction change* of various workflow characteristics based on new execution performance data available, in particular branch probabilities in conditional activities, number of iterations in sequential and parallel loops, or more accurate execution time estimations of computational activities;

- *resource change*, in particular in the availability of Grid sites (i.e. number of processors available) where workflow activities are scheduled, or when new powerful parallel computers become available;
- *performance contract violation* [146] which are caused by workflow executions that no longer follow the original optimised plan computed by the Scheduler.

Definition 7.13. *Let N be a submitted activity, W_N its underlying work assigned (i.e. floating point operations for CA activities, file size for DA activities), $T_N^{\mathcal{S}_N}$ its estimated execution time, and:*

$$start(N) = end(N) - T_N^{\mathcal{S}_N}$$

its start timestamp, where the end timestamp end(N) was defined in Section 6.1.2 (see Definition 6.7). We define the performance contract *[185] of an activity N at time instance t, such that $start(N) \leq t < end(N)$, as:*

$$PC(N, \mathcal{S}_N, t) = \frac{W_N}{W_N(t) \cdot T_N^{\mathcal{S}_N}} \cdot (t - start(N)),$$

where $W_N(t)$ is the work completed by activity N in the interval $[start(N), t]$.

The steering module of the Enactment Engine triggers a rescheduling event for activity N at time instance t whenever:

$$PC(N, \mathcal{S}_N, t) > f_N,$$

where f_N is the predefined *performance contract elapse factor* of activity N. Currently the value of the performance contract elapse factor f_N needs to be statically defined by the user for each activity (as activity properties in the workflow specification [70]) that represents a certain percentage from its predicted activity execution time $T_N^{\mathcal{S}_N}$. We provide two options for monitoring the amount of work $W_N(t)$ performed by an activity N based on online performance analysis sensors that we developed:

1. source code-based using the ZEN event directive specified in Section 3.2.12 (see Chapter 3);
2. binary code-based using the dynamic instrumentation technology described in Section 5.4.1 (see Chapter 5);

After rescheduling, the workflow activities are restarted or resumed from the last checkpoint, if available [122, 166] (see Section 7.3.6).

Steering Algorithm

The static workflow scheduling approach that we described in Section 7.2 suffers of two limitations:

1. loops are not comprised in the DAG-based workflow model used by the Scheduler;
2. the Grid is not considered as a dynamic environment where the resources can change runtime load and availability.

Definition 7.14. *An activity $N \in$ Nodes of the running workflow can be at a certain time instance t in one of the following* states: *queued, running, completed, or failed, denoted as* state(N, t).

In this section we propose a simple *steering algorithm* depicted in Algorithm 10 that is based on the repeated invocation of the static scheduling algorithm, as informally outlined by the following execution steps [146]:

1. the algorithm receives as input a DG-based scientific workflow compliant with the model presented in Section 7.1 (lines $1 - 2$);
2. the workflow is converted into a DAG and scheduled onto the Grid using optimisation heuristics as presented in Section 7.2 (lines $3 - 4$);
3. the workflow is submitted for execution based on the initial schedule (line 5);
4. the workflow is monitored until it completes its execution (lines $6 - 14$);
5. whenever one of the events presented in the previous section occur, a rescheduling event is triggered (line 7);
6. all activities that violate their performance contract are canceled and reported as failed (lines $8 - 11$);
7. the workflow is converted once again based on the new runtime information and rescheduled (lines $12 - 13$).

To efficiently handle workflow rescheduling at runtime, we extended the workflow conversion algorithm originally presented in Algorithm 5 with a new time axis that only considers the relevant (i.e. still to be executed) part of the workflow as part of the optimisation process (lines $17 - 30$). More specifically, the following activities are eliminated and not considered for rescheduling (lines $26 - 27$):

1. all properly running activities that fulfill their performance contract;
2. all completed activities that do not have sequential loops as parents and, therefore, will not be re-executed.

7.3.6 Fault Tolerance

Fault tolerance is sometimes called redundancy management, since one of the nature of distributed systems is redundancy which provides means for increased reliability. We handle failures as part of the Enactment Engine at three levels of abstractions:

Algorithm 10. The workflow steering algorithm.

```
 1: function STEERING(W, GRID)
 2:     W = (Nodes, C-edges, D-edges, IN-ports, OUT-ports)        ▷ Precondition
 3:     W' ← WF-CONVERTER(W, W, 0)                    ▷ Workflow conversion
 4:     S_W ← SCHEDULE(W')                           ▷ Workflow scheduling
 5:     EXECUTE(S_W)                                 ▷ Workflow execution
 6:     repeat
 7:         t ← SLEEP(n)                          ▷ Until scheduling event
 8:         for all N ∈ Nodes ∧ state(N, t) = running ∧ PC(N, S_N, t) > f_N do
 9:             CANCEL(N)                     ▷ Performance contract violation
10:             state(N) ← failed
11:         end for
12:         W' ← WF-CONVERTER(W, W, t)        ▷ Runtime workflow conversion
13:         S_W ← SCHEDULE(W')                       ▷ Workflow rescheduling
14:     until state(N, t) = completed, ∀ N ∈ Nodes ∧ succ(N) = ∅
15: end function
16:
17: function WF-CONVERTER(W_root, N, t)
18:     if N is a N_if then
19:         W_root ← BRANCH-EXPANSION(W_root, N)
20:     else if N is a N_loop then
21:         W_root ← SEQ-LOOP-UNROLLING(W_root, N)
22:     else if N is a N_par then
23:         W_root ← PAR-LOOP-UNROLLING(W_root, N)
24:     else if N is a W then
25:         W_root ← WF-INLINING(W_root, N)
26:     else if (state(N, t) = running ∧ PC(N, S_N, t) ≤ f_N) ∨
                (state(N, t) = completed ∧ (∄ n ∈ IN ∧ Parent^n(N) is a N_loop)) then
27:         ACTIVITY-ELIMINATION(N)              ▷ Completed or properly running
28:     end if
29:     return W_root
30: end function
```

1. *activity level fault tolerance* or activity crash failure:
   a) *retry* submits a computational activity multiple times on the same
      Grid site until it succeeds;
   b) *replicate* submits the same activities to different Grid sites simulta-
      neously, uses the results of the one that finishes first, and cancels the
      others;
2. *control flow level fault tolerance*:
   a) *checkpointing* saves the state of the workflow activities and URLs to
      their input and output data port instances in the Experiment Data
      Repository. Full backup copies of the data port instances are not
      saved;
   b) *migration* moves an activity to a different Grid site upon performance
      contract violation, as defined in Section 7.3.5. Upon migration, the

activity is resumed if an activity level checkpoint is available (see next section), otherwise it is restarted;

3. *workflow level fault tolerance*:

   a) *alternate task* uses in case of failure a different implementation of the same activity with different implementation characteristics;

   b) *workflow level redundancy* simultaneously launches different implementations of the same activity with different characteristics or quality of service parameters, hoping that one of the alternative jobs will finish successfully (e.g. a parallel high performance but unreliable MPI implementation versus a reliable but slow sequential version);

   c) *exception handling* consists of recovery methods based on user-defined exceptions or upon activity failures. Typical recovery methods include, for example, stop the workflow, checkpoint the workflow, or ignore the fault;

   d) *checkpointing* at the workflow level saves complete backup copies of the activity input and output data port instances in addition to control flow level checkpointing. This method is slower but has the advantage that the user can restore the workflow at any time and from any Grid location.

Checkpointing

Checkpointing and recovery are fundamental techniques for saving the application state during the normal execution and restoring the saved state after a failure to reduce the amount of lost work. There are two traditional approaches to checkpointing:

1. *system level checkpointing* saves to the disk the image of an entire operating system process, including registers, stack, code and data segments. This is known to be a rather expensive and platform dependent process which is very critical to apply for a large number of activities in heterogeneous Grid environments;

2. *application level checkpointing* is usually implemented within the application source code by programmers, or is automatically added to the application using compiler-based tools.

We therefore concentrate our checkpointing approach on application level checkpointing, as a portable and more reliable approach for being applied in heterogeneous Grid environments. Since it is not always possible to checkpoint everything that can affect the program behaviour, it is essential to identify what to include in a checkpoint to guarantee a successful recovery, which for our scientific workflow model consists of:

- the state of the workflow activities;
- the state of the data dependencies.

We configure the Enactment Engine to checkpoint a workflow application upon precise events defined, for example as part of the (XML-based) workflow specification through property and constraint constructs [70]. Typical checkpointing events occur when an activity fails, after the completion of an important number of activities (e.g. workflow phases, parallel loops, or sequential loop iterations), or after a user defined deadline (e.g. percentage of the overall expected or predicted execution time). Other checkpointing events may happen upon rescheduling certain workflow parts (see Section 7.3.5) due to the dynamic availability of Grid resources or due to variable or statically unknown number of activities in workflow parallel loops. Upon a checkpointing event, the control flow management module stops the workflow execution and invokes the fault management module that saves the status and the data flow ports into the Experiment Data Repository.

We designed and implemented a stack of three checkpointing mechanisms:

1. *activity level checkpointing* is based on existing system level checkpointing tools like Condor [123] or MOSIX [14] and saves the registers, stack, and memory segments for every individual activity running on a certain processor. The advantage of the activity level checkpoint is that an atomic activity can be recovered upon an internal or a system failure;

2. *control flow level checkpointing* saves the workflow state and (GASS and GridFTP-based) URLs to the files that instantiate activity runtime data ports. Checkpointing URLs rather than complete backup copies of large data files makes the control flow level checkpointing mechanism a very fast and light-weight mechanism. The disadvantage is that the input and output data port instances remain stored on possible unsecured and volatile file systems which makes this recovery approach appropriate only at runtime during the same workflow execution;

3. *workflow level checkpointing* enhances the control flow checkpointing by saving not only the workflow state, but also complete copies of the data port instances available at the execution point when the checkpoint is performed (see Definition 7.15). The advantage of the workflow level checkpointing is that the execution can be restored and resumed at anytime and from any Grid location. The disadvantage is that the checkpointing overhead grows significantly for large files that instantiate the data ports and is therefore less suitable for immediate runtime recovery. This approach is more appropriate for resuming the execution at a later time, possibly with a different schedule or within a different experimental context.

Definition 7.15. *Let* $\mathcal{W}$ = (*Nodes, C-edges, D-edges, IN-ports, OUT-ports*) *be a workflow application. We define a* workflow checkpoint *at the time instance t as a set of tuples:*

$$CKPT(\mathcal{W}, t) = \left(\bigcup_{\substack{\forall\, (N_1, N_2, D\text{-}port) \in D\text{-}edges\, \wedge \\ state(N_1, t) = completed\, \wedge \\ state(N_2, t) \neq completed}} (N_2, state\,(N_2, t)\,, D\text{-}port)\,, \quad t \right).$$

As we can notice, there are multiple options for the checkpointed state $state\,(N_2)$ of a not yet completed activity N_2, where the activity state was defined in Section 7.3.5 (see Definition 7.14). We propose three solutions to this problem:

1. checkpoint immediately and regard the activity as running;
2. wait for the activity to terminate and set its state to completed if the execution was successful, otherwise set the state to failed. Both solutions are not obviously perfect and, therefore, we propose a third option that uses the predicted execution time of the job, as follows:
3. delay the checkpoint for a significantly shorter amount of time, based on the following parameters:
   a) *predicted execution time* T_N is the time that activity N is expected to execute, computed using analytical models and regression techniques, as presented in Sections 6.1.2 and 6.3.1;
   b) *checkpoint deadline* CD is a predefined maximum time the checkpoint can be delayed, usually equal to the overhead time required for performing the entire checkpoint;
   c) *activity elapsed time* t_N is the activity execution time from the its start until the checkpoint time t.

We compute the state of an activity N using the following formula:

$$state(N, t) = \begin{cases} running, & T_N - CD \geq t_N; \\ completed, & T_N - CD < t_N. \end{cases}$$

This solution saves the checkpointing overhead and lets the checkpoint complete within a shorter time frame.

Another important factor that affects the overhead of the workflow checkpointing is the size of the data port instances to be checkpointed. We propose two solutions to this problem:

1. *output data checkpointing* stores all the output files of the executed activities that were not previously checkpointed;
2. *input data checkpointing* stores all the input files of the activities not yet executed that will be used later in the execution.

For a centralised Enactment Engine, the input data checkpointing is obviously the better choice because it ignores all the data files that will not be used which saves significant data transfer overhead. In case of a distributed architecture, the slave engines do not know which of the current data files will be used later and, therefore, must use the output checkpointing mechanism.

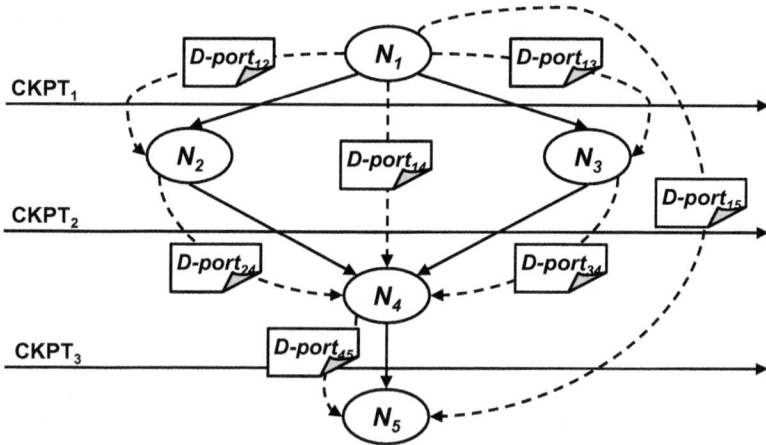

Fig. 7.16. A workflow checkpointing example.

Table 7.4. The input and output data checkpointing for the workflow example depicted in Figure 7.16.

	Output data checkpointing	Input data checkpointing
CKPT$_1$	D-port$_{12}$, D-port$_{13}$, D-port$_{14}$	D-port$_{12}$, D-port$_{13}$, D-port$_{14}$
CKPT$_2$	D-port$_{24}$, D-port$_{34}$	D-port$_{14}$, D-port$_{24}$, D-port$_{34}$
CKPT$_3$	D-port$_{45}$	D-port$_{15}$, D-port$_{45}$

The advantage, however, is that the checkpoint is performed locally by each slave engine which saves important network file transfer overhead. Table 7.4 shows the difference between the two checkpointing approaches for the three checkpoints defined on the sample workflow depicted in Figure 7.16.

7.3.7 WIEN2k Execution Experiments

We use the WIEN2k application that we introduced in Section 6.3.1 for validating the design and functionality of the Enactment Engine with a problem size that produces at runtime 250 parallel k-points which means a total of over 500 workflow activities (see Figures 6.6 and 7.15). The workflow execution experiments presented in this section logically follow the initial scheduling step that we analysed for this application in Section 7.2.4. We executed the WIEN2k workflow in a subset of the Austrian Grid infrastructure [2] consisting of a number of parallel computers and workstation networks accessible through the Globus toolkit and local job managers as separate Grid sites. We first executed the workflow application on the fastest site available (i.e. altix1.jku in Linz) that gives us the indication of what can be achieved for this application by using only local compute resources. Then we incrementally added the next fastest sites for this application as indicated by the rank

Table 7.5. The Austrian Grid testbed for WIEN2k execution experiments.

Rank	Site	Architecture	Size	Processor	GHz	Job Mgr.	Location
1	altix1.jku	ccNUMA, SGI Altix 3000	16	Itanium 2	1.6	Fork	Linz
2	altix1.uibk	ccNUMA, SGI Altix 350	16	Itanium 2	1.6	Fork	Innsbruck
3	schafberg	ccNUMA, SGI Altix 350	16	Itanium 2	1.6	Fork	Salzburg
4	agrid1	NOW, Fast Ethernet	16	Pentium 4	1.8	PBS	Innsbruck
5	arch19	NOW, Fast Ethernet	20	Pentium 4	1.8	PBS	Innsbruck
6	arch21	NOW, Fast Ethernet	20	Pentium 4	1.8	PBS	Innsbruck

column in Table 7.5 and observed the benefits or losses obtained by executing the same problem size in a larger Grid environment. We compare in these experiments the performance delivered by three of our workflow enactment techniques: control and data flow optimisation, control and data flow optimisation plus dynamic steering, and VSEE.

Figure 7.17(a) presents the number of WIEN2k partitions computed by the partitioning algorithm for each Grid site configuration. The number of partitions depends on the workflow structure and the execution plan computed by the Scheduler and is proportional with the number of sites used for each execution. Figure 7.17(b) shows the execution times for running the same WIEN2k problem on different Grid size configurations ranging from one to six aggregated sites. Similarly, Figure 7.17(c) displays the speedup computed as the ratio between the Grid execution time on multiple distributed sites and the execution time on the fastest local site available (altix1.jku in Linz). Without any optimisation, the performance and the speedup deteriorate with the increase in the number of Grid sites used for scheduling and running the workflow. With optimisation and steering, the WIEN2k execution time improves because of the simplified data flow and balanced execution of the LAPW1 and LAPW2 parallel loops. We exhibit, however, a slow down from five to six Grid sites using control and data flow optimisation because of the increased communication time across six distributed sites.

Figures 7.18(a) and 7.18(b) show that the number of file transfers, respectively remote job submissions, are considerably reduced when optimisation is applied which explains the performance results obtained. Figure 7.18(c) displays the average GridFTP and GRAM latencies experienced in our runs, measured for each job from the submission time until it becomes active, which ranges from one to 18 seconds when a local queuing system is used underneath. Figure 7.19(a) shows that the size of transferred data under VSEE is obviously larger than in the other cases, however, VSEE offers the biggest execution improvement since it reduces the number of file transfers by three orders of magnitude that drastically reduces the latencies (i.e. mutual authentication to the GridFTP service). The steering improvement is due to several external jobs that we submitted to the fastest Grid site which caused several LAPW1 and LAPW2 activities wait in the queue. The consequence is an increased load imbalance in the execution of the LAPW1 and LAPW2 parallel loops, which is reduced to half through dynamic steering as shown in Figure 7.19(b).

Figure 7.19(c) compares the data transfer overheads of the activity migration upon control and data flow optimisation with and without the VSEE mechanism. One important aspect is that the data transfer overhead upon migrating LAPW1 and LAPW2 activities is zero when using the VSEE mechanism. The reason is that the sequential activities LAPW0 and LAPW2_FERMI replicate all their output files to the sites where the following LAPW1 and LAPW2 parallel loop activities are scheduled. Therefore, these activities will find their inputs already prepared on the sites where they are migrated which eliminates the data transfer overhead.

7.3.8 Steering Experiments

Our steering algorithm is based on the repeated invocation of the scheduling heuristic engne at well-defined scheduling events in attempt to adjust the optimised workflow schedule to the dynamically changing Grid resources. To evaluate the algorithm, we generated three experimental WIEN2k workflow instances (i.e. two DAG and one DG-based) that correspond to different application input cases (i.e. the number of atoms and matrix sizes) with different parallelization sizes (i.e. number of k-points). We use a static value of 50% as the performance contract elapse factor of all workflow activities (see Section 7.3.5).

Figure 7.20(a) traces the value of makespan objective function optimised by the genetic algorithm at consecutive scheduling events during the execution of each experimental workflow. As the workflow activities are scheduled, execute, and complete, the makespan of the remaining DAG1 and DAG2 sub-workflows obviously decreases with the number of scheduling events. The abrupt decreases of the makespan happen after the submission of all the LAPW1 k-points, which are the most time consuming workflow activities that no longer need to be considered by the Scheduler. The abrupt increases of the makespan are due the LAPW1 activities that violate their performance contract which need to be reconsidered by the Scheduler for rescheduling, migration, and restart. In case of the DG-based workflow, the Scheduler always receives the complete workflow as input but with different control precedence relation between nodes, which explains why the makespan does not decrease with the scheduling events.

Figure 7.20(b) traces the overall predicted workflow makespan (i.e. the overall time the entire workflow is expected to execute) at consecutive scheduling events during the workflow execution. There are several high peaks in the histogram which are due to severe perturbations applied to the Grid sites running the LAPW1 k-points. As a consequence of the performance contract violation, the Enactment Engine rescheduled the critical activities to new machines at the next scheduling event which drops the next predicted

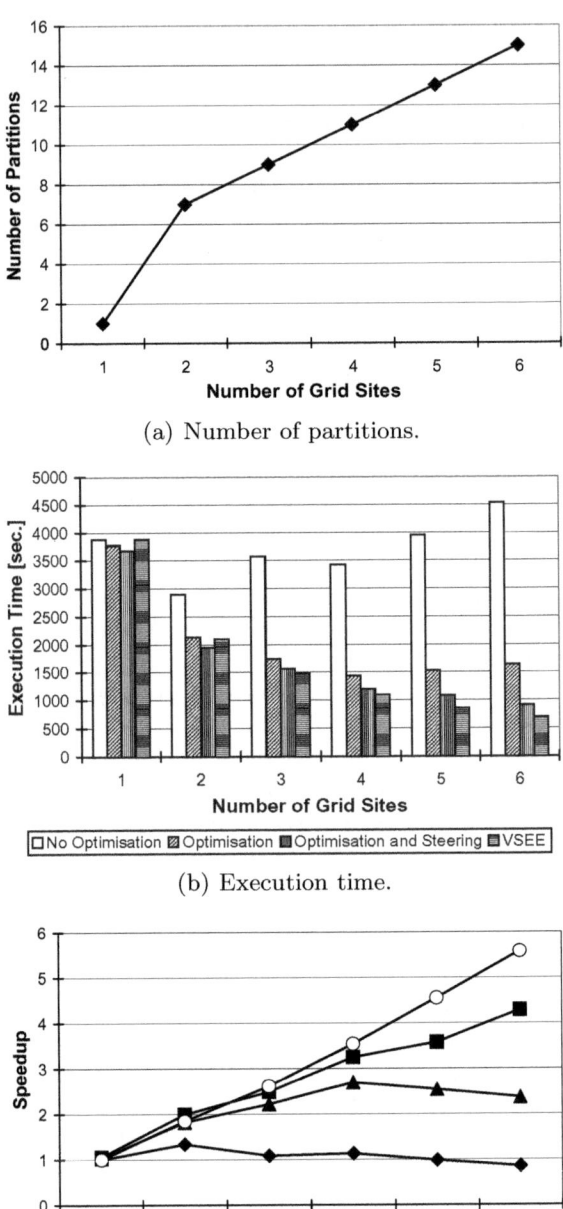

(a) Number of partitions.

(b) Execution time.

(c) Speedup.

Fig. 7.17. The WIEN2k execution results (I).

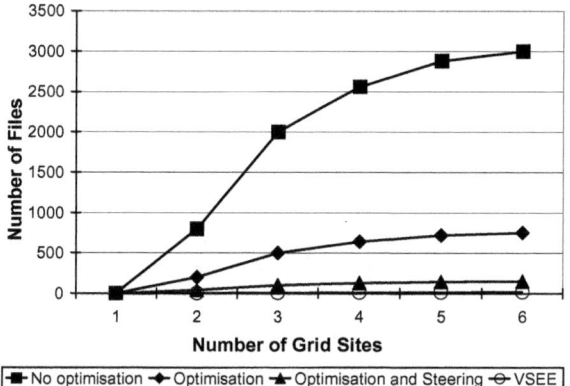

(a) Number of file transfers.

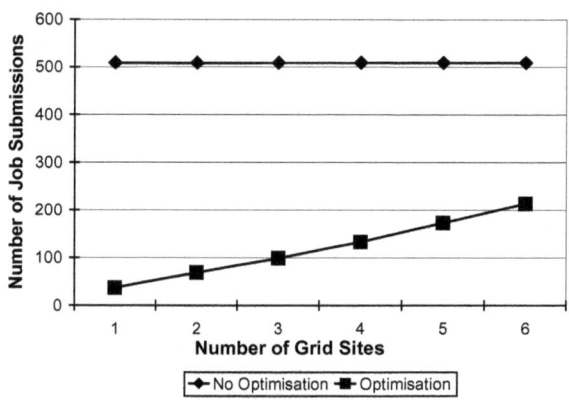

(b) Number of job submissions.

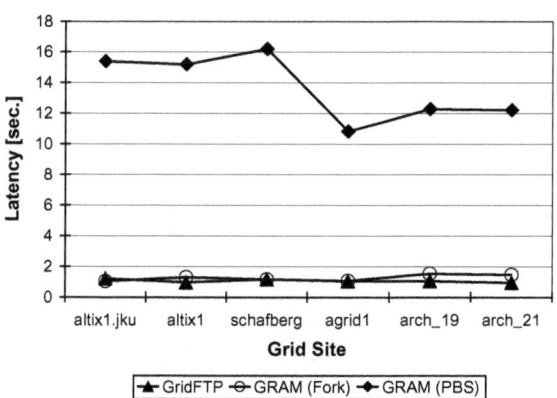

(c) Latency of GridFTP and GRAM.

Fig. 7.18. The WIEN2k execution results (II).

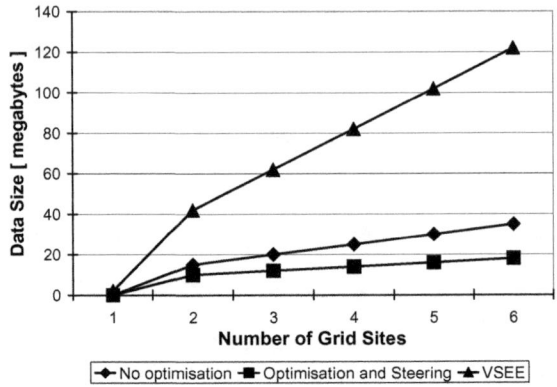

(a) Size of transferred files.

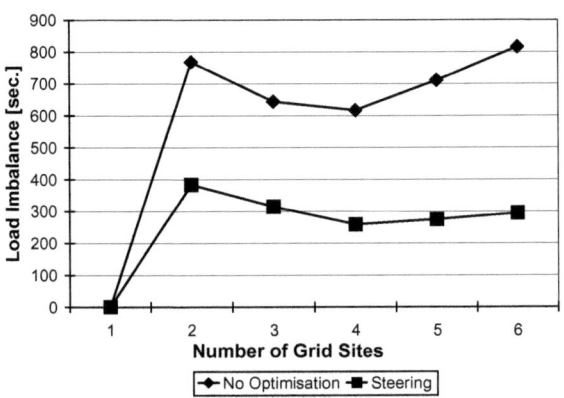

(b) Overhead of load imbalance.

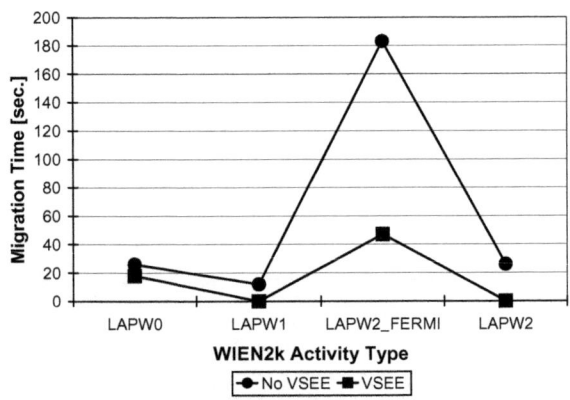

(c) Overhead of activity migration.

Fig. 7.19. The WIEN2k execution results (III).

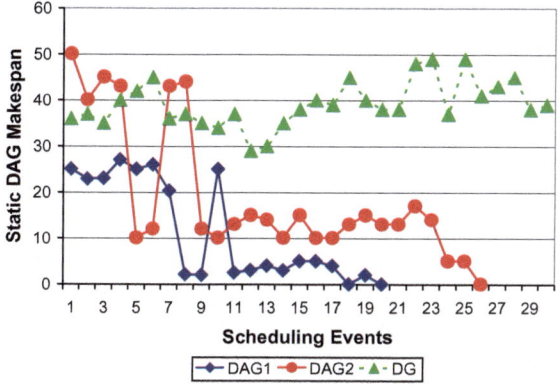

(a) Static DAG makespan.

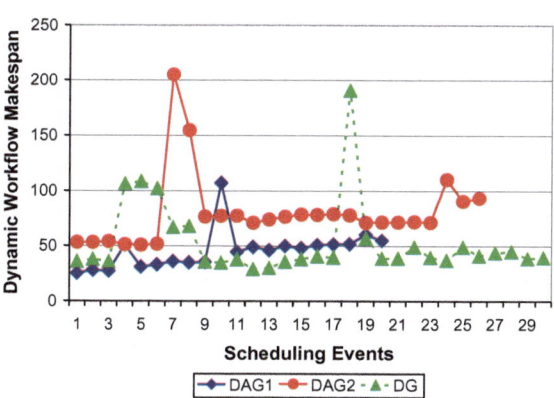

(b) Dynamic workflow makespan.

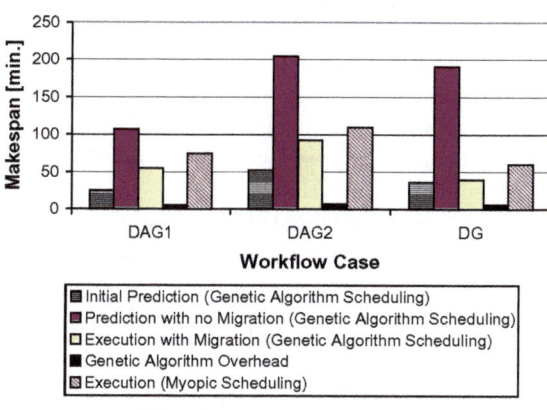

(c) Schedule comparison.

Fig. 7.20. The workflow steering executions traces.

makespan close to the original predicted value. We achieve through rescheduling an estimate of about two fold improvement in the overall makespan (see Figure 7.20(c)). Since the workflow referred as DAG2 represents a larger problem size than DAG1, the benefit obtained through rescheduling and activity migration is higher. The final makespan of the DAG-based workflows is, however, about twice as large as it was originally predicted by the Scheduler. While most of the performance loss is the consequence of activity restarts (i.e. due to duplicated file transfers and LAPW1 task computations), a fraction (i.e. about 10%) is due to genetic algorithm execution overhead. For the DG-based workflow, we could not estimate the makespan of the entire workflow (i.e. beyond the execution of one sequential loop iteration) since the number of loop iterations is statically unknown. As a consequence, Figure 7.20 represents the DG makespan of one workflow iteration only, which is successfully kept relatively constant through activity migration in two critical occasions.

Figure 7.20(c) compares the use of the genetic algorithm for repeated scheduling of the workflow against the myopic just-in-time approach. We performed the experiments on the same workflow cases and under similar (logged) Grid conditions as for the previous experiments. For the myopic algorithm, we generate rescheduling events upon the completion of each workflow activity and the successor activities are immediately scheduled on the resources that produce the lowest execution times (with $\mathcal{O}(n)$ complexity). The overall workflow makespans obtained when using the myopic algorithm were in average 25% higher, because the genetic algorithm was able to find better workflow mappings by looking ahead at the entire workflow.

7.4 Overhead Analysis

The ultimate goal of the Enactment Engine service is to support reliable high performance execution of scientific applications on the Grid. While fault tolerance techniques and distributed executions have important advantages that ensure fast and proper completion of the application, they are also the source of a broad set of additional overheads. In this section we try to classify and understand the nature of these overheads and their contribution to the overall workflow execution time [133].

Figure 7.21 presents a hierarchical classification of a set of *overheads* from the Enactment Engine perspective that we classify in six main categories, as follows:

1. *Middleware overhead* is due communication with the middleware services, which we further divide in:
   a) *Scheduling overhead* represents the time spent by the Scheduler service to appropriately map the workflow activities onto the Grid. The *rescheduling* sub-overhead represents the time to needed to re-map the remaining workflow activities onto other Grid resources upon rescheduling events;

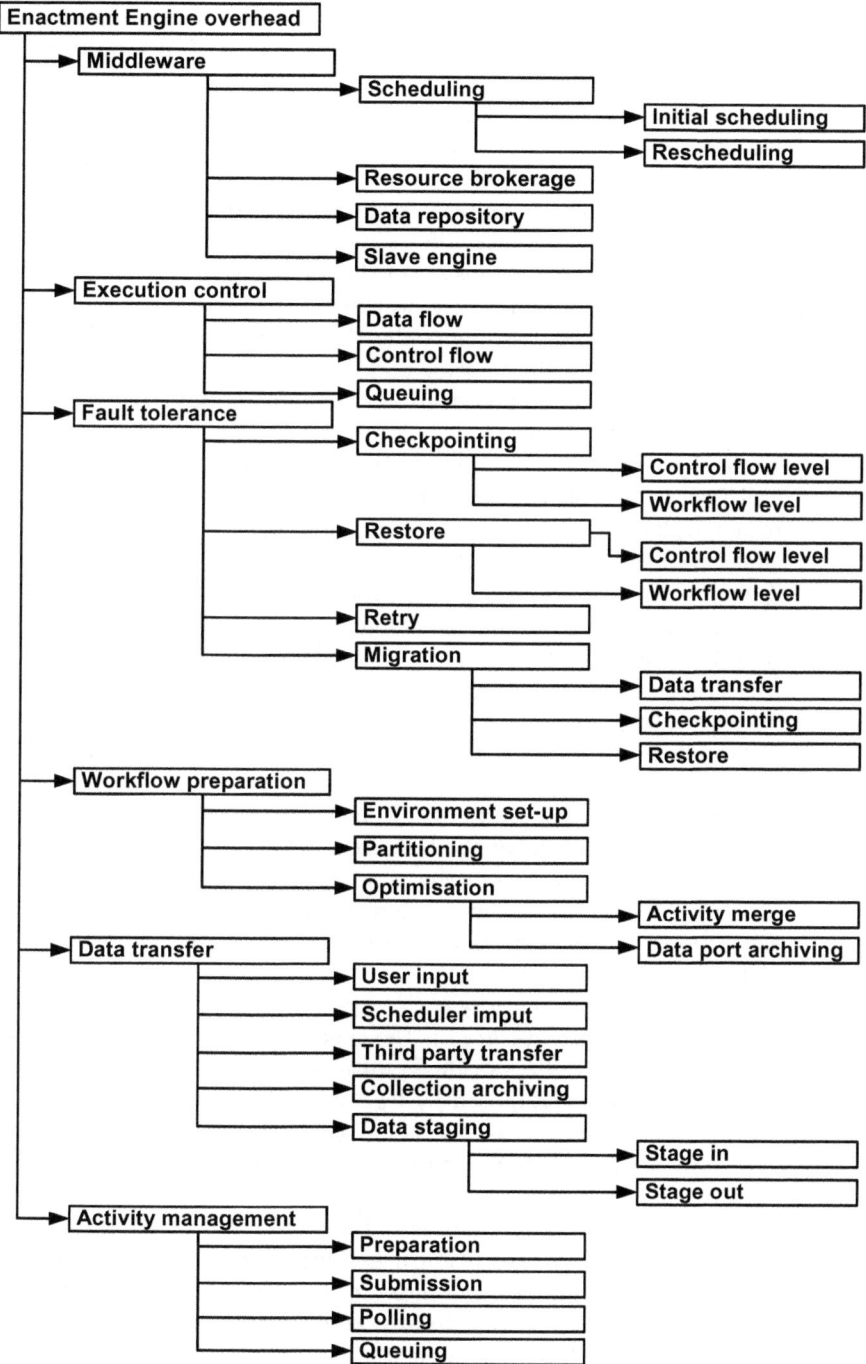

Fig. 7.21. The execution overhead classification.

b) *Resource brokerage overhead* accounts for the time needed to query and retrieve the available resources from the MDS information service;

c) *Data repository overhead* represents the time to access the remote Experimental Data Repository to store, e.g. performance data and checkpoint information;

d) *Slave engine overhead* represents the time needed by the master engine to communicate with other remote slave engines;

2. *Execution control overhead* consists of the following sub-overheads required to control the execution of the workflow:

   a) *Data flow overhead* represents the time required by the Enactment Engine to dynamically analyse and optimise (i.e. archive, compress) the data dependencies and decrease the number and size of file transfers (see Section 7.3.3);

   b) *Control flow overhead* represents the time needed to process the control flow dependencies, like fork a set of activities at the beginning of a parallel loop, or join (synchronise) them at the end (see Section 7.3.2);

   c) *Queuing overhead* represents the time to control the maximum number of parallel jobs submitted to one Grid site, which avoids overloading the GRAM gatekeepers on slower front-end computers;

3. *Fault tolerance overhead* comprises:

   a) *Checkpointing overhead* represents the time required to stop the execution of the workflow and store the state into the Experiment Data Repository;

   b) *Restore overhead* represents the time taken to restore and resume a workflow execution from the last checkpoint;

   c) *Retry overhead* represents the time required to re-execute a failed activity on the same or on a different Grid site;

   d) *Migration overhead* represents the time needed to checkpoint, reschedule, and resume an activity;

4. *Workflow preparation* comprises:

   a) *Environment setup overhead* is the time needed to prepare the execution environment of a workflow, for example to create the necessary directory structure required by legacy applications;

   b) *Partitioning overhead* is the time required to partition the workflow into smaller parts to be executed by the slave engines (see Section 7.3.1);

   c) *Optimisation overhead* represents the time required to optimise the workflow before the execution using the control flow and data flow optimisation techniques presented in Sections 7.3.2 and 7.3.3;

5. *Data transfer overhead* is due to any kind of data transfer that implements the workflow data dependencies, including:

   a) *User input overhead* (interactive);

b) *Input from scheduler overhead* for runtime location of data dependencies (see Section 7.3.3);
c) *Third party transfer overhead* between two remote Grid sites;
d) *Collection archiving* for archiving and compressing a data collection
   before initiating a third party data transfer;
e) *Data staging overhead* including stage in from the local user machine
   to the remote Grid site where the workflow input is needed by the
   first activities, and stage out of the workflow output from the remote
   site to the local machine;

6. *Activity management overhead* comprises the following sub-overheads:
   a) *Preparation overhead* corresponds, for example, to the time required
      to uncompress data archives or create remote directory structures;
   b) *Submission overhead* represents the time needed to submit a compu-
      tational activity on a Grid site;
   c) *Polling overhead* is the time required to poll for job termination to
      the GRAM gatekeeper;
   d) *Queuing overhead* is related to jobs waiting in the local queuing sys-
      tem of the parallel machines available as Grid sites.

7.4.1 Experiments

For validating our overhead analysis approach, we use again the WIEN2k
material science workflow (presented first in Section 6.3.1) which we executed
in the Austrian Grid testbed depicted in Table 7.6. Our experiments try to
answer multiple questions, such as:

- what speedups can we obtain by running the application on several distributed Grid sites compared to the fastest parallel computer available?
- what are the most important sources of overheads that slow down the
  execution of the Grid application?
- how does the distributed Enactment Engine architecture improve the
  workflow execution time?
- what are the overheads of the two workflow level checkpointing approaches
  proposed?

Table 7.6. The Austrian Grid testbed for overhead analysis experiments.

Rank	Site	Architecture	Size	CPU	GHz	Job Mgr.	Location
1	altix1.jku	ccNUMA, SGI Altix 3000	10	Itanium 2	1.6	Fork	Linz
2	gescher	COW, Gigabit Ethernet	10	Pentium 4	3	PBS	Vienna
3	altix1.uibk	ccNUMA, SGI Altix 350	10	Itanium 2	1.6	Fork	Innsbruck
4	schafberg	ccNUMA, SGI Altix 350	10	Itanium 2	1.6	Fork	Salzburg
5	agrid1	NOW, Fast Ethernet	10	Pentium 4	1.8	PBS	Innsbruck
6	arch19	NOW, Fast Ethernet	10	Pentium 4	1.8	PBS	Innsbruck

We used an average WIEN2k problem size of 100 parallel k-points that generates a total of over 200 workflow activities. We first ranked the Grid sites according to their individual speed in executing the WIEN2k application, as presented in Table 7.6. Thereafter, we executed the workflow on the fastest Grid site available (in Linz) and then we incrementally added new sites to the execution environment. Figure 7.22(a) shows that this modest WIEN2k problem case considerably benefits from a distributed Grid execution until three sites. The improvement comes from the parallel execution of WIEN2k on multiple Grid sites that significantly decreases the computation of the LAPW1 and LAPW2 parallel loop activities. Beyond four Grid sites we did not obtain further improvements due to a slow interconnection network of one megabit per second to the Grid site in Salzburg. As expected, the overheads increase with the number of aggregated Grid sites, as shown in Figures 7.22(c) (5.669%) and 7.23(a) (25.933%).

We can rank the importance of the measured overheads as follows:

1. *Data transfer overhead* increases with the number of Grid sites due to a high number of GridFTP third party file transfers;
2. *Load imbalance overhead* increases with the number of Grid sites, mainly because of heterogeneity. We define the load imbalance as the difference between the maximum and the average termination time of the activities in a workflow parallel loop (e.g. LAPW1 and LAPW2). Figure 7.22(b) displays the distribution of activities to the Grid sites in each Grid configuration, as computed by the HEFT algorithm used to schedule the workflow;
3. *Workflow preparation overhead* increases since more preparatory tasks are required when multiple sites are used;
4. *Checkpointing overhead* increases with the number of checkpoints performed;
5. *Middleware overhead*, including scheduling and resource brokerage overheads, remains relatively constant since is done once for every single execution using the same algorithms;
6. *Activity management overhead*, in contrast, decreases with the number of Grid sites since the more activities are executed in parallel, the more job preparations overheads will overlap.

The most important overhead for this application is, therefore, the data transfer. Figures 7.23(b), 7.23(c), 7.24(a), and 7.24(b) display the breakdown of the data transfer overhead from one to four Grid site configurations. The percentages of the input data staging, output data staging, and input from Scheduler overheads decrease significantly since they are relatively constant in each execution. The third party GridFTP-based file transfer is the main source of overhead, which increases from 0% for one site to 94.942% on four sites.

We configured Enactment Engine to perform a checkpoint after each main phase of the WIEN2k execution, i.e. LAPW0, LAPW1, and LAPW2. In ad-

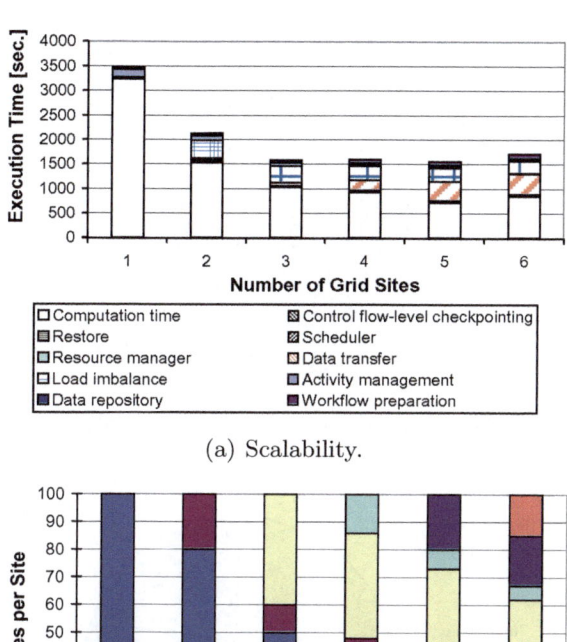

(a) Scalability.

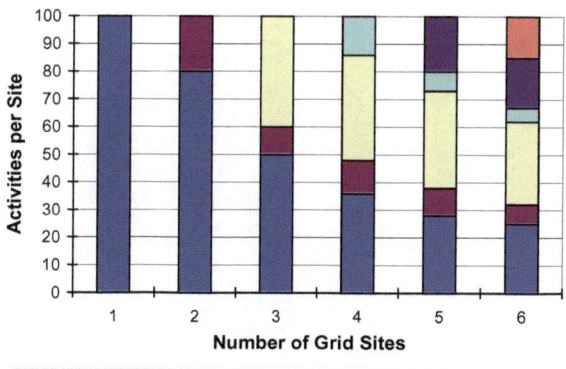

(b) Distribution of parallel activities.

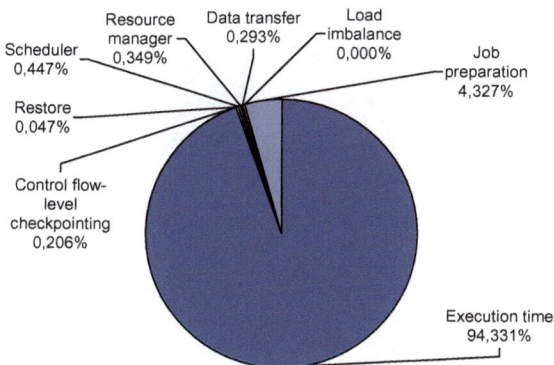

(c) All overheads on one Grid site (altix1.jku).

Fig. 7.22. The WIEN2k overhead analysis (I).

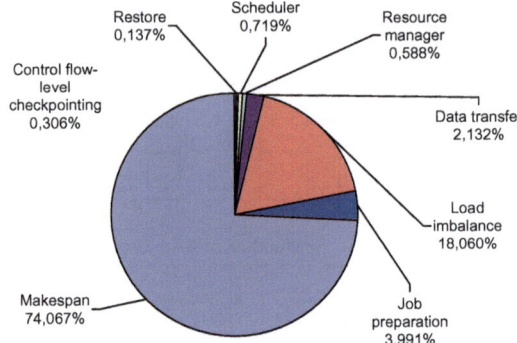

(a) All overheads on two Grid sites (altix1.jku, gescher).

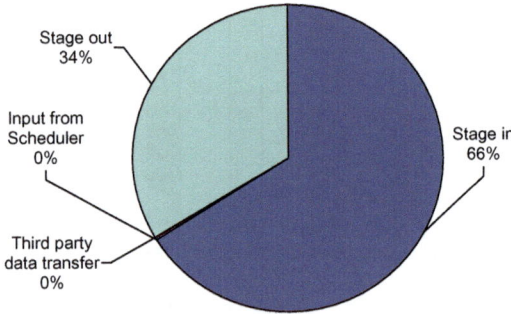

(b) Data transfer overheads on one Grid site (altix1.jku).

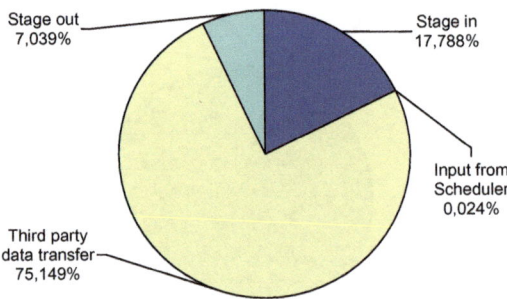

(c) Data transfer overheads on two Grid sites (altix1.jku, gescher).

Fig. 7.23. The WIEN2k overhead analysis (II).

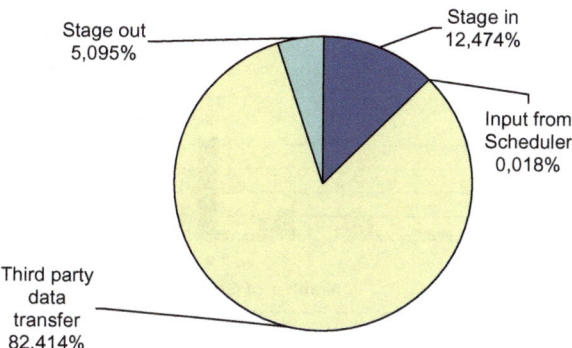

(a) Data transfer overheads on three Grid sites (altix1.jku, gescher, altix1.uibk).

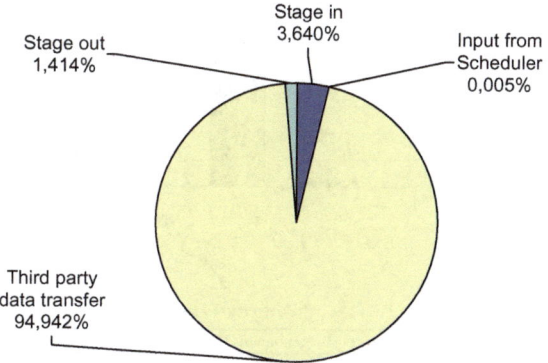

(b) Data transfer overheads on four Grid sites (altix1.jku, gescher, altix1.uibk, schafberg).

Fig. 7.24. The WIEN2k overhead analysis (III).

dition, we configured the master engine to perform input data checkpointing and the slave engines to do output data checkpointing. Figure 7.25(a) compares the overheads of the control flow level checkpointing and the workflow level checkpointing for a centralised and a distributed Enactment Engine. The overhead of the control flow level checkpointing is, as expected, very low and relatively constant since it only stores the workflow state and URLs to data dependencies. The overhead of the workflow level checkpointing for a centralised Enactment Engine increases with the number of Grid sites because more checkpointing data needs to be transferred to the Experiment Data Repository. For a distributed Enactment Engine, the workflow level checkpointing overhead is much lower since every slave engine uses a local

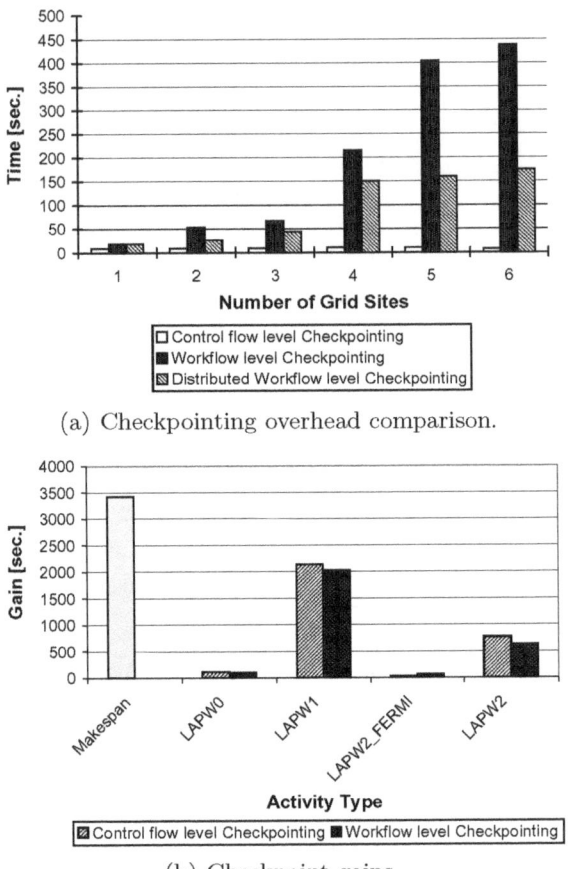

(a) Checkpointing overhead comparison.

(b) Checkpoint gains.

Fig. 7.25. The WIEN2k checkpointing results (I).

repository to store the checkpointed data files, which eliminates the wide area network file transfers.

Figure 7.25(b) presents the gains we obtained in the single site workflow execution because of checkpointing. We define the *gain* as the difference between the timestamp when the last checkpoint is performed t_{CKPT} minus the timestamp of the previous checkpoint t'_{CKPT}:

$$Gain = t_{\text{CKPT}} - t'_{\text{CKPT}}.$$

The largest gains are obtained after checkpointing the parallel loops LAPW1 and LAPW2. The gain for workflow level checkpointing is lower since it subtracts the time required to copy the data to the Experiment Data Repository.

Figure 7.26(a) shows that the size of the data checkpointed at the workflow level is bigger than the overall size of data needed to be transferred for a

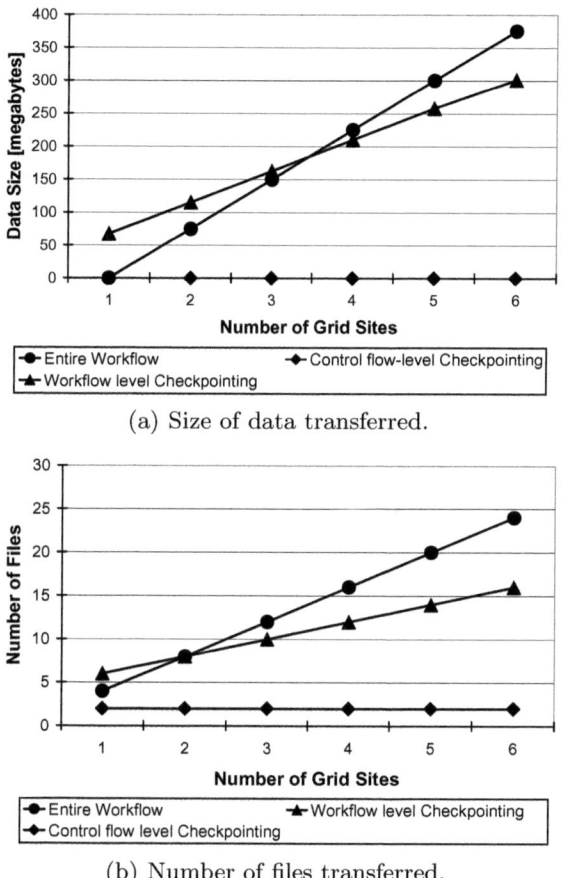

(a) Size of data transferred.

(b) Number of files transferred.

Fig. 7.26. The WIEN2k checkpointing results (II).

small number of Grid sites (up to three, when scalability is achieved). Beyond four sites, the size of the data dependencies exceeds the workflow level checkpointing data size. The data size of the control flow level checkpointing is, of course, negligible. The number of files transferred preserves, more or less, this behaviour (see Figure 7.26(b)).

7.5 Summary

In this section we introduced an abstract hierarchical model for representing large and complex scientific workflows supported by a comprehensive Grid computing runtime environment. A Scheduler service enhances the optimisation framework presented in Chapter 6 with new techniques for converting dynamic workflows into flat static DAGs that can be effectively scheduled using graph-based heuristic algorithms. An Enactment Engine distributed across several Grid sites ensures scalable and fault tolerant execution of large scientific workflows through techniques such as partitioning, control and data flow optimisation, runtime steering adaptation, and various levels of checkpointing. We validated our approach by modeling, scheduling, and executing two real-world applications from the material science and meteorological fields in a real Grid environment (i.e. Austrian Grid). Finally, we classified the major sources of overheads that occur when executing workflows in distributed Grid environments and presented a large number of experiments and scenarios that illustrate how to gain performance in a real, heterogeneous, and dynamic Grid environment.

8
Related Work

The work presented in this monograph is centred around six different research fields: experiment management, performance studies, parameter studies, tool integration, scheduling, and scientific workflows. In the following sections we outline the most relevant related work in each of these areas.

8.1 Experiment Management

ZOO [104] project took place in the late 1990s at the University of Wisconsin-Madison to support scientific experiment management based on a desktop environment. The project defines a clear lifecycle of a scientific experiment, which iterates through three steps: experiment design, data collection, and data exploration. Experiments are designed by using an object-oriented data description language, while input data is provided through a special experiment database. A transformation mechanism maps the contents of the database to application specific input and output files. In contrast, ZENTURIO and the ZEN language do not restrict the parametrisation to input files, but enable the parameter specification within arbitrary application files.

UNICORE (Uniform Interface for COmputing REsources) [65] facilitates the use of parallel computers on the Grid by using modern browser technology. Experiments have to be manually defined by the users, including source, input, and output file staging, as well as and eventual compilation processes. There is no support for experiment set specification and automatic experiment management. Performance analysis is supported for single experiments by providing an interface to the Vampir performance tool [132].

8.2 Performance Study

Paradyn parallel performance tools [107], developed at the University of Wisconsin-Madison, supports experiment management through a representation of the execution space of performance experiments, techniques for the quantitative comparison of several experiments, and performance diagnosis based on dynamic instrumentation. The experiments have to be set up manually by the user, whereas performance analysis is done automatically by the tool for every experiment with using historical data [108]. Paradyn is based on dynamic instrumentation which is difficult or impossible to apply for high level programming paradigms like OpenMP and HPF. In contrast, the ZEN performance directives of ZENTURIO support compile-time instrumentation of arbitrary source code regions and high level language specific performance overheads.

National Institute of Standards and Technology (NIST) [43] developed a prototype for an automated benchmarking tool-set to reduce the manual effort in running and analysing the results of parallel benchmarks. A data collection and storage module implements a central repository for gathering the performance data. A visualisation module provides an integrated mechanism to analyse and visualise the data stored in the repository. An experiment control module assists the user in designing and executing the experiments. In contrast to ZENTURIO, the experiment specification is restricted to predefined parameters available through a special purpose graphical user interface.

SKaMPI [154], developed at the University of Karlsruhe, provides a benchmarking environment for MPI applications with the goal of analysing the runtime performance of the MPI routines. A predefined set of measurements, machine, and problem size parameters can be controlled by the programmer through a special purpose planning script. A public performance database allows to store the benchmark data and perform interactive comparison of various MPI performance aspects across different implementations and computer architectures. The project, however, exclusively focuses on benchmarking various MPI implementations.

Tracefile Testbed [71] is a community repository for organising the performance data of parallel applications which allows the users to flexibly search and retrieve the trace file metadata based on specific parameters such as the computer architecture used, the types of events recorded, or the class of applications. The automatic execution of experiments and the automatic data collection are not addressed.

XPARE (eXPeriment Alerting and REporting) [52] tools are designed at the University of Oregon to specify automated benchmark regression testings for a given set of performance metrics of parallel applications. The tool provides a historical panorama of the evolution of various performance metrics across software versions. Apart from software version control, no other parametrisation is addressed.

The APART working group, funded by the European Union's Information Society Technologies framework, developed a generic design of an automatic performance analysis system that defines and categorises performance analysis experiments [130]. In this context, ZENTURIO represents an implementation of some of the design ideas built within APART.

Automatically Tuned Linear Algebra Software (ATLAS) [188] is an empirical approach for automatic generation and optimisation of numerical software for processors with deep memory hierarchies and pipelined functional units. Benchmarking data is organised and stored in a special purpose performance database server [24]. The scope of ATLAS is, however, limited to linear algebra software and comprises a predefined set of parameters and optimisation metrics.

8.3 Parameter Study

Nimrod [5] is a tool developed at the Monash University that manages the execution of parameter studies across distributed computers by hiding the low level issues of distributing files to remote systems, performing remote computations, and gathering results. A parameterised experiment is specified by a declarative plan file which describes the parameters, their default values, and the commands necessary for performing the work. Nimrod generates one job for each unique combination of parameter values by taking the cross product of all the instantiation values available. The set of possible parameter value combinations cannot be constrained to a meaningful subset like in the ZEN language. Another limitation is that the parametrisation is restricted to global variables which requires appropriate adaptation of the application. Remote source code compilation is also not addressed. Nimrod provides several application specific interfaces whereas ZENTURIO provides a generic user portal for parameterisations, execution, and analysis.

The ILAB [197] project developed by NASA controls parameter studies through graphical annotations of input files. Value sets can be specified by enumeration lists or by *min:max:inc* patterns. So called masking of parameter values equivalent to the constraints provided by the ZEN language is supported via *Perl* scripts. Program variables cannot be controlled.

8.4 Optimisation and Scheduling

Directed Acyclic Graph Manager (DAGMan) [1], developed by the Condor [123] project at the University of Wisconsin-Madison, allows the specification of DAG-based workflows using a special input script where each workflow node is described by a Condor job description file. DAGMan manages the control flow dependencies between jobs and their input and output data at a higher level of abstraction than the Condor scheduler. The concrete scheduling is based on Condor specific opportunistic techniques such as resource matchmaking and cycle stealing with no support for advanced optimisation heuristics.

Pegasus [53] system, developed at the University of Southern California, advocates artificial intelligence-based planning techniques [28] to approach the workflow scheduling problem. Workflows are based on the Condor DAGMan model and, therefore, restricted to DAGs. Pegasus reduces large workflows to more manageable quantities based on the Chimera virtual data availability model [81]. The workflow activities are scheduled randomly to the Grid sites where the virtual data is available. Additional research results report simulation-based scheduling using a weighted min-min heuristic.

AppLeS Parameter Sweep Template (APST) [36] uses application level scheduling techniques developed by the Application Level Scheduling (AppLeS) [22] project at the University of California for efficient deployment of parameter study applications on the Grid. The throughput optimisation algorithms addressed comprise min-min, max-min, and suffrage heuristics [125].

Grid Application Development Software (GrADS) project [50] continues the tradition of the AppLeS effort on developing techniques for scheduling MPI, iterative, and master-slave applications on the Grid, with recent focus on DAG-based workflows [42]. Unlike in ZENTURIO, workflow loops are not addressed. Scheduling is approached through max-min, min-min, and suffrage heuristics which were originally developed for throughput scheduling of independent tasks. Additionally, the project investigated the use of a simulated annealing algorithm for static scheduling of ScaLAPACK MPI applications [27, 196].

Nimrod/O [4] is a variation of the Nimrod parameter study tool that uses a broad range of heuristics for output parameter optimisations. Performance-oriented optimisations are not addressed and genetic algorithms are not used.

Nimrod/G [3] is a Grid aware version of Nimrod enhanced with ad-hoc techniques for throughput scheduling of parameter studies on multiple Grid sites based on a user-defined budget and deadline functionality. The Nimrod/G scheduler is based on a computational economy model called GRACE (GRid Architecture for Computational Economy) and does not target general NP-complete optimisations.

The problem of scheduling task graphs through genetic algorithms has been addressed in the past [117], however, restricted to homogeneous parallel computers with a rather limited number of processors.

In [162], a hierarchical genetic algorithm was successfully applied for automatic optimisation of HPF array distributions within Fortran 90 compilers. The definition of the objective function is based on training set pre-measurements.

8.5 Tool Integration

The Annai [40] tool environment was the outcome of the collaboration between the Swiss Centre for Scientific Computing and NEC in developing an integrated parallel application engineering environment for parallel processing. Annai consisted of an extended HPF compiler, a parallel performance monitor and analyser, and a parallel debugger for distributed memory parallel processors. While integration of different tools was achieved by the specification of well-defined interfaces and communication protocols, further extensions were only possible after rethinking, redesigning, and rebuilding the entire system.

Portable Parallel Distributed Debugger (p2d2) [100] developed by NASA Ames Research Center promoted the idea of client-server tools, with platform dependencies confined to the server back-end, and the client front-end implemented in a portable manner. The debugger defined a server interface that should be provided by any vendor which allows third party front-end clients be implemented in a platform independent manner.

The Tool-Set [191] integrated tool environment and the *Online Monitoring Interface Specification (OMIS)* [124], both developed at the Technical University of Munich, built on the ideas of *p2d2* affirming that a monitoring system should separate the application processes from the tools, thereby encapsulating the platform dependencies. OMIS defines an open interface for connecting runtime development tools in a distributed environment with tool interoperability as a major requirement. Neither *p2d2* nor OMIS, however, built their ideas on top of modern Grid technologies such as Web services.

DDBG/PDBG/TDBG [44] developed at the University Nova of Lisbon is a suite of distributed debuggers integrated into a wider scope problem solving environment. DDBG has been interfaced to a graphical parallel programming tool for high level debugging of parallel programs, and a static analysis and testing tool for controlled execution of previously generated testing scenarios.

Parallel tools consortium (PTools) coordinated projects in the late 1990s with the purpose to define, develop, and promote parallel tools for scalable portable applications. These tools provide flexible open interfaces which facilitate their integration and reuse, however, the possibility of integration and interoperability was not addressed.

High Performance Debugging Forum (HPDF) [118] defined within the PTools umbrella a useful and appropriate set of standards relevant to debugging tool development for high performance computers that influenced some of our design decisions.

Dyninst [31] library developed at the University of Maryland exports a platform independent interface to the dynamic instrumentation technology provided by the Paradyn project for portable dynamic instrumentation of single processes.

Dynamic Probe Class Library (DPCL) [99] is an object-based C++ class library developed by IBM that provides the tool developers with an advanced infrastructure for building parallel and serial tools based on the dynamic instrumentation technology. DPCL allows the tool researchers focus on developing tools rather than deal with compiler details or distributed infrastructure development.

8.5.1 Scientific Workflows

DAGMan [1] is a centralised scheduler and enactment engine for Condor jobs organised in a DAG. The workflow model supported by DAGMan is rather primitive and misses important control flow constructs such as conditional activities and loops (both sequential and parallel). Fault tolerance is addressed through a rescue DAG mechanism, automatically generated whenever an activity instance fails. Our checkpointing mechanism, in contrast, addresses also the case when the Enactment Engine itself crashes.

Pegasus [53] uses DAGMan (limited therefore to DAG-based workflows) as enactment engine, enhanced with data derivation techniques that simplify the workflow at runtime based on data availability. Pegasus provides a layered partitioning scheduling approach which we demonstrated to be problematic for strongly imbalanced workflows. In contrast, our Enactment Engine performs workflow partitioning after the scheduling phase which has significant performance benefits due to decentralised coordination, as opposed to the centralised approach taken by DAGMan. In [109], several task and workflow-based scheduling approaches were compared based on simulation rather than real executions as in our experiments. The conclusion of this simulation was that workflow-based approaches perform better for data intensive cases while task-based approaches are suited for compute intensive workflows. In this monograph we presented a new mechanism called VSEE suited for compute intensive workflows with large amounts of small data dependencies which was not considered by Pegasus. [109] also studies the impact of uncertainty to the overall workflow schedule but does not propose any runtime steering techniques as we did.

Triana [175] developed at the University of Cardiff uses the Grid Application Toolkit [161] interface to the Grid through Web services, but misses compact mechanisms for expressing large parallel loops. Scheduling is done just-in-time with no optimisations or performance estimates. Triana has a distributed engine to partition sections of a workflow to remote machines. The user has to understand the Grid and the workflow execution, while our approach partitions and distributes the workflow automatically.

Imperial College E-science Networked Infrastructure (ICENI) [127] supports low level enactment engine specific constructs such as start and stop in the workflow definition. Scheduling is done using random, best of n-random, simulated annealing, and game theory algorithms.

Taverna's [136] workflow language called SCUFL is also limited to DAGs. Scheduling is done just-in-time, while fault tolerance is addressed at activity level through retry and alternate resource mechanisms only. Taverna focuses on data integration, fault tolerance, and user friendly interfaces for for bioinformatics, while our approach targets generic scientific workflows that are not designed for specific domains.

GridAnt [10] centralised workflow engine, developed at the Argonne National Laboratory, extends the *Ant* [180] commodity tool for controlling the application composition process in Java using low level constructs such as `grid-copy` and `grid-execute`. Scheduling is done manually and fault tolerance is not addressed.

GrADS project [42] restricts workflows to a DAG model and does not propose any workflow model or language. The architecture is centralised and does not consider any service-oriented Grid technology. Similar to our approach, performance prediction models are derived from historical executions based on processor operations and memory access patterns. The GrADS project introduced for the first time the term performance contract [185] and applied it in the context of single site Grid applications, rather than workflows as we did.

UNICORE [65] provides graphical composition of DG-based workflows, comprising file transfers and binary or script file executions (including compilation and link tasks). The workflow jobs can be organised in groups. The UNICORE workflow model does not support parallel loop constructs. Scheduling is user-directed (manual) and fault tolerance is not addressed.

Gridbus [34] support to workflow management at the University of Melbourne provides an XML-based workflow language oriented towards QoS requirements and parametrisation, in particular Grid economy mechanisms. Fault tolerance is limited to activity level using replication.

GridFlow [35] comprises a user portal and a set of services for global Grid workflow management and local Grid sub-workflow scheduling. Simulation, execution, and monitoring functionalities are provided at the global Grid level on top of an existing agent-based Grid resource management system. At each local Grid, sub-workflow scheduling and conflict management are processed on top of an existing performance prediction-based task scheduling system. A fuzzy timing technique is applied for workflow management in a cross-domain and highly dynamic Grid environment.

Our approach to scientific workflows differs in several aspects from the above mentioned related projects. Our model (appropriately supported by an implementation language [70]) allows scalable specification of large numbers of parallel activities typical to scientific workflows, by using compact parallel loops. The Enactment Engine effectively handles large data collections generated by large scale control and data flow constructs. Additionally, we provide two levels of workflow checkpointing for restoring and resuming the execution in case of failures of the engine itself. Moreover, none of these projects provide support for scientific workflows with dynamic control and data flow structure (statically unknown before the execution) that may change at runtime based on the computations performed by certain activities.

9
Conclusions

9.1 Contributions

In this section we conclude this research monograph by summarising our main contributions in the areas of experiment management, scheduling, tool integration, and scientific workflow management in Grid computing.

9.1.1 Experiment Specification

We designed in Chapter 3 a new *directive-based language* called ZEN [139, 143] to specify a large number of experiments for performance, parameter, or optimisation studies in a compact and friendly manner. We defined so called ZEN directives as program comments that annotate arbitrary application files and, therefore, do not change the semantics of the code, as they are ignored by compilers or interpreters which are not aware of their semantics.

We defined four types of directives as part of the ZEN experiment specification language:

1. *Substitute directives* allow flexible specification of arbitrary application parameters through string substitution semantics. The ZEN substitute directives are useful for defining application parameters beyond ordinary program variables, like (HPF) array distributions, (OpenMP) loop scheduling strategies, data locations, compiler options, target execution sites, software libraries, and so on;

2. *Assignment directives* are used to parameterise program variables in cases when the substitute directives are inconvenient or impossible to be used. A typical case for using the assignment directive is the parametrisation of variables with short names (e.g. N) for which the substitute directive would also replace other equal but invalid string occurrences (e.g. in language specific keywords like END);

3. *Constraint directives* are used to restrict the number of experiments to a meaningful subset;

4. *Performance directives* are used to the specify high level performance metrics (i.e. OpenMP, MPI, and HPF specific) to be measured and computed for fine grained code regions, without altering the application source code with instrumentation probes.

The scope of the ZEN directives can be global to the entire enclosing application file or restricted to arbitrary code regions.

Our approach to specify parameters through ZEN directive-based language presents the following advantages over existing ad-hoc scripting [5] or graphical [197] parameter specification alternatives:

1. it does not require special preparation of the application which is an essential requirement for a tool to achieve general acceptance;
2. it does not restrict parametrisation to global variables to be exported outside the scope of the source code;
3. it can parameterise arbitrary local variables with arbitrary names (including homonyms);
4. it can parameterise arbitrary application characteristics beyond those envisaged during the design phase (e.g. parallelization options like array and loop distributions, software libraries, problem and machine sizes, target execution Grid sites, communication networks, or compilation options);
5. it can be applied at arbitrary fine grained scopes within the application source files.

We illustrated in Chapter 4 a variety of real-world scenarios [138, 148] how a large set (e.g. thousands) of experiments can be expressed through a small number (e.g. under 10) of short (e.g. under 50 characters) ZEN directives.

9.1.2 Experiment Management

We designed in Chapter 4 a general purpose *experiment management tool* called ZENTURIO [140, 144] for *multi-experimental performance and parameter studies* of parallel and Grid applications. ZENTURIO employs the ZEN directive-based language to define wide value ranges for arbitrary application parameters, including program variables, file names, compiler options, target Grid sites, machine sizes, scheduling strategies, or data distributions, without altering the source code or requiring any application modification. A lightweight graphical User Portal easy to be installed and managed by non-expert users allows them to create, control, and monitor the experiments as they progress from arbitrary Grid locations (i.e. client sites, local laptops). After the manual annotation of the application with ZEN directives, ZENTURIO automatically generates and conducts the complete set of experiments. Upon completion of each experiment, the performance and output data are automatically stored into a relational Experiment Data Repository for post-mortem analysis. We designed an advanced Application Data Visualiser to automatically query the repository and visualise the variation of any performance metric or output parameter as a function of arbitrary application parameters across multiple experiments (i.e. ZEN variables).

The multi-experimental performance analysis automatically performed by ZENTURIO is a unique contributing research feature. The general experiment specification approach taken by the ZEN language allowed us to support parameter studies within ZENTURIO with minimum extra design and implementation effort. We demonstrated the practical usefulness of ZENTURIO as a performance and parameter study tool on a variety real-world parallel applications [148]. Additionally, we installed ZENTURIO at the Paul Scherrer Institute (Swiss Federal Institute of Technology) for benchmarking three-dimensional FFT kernels as part of an international cooperation [138].

9.1.3 Optimisation

In Chapter 6 we extended the ZENTURIO experiment management tool with a generic *optimisation framework* [145] that employs general purpose meta-heuristics to reduce the parameter space defined through ZEN directives while searching for experiments that optimise a certain output parameter or performance metric. We designed the framework modularly so that it can be easily instantiated for a wide variety of performance and parameter optimisation problems by simply supplying the objective function to be maximised, for example by means of ZEN performance directives. The platform dependency of the objective function is hidden under problem independent interface. We illustrated a first generic encoding of the optimisation search engine using a genetic algorithm.

As case studies, we illustrated the following framework instantiations:

1. *Static scheduling of single workflow applications on the Grid* using genetic algorithms. We have successfully applied this feature on a real-world material science workflow application;
2. *Throughput scheduling of large sets of independent tasks on the Grid* using genetic algorithms;
3. *Optimisation of parallel applications* through repeated experimentation by defining parallelization parameters as ZEN variables and the objective function as a ZEN performance directive. In this context, we formally presented a novel concrete instantiation of the framework for optimising HPF applications on heterogeneous Grid resources using irregular array distributions.

9.1.4 Tool Integration Design

We designed the ZENTURIO experiment management tool within a broad *tool integration framework for interoperability* compliant with OGSA that we presented in detail in Chapter 5. Our architecture brings the following design contributions [110, 111]:

1. We designed *a layered architecture* that isolates the platform dependencies under a portable interface that significantly increases the tool availability and portability. The recommendation that each vendor provide the required set of platform dependent sensors (and eventual services) using a platform independent interface significantly increases the tool availability and, therefore, the acceptance of new computing platforms in the user community;
2. We carefully developed our light-weight and low level senors such that they comprise and *isolate all hardware and operating system dependencies* under a portable interface;
3. We designed and implemented *a broad set of high level services and sensors* that support and ease the development of portable tools:
   a) A *Process Manager* sensor encapsulates the platform dependencies for manipulation and dynamic runtime instrumentation of single processes;
   b) *Experiment Generator* service encapsulates the platform dependencies (including proprietary software libraries) of the Vienna Fortran Compiler on which we base the implementation of ZEN performance directives;
   c) *Experiment Executor* is a general purpose service for remote execution and management of experiments on the Grid which we interfaced to a variety of local resource management systems [29, 102, 123, 172, 201];
   d) *Dynamic Instrumentor* service exports a platform independent interface for low level process management, on-the-fly runtime dynamic instrumentation, and online performance data collection;
   e) *Scheduler* service employs advanced heuristics like genetic or HEFT algorithms for optimised mappings of complex scientific workflows onto heterogeneous Grid resources;
   f) *Enactment Engine* service supports scalable execution of scientific workflows in dynamic Grid environments using advanced partitioning, fault tolerance, and overhead analysis techniques.
4. We carefully designed the services to support *concurrent access* from multiple clients which enables end-user tools interoperate through the common use of services;
5. We designed and promoted *light-weight clients* or user tools which are easy to be installed and managed by non-expert users. The client tool functionality is built through the concurrent use of the underlying high level Grid services;
6. We classified several levels of *tool interoperability* and presented various concrete scenarios how concurrent use of online tools, comprising profilers, debuggers, code coveragers, memory access tools, or tracers, can improve the application engineering process [111, 150]. In addition, we de-

signed a relational *Experiment Data Repository* that enables postmortem performance and output data sharing across multiple users and tools.

9.1.5 Web Services for the Grid

We contributed with early techniques regarding the use of *standard Web services technologies* for *modeling stateful Grid resources* which anticipated several standardisation efforts [142, 144]:

1. We designed a general purpose *factory* service for creating service instances on remote Grid sites;
2. We designed a general purpose light-weight *registry* service for high throughput service discovery based on white, yellow, and green pages lookup operations;
3. We defined the *WSDL compatibility* operation which defines whether two Grid services implement the same functionality required by green pages lookup operations;
4. We redesigned the *UDDI best practices standard* for publishing and accommodating transient Grid services implementations rather than persistent Web services instances;
5. We implemented operations for manipulating the *service state and lifecycle* based on the non-standard facilities provided by existing Web services hosting environments;
6. We designed an *event framework* based on existing Web services technologies that preceded the OASIS WS-Notification [90] standard;
7. We continuously monitored the emergence of new Grid standards and comparatively evaluated against the own infrastructure which gave useful feedback to the community [141, 144].

9.1.6 Scientific Workflows

In Chapter 7 we gave a timely contribution to the Grid research community in the area of scientific workflow modeling, scheduling, execution, and analysis:

1. We introduced a *formal workflow model* for specifying scientific workflow applications at a high level of abstraction that shields the user from low level Grid technology details like explicit job submission or file transfer. Our workflow specification is generic (see [70] for an implementation) and supports advanced constructs that we identified as being characteristic to scientific workflows in Grid environments:
   a) a *hierarchical specification* allows the user to effectively split and focus the workflow definition at various levels of abstraction;
   b) *sequential loops* transform DAGs into more complex DG-based workflows which allow the specification of iterative recursive computations with dynamic convergence criteria (and therefore statically unknown

number of loop iterations) that is a common characteristic of scientific applications;

c) *parallel loops* allow the specification of large scale workflows consisting of hundreds to thousands of atomic activities in a compact and intuitive manner for the end-user;

d) so called *cardinality ports* allow scientific workflows to dynamically change their shape during execution depending on the intermediate results of the runtime computation;

e) *conditional activities* implement `if` and `switch`-like statements that change the workflow control flow depending on the runtime results of the computation;

f) advanced *collective communication patterns* like broadcast, scatter, gather, or parallel broadcast allow convenient specification of data flow between a large number of activities;

2. We addressed various techniques for *scheduling scientific workflows* in heterogeneous Grid environments, in particular [189, 190]:

a) a *workflow conversion algorithm* for transforming complex hierarchical scientific workflows into flat DAGs, which are appropriate for optimised mapping on the Grid using classical scheduling heuristics;

b) a comparative analysis of various optimisation heuristics, like *genetic, myopic (or opportunistic just-in-time), HEFT, and layered partitioning algorithms*, applied on real-world scientific workflows [160, 178] in a real Grid environment [2];

3. We proposed advanced mechanisms for *executing scientific workflows* in dynamic Grid environments, more precisely [59, 60, 61]:

a) a *partitioning algorithm* and a *distributed Enactment Engine architecture* for decentralised workflow execution across various slave engines that offer reduced coordination overhead and improved fault tolerance;

b) various workflow *runtime optimisation techniques*, including coalescing of several activities and compressing and archiving of multiple data dependencies;

c) a new method called *Virtual Single Execution Environment (VSEE)* that optimises the execution of peculiar scientific workflows containing a very large number of small sized data dependencies;

d) a systematic *workflow steering algorithm* that reacts upon well-defined *rescheduling events* and adjusts workflow schedules that no longer follow the original optimised mapping computed by the Scheduler;

e) various *fault tolerance techniques* including two *checkpointing* mechanisms;

4. We proposed a systematic *overhead analysis* approach to understand the sources of bottlenecks that slow down the distributed execution of scientific workflows based on a well-defined *hierarchical overhead classification* [133].

10

Appendix

10.1 Notations

Symbol	Description
$\sum_{i=1}^{n} e_i$	$e_1 + e_2 + \ldots + e_n$
$\Pi_{i=1}^{n} e_i$	$e_1 \cdot e_2 \cdot \ldots \cdot e_n$
$\mathcal{O}(m^n)$	Algorithm complexity of m^n
$avg\{S\}$	Average element from the set S of real numbers
$\overline{\mathcal{F}}$	Average population fitness
$\mathcal{B}(M_1, M_2)$	Bandwidth between sites M_1 and M_2
$D\text{-}port_{card}$	Cardinality input port
$|S|$	Cardinality of set S
$\mathrm{CKPT}(\mathcal{W}, t)$	Checkpoint of workflow $\mathcal{W}$ at time instance t
$\mathcal{CR}$	Code region
C_n^2	Combinations of n elements taken two at a time
CA	Computational activity
N_{if}	Conditional activity
$\mathcal{C}$	Constant
(N_1, N_2)	Control flow dependency from activity N_1 to activity N_2
$\prec_c$	Control flow precedence relation
$\times$	Cross product
$\oplus$	Crossover operator
$(N_1, N_2, D\text{-}port)$	Data flow dependency from activity N_1 to activity N_2
$\prec_d$	Data flow precedence relation
$D\text{-}port$	Data port
ω_N	Data port evaluation function of activity N
DA	Data transfer activity
$\emptyset$	Empty set
T	Execution time
T_N^M	Execution time of activity N scheduled on site M
$\exists$	Exists
ϵ	Experiment

Symbol	*Description*
$false$	False boolean value
$flops$	Floating point operations
$\forall$	For all
$\{x\}$	Fractional part of real number $x \in \mathbb{R}$
$\rightarrow$	Function mapping
$\mathcal{G}$	Gantt chart
GRID	Grid
M	Grid site
$\Longleftrightarrow$	If and only if equivalence
$\Longrightarrow$	Implication
$\mathcal{I}^z$	Index domain of ZEN variable z
ϑ^{-1}	Index function
$IN\text{-}ports^N$	Input data ports of activity N
$IN\text{-}ports^{\mathcal{W}}$	Input data ports of workflow $\mathcal{W}$
$\lfloor x \rfloor$	Integer part of real number $x \in \mathbb{R}$
$\mathcal{L}(M_1, M_2)$	Latency between sites M_1 and M_2
$\wedge$	Logical conjunction
$\vee$	Logical disjunction
$\neg$	Logical negation
$\max\{S\}$	Maximum element from the set S of real numbers
$\min\{S\}$	Minimum element from the set S of real numbers
$\ominus$	Mutation operator
$\nu(z)$	Name of ZEN variable z
$\mathcal{F}$	Objective or fitness function
ϵ	Output data
$OUT\text{-}ports^N$	Output data ports of activity N
$OUT\text{-}ports^{\mathcal{W}}$	Output data ports of workflow $\mathcal{W}$
$\mathcal{Z}_o$	Output file
$\mathcal{OP}$	Output parameter
$\mathcal{OP}(\mathcal{A})$	Set of output parameters of ZEN application $\mathcal{A}$
N_{par}	Parallel loop activity
$Parent(N)$	Parent of activity N
$Parent^n(N)$	Parent of rank n of activity N
f_N	Performance contract elapse factor of task N
$PC(N, \mathcal{S}_N, t)$	Performance contract of activity N at time instance t
δ	Performance data
$\delta_M(\mathcal{M}, \mathcal{AI})$	Perf. data for measurement $\mathcal{M}$ of application $\mathcal{AI}$ on site M
$\mathcal{M}$	Performance measurement
$\mathcal{M}(m, \mathcal{CR})$	Performance measurement of metric m for code region $\mathcal{CR}$
$\mathcal{M}(d)$	Performance measurements defined by directive d
$\mathcal{M}(\mathcal{A})$	Performance measurements defined by ZEN application $\mathcal{A}$
POP	Population of individuals
$\mathcal{P}(S)$	Power set of S

Symbol	Description
$pred(N)$	Predecessor of activity N
$pred^p(N)$	Predecessor of rank p of activity N
$\overline{T}$	Probabilistic predicted time
Pr	Probability
$Pr(N)$	Probability of execution of activity N
PROC	Processor
$\Pi_P S$	Projection operator from space S to subspace P
$\overline{R}_N$	Rank of activity N
$\mathcal{S}_N$	Schedule of activity N
$\mathcal{S}_\mathcal{A}$	Schedule of ZEN application $\mathcal{A}$
$\mathcal{S}_\mathcal{W}$	Schedule of workflow $\mathcal{W}$
$scope(d)$	Scope of ZEN directive d
$Nodes^{CA}$	Set of CA activities
$Nodes^{DA}$	Set of DA activities
$\setminus$	Set difference
$[a..b]$	Set of integer numbers from a to b
$\cap$	Set intersection
$\bigcap_{i=1}^{n} S_i$	$S_1 \cap S_2 \cap \ldots \cap S_n$
$\in$	Set membership
$\mid$	Set restriction
$C\text{-}edges$	Set of control flow dependencies
$D\text{-}edges$	Set of data flow dependencies
$\mathbb{N}$	Set of natural numbers
$\mathbb{N}^*$	Set of non-zero natural numbers
$\mathbb{R}_+$	Set of positive real numbers
$\mathbb{R}_+^*$	Set of positive non-zero real numbers
$\mathbb{R}$	Set of real numbers
$[a, b]$	Set of real numbers from a to b
$Nodes$	Set of workflow activities
$\cup$	Set union
$\bigcup_{i=1}^{n} S_i$	$S_1 \cup S_2 \cup \ldots \cup S_n$
N_{loop}	Sequential loop activity
v	Speed
$start(N)$	Start timestamp of activity N
$state(N, t)$	State of activity N at time instance t
$\subset$	Subset of
$\subseteq$	Subset of or equal
$succ(N)$	Successor of activity N
$succ^p(N)$	Successor of rank p of activity N
$end(N)$	Termination timestamp of task N
t	Timestamp
$\prec$	Totally ordered set precedence
$true$	True boolean value

Symbol	Description
$\otimes$	Tuple composition operator
$\tau(z)$	Type of ZEN variable z
ϑ	Value function
$\mathcal{V}^z$	Value set of ZEN variable z
$\mathcal{V}^{\mathcal{A}}$	Value set of ZEN application $\mathcal{A}$
$\overline{w}$	Weight
W	Work
$\mathcal{W}$	Workflow
N	Workflow activity
$\mathcal{W}_{sub}$	Workflow composite activity (sub-workflow)
ρ	Workflow path
$\mathcal{A}$	ZEN application
$\mathcal{AI}$	ZEN application instance
γ	ZEN constraint function
d	ZEN directive
e	ZEN element
$\mathcal{Z}$	ZEN file
$\mathcal{ZI}$	ZEN file instance
ε	ZEN set evaluation function
z	ZEN variable

10.2 Code Regions

Mnemonic	Description
CR_P	Main program
CR_A	Arbitrary code region
CR_L	All loops
CR_U	Outermost loop
CR_B	Branch code region
CR_W	IO write operation
CR_R	IO read operation
CR_O	IO open operation
CR_C	IO close operation
CR_Y	Function or subroutine body
CR_S	Subroutine call
CR_F	Function calls
CR_COMALL	All common code regions
CR_I	HPF INDEPENDENT loop
CR_D	HPF work distribution
CR_N	HPF inspector
CR_X	HPF executor
CR_G	HPF gather

Mnemonic	Description
CR_T	HPF scatter
CR_HPFALL	All HPF code regions
CR_OMPPA	OMP PARALLEL
CR_OMPPD	OMP PARALLEL DO
CR_OMPPS	OMP PARALLEL SECTIONS
CR_OMPPW	OMP PARALLEL WORKSHARE
CR_OMPDO	OMP DO
CR_OMPSE	OMP SECTIONS
CR_OMPWO	OMP WORKSHARE
CR_OMPSI	OMP SINGLE
CR_OMPMA	OMP MASTER
CR_OMPBA	OMP BARRIER
CR_OMPCR	OMP CRITICAL
CR_OMPAT	OMP ATOMIC
CR_OMPOR	OMP ORDERED
CR_OMPFL	OMP FLUSH
CR_OMPSE	OMP SECTION
CR_OMPICR	OMP CRITICAL
CR_OMPIOR	OMP ORDERED
CR_OMPISE	OMP SINGLE
CR_OMPBPA	OMP PARALLEL directive
CR_OMPEPA	OMP END PARALLEL directive
CR_OMPIDO	OMP DO body
CR_OMPLO	OpenMP locks
CR_OMPALL	All OpenMP code regions
CR_MPISTARTUP	MPI_Init and MPI_Finalize
CR_MPIP2P	MPI P2P communication
CR_MPISEND	MPI send
CR_MPIRECV	MPI receive
CR_MPICOL	MPI collective communication
CR_MPITP	MPI data type conversions
CR_MPIBA	MPI barrier
CR_MPIALL	All MPI code regions
CR_OTHERREP	Replicated code regions
CR_OTHERSEQ	Sequential code regions

10.3 Abbreviations

Abbreviation	Description
3DPIC	Three-Dimensional Particle-In-Cell
AGWL	Abstract Grid Workflow Language
AMD	Advanced Micro Devices, Inc.

Abbreviation	Description
API	Application Programming Interface
ASCII	American Standard Code for Information Interchange
ccNUMA	Cache Coherent Non-Uniform Memory Access
CoG	Commodity Grid kit
CORBA	Common Object Resource Broker Architecture
COW	Clusters of Workstations
CPU	Central Processing Unit
DAG	Directed Acyclic Graph
DCE	Distributed Computing Environment
DCOM	Distributed Component Object Model
DHCP	Dynamic Host Configuration Protocol
DG	Directed Graph
DUROC	Dynamically-Updated Request Online Coallocator
FFT	Fast Fourier Transform
FFTW	Fastest Fourier Transform in the West
FIFO	First In First Out
flops	Floating point operations
FTP	File Transfer Protocol
GASS	Global Access to Secondary Storage
GHz	Gigahertz
GIIS	Grid Index Information Service
GRAM	Grid Resource Allocation Manager
GRIS	Grid Resource Information Service
GSI	Grid Security Infrastructure
GT	Globus toolkit
GT2	Globus toolkit version 2
GT3	Globus toolkit version 3
HEFT	Heterogeneous Earliest Finish Time
HPF	High Performance Fortran
HTTP	Hyper Text Transfer Protocol
Hz	Hertz
IBM	International Business Machines Corporation
IIOP	Internet Inter-Orb Protocol
IO	Input-Output
IP	Internet Protocol
J2EE	Java 2 Enterprise Edition
JAXM	Java API for XML Messaging
JAX-RPC	Java API for XML Remote Procedure Call
JAX-WS	Java API for XML Web Services
JDBC	Java Database Connectivity
JRMP	Java Remote Method Protocol
LAM	Local Area Multicomputer
LAPW	Linearised Augmented Plane Wave

Abbreviation	Description
MDS	Monitoring and Discovery Service
MIMD	Multiple Instructions Multiple Data
MPI	Message Passing Interface
MPICH	MPI Chameleon
MPMD	Multiple Program Multiple Data
MPP	Massively Parallel Processors
MQ	Message Queue
N	Notification
NFS	Network File System
NOW	Network of Workstations
NP	Non-deterministic Polynomial time
NUMA	Non-Uniform Memory Access
NWS	Network Weather Service
OASIS	Organisation for the Advancement of Structured Information Standards
OGSA	Open Grid Services Architecture
OGSI	Open Grid Services Infrastructure
OpenMP	Open Multiprocessing
ORB	Object Request Broker
ORPC	Object Remote Procedure Call
PBS	Portable Batch System
PKI	Public Key Infrastructure
PS	Publish-Subscribe
QR	Query-Response
RMI	Remote Method Invocation
RPC	Remote Procedure Call
RSL	Resource Specification Language
(μ)sec.	(micro-) Second
SIMD	Single Instruction Multiple Data
SISD	Single Instruction Single Data
SMP	Symmetric Multiprocessor
SMTP	Simple Mail Transfer Protocol
SOA	Service-oriented Architecture
SOAP	Simple Object Access Protocol
SPMD	Single Program Multiple Data
SQL	Structured Query Language
ssh	Secure Shell
SSL	Secure Socket Layer
TCP	Transmission Control Protocol
TLB	Translation Lookaside Buffer
TLS	Transport Layer Security
UDDI	Universal Description, Discovery and Integration
UMA	Uniform Memory Access
UML	Unified Modeling Language

Abbreviation	Description
URL	Uniform Resource Locator
VSEE	Virtual Single Execution Environment
WASP	Web Application and Services Platform
WSDL	Web Service Description Language
WSIF	Web Services Invocation Framework
WSIL	Web Services Inspection Language
WSRF	Web Services Resource Framework
WWW	World Wide Web
XML	eXtensive Markup Language

10.4 Performance Metrics

Mnemonic	Date Type	Unit	Description
WTIME	double	μsec.	Wall-clock time
UTIME	double	μsec.	User CPU time
STIME	double	μsec.	System CPU time
CTIME	double	μsec.	CPU Time (user + system)
NCALLS	int64	counter	Number of calls
NSUBS	int64	counter	Number of code region calls
MAJT	int64	counter	Page faults requiring physical IO
MINT	int64	counter	Page faults not requiring physical IO
NSWAP	int64	counter	Number of swaps
L1_DCM	int64	counter	Level data cache misses
L1_ICM	int64	counter	Level 1 instruction cache misses
L2_DCM	int64	counter	Level 2 data cache misses
L2_ICM	int64	counter	Level 2 instruction cache misses
L3_DCM	int64	counter	Level 3 data cache misses
L3_ICM	int64	counter	Level 3 instruction cache misses
L1_TCM	int64	counter	Level 1 cache misses
L2_TCM	int64	counter	Level 2 cache misses
L3_TCM	int64	counter	Level 3 cache misses
CA_SNP	int64	counter	Requests for a snoop
CA_SHR	int64	counter	Exclusive access to shared cache line
CA_CLN	int64	counter	Exclusive access to clean cache line
CA_INV	int64	counter	Cache line invalidation
CA_ITV	int64	counter	Cache line intervention
L3_LDM	int64	counter	Level 3 load misses
L3_STM	int64	counter	Level 3 store misses
BRU_IDL	int64	counter	Cycles branch units are idle
FXU_IDL	int64	counter	Cycles integer units are idle
FPU_IDL	int64	counter	Cycles floating point units are idle
LSU_IDL	int64	counter	Cycles load/store units are idle
TLB_DM	int64	counter	Data TLB misses
TLB_IM	int64	counter	Instruction TLB misses

Mnemonic	Date Type	Unit	Description
TLB_TL	int64	counter	Total TLB misses
L1_LDM	int64	counter	Level 1 load misses
L1_STM	int64	counter	Level 1 store misses
L2_LDM	int64	counter	Level 2 load misses
L2_STM	int64	counter	Level 2 store misses
BTAC_M	int64	counter	Branch target address cache misses
PRF_DM	int64	counter	Data prefetch cache misses
L3_DCH	int64	counter	Level 3 data cache hits
TLB_SD	int64	counter	TLB shootdowns
CSR_FAL	int64	counter	Failed store conditional instructions
CSR_SUC	int64	counter	Successful store conditional instructions
CSR_TOT	int64	counter	Total store conditional instructions
MEM_SCY	int64	counter	Cycles stalled waiting for memory accesses
MEM_RCY	int64	counter	Cycles stalled waiting for memory reads
MEM_WCY	int64	counter	Cycles stalled waiting for memory writes
STL_ICY	int64	counter	Cycles with no instruction issued
FUL_ICY	int64	counter	Cycles with maximum instruction issued
STL_CCY	int64	counter	Cycles with no instructions completed
FUL_CCY	int64	counter	Cycles with maximum instructions completed
HW_INT	int64	counter	Hardware interrupts
BR_UCN	int64	counter	Unconditional branch instructions
BR_CN	int64	counter	Conditional branch instructions
BR_TKN	int64	counter	Conditional branch instructions taken
BR_NTK	int64	counter	Conditional branch instructions not taken
BR_MSP	int64	counter	Conditional branch instructions mispredicted
BR_PRC	int64	counter	Conditional branch instructions predicted
FMA_INS	int64	counter	FMA instructions completed
TOT_IIS	int64	counter	Instructions issued
TOT_INS	int64	counter	Instructions completed
INT_INS	int64	counter	Integer instructions
FP_INS	int64	counter	Floating point instructions
LD_INS	int64	counter	Load instructions
SR_INS	int64	counter	Store instructions
BR_INS	int64	counter	Branch instructions
VEC_INS	int64	counter	Vector/SIMD instructions
FLOPS	int64	counter	Floating point instructions per second
RES_STL	int64	counter	Cycles stalled on any resource
FP_STAL	int64	counter	Cycles stalled on floating point units
TOT_CYC	int64	counter	Total cycles
IPS	int64	counter	Instructions per second
LST_INS	int64	counter	Load/store instructions completed
SYC_INS	int64	counter	Synchronisation instructions completed
L1_DCH	int64	counter	Level 1 data cache hits
L2_DCH	int64	counter	Level 2 data cache hits
L1_DCA	int64	counter	Level 1 data cache accesses
L2_DCA	int64	counter	Level 2 data cache accesses

Mnemonic	Date Type	Unit	Description
L3_DCA	int64	counter	Level 3 data cache accesses
L1_DCR	int64	counter	Level 1 data cache reads
L2_DCR	int64	counter	Level 2 data cache reads
L3_DCR	int64	counter	Level 3 data cache reads
L1_DCW	int64	counter	Level 1 data cache writes
L2_DCW	int64	counter	Level 2 data cache writes
L3_DCW	int64	counter	Level 3 data cache writes
L1_ICH	int64	counter	Level 1 instruction cache hits
L2_ICH	int64	counter	Level 2 instruction cache hits
L3_ICH	int64	counter	Level 3 instruction cache hits
L1_ICA	int64	counter	Level 1 instruction cache accesses
L2_ICA	int64	counter	Level 2 instruction cache accesses
L3_ICA	int64	counter	Level 3 instruction cache accesses
L1_ICR	int64	counter	Level 1 instruction cache reads
L2_ICR	int64	counter	Level 2 instruction cache reads
L3_ICR	int64	counter	Level 3 instruction cache reads
L1_ICW	int64	counter	Level 1 instruction cache writes
L2_ICW	int64	counter	Level 2 instruction cache writes
L3_ICW	int64	counter	Level 3 instruction cache writes
L1_TCH	int64	counter	Level 1 total cache hits
L2_TCH	int64	counter	Level 2 total cache hits
L3_TCH	int64	counter	Level 3 total cache hits
L1_TCA	int64	counter	Level 1 total cache accesses
L2_TCA	int64	counter	Level 2 total cache accesses
L3_TCA	int64	counter	Level 3 total cache accesses
L1_TCR	int64	counter	Level 1 total cache reads
L2_TCR	int64	counter	Level 2 total cache reads
L3_TCR	int64	counter	Level 3 total cache reads
L1_TCW	int64	counter	Level 1 total cache writes
L2_TCW	int64	counter	Level 2 total cache writes
L3_TCW	int64	counter	Level 3 total cache writes
FML_INS	int64	counter	Floating point multiply instructions
FAD_INS	int64	counter	Floating point add instructions
FDV_INS	int64	counter	Floating point divide instructions
FSQ_INS	int64	counter	Floating point square root instructions
FNV_INS	int64	counter	Floating point inverse instructions
ODATA	double	μsec.	Data movement
ODATA_L21	double	μsec.	Level two to level one cache misses
ODATA_L23	double	μsec.	Level three to level two cache misses
ODATA_SEND	double	μsec.	Send data
ODATA_RECV	double	μsec.	Receive data
ODATA_P2P	double	μsec.	Point to point communication
ODATA_COL	double	μsec.	Collective communication
ODATA_PUT	double	μsec.	Put remote data
ODATA_GET	double	μsec.	Get remote data
ODATA_FREAD	double	μsec.	File system read

Mnemonic	Date Type	Unit	Description
ODATA_FWRITE	double	μsec.	File system write
ODATA_FOTHER	double	μsec.	Other file system operations
OSYNC	double	μsec.	Synchronisation
OSYNC_BAR	double	μsec.	Barriers in single address space
OSYNC_LOCK	double	μsec.	Lock in single address space
OSYNC_COND	double	μsec.	Conditional variable in single address space
OSYNC_MPBAR	double	μsec.	Barriers in multiple address spaces
OSYNC_DCS	double	μsec.	Deferred communication synchronisation
OSYNC_CRS	double	μsec.	Collective RMA synchronisation
OSYNC_RLO	double	μsec.	RMA locks
OCTRP	double	μsec.	Control of parallelism
OCTRP_SCHED	double	μsec.	Schedule
OCTRP_INSP	double	μsec.	Inspector
OCTRP_EXEC	double	μsec.	Executor
OCTRP_FKJN	double	μsec.	Fork / join threads
OCTRP_IN	double	μsec.	Initialise / finalise message passing
OCTRP_SP	double	μsec.	Spawn processes
OADD	double	μsec.	Additional overhead
OADD_ALGR	double	μsec.	Overhead due to algorithm change
OADD_COMP	double	μsec.	Overhead due to compiler changes
OADD_DTC	double	μsec.	Overhead due to data type conversion
OADD_PUI	double	μsec.	Overhead of processing unit information
OLOPA	double	μsec.	Overhead of loss parallelism
OLOPA_UNPAR	double	μsec.	Unparallelised code
OLOPA_REPL	double	μsec.	Replicated code
OLOPA_PPAR	double	μsec.	Partial parallelised code
OALL_IDENT	double	μsec.	Identified overhead
OALL_UNID	double	μsec.	Unidentified overhead

References

1. DAGMan: Directed acyclic graph manager.
   http://www.cs.wisc.edu/condor/dagman/. Condor project, University of
   Wisconsin-Madison.
2. The Austrian Grid Consortium. http://www.austriangrid.at.
3. D. Abramson, R. Buyya, and J. Giddy. A computational economy for Grid
   computing and its implementation in the Nimrod-G resource broker. *Future
   Generation Computer Systems*, 18(8):1061–1074, 2002.
4. D. Abramson, A. Lewis, T. Peachey, and C. Fletcher. An automatic design
   optimization tool and its application to computational fluid dynamics. In
   Supercomputing Conference. ACM Press and IEEE Computer Society Press,
   2001.
5. D. Abramson, R. Sosic, R. Giddy, and B. Hall. Nimrod: a tool for performing
   parameterised simulations using distributed workstations. In *4th Symposium
   on High Performance Distributed Computing*, pages 520–528. IEEE Computer
   Society Press, 1995.
6. B. Allcock, J. Bester, J. Bresnahan, A. L. Chervenak, I. Foster, C. Kesselman, S. Meder, V. Nefedova, D. Quesnel, and S. Tuecke. Data management
   and transfer in high-performance computational Grid environments. *Parallel
   Computing*, 28(5):749–771, 2002.
7. M. N. Alpdemir, A. Mukherjee, N. W. Paton, A. A. A. Fernandes, P. Watson,
   K. Glover, C. Greenhalgh, T. M. Oinn, and H. J. Tipney. Contextualised
   workflow execution in MyGrid. In *European Grid Conference*, volume 3470 of
   Lecture Notes in Computer Science, pages 444–453. Springer Verlag, 2005.
8. G. M. Amdahl. Validity of the single processor approach to achieving large
   scale computing capabilities. In *AFIPS Conference*, pages 483–485, 1967.
9. K. Amin, M. Hategan, G. von Laszewski, and N. Zaluzec. Abstracting the
   Grid. In *12th Euromicro Conference on Parallel Distributed and Network based
   Processing*. IEEE Computer Society Press, 2004.
10. K. Amin, M. Hategan, G. von Laszewski, N. Zaluzec, S. Hampton, and
    A. Rossi. GridAnt: A client-controllable Grid workflow system. In *Hawaii
    International Conference on System Sciences*. IEEE Computer Society Press,
    2004.
11. Apache Software Foundation. Apache Axis. http://ws.apache.org/axis.

12. K. Ballinger, P. Brittenham, A. Malhotra, W. A. Nagy, and S. Pharies. Web services inspection language (WS-Inspection) 1.0. Specification, IBM Corporation and Microsoft, 2001.
ftp://www6.software.ibm.com/software/developer/library/ws-wsilspec.pdf.

13. T. Banks. Web Services Resource Framework (WSRF). Specification primer v1.2, Organization for the Advancement of Structured Information Standards (OASIS), 2006.

14. A. Barak and O. La'adan. The MOSIX multicomputer operating system for high performance cluster computing. *Future Generation Computer Systems*, 13(4–5):361–372, 1998.

15. D. Barbara, S. Mehrotra, and M. Rusinkiewicz. INCAS: a computation model for dynamic workflows in autonomous distributed environments. Technical report, Matsushita Information Technology Laboratory, 2 Research Way, 3rd Floor, Princeton , N.J. 08540 USA, 1994.

16. L. Baresi and R. Heckel. Tutorial introduction to graph transformation: A software engineering perspective. In *1st International Conference on Graph Transformation*, pages 402–429. Springer Verlag, 2002.

17. D. Barkai. *Peer-To-Peer Computing: Technologies for Sharing and Collaborating on the Net.* Intel Press, 2002.

18. R. Bell, A. D. Malony, , and S. Shende. A portable, extensible, and scalable tool for parallel performance profile analysis. In *9th International Europar Conference*, Lecture Notes in Computer Science. Springer Verlag, 2003.

19. M. Benantar. *Introduction to the Public Key Infrastructure for the Internet.* P T R Prentice-Hall, Englewood Cliffs, NJ 07632, USA, 2002.

20. S. Benkner. HPF+: High Performance Fortran for advanced industrial applications. *Lecture Notes in Computer Science*, 1401, 1998.

21. S. Benkner. VFC: the vienna fortran compiler. *Scientific Programming, IOS Press*, 7(1):67–81, 1999.

22. F. D. Berman, R. Wolski, S. Figueira, J. Schopf, and G. Shao. Application-level scheduling on distributed heterogeneous networks. In *Supercomputing Conference*. IEEE Computer Society Press, 1996.

23. J. Berry. Assessing CPU utilization. *Sys Admin: The Journal for UNIX Systems Administrators*, 7(5):57–60, 1998.

24. M. W. Berry, J. J. Dongarra, B. H. LaRose, and T. A. Letsche. PDS: a performance database server. *Scientific Programming*, 3(2):147–156, 1994.

25. J. Bester, I. Foster, C. Kesselman, J. Tedesco, and S. Tuecke. GASS: A data movement and access service for wide area computing systems. In *6th Workshop on Input/Output in Parallel and Distributed Systems*, pages 78–88. ACM Press, 1999.

26. D. Bhatia, V. Burzevski, M. Camuseva, G. Fox, W. Furmanski, and G. Premchandran. WebFlow – a visual programming paradigm for Web/Java based coarse grain distributed computing. *Concurrency: Practice and Experience*, 9(6):555–577, 1997.

27. L. S. Blackford, J. Choi, A. Cleary, J. Demmel, I. Dhillon, J. Dongarra, S. Hammarling, G. Henry, A. Petitet, K. Stanley, D. Walker, and R. C. Whaley. ScaLAPACK: a linear algebra library for message-passing computers. In *Conference on Parallel Processing*. Society for Industrial and Applied Mathematics, 1997.

28. J. Blythe, E. Deelman, Y. Gil, C. Kesselman, A. Agarwal, G. Mehta, and K. Vahi. The role of planning in Grid computing. In *13th International Conference on Automated Planning and Scheduling*. AAAI Press, 2003.

29. B. Bode, D. M. Halstead, R. Kendall, Z. Lei, and D. Jackson. The portable batch scheduler and the maui scheduler on linux clusters. In *4th Annual Showcase and Conference (LINUX-00)*, pages 217–224. USENIX Association, 2000.

30. M. Bubak, W. Funika, B. Baliś, and R. Wismüller. Performance measurement support for MPI applications with PATOP. In *Workshop on Applied Parallel Computing*, 2000.

31. B. Buck and J. K. Hollingsworth. An API for runtime code patching. *High Performance Computing Applications*, 14(4):317–329, 2000.

32. D. Bunting, M. Chapman, O. Hurley, M. Little, J. Mischkinsky, E. Newcomer, J. Webber, and K. Swenson. Web services context (WS-Context). Specification, Arjuna Technologies Ltd., Fujitsu Limited, IONA Technologies Ltd., Oracle Corporation, and Sun Microsystems, Inc., 2003.

33. G. Burns, R. Daoud, and J. Vaigl. LAM: An open cluster environment for MPI. In *Supercomputing Conference*, pages 379–386, 1994.

34. R. Buyya and S. Venugopal. The Gridbus toolkit for service oriented Grid and utility computing: An overview and status report. In *1st International Workshop on Grid Economics and Business Models*, pages 19–36. IEEE Computer Society Press, 2004.

35. J. Cao, S. A. Jarvis, S. Saini!, and G. R. Nudd. GridFlow: workflow management for Grid computing. In *3rd International Symposium on Cluster Computing and the Grid*. IEEE Computer Sociery Press, 2003.

36. H. Casanova, G. Obertelli, F. Berman, and R. Wolski. The AppLeS parameter sweep template: User-level middleware for the Grid. In *Supercomputing Conference*, pages 75–76. ACM Press and IEEE Computer Society Press, 2000.

37. C. Catlett. Standards for Grid computing: Global Grid Forum. *Journal of Grid Computing*, 1(1):3–7, 2003.

38. E. Christensen, F. Curbera, G. Meredith, and S. Weerawarana. Web Services Description Language (WSDL). Technical report, The World Wide Web Consortium, March 2001. http://www.w3.org/TR/wsdl.

39. J. Clark and S. J. DeRose (Eds). "XML Path Language (XPath) Version 1.0". Recommendation, World Wide Web Consortium, 1999. http://www.w3.org/TR/xpath.

40. C. Clémençon, A. Endo, J. Fritscher, A. Müller, R. Rühl, and B. J. N. Wylie. Annai: An integrated parallel programming environment for multicomputers. In *Tools and Environments for Parallel and Distributed Systems*, volume 2 of *Kluwer International Series in Software Engineering*, chapter 2, pages 33–59. Kluwer Academic Publishers, 1996.

41. J. Colgrave and K. Januszewski. Using WSDL in a UDDI registry. UDDI Technical Note, Organization for the Advancement of Structured Information Standards, 2004. http://www.oasis-open.org/committees/uddi-spec/doc/tn/uddi-spec-tc-tn-wsdl-v2.htm.

42. K. Cooper, A. Dasgupta, K. Kennedy, C. Koelbel, A. Mandal, G. Marin, M. Mazina, J. Mellor-Crummey, F. Berman, H. Casanova, A. Chien, H. Dail, X. Liu, A. Olugbile, O. Sievert, H. Xia, L. Johnsson, B. Liu, M. Patel, D. Reed, W. Deng, C. Mendes, Z. Shi, A. YarKhan, and J. Dongarra. New Grid scheduling and rescheduling methods in the GrADS project. In *International Parallel and Distributed Processing Symposium, Next Generation Software Workshop*. IEEE Computer Society Press, 2004.

43. M. Courson, A. Mink, G. Marcais, and B. Traverse. An automated benchmarking toolset. In *8th European High-Performance Computing and Networking Conference*, Lecture Notes in Computer Science, pages 497–506. Springer Verlag, 2000.

44. J. C. Cunha, c. João Louren and T. A. ao. An experiment in tool integration: the DDBG parallel and distributed debugger. *Euromicro Journal of Systems Architecture*, 45(11):897–907, 1999.

45. F. Curbera, H. Dholakia, Y. G. Bea, J. K. Microsoft, F. Leymann, K. L. Sap, D. R. Ibm, D. Smith, S. Systems, S. Thatte, I. T. Sap, and S. Weerawarana. Business process execution language for web services. Specification version 1.1, BEA, IBM, Microsoft, and Siebel Systems, 2003.

46. K. Czajkowski, D. Ferguson, I. Foster, J. Frey, S. Graham, T. Maguire, D. Snelling, and S. Tuecke. From Open Grid Services Infrastructure to WSResource Framework: Refactoring and evolution. Version 1.1, Global Grid Forum and Globus Alliance, 2004.
http://www.globus.org/wsrf/specs/ogsi_to_wsrf_1.0.pdf.

47. K. Czajkowski, I. Foster, N. Karonis, S. Martin, W. Smith, and S. Tuecke. A resource management architecture for metacomputing systems. In *Job Scheduling Strategies for Parallel Processing Workshop*, volume 1459 of *Lecture Notes Computer Science*, pages 62–82. Springer Verlag, 1998.

48. K. Czajkowski, I. Foster, and C. Kesselman. Co-allocation Services for Computational Grids. In *High Performance Distributed Computing Symposium*. IEEE Computer Society Press, 1999.

49. L. Dagum and R. Menon. OpenMP: An industry-standard API for shared-memory programming. *IEEE Computational Science and Engineering*, 5(1):46–55, 1998.

50. H. Dail, O. Sievert, F. Berman, H. Casanova, A. YarKhan, S. Vadhiyar, J. Dongarra, C. Liu, L. Yang, D. Angulo, and I. Foster. Scheduling in the Grid Application Development Software Project. *Resource Management in the Grid*, 2003.

51. J. Davies, D. Fensel, and F. van Harmelen. *Towards the Semantic Web: Ontology-Driven Knowledge Management*. John Wiley & Sons, 2003.

52. J. D. de St. Germain, A. Morris, S. G. Parker, A. D. Malony, and S. Shende. Integrating performance analysis in the uintah software development cycle. In *4th International Symposium on High Performance Computing*, pages 190–206, 2002.

53. E. Deelman, J. Blythe, Y. Gil, C. Kesselman, G. Mehta, K. Vahi, K. Blackburn, A. Lazzarini, A. Arbree, R. Cavanaugh, and S. Koranda. Mapping abstract complex workflows onto Grid environments. *Journal of Grid Computing*, 1(1):25–39, 2003.

54. L. P. Deutsch and J.-L. Gailly. RFC 1950: ZLIB compressed data format specification version 3.3, 1996.
55. E. Dockner and H. Moritsch. Pricing constant maturity floaters with embeeded options using monte carlo simulation. Aurora technical report aur_99-04, University of Vienna, 1999.
56. J. J. Dongarra, P. Luszczek, and A. Petitet. The LINPACK benchmark: past, present and future. *Concurrency and Computation: Practice and Experience*, 15(9):803–820, 2003.
57. J. J. Dongarra, H. W. Meuer, and E. Strohmaier. TOP500 supercomputer sites. *Supercomputer*, 11(2–3):133–163, 1995.
58. R. Duan, T. Fahringer, R. Prodan, J. Qin, A. Villazon, and M. Wieczorek. Real world workflow applications in the ASKALON Grid environment. In *European Grid Conference*, Lecture Notes in Computer Science. Springer Verlag, 2005.
59. R. Duan, R. Prodan, and T. Fahringer. DEE: A distributed fault tolerant workflow enactment engine for Grid computing. In *International Conference on High Performance Computing and Communications*, volume 3726 of *Lecture Notes in Computer Science*. Springer Verlag, 2005.
60. R. Duan, R. Prodan, and T. Fahringer. Data mining-based fault prediction and detection on the Grid. In *International Symposium on High Performance Distributed Computing*. IEEE Computer Society Press, 2006.
61. R. Duan, R. Prodan, and T. Fahringer. Run-time optimization for Grid workflow applications. In *International Conference on Grid Computing*. IEEE Computer Society Press, 2006.
62. M. J. Duftler, N. K. Mukhi, A. Slominski, and S. Weerawarana. Web Services Invocation Framework (WSIF). In *Object-Oriented Web Services Workshop*. Object Oriented Programming Systems Languages and Architecture Conference, 2001.
63. M. Dumas and A. Hofstede. UML activity diagrams as a workflow specification language. In *4th International Conference on UML*, number 2185 in Lecture Notes In Computer Science. Springer Verlag, 2001.
64. W. K. Edwards. *Core Jini*. P T R Prentice-Hall, 2001.
65. D. W. Erwin. UNICORE – a Grid computing environment. *Concurrency and Computation: Practice and Experience*, 14(13-15):1395–1410, 2002.
66. S. E. Fagan. Tracing BSD system calls. *Dr. Dobb's Journal of Software Tools*, 23(3):38, 40, 42–43, 105, 1998.
67. T. Fahringer. ASKALON visualization diagrams. http://www.par.univie.ac.at/project/askalon/visualization/index.html.
68. T. Fahringer. *Automatic Performance Prediction of Parallel Programs*. Kluwer Academic Publishers, 1996.
69. T. Fahringer, R. Prodan, R. Duan, F. Nerieri, S. Podlipnig, J. Qin, M. Siddiqui, H.-L. Truong, A. Villazon, and M. Wieczorek. ASKALON: a Grid application development and computing environment. In *6th International Workshop on Grid Computing*. IEEE Computer Society Press, 2005.
70. T. Fahringer, J. Qin, and S. Hainzer. Specification of Grid workflow applications with AGWL: An abstract Grid workflow language. In *International Symposium on Cluster Computing and the Grid*. IEEE Computer Society Press, 2005.

71. K. Ferschweiler, M. Calzarossa, C. Pancake, D. Tessera, and D. Keon. A community databank for performance tracefiles. In *8th Europen PVM/MPI Conference*, volume 2131 of *Lecture Notes in Computer Science*, pages 233–240. Springer Verlag, 2001.

72. S. Fitzgerald, I. Foster, C. Kesselman, G. von Laszewski, W. Smith, and S. Tuecke. A directory service for configuring high-performance distributed computations. In *6th Symposium on High-Performance Distributed Computing*, pages 365–375. IEEE Computer Society Press, 1997.

73. M. Fleury and F. Reverbel. The JBoss extensible server. In *International Middleware Conference*, volume 2672 of *Lecture Notes in Computer Science*, pages 344–373. Springer Verlag, 2003.

74. M. J. Flynn. Some computer organizations and their effectiveness. *IEEE Transactions on Computers*, C-21(9):948–960, 1972.

75. I. Foster and N. T. Karonis. A Grid-enabled MPI: Message passing in heterogeneous distributed computing systems. In *Supercomputing Conference*. IEEE Computer Society Press, 1998.

76. I. Foster and C. Kesselman. Globus: A metacomputing infrastructure toolkit. *International Journal of Supercomputer Applications and High Performance Computing*, 11(2):115–128, 1997.

77. I. Foster and C. Kesselman. *The Grid: Blueprint for a Future Computing Infrastructure*. Morgan Kaufmann, 2 edition, 2004.

78. I. Foster, C. Kesselman, G. Tsudik, and S. Tuecke. A security architecture for computational Grids. In *5th Computer and Communications Security Conference*, pages 83–92. ACM Press, 1998.

79. I. Foster, H. Kishimoto, and A. Savva. The open Grid services architecture. Specification, version 1.0, Global Grid Forum, 2003. https://forge.gridforum.org/projects/ogsa-wg.

80. I. Foster, D. Kohr, R. Krishnaiyer, and J. Mogill. Remote I/O: Fast access to distant storage. In *5th Workshop on I/O in Parallel and Distributed Systems*, pages 14–25. ACM Press, 1997.

81. I. Foster, J. Vockler, M. Wilde, and Y. Zhao. Chimera: A Virtual Data System For Representing, Querying, and Automating Data Derivation. In *14th International Conference on Scientific and Statistical Database Management*, 2002.

82. B. Friesenhahn. Autoconf makes for portable software — use of os features and a freeware scripting utility solves application portability across various flavors of Unix. *BYTE Magazine*, 22(11):45–46, 1997.

83. M. Frigo and S. Johnson. FFTW: An adaptive software architecture for the FFT. In *Acoustics Speech and Signal Processing*, volume 3, pages 1381–1384. IEEE Computer Society Press, 1998.

84. M. Frigo and S. G. Johnson. benchFFT. http://www.fftw.org/benchfft/.

85. M. R. Garey and D. S. Johnson. *Computers and Intractability / A Guide to the Theory of NP-Completeness*. W.H. Freeman and Company, San Francisco, 1978.

86. M. Geissler. *Interaction of High Intensity Ultrashort Laser Pulses with Plasmas*. PhD thesis, Vienna University of Technology, 2001.

87. G. A. Geist, M. T. Heath, B. W. Peyton, and P. H. Worley. A user's guide to PICL: a portable instumented communications library. Technical Report ORNL/TM-11616, Oak Ridge National Laboratory, Oak Ridge, Tennessee, 1992.

88. D. E. Goldberg. *Genetic Algorithms in Search, Optimization and Machine Learning.* Reading. Addison-Wesley, Massachusetts, 1989.

89. K. Gottschalk, S. Graham, H. Kreger, and J. Snell. Introduction to Web services architecture. *IBM Systems Journal,* 41(2):168–177, 2002.

90. S. Graham, D. Hull, and B. Murray. Web services base notification 1.3 (WS-BaseNotification). Specification, Organization for the Advancement of Structured Information Standards, 2006.

91. W. Gropp, E. Lusk, N. Doss, and A. Skjellum. High-performance, portable implementation of the MPI Message Passing Interface standard. *Parallel Computing,* 22(6):789–828, 1996.

92. W. Gropp, E. Lusk, and R. Thakur. *Using MPI-2: Advanced Features of the Message Passing Interface.* Scientific and Engineering Computation. MIT Press, Cambridge, MA, 1999.

93. W. Grosso. *Java RMI.* O'Reilly & Associates, Inc., 981 Chestnut Street, Newton, MA 02164, USA, 2002.

94. E. R. Harold. *XML: EXtensible Markup Language.* IDG Books, San Mateo, CA, USA, 1998.

95. R. Hastings and B. Joyce. Purify: Fast detection of memory leaks and access errors. In *Winter USENIX Conference,* pages 125–136, 1992.

96. R. Herzog. PostgreSQL – the Linux of databases. *Linux Journal,* 46, 1998.

97. R. H. High Jr. and M. Kloppmann. WebSphere programming model and architecture. *Datenbank-Spektrum,* 8:18–31, 2004.

98. High Performance Fortran Forum. High Performance Fortran language specification. *Scientific Programming,* 2(1-2):1–170, 1993.

99. J. K. Hollingsworth, L. Derose, and T. Hoover. The dynamic probe class library - an infrastructure for developing instrumentation for performance tools. In *15th International Parallel and Distributed Processing Symposium.* IEEE Computer Society Press, 2001.

100. R. Hood. The *p2d2* project: Building a portable distributed debugger. In *1st Symposium on Parallel and Distributed Tools.* ACM Press, 1996.

101. S. Hwang and C. Kesselman. Grid workflow: A flexible failure handling framework for the Grid. In *12th International Symposium on High Performance Distributed Computing,* pages 126–137. IEEE Computer Society Press, 2003.

102. IBM Corporation. *Using and Administering LoadLeveler – Release 3.0,* 4 edition, 1996. Document Number SC23-3989-00.

103. IBM Corporation. Emerging technologies toolkit for Web services, 2003. http://www.alphaworks.ibm.com/tech/ettkws.

104. Y. E. Ioannidis, M. Livny, S. Gupta, and N. Ponnekanti. ZOO: A desktop experiment management environment. In T. M. Vijayaraman, A. P. Buchmann, C. Mohan, and N. L. Sarda, editors, *22th International Conference on Very Large Data Bases,* pages 274–285. Morgan Kaufmann, 1996.

105. R. Johnson. J2EE Development Frameworks. *IEEE Computer,* 38(1):107–110, 2005.

106. A. Jugravu and T. Fahringer. JavaSymphony, a programming model for the Grid. In *International Conference on Computational Science*, Lecture Notes In Computer Science. Springer Verlag, 2004.

107. K. L. Karavanic and B. P. Miller. Experiment management support for performance tuning. In *Supercomputing Conference*. ACM Press and IEEE Computer Society Press, 1997.

108. K. L. Karavanic and B. P. Miller. Improving online performance diagnosis by the use of historical performance data. In *Supercomputing Conference*. ACM Press and IEEE Computer Society Press, 1999.

109. K. Kennedy, J. Blythe, S. Jain, E. Deelman, Y. Gil, K. Vahi, and A. Mandal. Task scheduling strategies for workflow-based applications in Grids. In *International Symposium on Cluster Computing and the Grid*. IEEE Computer Society Press, 2005.

110. J. M. Kewley and R. Prodan. A distributed object-oriented framework for tool development. In *34th International Conference on Technology of Object-Oriented Languages and Systems*, pages 353–62. IEEE Computer Society Press, 2000.

111. J. M. Kewley and R. Prodan. Interoperable performance and debugging tools using dynamic instrumentation. *Parallel and Distributed Computing Practices*, 4(3):245–260, 2001. Special Issue on Monitoring Systems and Tool Interoperability.

112. C. Kostick. IP masquerading with Linux. *Linux Journal*, 27, 1996.

113. H. Kreger. Web services conceptual architecture (WSCA 1.0). Prepared for sun microsystems, inc., IBM Software Group, 2001. http://www-4.ibm.com/software/solutions/webservices/pdf/WSCA.pdf.

114. S. Krishnan, R. Bramley, D. Gannon, M. Govindaraju, R. Indurkar, A. Slominski, B. Temko, J. Alameda, R. Alkire, T. Drews, and E. Webb. The XCAT science portal. In *Supercomputing Conference*. ACM Press and IEEE Computer Society Press, 2001.

115. S. Krishnan, P. Wagstrom, and G. von Laszewski. GSFL: A workflow framework for Grid services. Technical report, Argonne National Laboratory, 9700 S. Cass Avenue, Argonne, IL 60439, U.S.A., 2002.

116. K. Kunchithapadam and B. P. Miller. Integrating a debugger and a performance tool for steering. In *Debugging and Performance Tools for Parallel Computing Systems*, pages 53–64. IEEE Computer Society Press, 1996.

117. Y.-K. Kwok and I. Ahmad. Efficient scheduling of arbitrary task graphs to multiprocessors using a parallel genetic algorithm. *Journal of Parallel and Distributed Computing*, 47(1):58–77, 1997.

118. D. LaFrance-Linden. Challenges in designing an HPF debugger. *DIGITAL Technical Journal*, 9(3), Jan. 1998.

119. R. M. Lerner. At the forge: Server-side Java with Jakarta-Tomcat. *Linux Journal*, 84:50, 52–54, 56–58, 2001.

120. D. S. Linthicum. CORBA 2.0? *Open Computing*, 12(2), 1995.

121. M. A. Linton. The evolution of Dbx. In *USENIX Summer Conference*, pages 211–220, 1990.

122. M. Litzkow, T. Tannenbaum, J. Basney, and M. Livny. Checkpoint and migration of UNIX processes in the Condor distributed processing system. Technical Report UW-CS-TR-1346, University of Wisconsin - Madison, Computer Sciences Department, 1997.

123. M. J. Litzkow, M. Livny, and M. W. Mutka. Condor: A hunter of idle workstations. In *8th International Conference on Distributed Computing Systems*, pages 104–111. IEEE Computer Society Press, 1988.

124. T. Ludwig and R. Wismüller. OMIS 2.0 – a universal interface for monitoring systems. In *4th European PVM/MPI User's Group Meeting*, Lecture Notes in Computer Science, pages 267–276. Springer Verlag, 1997.

125. M. Maheswaran, S. Ali, H. J. Siegel, D. Hensgen, and R. F. Freund. Dynamic mapping of a class of independent tasks onto heterogeneous computing systems. *Journal of Parallel and Distributed Computing*, 59(2):107–131, 1999.

126. M. L. Massie, B. N. Chun, and D. E. Culler. The Ganglia distributed monitoring system: Design, implementation, and experience. *Parallel Computing*, 30(7):817–840, 2004.

127. A. Mayer, S. McGough, N. Furmento, W. Lee, S. Newhouse, and J. Darlington. ICENI dataflow and workflow: Composition and scheduling in space and time. In *UK e-Science All Hands Meeting*, pages 627–634, Nottingham, UK, 2003.

128. M. K. McKusick. gprof: A call graph execution profiler. In *USENIX Summer Conference*, pages 81–88, 1983.

129. Mercury Interactive Corporation. Systinet server for Java. http://www.systinet.com/products/ssj/overview.

130. B. Mohr. Design of automatic performance analysis systems. Workpackage 3: Implementation issues, EU IST APART, 2000. http://www.kfa-juelich.de/apart.

131. A. Nadalin, C. Kaler, R. Monzillo, and P. Hallam-Baker. Web services security: SOAP message security 1.1 (WS-Security 2004). Standard specification, Organization for the Advancement of Structured Information Standards, 2006.

132. W. E. Nagel, A. Arnold, M. Weber, H.-C. Hoppe, and K. Solchenbach. VAMPIR: Visualization and analysis of MPI resources. *Supercomputer*, 12(1):69–80, 1996.

133. F. Nerieri, R. Prodan, T. Fahringer, and H. L. Truong. Overhead analysis of Grid workflow applications. In *International Conference on Grid Computing*. IEEE Computer Society Press, 2006.

134. G. Nyberg. *WebLogic 6.1 Server Workbook for Enterprise JavaBeans*. O'Reilly & Associates, Inc., 981 Chestnut Street, Newton, MA 02164, USA, 3 edition, 2002.

135. Organization for the Advancement of Structured Information Standards. http://www.oasis-open.org.

136. T. Oinn, M. Addis, J. Ferris, D. Marvin, M. Senger, M. Greenwood, T. C. adn K. Glover, M. Pocock, A. Wipat, and P. Li. Taverna: a tool for the composition and enactment of bioinformatics workflows. *Bioinformatics*, 20(17):3045–3054, 2004.

137. Organization for the Advancement of Structured Information Standards. UDDI: Universal Description, Discovery and Integration. Standard Specification version 3.0, 2005.

138. R. Prodan, A. Bonelli, A. Adelmann, T. Fahringer, and C. Überhuber. Benchmarking parallel three-dimensional FFT kernels with ZENTURIO. In *International Conference on Computational Science*, volume 3037 of *Lecture Notes in Computer Science*, pages 459–467. Springer Verlag, 2004.

139. R. Prodan and T. Fahringer. ZEN: a directive-based language for automatic experiment management of parallel and distributed programs. In *31st International Conference on Parallel Processing*. IEEE Computer Society Press, 2002.

140. R. Prodan and T. Fahringer. ZENTURIO: An experiment management system for cluster and Grid computing. In *4th International Conference on Cluster Computing*. IEEE Computer Society Press, 2002.

141. R. Prodan and T. Fahringer. From Web services to OGSA: Experiences in implementing an OGSA-based Grid application. In *4th International Workshop on Grid Computing*. IEEE Computer Society Press, 2003.

142. R. Prodan and T. Fahringer. A Web service-based experiment management system for the Grid. In *17th International Parallel and Distributed Processing Symposium*. IEEE Computer Society Press, 2003.

143. R. Prodan and T. Fahringer. ZEN: A directive-based experiment specification language for performance and parameter studies of parallel and distributed scientific applications. *International Journal of High Performance Computing and Networking*, 5(2/3):103–121, 2004.

144. R. Prodan and T. Fahringer. ZENTURIO: A Grid middleware-based tool for experiment management of parallel and distributed applications. *Journal of Parallel and Distributed Computing*, 64/6:693–707, 2004.

145. R. Prodan and T. Fahringer. ZENTURIO: A Grid service-based tool for optimising parallel and Grid applications. *Journal of Grid Computing*, 2(1):15–29, 2004.

146. R. Prodan and T. Fahringer. Dynamic scheduling of scientific workflow applications on the Grid using a modular optimisation tool: A case study. In *20th Symposion of Applied Computing*. ACM Press, 2005.

147. R. Prodan and T. Fahringer. Optimising parallel applications on the Grid using irregular array distributions. In *European Grid Conference*, volume 3470 of *Lecture Notes in Computer Science*. Springer Verlag, 2005.

148. R. Prodan, T. Fahringer, F. Franchetti, M. Geissler, G. Madsen, and H. Moritsch. On using ZENTURIO for performance and parameter studies on clusters and Grids. In *11th Euromicro Conference on Parallel Distributed and Network based Processing*. IEEE Computer Society Press, 2003.

149. R. Prodan and J. M. Kewley. FIRST: A framework for interoperable resources, services, and tools. In *International Conference on Parallel and Distributed Processing Techniques and Applications*, volume 4, pages 1790–96. CSREA Press, 1999.

150. R. Prodan and J. M. Kewley. A framework for an interoperable tool environment. In *Euro-Par Conference*, volume 1900 of *Lecture Notes in Computer Science*, pages 65–69. Springer Verlag, 2000.

151. J. Qin, T. Fahringer, and S. Pllana. UML-based Grid workflow modelling under ASKALON. In *6th Austrian-Hungarian Workshop on Distributed and Parallel Systems*. Springer Verlag, 2006.

152. R. Raman, M. Livny, and M. Solomon. Policy driven heterogeneous resource co-allocation with gangmatching. In *High Performance Distributed Computing Symposium*, pages 80–89. IEEE Computer Society Press, 2003.

153. D. A. Reed, R. A. Aydt, R. J. Noe, P. C. Roth, K. A. Shields, B. W. Schwartz, and L. F. Tavera. Scalable performance analysis: The Pablo performance analysis environment. In *Scalable Parallel Libraries Conference*, pages 104–113. IEEE Computer Society Press, 1993.

154. R. Reussner, P. Sanders, and J. L. Träff. SKaMPI: a comprehensive benchmark for public benchmarking of MPI. *Scientific Programming*, 10(1):55–65, 2002.

155. M. Ronsse, K. D. Bosschere, and C. de Kergommeaux. Execution replay and debugging. In *4th International Workshop on Automated Debugging*, pages 5–18. Computer Research Repository, 2000.

156. W. Rosenberry and J. Teague. *Distributing Applications Across DCE and Windows NT*. O'Reilly & Associates, Inc., 981 Chestnut Street, Newton, MA 02164, USA, 1993.

157. B. Roth. An introduction to Enterprise Java Beans technology. *Java Report: The Source for Java Development*, 3, 1998.

158. W. Rubin and M. Brain. *Understanding DCOM*. P T R Prentice-Hall, 1999.

159. B. Satdeva. DHCP: The next generation host configuration scheme. *Sys Admin: The Journal for UNIX Systems Administrators*, 4(1), 1995.

160. K. Schwarz, P. Blaha, and G. K. H. Madsen. Electronic structure calculations of solids using the wien2k package for material sciences. *Computer Physics Communications*, 147(71), 2002.

161. E. Seidel, G. Allen, A. Merzky, and J. Nabrzyski. GridLab: A Grid application toolkit and testbed. *Future Generation of Computer Systems*, 18(8):1143–1153, 2002.

162. U. N. Shenoy, Y. N. Srikant, V. P. Bhatkar, and S. Kohli. Automatic data partitioning by hierarchical genetic search. *Parallel Algorithms and Applications*, 14(1):1–29, 2000.

163. C. Sivula. A call for distributed computing (RPC. *Datamation*, 36(1):75–76, 78, 80, 1990.

164. M. Snir, S. W. Otto, S. Huss-Lederman, D. W. Walker, and J. Dongarra. *MPI: The Complete Reference*. Scientific and Engineering Computation Series. MIT Press, Cambridge, MA, 1996.

165. R. Stallman. *Debugging with GDB: the GNU source-level debugger*. Free Software Foundation, Inc., 1996.

166. G. Stellner. CoCheck: checkpointing and process migration for MPI. In *10th International Parallel Processing Symposium*, pages 526–531. IEEE Computer Society Press, 1996.

167. T. L. Sterling and H. P. Zima. Gilgamesh: A multithreaded processor-in-memory architecture for petaflops computing. In *Supercomputing Conference*. ACM Press and IEEE Computer Society Press, 2002.

168. W. R. Stevens and S. Rago. *Advanced Programming in the UNIX Environment*. Addison-Wesley, Reading, MA, USA, second edition, 2005.

169. H. Stockinger, A. Samar, B. Allcock, I. Foster, K. Holtman, and B. Tierney. File and object replication in data Grids. *Cluster Computing*, 5(3):305–314, 2002.

170. H. M. Stommel. The western intensification of wind-driven ocean currents. *Transactions American Geophysical Union*, 29:202–206, 1948.

171. X.-H. Sun and D. T. Rover. Scalability of parallel algorithm-machine combinations. *IEEE Transactions on Parallel and Distributed Systems*, 5(6):599–613, 1994.

172. Sun Microsystems. Sun Grid Engine. http://gridengine.sunsource.net/.

173. Sun Microsystems. The Web Services Development Pack. http://java.sun.com/webservices/webservicespack.html.

174. Sun Microsystems, Inc. NFS: Network file system protocol specification. RFC 1094, Network Information Center, SRI International, 1989.

175. I. Taylor, M. Shields, I. Wang, and R. Rana. Triana applications within Grid computing and peer to peer environments. *Journal of Grid Computing*, 1(2):199–217, 2003.

176. C. Temperton. Self-sorting in-place fast Fourier transforms. *SIAM Journal on Scientific and Statistical Computing*, 12(4):808–823, 1991.

177. R. Thakur, W. Gropp, and E. Lusk. An abstract-device interface for implementing portable parallel-I/O interfaces. In *6th Symposium on the Frontiers of Massively Parallel Computation*, pages 180–187, 1996.

178. D. Theiner and P. Rutschmann. An inverse modelling approach for the estimation of hydrological model parameters. In *Journal of Hydroinformatics*. IWA Publishing, 2005.

179. B. Tierney, R. Aydt, D. Gunter, W. Smith, V. Taylor, R. Wolski, and M. Swany. A Grid monitoring architecture. Technical report, Global Grid Forum, 2002. http://www-didc.lbl.gov/GGF-PERF/GMA-WG/papers/GWD-GP-16-2.pdf.

180. J. E. Tilly and E. M. Burke. *Ant: The Definitive Guide*. O'Reilly & Associates, Inc., 2002.

181. H.-L. Truong and T. Fahringer. SCALEA: A performance analysis tool for parallel programs. *Concurrency and Computation: Practice and Experience*, 15(11-12):1001–1025, 2003.

182. H.-L. Truong and T. Fahringer. SCALEA-G: a unified monitoring and performance analysis system for the Grid. In *2nd European Across Grid Conference*, Lecture Notes in Computer Science. Springer Verlag, 2004.

183. J. Ullman. NP-complete scheduling problems. *Journal of Computer and System Sciences*, 10:384–393, 1975.

184. G. von Laszewski, I. Foster, J. Gawor, and P. Lane. A Java commodity Grid kit. *Concurrency and Computation: Practice and Experience*, 13(8–9):645–662, 2001.

185. F. Vraalsen, R. A. Aydt, C. L. Mendes, and D. A. Reed. Performance contracts: Predicting and monitoring Grid application behavior. In *2nd International Grid Computing Workshop*, volume 2242 of *Lecture Notes in Computer Science*, pages 154–166. Springer Verlag, 2001.

186. webMethods Corporation. webMethods Glue and Integration Server. http://www.webmethods.com/Products/ESP/WebServicesDev.

187. The Workflow Management Coalition. http://www.wfmc.org/.

188. R. C. Whaley and J. J. Dongarra. Automatically tuned linear algebra software (ATLAS). In *Supercomputing Conference*. ACM Press and IEEE Computer Society Press, 1998.

189. M. Wieczorek, R. Prodan, and T. Fahringer. Comparison of workflow scheduling strategies on the Grid. In *International Conference on Parallel Processing and Applied Mathematics*, Lecture Notes in Computer Science. Springer-Verlag, 2005.

190. M. Wieczorek, R. Prodan, and T. Fahringer. Scheduling of scientific workflows in the ASKALON Grid environment. *SIGMOD Record*, 34(3):56–62, 2005. Special Issue on Scientific Workflows.

191. R. Wismüller and T. Ludwig. The Tool-set – an integrated tool environment for PVM. In *High-Performance Computing and Networking*, volume 1067 of *Lecture Notes in Computer Science*. Springer Verlag, 1995.

192. R. Wolski, N. T. Spring, and J. Hayes. The Network Weather Service: a distributed resource performance forecasting service for metacomputing. *Future Generation Computer Systems*, 15(5–6):757–768, 1999.

193. World Wide Web Consortium. Web Services Activity.
http://www.w3.org/2002/ws/.

194. World Wide Web Consortium. Web Services Architecture.
http://www.w3.org/TR/2002/WD-ws-arch-20021114/, 2002.

195. World Wide Web Consortium. XML Schemas: Datatypes.
http://www.w3.org/TR/xmlschema-2/, 2004.

196. A. YarKhan and J. J. Dongarra. Experiments with scheduling using simulated annealing in a Grid environment. *Lecture Notes in Computer Science*, 2536:232–244, 2002.

197. M. Yarrow, K. M. McCann, R. Biswas, and R. F. V. der Wijngaart. ILab: An advanced user interface approach for complex parameter study process specification on the Information Power Grid. In *International Workshop on Grid Computing*. ACM Press and IEEE Computer Society Press, 2000.

198. J. Yu and R. Buyya. A taxonomy of scientific workflow systems for Grid computing. *SIGMOD Record, Special Issue on Scientific Workflows*, 34(3):44–49, 2005. Special Issue on Scientific Workflows.

199. O. Zaki, E. Lusk, W. Gropp, and D. Swider. Toward scalable performance visualization with Jumpshot. *International Journal of High-Performance Computing and Applications*, 13(3):277–288, 1999.

200. H. Zhao and R. Sakellariou. An experimental investigation into the rank function of the heterogeneous earliest finish time scheduling algorithm. In *Euro-Par Conference*, pages 189–194, 2003.

201. S. Zhou. LSF: load sharing in large-scale heterogeneous distributed systems. In *Workshop on Cluster Computing*, 1992.

Index

Lecture Notes in Computer Science

For information about Vols. 1–4264

please contact your bookseller or Springer

Vol. 4306: Y. Avrithis, Y. Kompatsiaris, S. Staab, N.E. O'Connor (Eds.), Semantic Multimedia. XII, 241 pages. 2006.

Vol. 4305: A.A. Shvartsman (Ed.), Principles of Distributed Systems. XIII, 441 pages. 2006.

Vol. 4304: A. Sattar, B.-h. Kang (Eds.), AI 2006: Advances in Artificial Intelligence. XXVII, 1303 pages. 2006. (Sublibrary LNAI).

Vol. 4303: A. Hoffmann, B.-h. Kang, D. Richards, S. Tsumoto (Eds.), Advances in Knowledge Acquisition and Management. XI, 259 pages. 2006. (Sublibrary LNAI).

Vol. 4302: J. Domingo-Ferrer, L. Franconi (Eds.), Privacy in Statistical Databases. XI, 383 pages. 2006.

Vol. 4301: D. Pointcheval, Y. Mu, K. Chen (Eds.), Cryptology and Network Security. XIII, 381 pages. 2006.

Vol. 4300: Y.Q. Shi (Ed.), Transactions on Data Hiding and Multimedia Security I. IX, 139 pages. 2006.

Vol. 4299: S. Renals, S. Bengio, J.G. Fiscus (Eds.), Machine Learning for Multimodal Interaction. XII, 470 pages. 2006.

Vol. 4297: Y. Robert, M. Parashar, R. Badrinath, V.K. Prasanna (Eds.), High Performance Computing - HiPC 2006. XXIV, 642 pages. 2006.

Vol. 4296: M.S. Rhee, B. Lee (Eds.), Information Security and Cryptology – ICISC 2006. XIII, 358 pages. 2006.

Vol. 4295: J.D. Carswell, T. Tezuka (Eds.), Web and Wireless Geographical Information Systems. XI, 269 pages. 2006.

Vol. 4294: A. Dan, W. Lamersdorf (Eds.), Service-Oriented Computing – ICSOC 2006. XIX, 653 pages. 2006.

Vol. 4293: A. Gelbukh, C.A. Reyes-Garcia (Eds.), MICAI 2006: Advances in Artificial Intelligence. XXVIII, 1232 pages. 2006. (Sublibrary LNAI).

Vol. 4292: G. Bebis, R. Boyle, B. Parvin, D. Koracin, P. Remagnino, A. Nefian, G. Meenakshisundaram, V. Pascucci, J. Zara, J. Molineros, H. Theisel, T. Malzbender (Eds.), Advances in Visual Computing, Part II. XXXII, 906 pages. 2006.

Vol. 4291: G. Bebis, R. Boyle, B. Parvin, D. Koracin, P. Remagnino, A. Nefian, G. Meenakshisundaram, V. Pascucci, J. Zara, J. Molineros, H. Theisel, T. Malzbender (Eds.), Advances in Visual Computing, Part I. XXXI, 916 pages. 2006.

Vol. 4290: M. van Steen, M. Henning (Eds.), Middleware 2006. XIII, 425 pages. 2006.

Vol. 4289: M. Ackermann, B. Berendt, M. Grobelnik, A. Hotho, D. Mladenič, G. Semeraro, M. Spiliopoulou, G. Stumme, V. Svatek, M. van Someren (Eds.), Semantics, Web and Mining. X, 197 pages. 2006. (Sublibrary LNAI).

Vol. 4288: T. Asano (Ed.), Algorithms and Computation. XX, 766 pages. 2006.

Vol. 4287: C. Mao, T. Yokomori (Eds.), DNA Computing. XII, 440 pages. 2006.

Vol. 4286: P. Spirakis, M. Mavronicolas, S. Kontogiannis (Eds.), Internet and Network Economics. XI, 401 pages. 2006.

Vol. 4285: Y. Matsumoto, R. Sproat, K.-F. Wong, M. Zhang (Eds.), Computer Processing of Oriental Languages. XVII, 544 pages. 2006. (Sublibrary LNAI).

Vol. 4284: X. Lai, K. Chen (Eds.), Advances in Cryptology – ASIACRYPT 2006. XIV, 468 pages. 2006.

Vol. 4283: Y.Q. Shi, B. Jeon (Eds.), Digital Watermarking. XII, 474 pages. 2006.

Vol. 4282: Z. Pan, A. Cheok, M. Haller, R.W.H. Lau, H. Saito, R. Liang (Eds.), Advances in Artificial Reality and Tele-Existence. XXIII, 1347 pages. 2006.

Vol. 4281: K. Barkaoui, A. Cavalcanti, A. Cerone (Eds.), Theoretical Aspects of Computing - ICTAC 2006. XV, 371 pages. 2006.

Vol. 4280: A.K. Datta, M. Gradinariu (Eds.), Stabilization, Safety, and Security of Distributed Systems. XVII, 590 pages. 2006.

Vol. 4279: N. Kobayashi (Ed.), Programming Languages and Systems. XI, 423 pages. 2006.

Vol. 4278: R. Meersman, Z. Tari, P. Herrero (Eds.), On the Move to Meaningful Internet Systems 2006: OTM 2006 Workshops, Part II. XLV, 1004 pages. 2006.

Vol. 4277: R. Meersman, Z. Tari, P. Herrero (Eds.), On the Move to Meaningful Internet Systems 2006: OTM 2006 Workshops, Part I. XLV, 1009 pages. 2006.

Vol. 4276: R. Meersman, Z. Tari (Eds.), On the Move to Meaningful Internet Systems 2006: CoopIS, DOA, GADA, and ODBASE, Part II. XXXII, 752 pages. 2006.

Vol. 4275: R. Meersman, Z. Tari (Eds.), On the Move to Meaningful Internet Systems 2006: CoopIS, DOA, GADA, and ODBASE, Part I. XXXI, 1115 pages. 2006.

Vol. 4274: Q. Huo, B. Ma, E.-S. Chng, H. Li (Eds.), Chinese Spoken Language Processing. XXIV, 805 pages. 2006. (Sublibrary LNAI).

Vol. 4273: I. Cruz, S. Decker, D. Allemang, C. Preist, D. Schwabe, P. Mika, M. Uschold, L. Aroyo (Eds.), The Semantic Web - ISWC 2006. XXIV, 1001 pages. 2006.

Vol. 4272: P. Havinga, M. Lijding, N. Meratnia, M. Wegdam (Eds.), Smart Sensing and Context. XI, 267 pages. 2006.

Vol. 4271: F.V. Fomin (Ed.), Graph-Theoretic Concepts in Computer Science. XIII, 358 pages. 2006.

Vol. 4270: H. Zha, Z. Pan, H. Thwaites, A.C. Addison, M. Forte (Eds.), Interactive Technologies and Sociotechnical Systems. XVI, 547 pages. 2006.

Vol. 4269: R. State, S. van der Meer, D. O'Sullivan, T. Pfeifer (Eds.), Large Scale Management of Distributed Systems. XIII, 282 pages. 2006.

Vol. 4268: G. Parr, D. Malone, M. Ó Foghlú (Eds.), Autonomic Principles of IP Operations and Management. XIII, 237 pages. 2006.

Vol. 4267: A. Helmy, B. Jennings, L. Murphy, T. Pfeifer (Eds.), Autonomic Management of Mobile Multimedia Services. XIII, 257 pages. 2006.

Vol. 4266: H. Yoshiura, K. Sakurai, K. Rannenberg, Y. Murayama, S. Kawamura (Eds.), Advances in Information and Computer Security. XIII, 438 pages. 2006.

Vol. 4265: L. Todorovski, N. Lavrač, K.P. Jantke (Eds.), Discovery Science. XIV, 384 pages. 2006. (Sublibrary LNAI).